SOVIET
Air Power

SOVIET
Air Power

Bill Sweetman   Bill Gunston

a Salamander book

Published by Salamander Books Limited
LONDON

A Salamander Book

Published 1978 by Salamander Books Ltd,
27 Old Gloucester Street,
London WC1N 3AF
England

©Salamander Books Ltd 1978

ISBN 0 86101 015 9

Distributed in Australia/New Zealand
by Summit Books, a division of Paul Hamlyn Pty Ltd,
Sydney, Australia

Credits

Editor: Philip de Ste. Croix
Designer: Chris Steer
Project Manager: Ray Bonds

Colour three-views: Keith Fretwell,
©Salamander Books Ltd
Colour fold-out artwork: Terry Hadler,
©Salamander Books Ltd
Colour profile drawings
©Pilot Press Ltd and Salamander Books Ltd
Cutaway drawings and line diagrams:
©Pilot Press Ltd
Maps and charts prepared by Arka Graphics
©Salamander Books Ltd.

Filmset by SX Composing, England

Colour Reproduction by Culver Graphics Ltd, England
and Colourcraftsmen Ltd, England

Printed in Belgium by Henri Proost et Cie, Turnhout

Editor's Acknowledgments

The efforts of many people have contributed to this book—the most colourful study of contemporary Soviet air power yet published. In addition to authors Bill Sweetman, who wrote the chapters on the Warsaw Pact air forces, and Bill Gunston, who wrote the East v West chapter, the technical section and the introductions, we owe a debt of gratitude to John W. R. Taylor, who acted as consultant on the purely technical information here published. It should be pointed out that the political opinions expressed by each author are not those of the consultant, nor are they necessarily shared by his fellow author.

We are extremely grateful to Mark Hewish from whose original idea the form of the air forces chapters developed and who helped in their preparation, and to Maurice Allward who compiled the table of military satellite launches on page 35. We would also like to thank Keith Fretwell and Terry Hadler, who painted the magnificent colour three-views and fold-outs respectively, and Pilot Press Ltd whose cutaways, line three-views and profiles we have used. Thanks also go to the publishers of *Air Force* magazine upon whose diagram of major Warsaw Pact and NATO airfields our double page map is based.

Philip de Ste. Croix

Contents

In the entire history of mankind, there has never been a military machine as mighty as the integrated air and rocket forces now available to the Soviet Union and its Warsaw Pact allies. That assessment is not based on mere numbers of men and weapons, although such statistics are impressive in themselves. It also takes into account the capability of the individual weapons compared with those which oppose them in the West, the quality of the personnel who operate them, and the determination and ambitions of the governments which control them.

Western efforts to maintain peace through a balance of power are centred on what America refers to as its Triad of strategic weapons — intercontinental ballistic missiles (ICBMs) housed in underground launchers in the USA; submarine-launched ballistic missiles (SLBMs) carried by nuclear-powered submarines; and a force of manned long-range bombers.

There are 1,000 Minuteman and 54 Titan missiles in the US Air Force's ICBM inventory, compared with about 1,450 Soviet ICBMs. More significant is that most of the Soviet missiles are very new, with multiple, independently-targeted warheads, offering far higher standards of accuracy than the weapons they replaced. Already they represent nearly three times the total destructive power of America's ICBMs in terms of nuclear megatonnage. By the mid-eighties they are expected to provide the capability of destroying 85 to 90 per cent of the Minuteman/Titan force in its launch silos, by striking first in a nuclear war.

After doing this, the Soviet Union would still have 50 per cent of its ICBMs, and its complete force of 950 SLBMs, poised ready for a second strike. The US would have a few surviving Minuteman missiles, plus 656 Trident, Poseidon and Polaris SLBMs. The latter are, basically, city destroyers rather than weapons for use against ICBM sites. So, is it logical to imagine that the US would invite retaliation against its own huge centres of population by launching its SLBMs against Soviet cities? A first strike by the Soviet Union might, therefore, effectively eliminate America's ICBMs and render its SLBMs unusable.

This would leave the manned bombers — Strategic Air Command's 350 B-52 Stratofortresses (averaging 19 years old) and 65 smaller, supersonic FB-111s — for use against carefully selected targets. To reach their objectives, they would need to penetrate a Soviet home defence system that deploys currently more than 2,600 piloted interceptors and 12,000 surface-to-air missiles (SAMs). (By comparison, America's Aerospace Defense Command had 341 twenty-year-old F-106 interceptors and no SAMs in 1978.) The B-1 supersonic bombers that were to replace the ageing B-52s were cancelled by President Carter in June 1977.

Another factor of great importance is that recent expansion and modernisation of the Soviet armed services have been accompanied by the setting up of a civil defence system that is unique in the world. While America has to think in terms of 60 to 90 million dead in a full-scale nuclear exchange, the Soviet Union believes that it would suffer ''only'' 15 million casualties and could be back to something resembling normal within three years.

Its present political leaders experienced the worst horrors of World War II, when their nation lost some 20 million of its people. They are unlikely to consider any gain worth the death of another 15 million; but who will govern the Soviet Union (and the United States) in ten years' time?

Nor may we think only in terms of an all-out nuclear conflict. NATO leaders have begun to feel that the greater danger might be a military confrontation in Europe. There was a time when such a prospect held few worries for the West. Today, the Warsaw Pact air forces have a combined total of more than 3,000 tactical fighters,

The Shadow on the Wall

reconnaissance and bomber aircraft deployed along NATO's Central and lower Northern regions, and 920 along the Southern flank. Facing them are 1,700 NATO tactical aircraft in the Central and lower Northern regions, plus 710 more in the South. The Soviet aircraft include MiG-25s, fastest combat aircraft in the world; Sukhoi Su-19 attack fighters, each carrying about five times the weight of weapons five times as far as the aircraft they replaced; and many hundreds of Mil Mi-24 helicopters, which have given entirely new standards of hard-hitting mobility to Warsaw Pact ground forces.

The Soviet aircraft industry is manufacturing new military aircraft at the rate of 1,800 a year, including sufficient of the very latest types of combat aircraft to replace the equivalent of the entire first-line tactical strengths of the Royal Air Force and the German Luftwaffe annually. The time when such aircraft were poorly equipped has gone. Tupolev Tu-26 supersonic bombers have terrain-avoidance radar and Doppler navigation systems; reconnaissance MiG-25Rs have side-looking airborne radar; the ground attack aircraft have laser target seekers and rangefinders, used in conjunction with a whole range of homing air-to-surface missiles

and multi-barrel guns.

It shocked the West when the Soviet Union demonstrated its assault capability on 20–21 August, 1968, by setting down troops throughout Czechoslovakia in a nighttime air transport operation of great efficiency, in order to end the Dubcek "liberalisation"

of that country. More recent delivery of vast quantities of combat aircraft and other equipment to places as far apart as Peru and Ethiopia, by An-22s and other transports, reflects a continued impressive build-up of airlift capability.

Aircraft as diverse as the Yakovlev Yak-36 VTOL combat aircraft and Antonov An-72 advanced STOL transport emphasise that few modern techniques are beyond the capability of the Soviet aerospace industry; and that the Soviet government is prepared to exploit every technological development that will enhance the efficiency of its huge armed forces. This is very different from implying that its leaders seek a war with the West. Agreements reached under the SALT discussions, although sometimes one-sided, show what must be achieved before the introduction into service of far more terrible weapons. One of the most poignant photographs taken in Hiroshima in 1945 showed a wall seared by the blinding flash of the first atomic bomb dropped on Japan. On the wall was the man-shape shadow of an unkown person who had been sitting on the steps in front of it a millisecond before he was erased by a weapon he could never have imagined. Unless the leaders of East and West maintain a balance of deterrent power, and learn to scale it down

year by year, in step with each other and with China, future travellers may see from space not the "Good Earth" of 1968 Apollo astronaut Frank Borman but a harsh planet scarred with the shadow of mankind that once enjoyed its blessings.

The warning is printed on every page of this book.

John W.R. Taylor, Editor of *Jane's All the World's Aircraft*

The Soviet Union's relentless expansion of its arsenal of military hardware, and the ease with which it conducts a policy of intervention in areas of strategic importance such as the Horn of Africa must rate as one of the most disturbing historical developments of recent years. We in the West have made the assumption that even if numerically inferior, our forces have superior technology at their disposal, but today we are at the stage when we should think again. Soviet military technology now probably equals that of the West, and the quantitative gap between the two blocs is widening all the time.

In some vital areas there is almost no contest. The Soviet Union certainly has more SAMs than the rest of the world put together, and the disparity in numbers of global strategic weapons deployed is also increasing. The US Air Force worked hard to build a Triad, comprising ICBMs, manned bombers and Navy SLBMs, which would form an effective deterrent that could not be by-passed in any conceivable circumstance. Today the stage is set for deterrence to crumble: updating the SLBM force is in severe cost and schedule difficulties and will have small effect for many years, while replacements for the limited and

PART ONE

East v West

obsolescing ICBM and bomber forces are little but piles of proposals. The Soviet Union has never ceased to buy exactly the weapons it needs, including a full spectrum of ICBMs, mobile strategic missiles (as yet missing from the West's armoury entirely), intercontinental SLBMs and manned bombers.

The Warsaw Pact capability is formidable and growing, and Western observers must ask themselves why Soviet forces have been strengthened beyond the requirements of a purely defensive posture. Why has the Soviet Union completely gone over to offensive missions in the design and equipment of its tactical aircraft? Why is its army and tactical air equipment not merely mobile but, in nearly every case, air-portable and/or amphibious? If it is apprehensive about an invasion from the West, why does it not construct defences in depth against such an attack? Right across the board, in both major decisions and in detail hardware design, the Soviet armoury is geared totally to a war of fast-moving forward advance. No-one can view such a development without feeling apprehensive of future consequences, for the greater the imbalance between forces, the greater is the threat to peace.

Above: The Soviet Union has many times more nuclear missiles than all other countries combined. Several hundred, such as the "Scamp" (SS-14 "Scapegoat") system seen here, are mobile and dispersed around the frontiers of the Soviet Union.

Trying to present slick, readily assimilable "packaged" assessments of how the European NATO nations shape up in defence against the Warsaw Pact is a popular pastime among journalists, generals and the heads of nations. But it is also something that has to be done in deadly earnest, and it is not easy to do in a meaningful way. Many reviewers have an axe to grind. Some wish to scare Western populations and exaggerate the figures of Soviet or Warsaw Pact (WP) forces, often by including equipment items no longer in front-line use. (In fact, there is some justification for doing this. John W. R. Taylor, Editor of Jane's All the World's Aircraft and an authority on Soviet developments, recently said "I am often struck by the fact that, unlike us in the West, the Russians never throw anything away. It is all refurbished and re-equipped and used in a new role. If we looked hard enough we might even find a squadron of Ilya Mourometz bombers somewhere!" The IM series were bombers of 1913–17.)

The East/West Imbalance

More often the Western assessment seeks to assuage public fear by distorting the picture in the West's favour. The obvious way of doing this is to ignore the importance of timing, and include in the Soviet/WP balance sheet only the weapons known to be in use, while including in the West's line-up all the prototype or projected weapons that will not become operational for many years. Eight current assessments of strategic rocket strength—which in practice virtually boils down to US v Soviet ICBMs—include M-X in the "US" strength, even though it does not exist and could not be in use until after 1986. We suppose there must be several counterparts to M-X in the Soviet Union, but none are included in the balance-sheet. Likewise, all publicly available assessments of data on US v Soviet battle tanks include the American XM-1, a tank still years away from

production and likely still to undergo major changes or even give way to a different design. No allowance is made for whatever the Soviet Union is at present testing to replace the T-72, a tank in service in very large numbers and so far ahead technically of the latest available US tank, the M60, as to make comparison pointless.

Even the basic assessment of numbers is often done with inadequate explanation to a worried public eager for authoritative information. How many tanks face us in Europe? According to the US Congress official "American and Soviet Military Strength, Contemporary Trends Compared, 1970–76" the 1976 total was 16,000. According to the US Air Force Magazine, which has access to every kind of published information, the December 1976 total for tanks in combat units was 19,000 in Northern and Central Europe and 7,500 in Southern Europe; total tank holdings, allowing for reserves and vehicles being modified or repaired, were "materially higher". According to the Fiscal Year 1979 (FY79) Report of the Joint Chiefs of Staff to the US Congress "The Soviet tank force consists of 45,000–50,000 medium and heavy tanks . . ." Three other semi-official NATO assessments put the total facing NATO forces at between 27,000 and 35,000. Such figures are not terribly helpful, beyond driving home the idea—which is absolutely correct—that the true total is frighteningly great, and far superior to anything that can be mustered by the West. But too many wildly different figures can discredit the whole process of trying to arrive at a meaningful answer, and thus blur the true situation.

Unlike the Soviet Union, where the public knows better than to risk becoming "a dissident", there are plenty of articulate and noisy people in the West who will seize on any

excuse to reduce spending on national or collective defence. They appear to have little interest in the forces facing the NATO nations, to dislike any attempt to publish a factual balance-sheet, and deliberately to avoid any positive contribution to how the West should best defend itself against the largest peacetime array of firepower the world has ever seen. Such an attitude is intensely dangerous because, no matter how much one may try to argue against it, it is an inescapable truth that, the greater the imbalance between opposing forces, the greater the threat to peace.

Strategic Forces

Virtually all strategic weaponry comes within the general concept of "air power". The main subdivisions comprise manned bombers, and the missiles they launch, land-based intercontinental ballistic missiles (ICBMs) and submarine-launched ballistic missiles (SLBMs). Several naval bombardment missiles might be construed as strategic, in view of the fact that they can be carried to launch points wherever there is sea, but this review is confined to the SLBM which is generally considered to be targeted at enemy heartlands rather than ports or ships at sea.

Basic numbers of manned bombers are given below:

Above: White hope or white elephant? With the cancellation of the B-1 the Western world has knocked away one of the three props on which its credible nuclear deterrent rested. Unmanned missiles dare not be launched until too late.

Fundamental differences in philosophy are immediately apparent. While the USAF has kept its old B-52 in the front-line bomber inventory through sheer necessity (there being nothing else), the Soviet DA (Dal'naya Aviatsiya, or long-range aviation) has progressively rebuilt its M-4 "Bison" and Tu-20 "Bear" long-range bombers as multi-sensor and electronic warfare and reconnaissance aircraft, missile guidance platforms, tankers and for various other roles not calling for the penetration of hostile airspace. These aircraft, similar in vintage to the the West's B-52, are entirely capable of fulfilling their assigned duties. In their place in the attack squadrons are the swing-wing (Tu-26?) bombers called "Backfire" by NATO, while a rather larger bomber is believed to be well advanced in flight development. The fundamental contrast between the West, represented by the USAF, and the Soviet Union is therefore one of abandonment of strategic manned aircraft on the one hand and an orderly planned continuance of development on the other.

There has been surprising public debate in the United

Table I   Strategic bombers

Type	Service entry (original model)	Number in service	ASM missile capability	Flight-refuelling capability	Inter-continental range
B-52G and H	1955	349 (all versions)	yes	yes	yes
FB-111A	1970	66	yes	yes	no
Vulcan	1957	50	no	yes	no
Tu-16	1954	800	yes	yes	no
Tu-20 (Tu-95)	1957	90 (40 as bombers)	yes	yes	yes
M-4	1955	90	no	yes	marginal
Backfire	1974	120	yes	yes	marginal

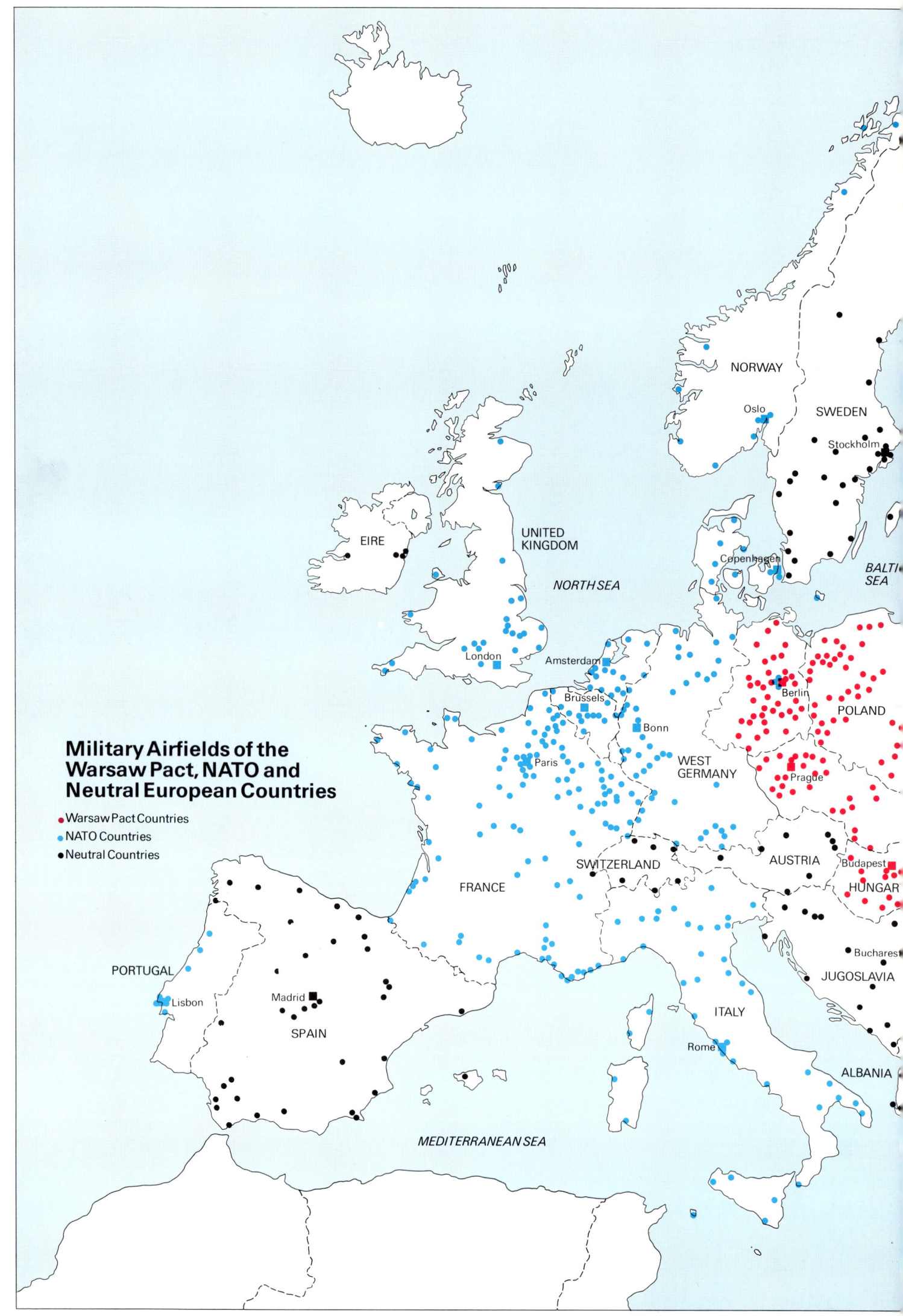

Military Airfields of the Warsaw Pact, NATO and Neutral European Countries

- ● Warsaw Pact Countries
- ● NATO Countries
- ● Neutral Countries

NORWAY

Oslo

SWEDEN

Stockholm

EIRE

UNITED KINGDOM

NORTH SEA

London

Amsterdam

Brussels

Bonn

Paris

WEST GERMANY

Copenhagen

BALTIC SEA

Berlin

POLAND

Prague

AUSTRIA

Budapest

HUNGARY

SWITZERLAND

FRANCE

Bucharest

JUGOSLAVIA

PORTUGAL

Lisbon

Madrid

SPAIN

ITALY

Rome

ALBANIA

MEDITERRANEAN SEA

Note: The purpose of this map is to show the concentration of military airfields in central Europe. It does not show airfields on the northern flank, north of Leningrad.

UNION OF SOVIET SOCIALIST REPUBLICS

Leningrad

Moscow

Warsaw

Kiev

ROMANIA

Belgrade

Sofia

BULGARIA

Istanbul

TURKEY

GREECE

Athens

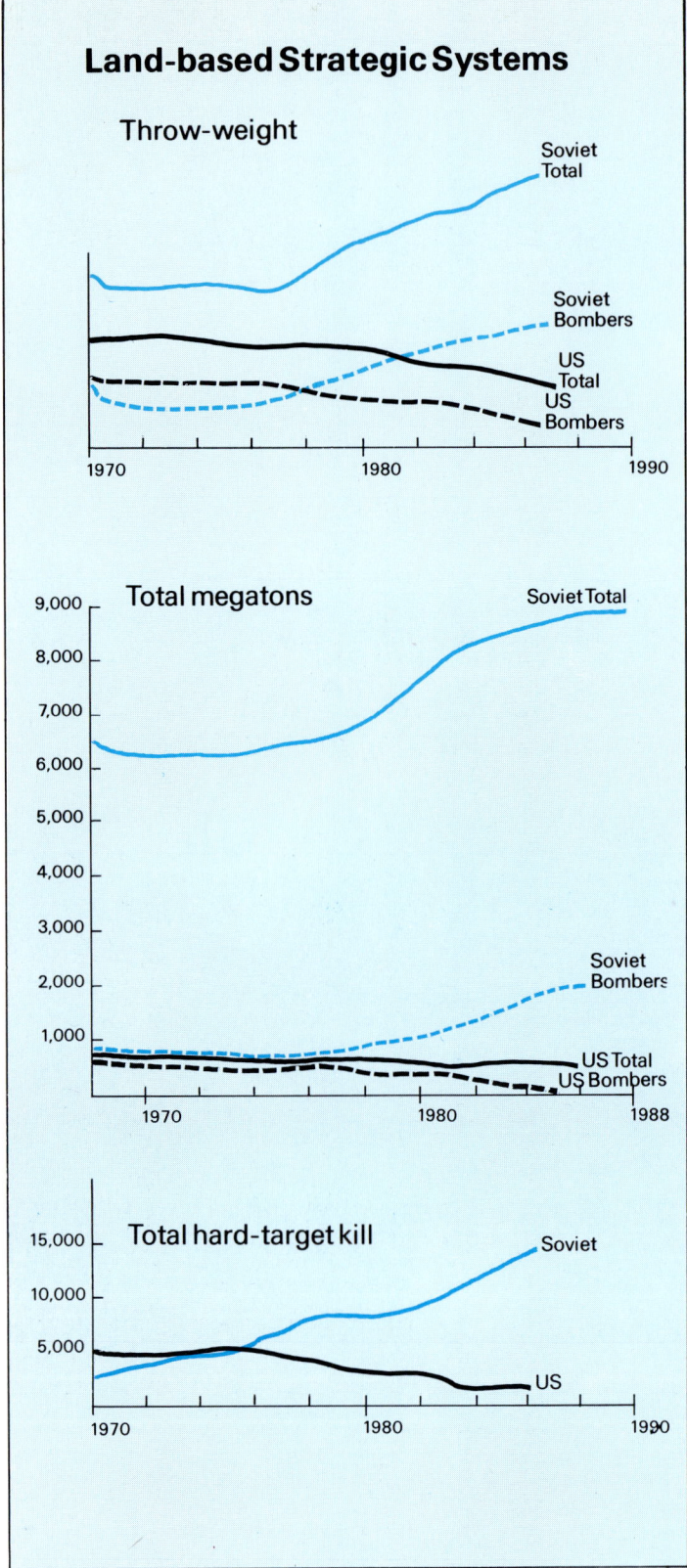

Land-based Strategic Systems

Throw-weight

- Soviet Total
- Soviet Bombers
- US Total
- US Bombers

1970 — 1980 — 1990

Total megatons

9,000
8,000
7,000
6,000
5,000
4,000
3,000
2,000
1,000

- Soviet Total
- Soviet Bombers
- US Total
- US Bombers

1970 — 1980 — 1988

Total hard-target kill

15,000
10,000
5,000

- Soviet
- US

1970 — 1980 — 1990

refuelling. Staging from Arctic bases and refuelled, the "Backfire" could cover virtually all of the United States on two-way high-altitude subsonic missions". All "Backfires" are believed to have a flight-refuelling probe.

So far (early 1978) about 120 "Backfires" have entered service, with production running at two or three per month. A total force of 250 to 400 is predicted. They are shared between the DA and the AV-MF (Naval Aviation) as noted later. All "Backfires" appear to have the capability of carrying the outstandingly accurate air-to-surface missile called AS-6 "Kingfish" by NATO. The story has it that, "If it was aimed at the Pentagon the guidance system could be adjusted to put it through the correct office window". For this reason many "Backfires" have been seen carrying one missile only. An alternative weapon is AS-4 "Kitchen", previously carried by the shorter-ranged Tu-22 "Blinder" supersonic bomber. Instead of missiles "Backfires" can carry modest loads of conventional or free-fall nuclear bombs, or carry out electronic warfare (EW) or reconnaissance missions, as they have been doing in many areas, especially off north-west Europe, since early 1975.

Bombers and ICBMs

In 1974 the Soviet Union was seen to be test-flying a larger strategic bomber with slender-delta wing similar to the Tu-144. This did not enter production, but since 1976 a newer bomber of different configuration has reportedly been under test. Fitted with double-delta wings broadly similar to the Swedish Viggen, it apparently combines very heavy weapon loads with short-field performance for dispersed operation away from paved runways. One report suggests it is a "military version of the Tu-144 SST", but this is certain to be a gross oversimplification. What is beyond dispute is the continuing Soviet strength in manned bombers.

Where strategic missiles are concerned the disparity in strength between the Soviet Union and the West is so great as to make it almost "no contest", an unprecedented and deeply worrying situation. Again the main numbers can be tabulated: (see Table II).

The West has virtually only one kind of ICBM, the USAF's Minuteman. This is a relatively small missile, much inferior in throw weight to most of the Soviet missiles. Only the 550 Minuteman III missiles can be considered modern, with MIRV (multiple independently-targeted re-entry vehicles) capability for directing self-guided warheads against a number of targets. The 54 Titan II ICBMs are old and costly to maintain, though the cost is being reduced by continuing modernization. The only other Western land-based missiles are hardly strategic: France has a small force of intermediate-range ballistic missiles (IRBMs) in south-west France, on the Plateau d'Albion.

At sea the submarine-based missile force of the US Navy

States concerning the capability of the "Backfire". For obvious reasons the Soviet negotiators at the SALT talks have insisted that "Backfire" is "not a strategic aircraft" and should not be included in the total of manned strategic aircraft of the Soviet Union. The US Central Intelligence Agency (CIA) has echoed this theme, claiming the aircraft is "primarily built for a peripheral role" against Western Europe, Britain, sea traffic and China. The CIA has never explicitly denied that "Backfire" can fly missions against the United States, but has been at pains to play down the idea, presumably for political reasons. Yet even the present "Backfire B" is a formidable strategic aircraft; it would be inconceivable if it were not, for it is a modern variable-geometry aircraft $2\frac{1}{2}$ times as heavy as the FB-111A. According to the US Defense Intelligence Agency (DIA) "On one-way Arctic-staged missions, recovering in friendly or neutral territory, the "Backfire" is capable of delivering weapons anywhere in the United States without aerial

Above: BGM-109 Tomahawk is intended eventually to be one of the substitutes for the B-1. But could it, even today, penetrate sophisticated hostile airspace? How about the 1980s?

Right: It is hard to grasp the enormity of the Soviet missile programmes. This is a silo-launch of SS-7 ''Saddler'', an old weapon largely replaced by SLBMs.

Table II ICBMs and MRBMs

Type	Year in service	Number	Range km	MIRV	Mobile	Throw-weight
Minuteman II	1965	450	11,250	no	no	small
Minuteman III	1970	550	13,000	yes	no	small
Titan II	1963	54	15,000	no	no	large
SSBS (France)	1971	18	2,750	no	no	small
SS-4	1960	500	2,000	no	some	small
SS-5	1963	100	3,500	?	no	large
SS-7/8	1964	209*	11,000	yes	no	large
SS-9	1965	288*	12,000	yes	no	large
SS-10	1965	?	8,000	possible	not deployed operationally	
SS-11	1966?	900*	10,000	no	no	small
SS-11 Mod 3	1973	conversions	10,000	yes	no	small
SS-13	1969?	60+	8,000	no	no	small
SS-14	1967?	large	4,000	no	yes	small
SS-16	1977?	?	10,000	?	yes	small
SS-17	1975	70?	10,000	yes	no	large
SS-18	1974	100+	10,500	yes	no	large
SS-19	1974	300	9,000+	yes	no	large
SS-20	1976	growing	5500	yes	yes	?
SS-XZ (Scrooge)	recent	?	6000+	?	yes	large

*Supposed to be diminishing

Table III SLBMs

Type	Year in service	Number	Range km	MIRV	Throw-weight	Tubes per sub
Polaris A3	1964	160	4630	yes	small	16
Poseidon C-3	1971	496	4630	yes	fair	16
Polaris UK	1970	64	4630?	yes	small	16
MSBS (France)	1971	64*	3000	no	small	16
SSN-5	1963	21	1500?	no	fair	varies
SSN-6	1968	544	3000	yes	fair	16
SSN-8	1973	260+	8000	yes	large	12 or 16

A Delta 3 class submarine carrying 20 or 24 N-8 missiles has been persistently reported.

Type	Year in service	Number	Range km	MIRV	Throw-weight	Tubes per sub
SSNX-17	1978?	new class of SLBM with MIRV capability, few details.				
SSNX-18	1978?	few yet	9500	yes	large	not known

has been overtaken by the Soviet Union with startling speed, just as was the land-based force of the USAF. Quite apart from the Soviet dominance in number of launchers, the size and range of the missiles in the later Soviet vessels gives cause for concern, for they far surpass anything available in the West. Table III gives the chief numbers.

Trident and Cruise Missiles

Today the entire Western effort on SLBMs is devoted to the US Navy's Trident programme. This has been almost ten years under development and is matched with a new class of extremely large submarine, but the latter has suffered delays and extremely serious cost-escalation and initial operational capability is not now expected in 1979 as originally had been forecast for this vessel.

When President Carter announced termination of the B-1 bomber in June 1977 he said instead increased emphasis would be placed on cruise missiles. Such weapons are miniature bombers, with internal self-contained guidance enabling them to follow any desired course or flight profile, finally releasing one or more independently targeted warheads and will presumably use the maximum sophistication in EW and ECM to assist them to pass safely through defended airspace. The Boeing AGM-86 and General Dynamics BGM-109 Tomahawk are well advanced in development and an advanced strategic air-launched missile (ASALM) is planned for USAF deployment in 1984. All these are winged weapons with flight ranges in the order of 1,000 miles (1600km), though limited to 600km from land or sea

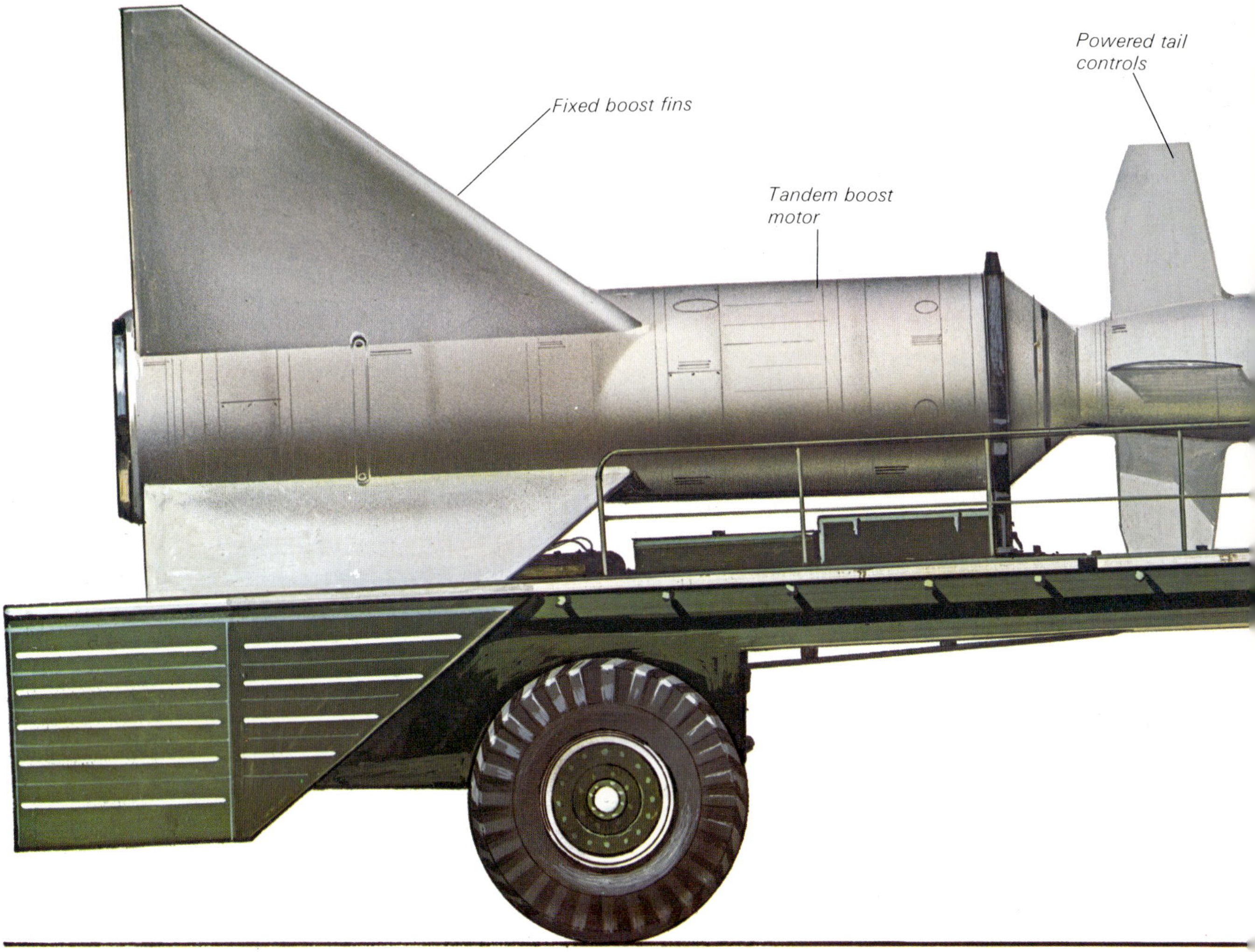

Fixed boost fins

Powered tail controls

Tandem boost motor

Four first-stage nozzles

SA-5 "Gammon"
Surface-to-Air Missile

Type: Long-range strategic SAM, believed to have some ABM (anti-ballistic missile) capability.

Propulsion: Tandem solid-propellant rocket boost motor, solid-propellant rocket sustainer.

Missile Data: Overall length 54ft 2in (16·50m); body diameter 34·0in (0·86m); launch weight estimated at 15,000lb (6800kg).

Operation: This missile has only been seen publicly on a transport vehicle which does not include a launcher. It is a very high-performance system much larger than most SAMs for use against manned aircraft and was first seen in 1963, when it was said to have an anti-missile (assumed ABM) capability. Formerly named "Griffon" by NATO, it was also called the Tallinn System from its early use near the Estonian capital. Guidance is entirely by radar tracking of target and missile, mainly by "Square Pair" radar, to an altitude well above 150,000ft (46,000m) and to a slant range at altitude estimated at 155 miles (250km). By 1975 about 1,100 were estimated to be in place on fixed launchers; a small additional number are believed to have been commissioned since.

SS-13 "Savage"
Surface-to-Surface Missile

Type: Solid-propellant ICBM for use from fixed hardened silos.

Propulsion: Three rocket stages, each with solid propellant and unknown thrust-vector control system.

Missile Data: Overall length (height) 65ft 6in (20m); body diameter (excluding first-stage skirt) 67·0in (1·7m); launch weight estimated at 70,000lb (31,750kg) (some sources put it at 80,000lb).

Operation: This was the first Soviet solid-propellant ICBM. It was first displayed on 9 May 1965, and has often been seen since, with small improvements to the tug and articulated transport trailer. The missile is lowered by a separate crane into a hardened vertical silo, of which some 60 were constructed near Plesetsk in 1968–70. Guidance appears to be inertial, with a CEP (circular error probable) of 1·25 miles (2km). The warhead is estimated at 1 megaton. Ultimate range is universally put at 5,000 miles (8,000km). The second and third stages, without the first/second-stage lattice thrust structure, are almost identical to the mobile SS-14 "Scamp" system. SS-13 is believed to have led to the mass-produced SS-16 system, deployed in much greater numbers since 1976.

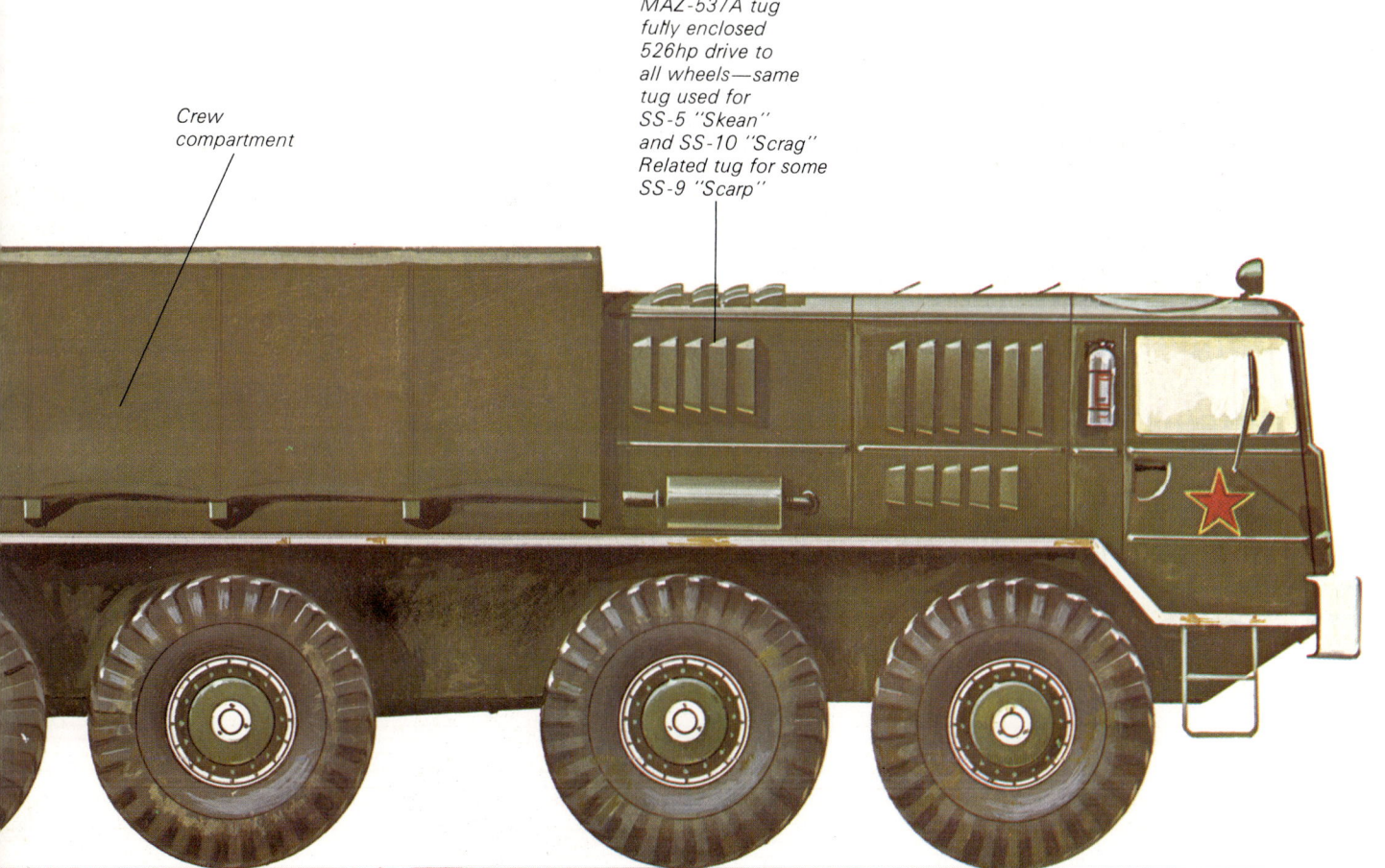

MAZ-537A tug fully enclosed 526hp drive to all wheels—same tug used for SS-5 "Skean" and SS-10 "Scrag" Related tug for some SS-9 "Scarp"

Crew compartment

SA-8 "Gecko" Surface-to-Air Missile

Type: Mobile tactical surface-to-air missile system.

Propulsion: Dual-thrust solid-propellant rocket motor.

Missile Data: Overall length 126in (3·2m); body diameter $8\frac{1}{4}$in (0·21m); launch weight (estimated) 420lb (190kg).

Operation: This whole system is air-portable and amphibious. Four rounds are carried on a rotatable launcher plus an estimated twelve in reload magazines. Two missiles are normally launched simultaneously at the same target, using different frequencies for radio command link giving ECM-resistant proportional-navigational guidance; the missile is believed to have IR homing. The slant range is estimated at 8 miles (12·9km) but the altitude limit is only about 20,000ft (6000m). The vehicle certainly includes optical (LLTV, low-light TV) and probably IR sensors for detecting and tracking targets and centering guidance radar around missile prior to mid-course phase. The missile itself is believed to have close kinship with the ship-launched SA-N-4.

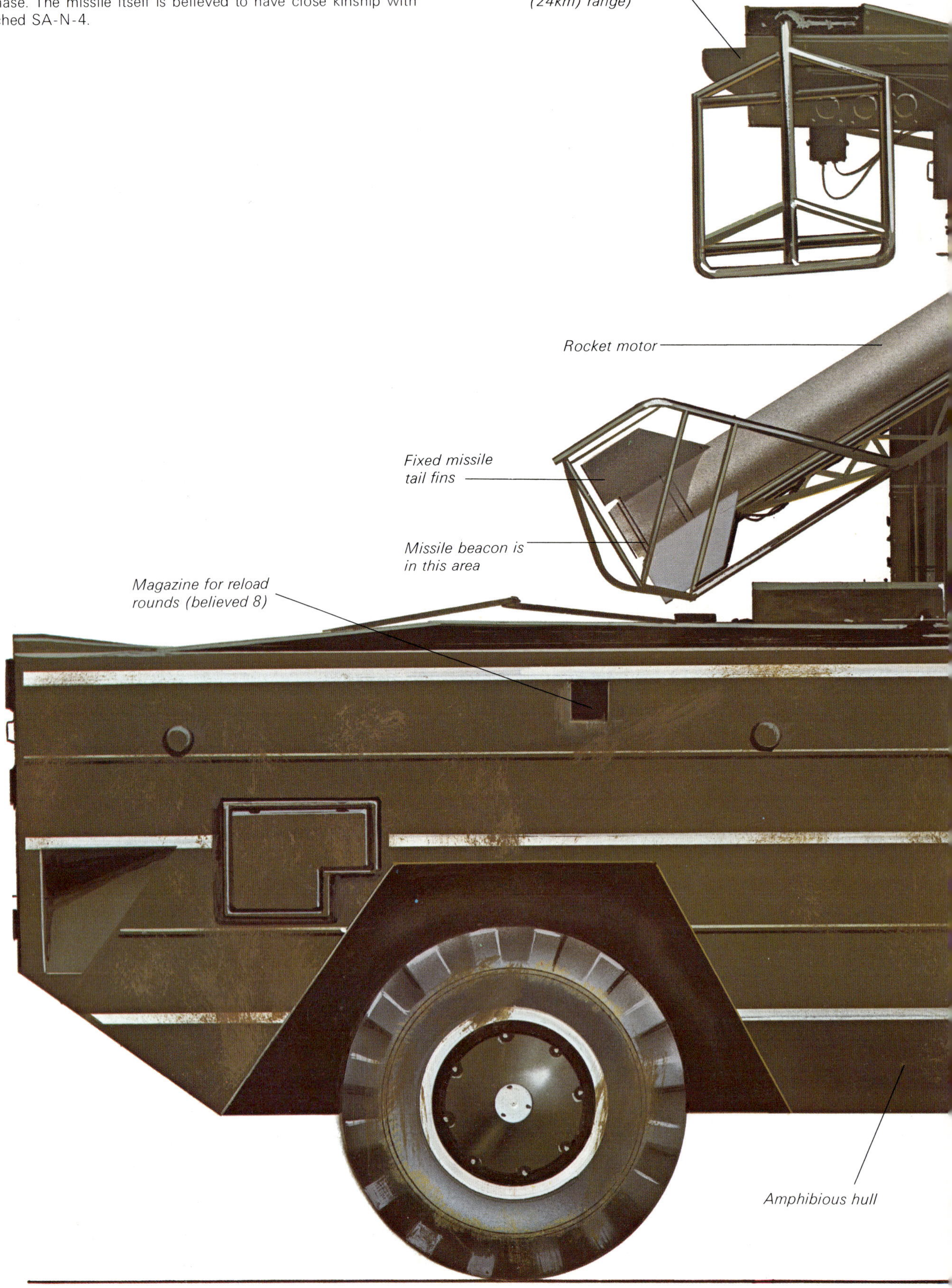

Surveillance radar folds down with launcher to fit An-22 airlifter (est. 15-mile (24km) range)

Rocket motor

Fixed missile tail fins

Missile beacon is in this area

Magazine for reload rounds (believed 8)

Amphibious hull

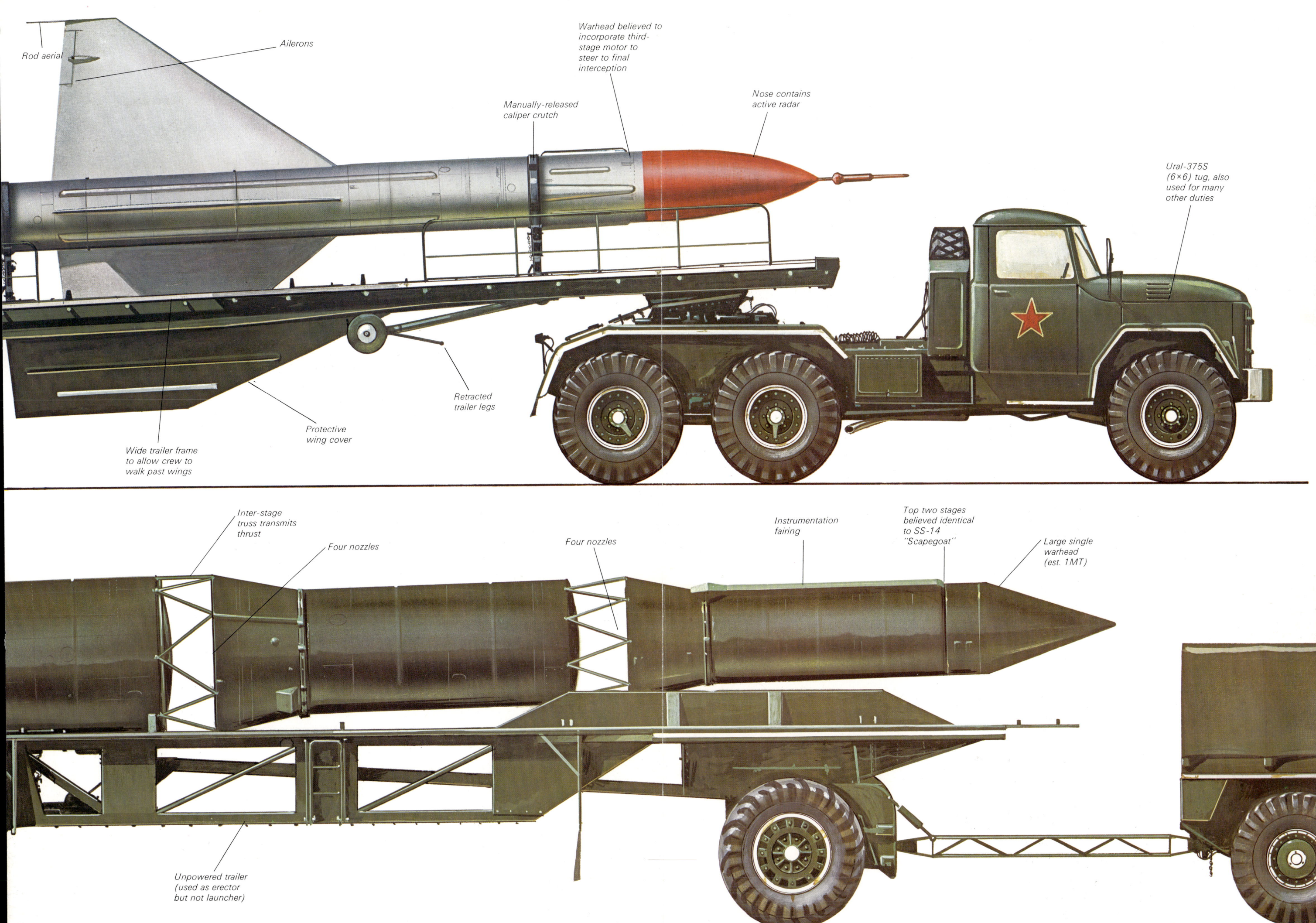

Rod aerial

Ailerons

Warhead believed to incorporate third-stage motor to steer to final interception

Manually-released caliper crutch

Nose contains active radar

Ural-375S (6×6) tug, also used for many other duties

Retracted trailer legs

Protective wing cover

Wide trailer frame to allow crew to walk past wings

Inter-stage truss transmits thrust

Four nozzles

Four nozzles

Instrumentation fairing

Top two stages believed identical to SS-14 "Scapegoat"

Large single warhead (est. 1MT)

Unpowered trailer (used as erector but not launcher)

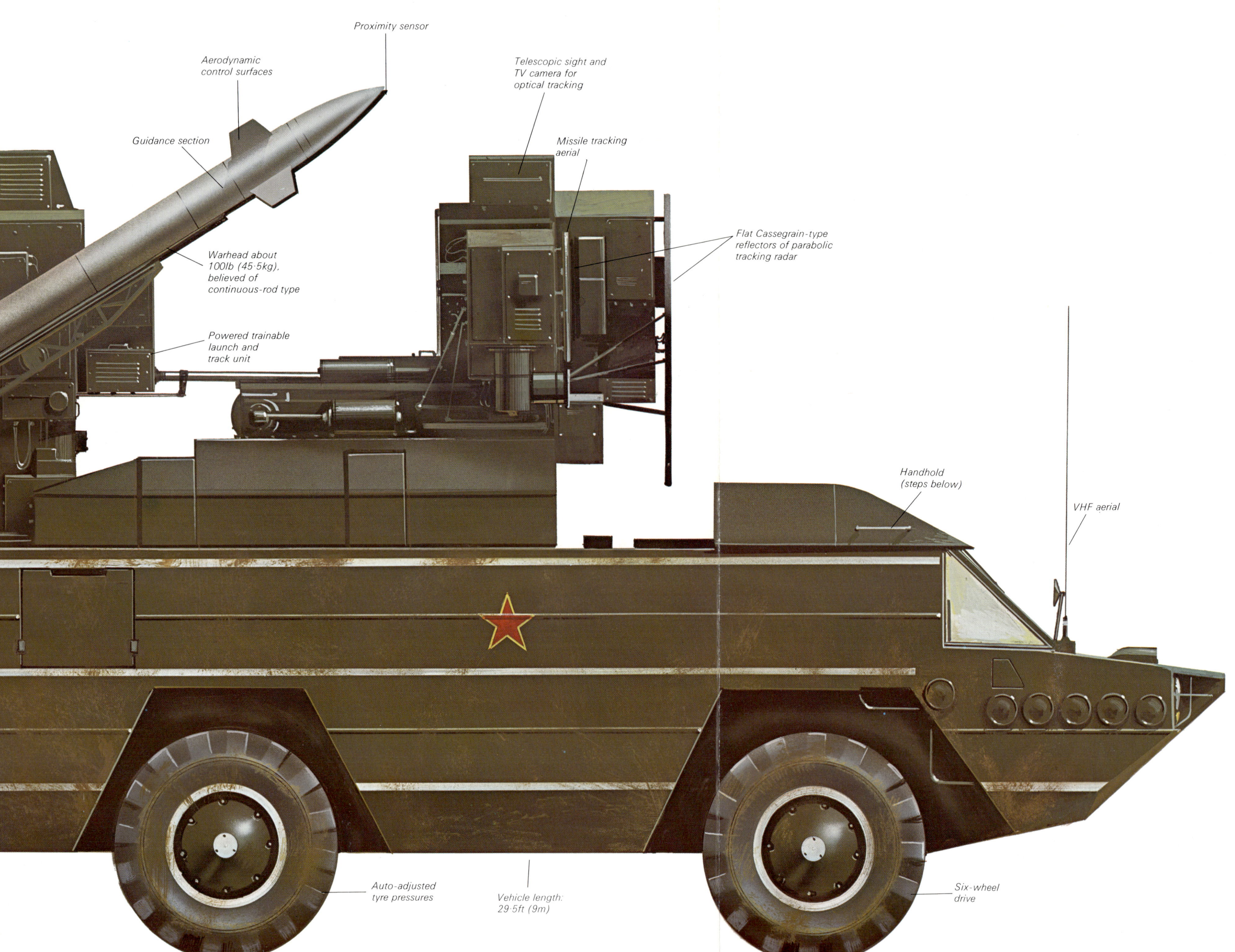

Aerodynamic
control surfaces

Proximity sensor

Guidance section

Telescopic sight and
TV camera for
optical tracking

Missile tracking
aerial

Warhead about
100lb (45·5kg),
believed of
continuous-rod type

Flat Cassegrain-type
reflectors of parabolic
tracking radar

Powered trainable
launch and
track unit

Right missile
tracking aerial
(receives missile
beacon signals)

Azimuth
pivot

Handhold
(steps below)

VHF aerial

Auto-adjusted
tyre pressures

Vehicle length:
29·5ft (9m)

Six-wheel
drive

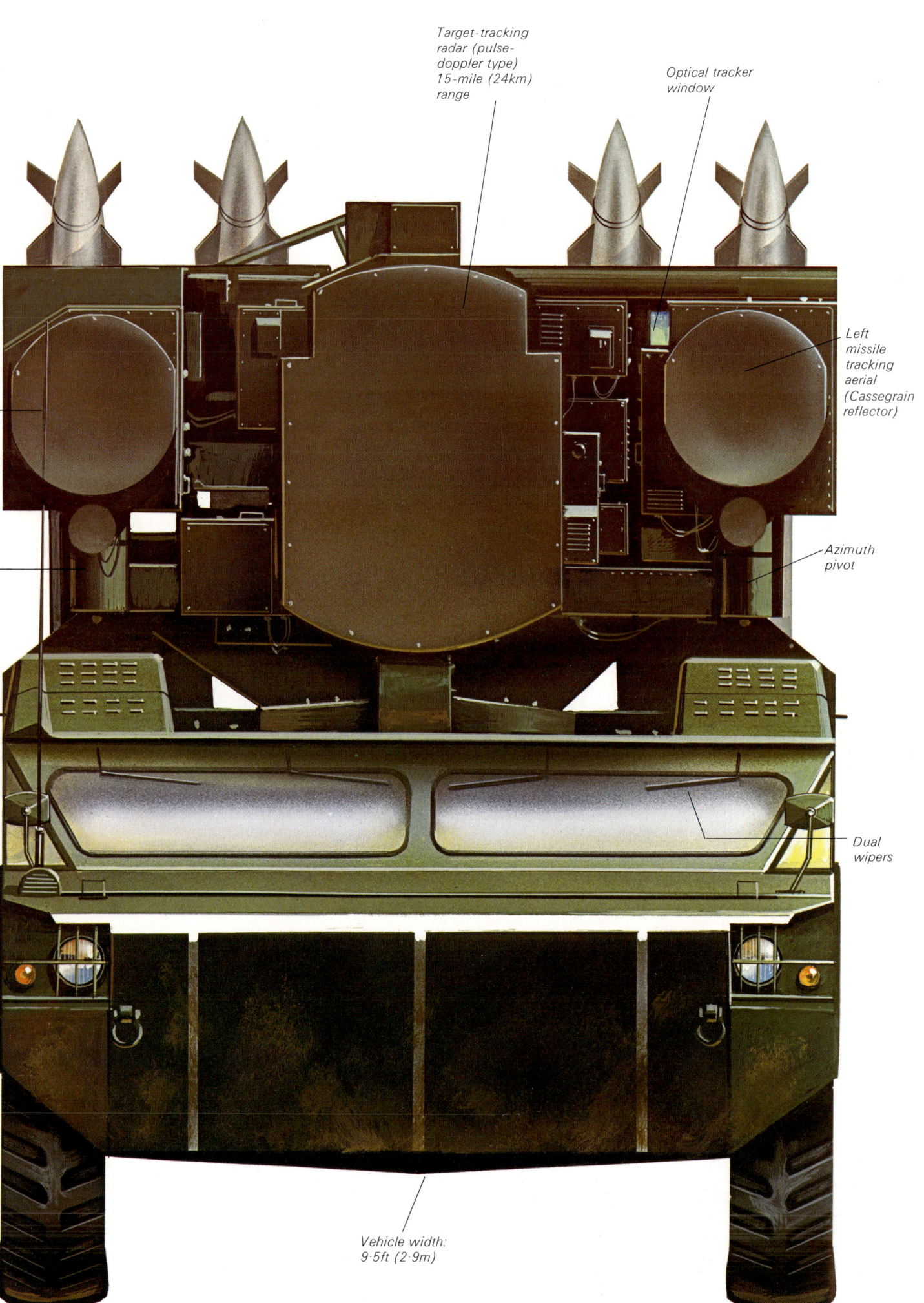

Target-tracking radar (pulse-doppler type) 15-mile (24km) range

Optical tracker window

Left missile tracking aerial (Cassegrain reflector)

Azimuth pivot

Dual wipers

Vehicle width: 9·5ft (2·9m)

25

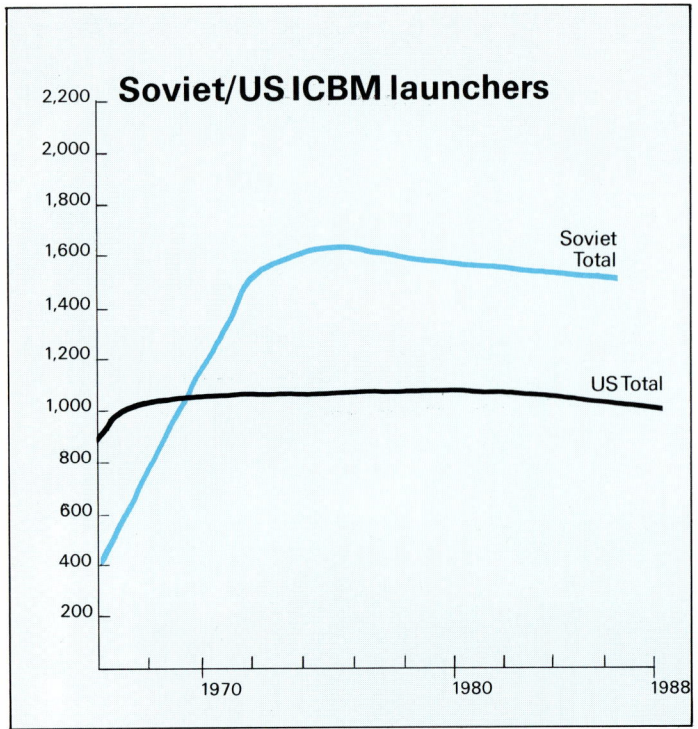

Soviet/US ICBM launchers

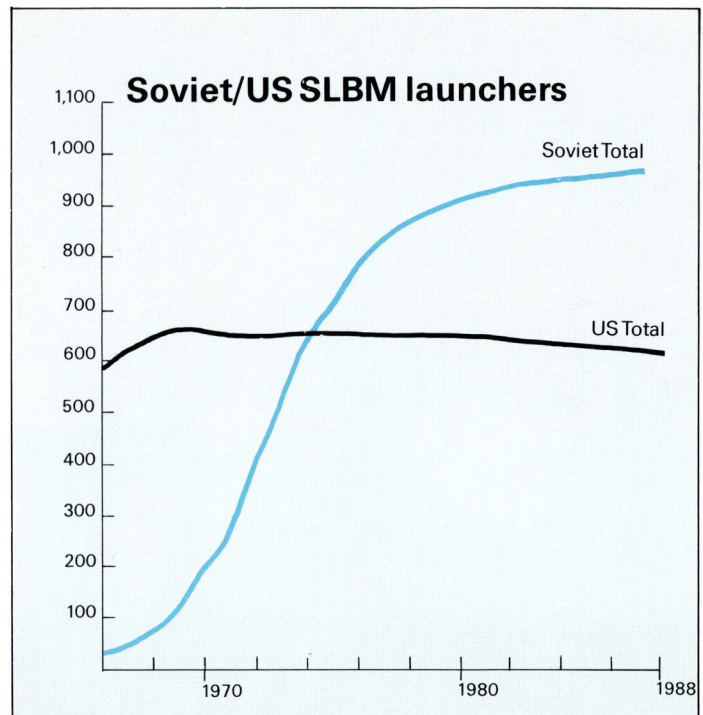

Soviet/US SLBM launchers

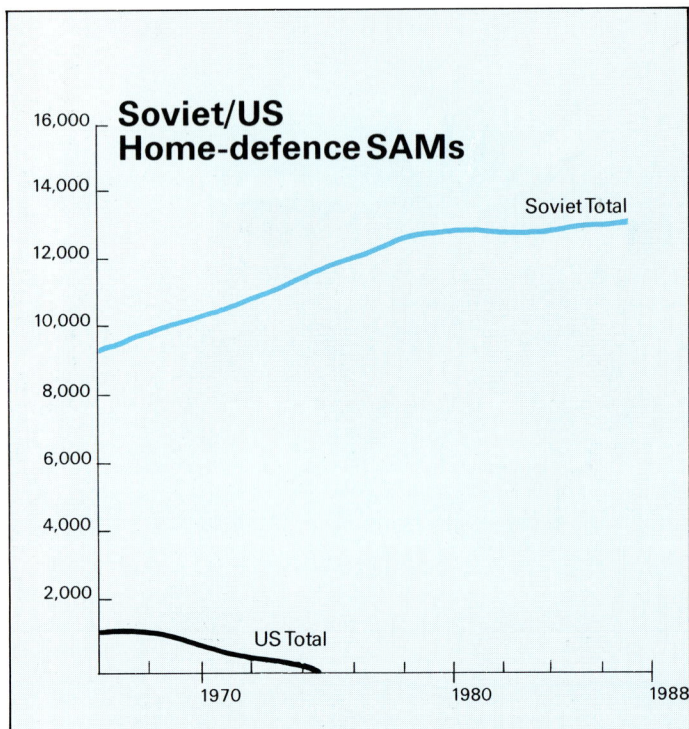

Soviet/US Home-defence SAMs

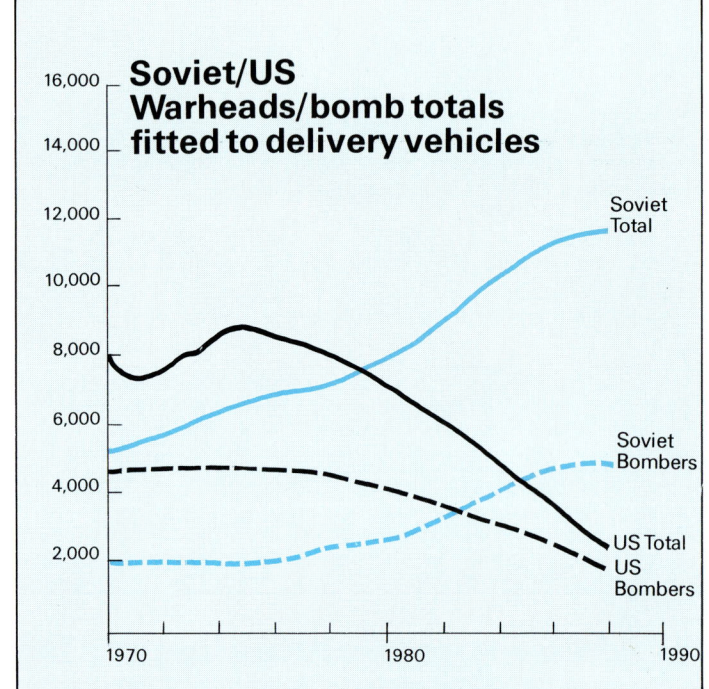

Soviet/US Warheads/bomb totals fitted to delivery vehicles

bases, 2,500km from air-launched platforms by the current three-year SALT protocol. The USSR does not need long-range cruise missiles, as most US targets are near to coast-lines or borders. This explains why Soviet cruise missiles with as long a range as the US ALCM have not been identified.

Tactical Airpower

Traditionally, the Soviet Union, and the Soviet Air Forces (VVS, Voyenno-vozdushnye-sily) in particular, have polarised their military thinking around the large land battle. The VVS throughout World War II was devoted almost entirely to close-support of field armies, and until the late 1960s its main strength was made up of fighters and fighter-bombers, generally somewhat inferior to those of the West. But by the late 1960s a dramatic transformation was taking place. The FA (Frontovaya Aviatsiya, frontal avia-tion), numerically the largest part of the VVS and the arm deploying the Soviet Union's tactical airpower, has been changed into the world's biggest and best-equipped offensive air force. This has been accomplished by the introduction of new types of aircraft carrying new ECM and other systems,

and matched with a wide range of new weapons. Whereas the previous generation of Soviet tactical aircraft, exem-plified by the MiG-21, Su-7B and Yak-27, were severely deficient in range, weapon load and equipment fit, today's replacements are second to none and superior to most air-craft currently in the front-line inventory of the West. The major types are shown in Table IV.

Compared with 1971 the aircraft deployed tactically by NATO in Europe could today deliver fractionally less ordnance if all went out together in a maximum-effort attack, while those of the WP air forces could deliver roughly 480 per cent more. In terms of numbers of aircraft deployed the WP forces overtook the West in 1971, a typical year for the cross-over of the basic strength curves, since when the two sides have continued to move further apart. Baseline numbers indicate a WP total of 3,000–3,300 tactical aircraft on the Central and lower Northern sectors in Europe, facing just half as many NATO aircraft of which 80 per cent are obsolescent or relatively limited through lack of capa-bilities. On the Southern front the situation is, on paper, more equal, with 920 WP against 710 of NATO.

Far and away the most important NATO tactical aircraft are the F-111E and F-111F swing-wing bombers of the 20th

Above: Essentially the West's only ICBM, Minuteman is a neat and refined weapon, but extremely small and limited in payload in comparison with the mighty Soviet missiles.

Above: Test firing of a Minuteman II, preceded by its smoke-ring (top left). New Soviet ICBMs use the superior "cold launch" technique, the rocket igniting above the silo.

Above: A test launch of the ALCM (Air-Launched Cruise Missile) from an NB-52G in 1976. The survivability of such relatively slow and unsophisticated missiles—essentially just small 600mph aircraft—is doubted.

Table IV   Tactical aircraft

Type	Service entry	Number	ASM	FR	Radar	Laser
A-7 Vought	1966	100*	yes	yes	yes	can be added
A-10A Fairchild	1974	30*	yes	yes	no	can be added
F-4C, F-4D MDD	1965	120*	yes	yes	yes	can be
F-5 (A, B versions) Northrop	1965	70	no	no	no	no
F-104G Lockheed	1963	550	yes	yes	yes	not usual
F-111 (E, F) GD	1968	170	could	yes	yes	can be
Jaguar Sepecat	1972	300	yes	yes	not usual	yes (RAF)
Mirage 5BA AMD-BA	1971	100*	?	no	no	no
MiG-27	1973	1,000	yes	no	yes (CW)	yes
Su-7BM	1959	550	?	no	no	not usual
Su-17	1970	400+	yes	no	yes	yes
Su-19	1974	480+	yes	?	yes	yes
Tu-22	1963	230	yes	yes	yes	probably

*With NATO air forces in Europe

and 48th Tactical Fighter Wings of USAFE, both based in England. These are the only Western aircraft available that can equal the capability of the Su-19 "Fencer", though the latter is deployed in much greater numbers. Next come the RAF Jaguar force, with outstanding range and weapon load, and excellent navigation and weapon-delivery systems but lacking multi-mode or terrain-following radar. No other Western tactical aircraft are capable of flying the required missions except under favourable daytime conditions or in airspace under NATO control. Two types possessed by NATO forces that appear not to have Soviet equals are the USAF A-10 and RAF Harrier. The former combines great air-to-ground lethality, survivability and other attributes that fit it well for front-line use, especially in its prime task of knocking out tanks and other point targets; but it lacks the essential all-weather capability and has yet to show how survivable it would be in a Soviet-style war involving vast concentrations of electronics and surface-to-air missiles. The Harrier has the major and so far unique (in the West) capability of not requiring an airfield. Though many Western combat types were intended to be capable of deployment to primitive hastily-prepared airstrips, all others do need an airstrip, and in any future war an airstrip is going to be one of the first things to be detected and attacked.

Off-Airfield Capabilities

Indeed, NATO air forces still use numerous aircraft, such as the F-104, F-5, most Mirages, the Buccaneer and (debatably) F-4 Phantom, which need a paved surface. Though some of these aircraft pay lip service to modern tactical operations—for example, the USAF F-4 versions have larger tyres than the original carrier-based F-4B—none of these aircraft has ever engaged in protracted or realistic off-airfield operation, and certainly not at gross weight. Neither have the F-111 and Jaguar; both were designed for rough-strip basing, and the Jaguar has convincingly demonstrated this capability—but not, so far as is known, in RAF or French service. This point is worth stressing, because without exception the Soviet FA uses oversize low-pressure tyres (they even make large bulges in the wing root or fuselage on some types) and operational units

Above: Late-model MiG-21 fighter-bombers in an underground hangar in Jugoslavia. Warsaw Pact countries, even more than the Jugoslavs, have concentrated on putting all their tactical air power in semi-hardened and dispersed installations which are often far from the nearest airstrip.

make a point of off-airfield deployment for up to two weeks at a time each year, in both warm and cold weather.

One would naturally expect Soviet tactical aircraft to have improved over the years, but the improvements have been impressively large and diverse. In structural materials, high-lift systems, weaponry and, above all, in the most difficult matters of ECM, sensors and weapon-guidance, the Soviets have virtually closed the technology gap between East and West which previously was used by Western governments to justify the large numerical gap. The only area where a technology gap appears still to exist is in gas-turbine engines, where such aggressive Western teams as GE, Pratt & Whitney and Turbo-Union appear hard to catch. But the engine gap is not enough to make a significant difference in aircraft capability, nor to justify widely differing numerical strengths.

Helicopters and Weaponry

The only other area in which the NATO forces appeared formerly to have had any kind of advantage was helicopters. Though the Eastern Bloc had large numbers of these aircraft, including types much larger and more capable than anything even considered in the West, the Soviets had nothing to equal the highly developed and effective "gunships", multi-sensor surveillance systems, and helicopter-fired guided missiles produced in the United States and to a lesser degree in France and Britain. Today most of the leeway has been made up, and before 1978 is out the fighting strength of Warsaw Pact helos will almost certainly outweigh that of NATO in Europe. Production of several formidable tactical derivatives of the Mi-24 assault transport is almost certainly running at maximum rate, and this single family of machines makes a gigantic contribution to Soviet battlefield capability. The combat versions appear to lack nothing in weapons, sensors and protection, and compare most favourably with types such as the Army Lynx, Hughes AH-64A and even machines still on paper such

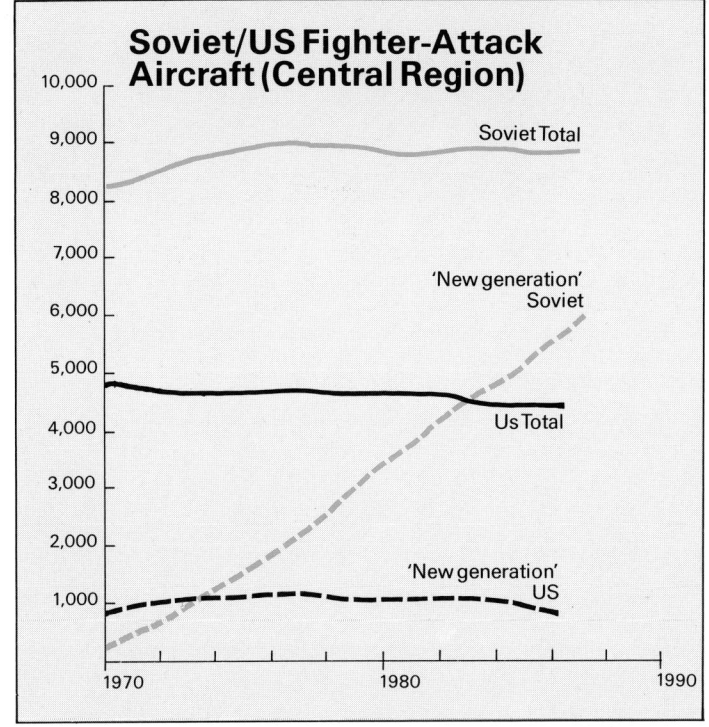

Soviet/US Fighter-Attack Aircraft (Central Region)

Soviet Total

'New generation' Soviet

Us Total

'New generation' US

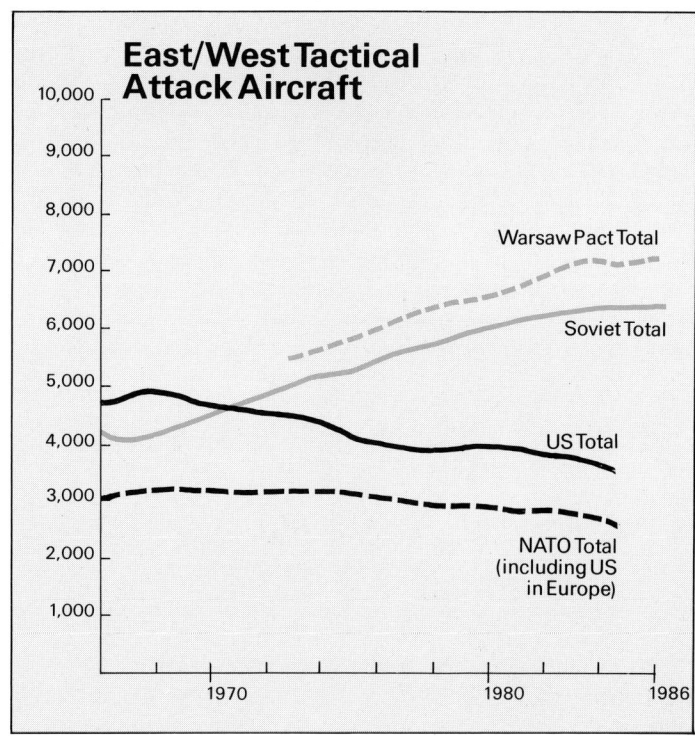

East/West Tactical Attack Aircraft

Warsaw Pact Total

Soviet Total

US Total

NATO Total (including US in Europe)

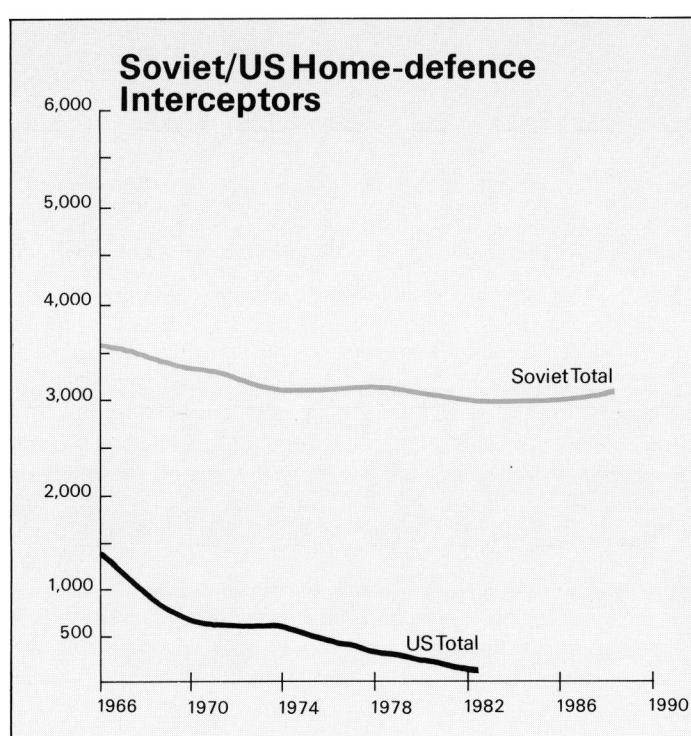

Soviet/US Home-defence Interceptors

Soviet Total

US Total

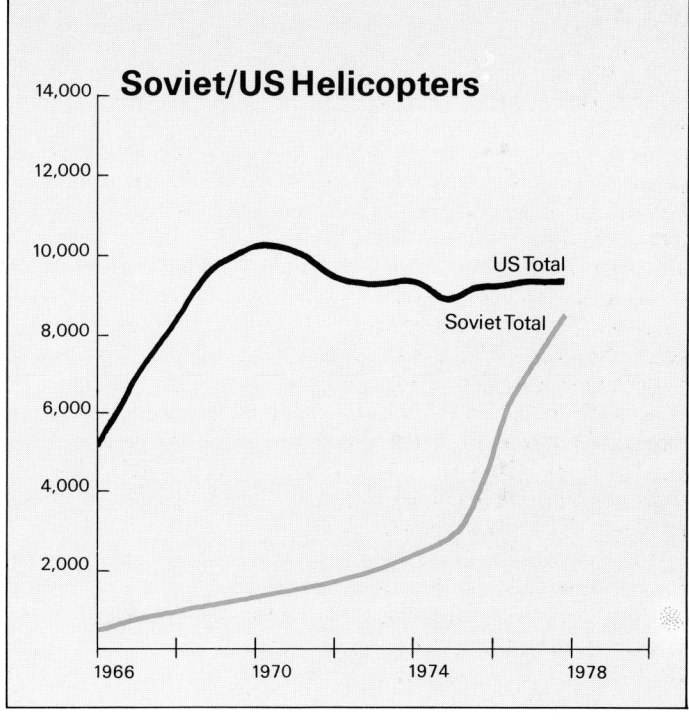

Soviet/US Helicopters

US Total

Soviet Total

as the PAH-2 project for West Germany. Likewise the assault transport Mi-24 stands up well even in comparison with the UH-60A Black Hawk, which like the AH-64A is still some way from service.

Some observers have made the point that the improved range of Soviet attack aircraft, with maximum or near-maximum weapon load, would allow a first strike to be flown, without warning, direct from normal peacetime bases. Until this decade it had been assumed in NATO planning that any attack launched by WP forces would be preceded by at least one full day of widespread repositioning of squadrons to advanced bases, probably mostly in East Germany.

To round off this section on tactical airpower it is necessary to compare NATO and WP weaponry. The Soviets have always been outstandingly good with aircraft guns (in World War II they were ahead of all other countries except Germany), and though today other nations have caught up the modern Soviet guns remain reliable, hard-hitting and adequate for their tasks. The chief calibres are 13·2, 23 and 30mm, with the last two by far the most important. Few 12·7 or 37mm guns remain, and none is thought to be in

any combat unit. The most important single-barrel gun is the NR-30, roughly equivalent to such Western guns as the Aden, DEFA and Oerlikon KCA. The twin-barrel GSh-23, widely used both for internal mounting and in the GP-9 clip-on pack, has almost double the impact kinetic energy of most Western 20mm ammunition and the high rate of fire of 3,000 shots/min. Little is known of Soviet multi-barrel "Gatling" cannon, of which several types have been in front-line service since 1973. A six-barrel gun, believed to be of 23mm calibre, appears to be fitted to all MiG-27s, probably with an ammunition tank of at least 500 rounds. A four-barrel gun, of calibre believed to be 13·2mm forms the main remotely sighted nose armament of the attack (gunship) derivative of the Mi-24.

Air/Surface Missile Systems

Though WP air forces use vast quantities of spin-stabilized rockets, mainly of 57mm (1·45in) calibre, in both air/air and air/ground operations, they have appeared so far strangely deficient in tactical guided missiles. Several types of extremely large air/surface missile appeared in the 1950s on strategic aircraft, and the well-known "Swatter" wire-guided anti-tank missile is carried by all known versions of the Mi-24 helicopter. But no tactical ASM was seen on any Soviet fixed-wing aircraft until very recently, and most of the information on such weapons in the West seems to be a mixture of supposition and guesswork. The reported types are: AS-7 ("Kerry"), said to be carried by the Su-19, to weigh 2,650lb (1200kg), have the remarkably short range of 6·2 miles (10km) with radio-command guidance, and exist in three versions; AS-8, a supposed "fire and forget" anti-armour missile carried by all versions of the Mi-24 helicopter, said to have the long range of 5 miles (8km); AS-X-9, a reported anti-radiation missile carried by the Su-19, said to have a range of 50–56 miles (80–90km); and AS-X-10, an EO (electro-optical) homing weapon with a range of 6·2 miles (10km), and possibly one of the versions of "Kerry". AS-8, X-9 and X-10 have not even been assigned published reporting names by NATO, suggesting that none has actually been seen by NATO observers. A still later missile, a supposed "Advanced TASM" (tactical air/surface missile) with a range of 25 miles (40km) has not even been given an AS-number.

All this contrasts strangely with the wealth of tactical air/surface guided missiles in the West, beginning with the US Navy Bullpup of 1954 and now too numerous to mention. The Soviets must have conducted extensive trials with such weapons for at least 20 years, and it is thought-provoking that not one has yet been seen in combat service.

Air Defence

For the first 25 years after World War II the PVO-Strany (air defence of the homeland) was the predominant arm of Soviet air power, with the largest number of aircraft and with most types of Soviet air-combat designs being created with this organization in mind. Vast sums were spent on every aspect of air defence, and the results achieved have been remarkable. Not even all Western defence budgets added together could fund an effective replacement-system for the Soviet Union, which is by far the largest country in the world; many of its 20-plus Military Districts are larger than any European country, and some in Asia are roughly the size of the whole of Western Europe. Even ignoring the "non-critical" frontiers or interior regions, the sheer size of the task of building an air-defence system for so enormous a land area would in the present Western fiscal environment appear out of the question. Yet it has not only been done, but the system has been continually updated and restructured to meet each new or predicted threat. (Some threats, such as the B-70 Valkyrie Mach-3 bomber, never materialized; that particular threat gave the Soviet Union the MiG-25 in all its high-performance versions.)

Dealing with manned interceptors first, the enormous forces of older fighters and all-weather interceptors have now been mainly retired from the IA-PVO (fighter aviation, PVO); but, true to Russian tradition, nearly all remain at work as EW (electronic-warfare) platforms and in various training or research/utility roles. In their place are today's fighters and interceptors (see Table V).

Clearly the MiG-25 is in a special position. Though its

Above: The most "penetrable" Western aircraft is the F-111 of the USAF. This is the ultimate model, the powerful F-111F (then serving in Idaho, now in England).

original role never came to pass, it remains a useful aircraft which has been developed in several versions and the interceptor sub-types are effective in commanding the upper airspace. Very much a "straight-line aircraft", in that it is not stressed for dogfighting but acts as an extremely fast high-flying platform for radar and missiles, the original "Foxbat A" typifies the Russian way of doing things in the late 1950s with a radar using thermionic valves (vacuum tubes) and relying on sheer power (600kW) to burn through any hostile jamming or other ECM. Even this version is equipped with a large, high-capacity and surprisingly versatile computer which links the aircraft into the Soviet electronic air-defence system and manages on-board data-processing. An aircraft of this type has virtually no need for a gun, though it does have a back-up optical sight. The prime armament comprises two IR (heat) and two radar guided missiles, known by the NATO designation AA-6 "Acrid". These are by far the largest air/air weapons in use in the world, though they cannot rival the multi-target 120-plus miles range of the US Navy AIM-54 Phoenix carried only by the F-14 Tomcat. A probable high-altitude range limit for "Acrid" is thought to be 50 miles (80km).

It is extremely important to note the mix of two guidance methods in each interceptor. IR-homing missiles work best in one set of environmental or ECM conditions, and semi-active radar homing works best in another set. There is evidence that in the IA-PVO it is normal technique to launch one of each kind against a single target, the IR weapon flying a fraction of a second in front so that it is not confused by the motor flame from its partner. Every Soviet interceptor normally carries at least one missile using each type of guidance, and this combination is much more difficult to evade than either radar or IR alone. Though on the whole Western AAMs (air/air missiles) are probably technically superior to Soviet types, no NATO fighter can fire missiles having a choice of guidance systems except for the Sidewinder family, which are close-ranged and pack relatively limited punch.

According to Lt V. Belenko, who defected to Japan in a MiG-25 in 1976, a later interceptor version exists with two additional missile pylons on the fuselage, and probably armed with a gun. The radar is also improved, and the engines up-rated. So much is to be expected, because the MiG-25 is almost 20 years old as a design and must have been subjected to improvement. But, surprisingly, Belenko is quoted as saying the improved model, called "Foxbat E", has an

Table V Fighters and interceptors

Type	Service entry	Number	AAM	FR	IR+radar	Internal gun
F-4E, F-4M MDD	1969	600	yes	yes	most	yes (not F-4M)
F-15 MDD	1975	48	yes	yes	yes	yes
F-104S Aeritalia/Lockheed	1969	205	yes	can be	no	not usual
Mirage F1-CG AMD-BA	1977 (Greece)	40	yes	no	yes	yes
MiG-21 (various)	various	2,200	yes	no	yes	yes
MiG-23	1971	850	yes	no	yes	yes
MiG-25	1969	400+	yes	no	yes	can be
Su-9, -11	1959, 1967	750	yes	no	yes	no
Su-15	1968	750	yes	no	yes	in some
Tu-28P	1961	150	yes	no	yes	no
Yak-28P	1962	550*	yes	no	yes	some

*Includes about 300 used as EW and multi-sensor platforms, interceptors phasing out

airframe stressed for supersonic flight at low level and for combat manoeuvres. Other versions of this exceedingly interesting aircraft include the MiG-25R strategic reconnaissance aircraft ("Foxbat B"), the MiG-25U dual trainer with stepped cockpits ("Foxbat C") and a later MiG-25R with larger SLAR (side-looking airborne radar) called "Foxbat D". None of these have any counterpart in the West, except for the handful of extremely specialized SR-71 "Blackbirds" used by USAF Strategic Air Command which, so far as is known, have never been considered for overflights of battle areas in Europe.

Fighters and AAMs

At one time the Su-9 was one of the most important IA-PVO interceptors, but its successor, Su-11, has already been overtaken by the much more advanced Su-15 ("Flagon"). The Su-11 marked a considerable advance in carrying the "Skip Spin" radar and associated AA-3 "Anab" missile in both radar and IR forms, with a slightly more powerful engine to maintain performance at least as good as the Su-9. In most respects the Su-11 is every bit as formidable as most Western interceptors, though it has the limited range common to all early Sukhoi 7/9/11 sub-types. Though almost certainly possessed of the same speed and missiles, the Su-15 ("Flagon") has considerably greater range and much longer-range radar, and the ability not only to carry additional armament and equipment but also to develop further in the course of time. Main current versions have a new wing ("Flagon D"), more power ("Flagon E") and a new radar with larger dish aerial requiring a fat ogival radome

Above: In-flight refuelling an FB-111A of USAF Strategic Air Command. Hit by inflation and budget problems, the 210 of this type were eventually cut to 76, supporting a mere two wings of only 30 aircraft each.

instead of a conical one ("Flagon F"). These are totally home-defence, or at least long-runway, aircraft; they affirm the continuing importance of the IA-PVO irrespective of the dwindling ability of the West to launch any manned-aircraft attack against the Soviet Union.

More numerous, and probably the chief "fighter" in the WP air forces today, the MiG-23 ("Flogger") has appeared in several forms and been exported to several foreign air forces. Curiously, no versions have yet been seen in service with any WP air force other than the GSFG (Group of Soviet Forces in Germany). Previously, though the Russians were always adamant that they alone were going to operate the latest bomber and tactical attack aircraft, they did allow modern defensive fighters to fly with as many units of as many WP air forces as could afford the money and manpower to do so. The policy may have changed, because the original MiG-23S was in operational service in East Germany seven years ago in 1971, and yet in 1978 not even the East German air force, nor those of Poland or Czechoslovakia, operate this purely defensive machine. It is not especially advanced in technology, and its fire control does not need the precise relative-wind information that results in the array of transducer vanes on a long boom on the nose of some other Soviet interceptors. On the other hand the multi-mode radar ("High Lark") is one of the more modern in Soviet service, and the two types of air/air missile (which are backed up by a laser ranger, optical sight and GSh-23

31

Above: Fastest military aircraft in the world, the technically amazing—and very expensive—Lockheed SR-71A is used for strategic reconnaissance. Is it vulnerable to SAMs?

This abundance of proven AAMs puts not only the IA-PVO but also the fighter elements of the FA (which use the MiG-23S) in a very strong position. No NATO air force has such a spectrum of air-combat missiles, and though lack of standardization within NATO results in a welter of different AAM types, the possible advantage of this in terms of Soviet countermeasures problems is nullified by the fact that the number used by each air force is often only one, and at the most two (ignoring F-14 Tomcats from US carriers).

SAM Networks

There is one major area in which the comparison between East and West is so staggering as to be meaningless. SAMs (surface/air missiles) are generally judged the most sure and cost/effective way to bring down hostile aircraft that penetrate one's own territory. All published war scenarios between NATO and the WP assume that it is the latter that invades the West; it is doubtful if a study has ever been done for an invasion in the opposite direction. This might be expected to result in a vast concentration of SAMs in the European NATO countries and very few in the East. The actual situation is the exact opposite. The Soviet Union almost certainly has more SAMs than the rest of the world put together. The European NATO nations have a scattered hodge-podge of designs which are either obsolescent, inadequate or not yet in effective service (see Table VI).

Current US Department of Defense assessments include the following totals: ABMs (anti-ballistic missile), US none, Soviet Union 64; strategically deployed SAMs, US none, Soviet Union 11,000. One wonders if these figures are widely appreciated by the noisy protesters who killed the American ABM, or who cosily believe that the US is protected by a vast network of SAMs? An equally disturbing

gun) are so new that little is known about them in the West. The bigger one, called AA-7 "Apex", is estimated to be larger than the familiar Sparrow, though its effective range is for some reason put at only 17 miles (27km). (The long-standing habit of Western, and especially NATO, observers to underrate Soviet performance has already been shown to be dangerously misleading, and seems to stem from the unfounded belief that the Russians simply cannot be as good as their rivals!) Both this range, and the figures published for other Soviet AAMs, ought to be looked at anew by intelligence experts able to view Soviet capability objectively. The smaller MiG-23S missile is called AA-8 "Aphid", and in configuration it appears to resemble the early Falcon missiles of the USAF. While "Apex" is known to exist in both IR and radar forms, "Aphid" is (probably incorrectly) not believed to exist in an IR-homing form. It is, of course, used for close-in dogfighting.

Table VI SAMs

Type	Service entry	Number on launchers ready to fire	Mobile	Blindfire capability
Blowpipe	recent	few	yes	no
Crotale	recent	80	yes	yes
Hawk/Improved Hawk	1958/72	482	some	yes
Nike Hercules	1958	472	no	yes
Rapier	1975?	few but rising	yes	most
Redeye	1965	1,400?	yes	no
Tigercat	1965?	few	yes	can have
* Rapier and Bloodhound	Very small numbers—information classified			
SA-1	1954	hundreds, falling	yes	yes
SA-2	1958	4,000, falling	yes	yes
SA-3	1961	2,000+	yes	yes
SA-4	1967?	1,000+	yes	yes
SA-6	1968	5,000	yes	yes
SA-7	1966?	20,000?	yes	no
SA-8	1976	rising fast	yes	yes
SA-9	1976	rising fast	yes	unlikely
ABM-1B (Galosh)	1966	64	no	yes

picture is seen in the vital matter of mobile battlefield air-defence systems. Much of the West's future protection rests on the Roland vehicle-mounted SAM system, originally planned by MBB and Aérospatiale (Euromissile) in 1964–68. A version has been adopted as the standard Shorads (short-range air-defense system) of the US Army, and at a cost exceeding $250,000,000 it has been modified to US standards and teamed with an American radar, on a different vehicle, though an attempt has been made to make the European and US systems grossly "compatible". Today, more than a year after fire units were planned to be in US Army service, the missile is still in its most crucial phase of testing against high-g aerial targets (what happens if the manoeuvrability of the missile should be found wanting?). The missiles available, Hawk and Nike Hercules, are obsolete, and the new-generation Patriot is fantastically costly and years late. Altogether the NATO air-defence missile scene is not merely in disarray, it is barely visible at all.

Naval Airpower

Though it lost two-thirds of its aircraft 16 years ago, when its fighters were transferred to the PVO, the AV-MF (Soviet independent naval air fleet) remains a large and diverse force which has been utterly transformed since 1970 by its deployment of what can be called "aircraft carriers". Since Czarist Russia there has been a separate naval air force, and except for the US Navy the AV-MF is the only large multi-role naval air force in the world. Its great size and effectiveness are beyond dispute. About 90 per cent of its aircraft are shore-based, a total of some 2,300 aircraft of which at least 800 are first-line operational types. Unlike even the US Navy these include the largest strategic aircraft, which fly all kinds of shore-based reconnaissance, Elint and EW missions and, in war, would work with the Soviet surface and submarine fleets to destroy Allied ships and direct missiles against Allied nations. These are duties unique to the AV-MF. Though nominally the AV-MF exists to support the Soviet fleets—Baltic Red Banner, Black Sea, Northern and Far East—its shore-based units also have the capability of independent operation in global strategic roles.

One of these roles, of course, is the Elint probing of NATO environments, including NATO exercises in distant waters. These duties used to be accomplished by several versions of Tu-20 (Tu-95 "Bear"), backed up by a much larger number of Tu-16 ("Badger") and a few M-4 ("Bison") sub-types, to a total of about 350 aircraft including supporting tankers. Now the "Backfire" has joined in this work, and a proportion that could exceed 50 per cent of the deliveries of "Backfire B" is being supplied to the AV-MF. To the uninitiated it is difficult to tell from a picture whether a Soviet strategic aircraft belongs to the AV-MF or DA; in "East v West"

Left: A rare picture of two F-102A Delta Dagger interceptors of the USAF (since withdrawn) escorting a Tu-20 "Bear C" long-range ocean-surveillance aircraft.

Above: Obviously expensive, the MiG-25 "Foxbat" interceptor has nevertheless spawned a valuable series of aircraft of ever-growing capability. We have not seen the last of it.

assessments it is important not to count such aircraft twice.

One of the prime duties of AV-MF strategic aircraft is to find distant targets for ship-based missile systems whose radars cannot yet see them because they are over the horizon from near sea level. Several of the Soviet naval missile systems have been planned from the start for in-flight guidance using radars mounted on sea or air platforms. Such guidance might be thought clumsy and primitive, especially in comparison with advanced Western inertial and Tercom (terrain-comparison) methods, but for use against ships it is not easy to find alternatives. The missile has to home on the ship, no matter what the latter may do, and unless it is possible to rely on a passive system, homing on IR or electronic emissions from the target, a semi-active system using an airborne emitter seems almost inevitable. (Thinking aloud, some of the Soviet satellites could well serve a target-illuminating function for ocean missile guidance, the advantages being that, even though the source might soon be detected, it could not quickly be shot down). The only alternative is to use active radar homing, as in the US Navy Tomahawk, but making a missile an emitter makes it almost simple to shoot down.

AV-MF uses numerous propeller-driven aircraft other than the Tu-20. The AI-20 turboprop powers both the main shore-based ASW types, the Il-38 ("May") and Be-12 ("Mail"). The latter is an extremely good and versatile amphibian which has no surviving counterpart in the West, except for Japan's PS-1 and fewer than a dozen Albatross still used by non-NATO countries in non-combatant duties. Whether an amphibian is an advantage in ASW missions is doubtful. Certainly the Il-38 has far greater speed and range, and bears comparison with the Orion (just which sub-type of Orion is arguable) and Atlantic. In view of Britain's outstanding success with the Nimrod it is noteworthy that no similar maritime rebuild has been seen of earlier bombers, except for Elint/recce duties. Many of the AV-MF's large force of strategic aircraft, various types of Tu-16 and Tu-20, were originally equipped to launch and guide large cruise missiles on their own account. The weapons included some of the largest air weapons of all time (AS-2 "Kipper", AS-3 "Kangaroo", AS-4 "Kitchen" and AS-5 "Kelt"), and though old most are still in operational service. One of the last types to carry such early stand-off missiles was the Tu-22 ("Blinder") supersonic bomber, of which at least half serve with the AV-MF. In this case the extra range conferred by the missile could be important, in view of the limited radius of the parent aircraft.

One of the most numerous AV-MF types is the Ka-25 ("Hormone") helicopter, a compact co-axial-rotor machine which has now appeared in more than seven versions (if minor differences are included) and which has never ceased to be updated. Powered by two 900shp turbines, it has proved capable of a degree of development rivalled by few Western

helicopters, and a close look at any recent example cannot fail to impress. Though many of the knobs, bulges, aerials, dielectric panels and strange devices remain enigmas, it is doubtful that any Western helicopter carries so many items of operational equipment. Mated with an obviously efficient capture/haul-down system, this useful machine serves aboard many major units of the surface fleet, including all *Kresta* and *Kara* cruisers, the ASW cruisers *Moskva* and *Leningrad* and the much larger V/STOL carrier *Kiev*. Obviously, the greater the number of equipment items, the smaller the fuel/weapon load. This must have put pressure on the Kamov bureau to produce an enlarged (three-engined?) derivative. Meanwhile in the past two years the Mil bureau has seen its Mi-8 derivative (called "Haze" by NATO) enter service in the ASW role. This is a considerably larger machine (bigger and heavier than the S-61 Sea King), and it obviously carries a much greater load of sensors, other equipment and weapons. But does it go to sea, as does Sea King? If it is judged too big for cruiser platforms it cannot properly be considered a replacement for the trusty Kamov, though there should be no difficulty in basing a unit of "Hazes" on the mighty *Kiev*.

V/STOL Platforms

Kiev, now a mature ship, is the first of at least four of the so-called *Kuril* class of multi-role carriers. They did not stem merely from Admiral Gorshkov's aggressive wish to transform the Soviet Navy into a powerful across-the-board global force; these new ships have immense potential and almost certainly represent better value for money than the traditional super-CVA with catapults, angled deck, arresters and 5,000 souls on board. (Equally, Britain is certainly wrong to have taken so emotive a stance against fixed-wing air power at sea, a stance which without the possibility of the Sea Harrier could have proved serious indeed.) Most observers judge the displacement of *Kiev* to be about 40,000 tons; her next two sisters are similar, *Minsk* being about ready to commission as this is written, but the fourth ship is much larger and tentatively put in the 60,000-ton class. *Kiev* has already gained considerable experience in sea operations with the jet VTOL Yak-36 ("Forger"), but it is doubtful that this is the definitive fixed-wing aircraft for use from the *Kuril* vessels. There is every reason to predict a more powerful and more versatile V/STOL with better role equipment and designed for rolling ski-jump takeoffs. Of course, such an aircraft does not need a 60,000-ton or even 40,000-ton ship, and the *Kuril* class, despite their vast amount of equipment for many types of duty, will probably be followed by V/STOL platforms of less than half the displacement.

The AV-MF has never shown the slightest inclination to deploy traditional fixed-wing airpower at sea. It is most unlikely it will attempt to do so, even though the fourth *Kuril* hull could in theory have ample capability to operate aircraft as large as the Su-19.

Space

Whereas in the 1960s the Americans, notably the US Air Force, funded an unrivalled long-term space programme totally military in character, the boot is today on the other foot. As the US military space budget has dwindled, so has the Soviet budget risen. This determines what can be achieved, and though few details of missions have leaked into the public arena it is blindingly obvious that today the Soviet Union is taking six or more steps in military space for each one by the United States. The list of missions, potential missions, research projects and possibilities in military space programmes are almost endless, and most are extremely exciting. There is no room here to elaborate, but few nations have any substantial military space programmes apart from the two super-powers. The list of military launches in 1977 (which even today may be incomplete, because no complete official list is issued by either country) gives an indication of the military space effort by both:

Summing Up

In most basic parameters—population, GNP, industrial strength—the West is far ahead of the East: even Western Europe alone can rival the Eastern (WP) Bloc on most such measures. But in terms of military strength and military potential the position is markedly different. In the totalitarian WP states the military effort is laid down by government without the participation of the people— who in any case have a limited source of information other than a totally "managed" press, radio and TV. It is simple in such a society to elevate war, or preparation for war, to a high position, chiefly by incessantly harping on the menace of the Capitalist powers. As a result the armed forces, in the Soviet Union rather more than in other WP nations, are— quite rightly—a major focal point of a passionately patriotic society. Attitudes towards the services, and towards military service itself, are intensely positive.

Many of the Western countries enjoyed similar patriotism and national pride in their armed forces early in this century, and during World War II, but recent years have been marked by a dramatic change in attitude. Nowhere is this more complete than in the United States, but it is also found throughout NATO. It goes much deeper than mere lethargy or pacifism, has complex origins, and is part of other equally deep changes in social attitudes and beliefs. Sadly, there has not been a change in another kind of attitude which, from the signing of the North Atlantic Treaty in 1949, has bedevilled NATO's entire operation. This is the passionate wish of the 15 nations to exert their "full national sovereignty". Nothing like this happens in the WP camp; when the chips are down, the Soviet Union—by no means universally liked or even respected, but simply the biggest— lays on the line what will be done. In the NATO councils any agreement at all is a major achievement, and it usually turns out to be an inefficient compromise.

This is manifest in every facet of every kind of military endeavour. The United States wants to sell military hardware, and views European weapon efforts either with suspicion or patronizing disbelief, whilst wishing its weak and spineless European Allies would get up and pull their weight instead of leaving it all to the Americans (this is the theme of an avalanche of reports and magazine articles that pour across Western desks). The Europeans, nettled by their continual failure to compete, achieve standardization, or withstand the onslaught of US technical and industrial domination, fumble with national projects and talk interminably about multinational collaboration. US industry jealously resists "giving away its vital technological secrets" to a supposedly backward and grasping

USSR Military Satellites 1977

Date	Name	Launch Weight Kg	lb	Apogee Km	Miles	Perigee Km	Miles	Inclination	Lifetime	Probable purpose
6 January	Cosmos 888	4,000	8,800	325	202	170	106	65·00	13 days	Reconnaissance satellite?
20 January	Cosmos 889	4,000	8,800	329	204	202	126	71·38	12 days	Reconnaissance satellite?
20 January	Cosmos 890	700	1,543	1,020	634	983	611	83·00	1,200 yrs	Navigation satellite?
2 February	Cosmos 891	—	—	516	321	473	294	65·84	10 yrs	Purpose not known
9 February	Cosmos 892	4,000	8,800	427	265	159	99	73·00	13 days	Reconnaissance satellite?
21 February	Cosmos 894	700	1,543	1,004	624	971	603	83·00	1,200 yrs	Navigation satellite?
26 February	Cosmos 895	2,500	5,500	635	395	611	380	81·00	60 yrs	Electronic surveillance satellite?
3 March	Cosmos 896	4,000	8,800	343	213	177	110	73·00	13 days	Reconnaissance satellite?
10 March	Cosmos 897	4,000	8,800	340	211	171	106	73·00	13 days	Reconnaissance satellite?
17 March	Cosmos 898	4,000	8,800	230	143	216	134	81·00	13 days	Reconnaissance satellite?
24 March	Cosmos 899	900	2,000	547	340	503	313	74·00	10 yrs	Electronic surveillance satellite?
5 April	Cosmos 901	400	882	820	510	269	167	71·00	17 mths	Radar calibration?
7 April	Cosmos 902	6,000	13,230	279	173	168	104	81·39	13 days	Reconnaissance satellite?
11 April	Cosmos 903	1,250	2,755	40,153	24,950	603	375	62·84	10 yrs	Early warning satellite?
20 April	Cosmos 904	5,500	12,125	328	204	203	126	71·37	14 days	Reconnaissance satellite?
26 April	Cosmos 905	6,000	13,230	339	211	171	106	67·00	30 days	Reconnaissance satellite? Recovered.
5 May	Cosmos 907	6,000	13,230	364	226	181	112	62·80	11 days	Reconnaissance satellite?
17 May	Cosmos 908	5,500	12,125	288	179	174	108	52·00	14 days	Reconnaissance satellite?
19 May	Cosmos 909	—	—	2,109	1,310	990	615	65·87	4,000 yrs	Target for interception test?
23 May	Cosmos 910	—	—	1,774	1,102	300	186	65·86	1·2 hrs	Intended to intercept Cosmos 909? Failed.
25 May	Cosmos 911	—	—	1,004	624	970	603	83·00	1,200 yrs	Navigation satellite?
30 May	Cosmos 913	550	1,213	520	323	472	293	74·00	6 yrs	Ferret mission satellite?
31 May	Cosmos 914	5,500	12,125	306	190	203	126	65·00	13 days	Reconnaissance satellite?
8 June	Cosmos 915	6,000	13,230	289	180	173	107	62·80	13 days	Reconnaissance satellite?
10 June	Cosmos 916	6,000	13,230	298	185	246	153	62·80	12 days	Reconnaissance satellite?
16 June	Cosmos 917	1,250	2,755	40,176	24,964	585	364	62·91	10 yrs	Early warning satellite?
17 June	Cosmos 918	—	—	243	151	128	80	65·11	1 day	'Intercepted' Cosmos 909.
18 June	Cosmos 919	400	882	822	511	269	167	71·00	7 mths	Electronic surveillance satellite?
22 June	Cosmos 920	6,000	13,230	342	213	173	107	65·00	13 days	Reconnaissance satellite?
30 June	Cosmos 922	5,500	12,125	299	186	205	127	62·81	13 days	Reconnaissance satellite?
1 July	Cosmos 923	750	1,653	817	508	799	496	74·03	120 yrs	Communications satellite?
4 July	Cosmos 924	900	2,000	550	342	513	319	74·02	10 yrs	Electronic surveillance satellite?
7 July	Cosmos 925	2,200	4,850	634	394	609	378	81·20	60 yrs	Electronic surveillance satellite?
8 July	Cosmos 926	700	1,543	1,011	628	976	606	82·94	1,200 yrs	Navigation satellite?
12 July	Cosmos 927	6,000	13,230	361	224	153	95	72·87	13 days	Reconnaissance satellite?
12 July	Cosmos 928	700	1,543	1,011	628	956	594	82·96	1,200 yrs	Navigation satellite?
20 July	Cosmos 931	1,250	2,755	40,065	24,895	604	375	62·96	12 yrs	Early warning satellite?
20 July	Cosmos 932	6,000	13,230	311	193	149	93	65·00	13 days	Reconnaissance satellite?
22 July	Cosmos 933	—	—	408	254	384	239	65·84	2 yrs	Radar calibration?
27 July	Cosmos 934	6,000	13,230	255	158	231	144	62·81	13 days	Reconnaissance satellite?
29 July	Cosmos 935	5,500	12,125	251	156	217	135	81·33	13 days	Reconnaissance satellite?
24 August	Cosmos 937	—	—	444	276	424	263	65·00	6 yrs	Ocean surveillance satellite?
24 August	Cosmos 938	6,000	13,230	340	211	181	112	62·81	13 days	Reconnaissance satellite?
24 August	Cosmos 939-946	40	88	1,490	926	1,470	913	74·00	8,000 yrs	Communications satellites?
27 August	Cosmos 947	5,500	12,125	321	199	203	126	72·85	13 days	Reconnaissance satellite?
6 September	Cosmos 949	6,700	14,770	325	202	177	110	62·80	29 days	Reconnaissance satellite?
13 September	Cosmos 950	5,500	12,125	282	175	205	127	62·8	13 days	Reconnaissance satellite?
13 September	Cosmos 951	700	1,543	1,017	632	968	601	83·00	1,200 yrs	Navigation satellite?
16 September	Cosmos 952	—	—	265	165	251	156	65·00	600 yrs	Ocean surveillance satellite?
16 September	Cosmos 953	6,000	13,230	330	205	180	112	62·80	13 days	Reconnaissance satellite?
18 September	Cosmos 954	—	—	265	165	251	156	65·00	129 days	Nuclear powered sea surveillance satellite. Remains came down over Canada.
20 September	Cosmos 955	2,500	5,511	265	165	251	156	81·2	60 yrs	Electronic surveillance satellite?
30 September	Cosmos 957	6,000	13,230	361	224	171	106	65·00	13 days?	Reconnaissance satellite?
11 October	Cosmos 958	6,000	13,230	351	218	257	160	62·80	13 days	Reconnaissance satellite?
21 October	Cosmos 959	—	—	850	528	146	91	65·84	40 days	Target satellite?
25 October	Cosmos 960	900	2,000	546	339	502	312	74·0	10 yrs	Electronic surveillance satellite?
26 October	Cosmos 961	—	—	302	188	125	78	66·00	1 day	Intended to intercept Cosmos 959?
28 October	Cosmos 962	700	1,543	1,012	629	968	601	83·00	1,200 yrs	Navigation satellite?
24 November	Cosmos 963	650	1,433	1,210	752	1,182	734	82·93	3,000 yrs	Navigation satellite?
4 December	Cosmos 964	6,000	13,230	362	225	171	106	72·88	13 days	Reconnaissance satellite?
8 December	Cosmos 965	550	1,212	516	321	465	289	74·03	6 yrs	Electronic surveillance satellite?
12 December	Cosmos 966	6,000	13,230	296	184	204	127	65·00	12 days	Reconnaissance satellite?
13 December	Cosmos 967	—	—	1,005	624	963	598	65·84	1,200 yrs	Target for Cosmos 970?
16 December	Cosmos 968	—	—	810	503	782	486	74·03	120 years	Communications satellite?
20 December	Cosmos 969	6,000	13,230	317	197	180	112	62·81	14 days	Reconnaissance satellite?
21 December	Cosmos 970	—	—	861	535	144	89	65·16	—	Interception satellite? Passed close to Cosmos 967 then exploded.
23 December	Cosmos 971	700	1,543	1,010	628	980	609	83·00	1,200 yrs	Navigation satellite?
27 December	Cosmos 973	6,000	13,230	325	202	203	126	71·45	13 days	Reconnaissance satellite?

US Military Satellites 1977

Date	Name	Launch Weight Kg	lb	Apogee Km	Miles	Perigee Km	Miles	Inclination	Lifetime	Probable Purpose
28 January	NATO 3B	700	1,543	35,797	22,243	35,777	22,231	2·6	Unlimited	NATO communications satellite.
6 February	USAF	—	—	35,860	22,282	35,620	22,133	0·5	Unlimited	Early warning satellite, with infrared sensors to detect launches of satellites from Asia.
13 March	USAF	3,000	6,614	348	216	124	77	96·40	74 days	Purpose not known.
12 May	DSCS	565	1,246	35,762	22,222	35,438	22,020	2·44	Unlimited	Military communications satellite
23 May	USAF	—	—	35,855	22,279	35,679	22,170	0·2	Unlimited	Purpose not known.
5 June	AMS-2	450	992	869	540	811	504	99·20	80 yrs	Advanced Meteorological Satellite.
23 June	NTS-2	431	950	20,187	12,544	19,545	12,145	63·28	Unlimited	Purpose not known.
27 June	USAF	13,300	29,321	239	149	155	96	97·02	179 days	'Big Bird' reconnaissance satellite.
23 September	USAF	3,000	6,614	352	219	125	78	96·49	76 days	Purpose not known.
28 October	Transat	—	—	1,107	688	1,069	664	89·92	2,000 yrs	Purpose not known
11 December	USAF	700	1,543	41,002	25,478	191	119	28·20	Unlimited	Purpose not known.

Note: All weights are estimated.

Europe. Each of the European nations eagerly agrees on a standardized NATO product, provided it is its own offering that is selected. Declining national defence budgets, unionization of the armed forces, and decaying national will all pour additional sand in the works of what was meant to be effective collective security.

Western citizens know in their hearts they enjoy greater freedom than those in the Communist nations. They believe they have a fuller and more impartial view of world affairs, and almost without exception they believe their way of life to be preferable. Yet in defence planning and procurement the East has the West beaten, hands-down. True, there is inefficiency in the Warsaw Pact, often on a giant scale; and few would be so naive as to suppose there are no internecine rivalries or friction. Yet what an advantage the WP air forces have in central direction, which in the matter of major procurement items stems from the Kremlin! Every cable connector fits the next nation's sockets. Every fighter can use the next nation's fuel, ammunition and ground power units. Every member of every ground staff knows that what he has learned reads right across the Pact. The WP air forces are superbly efficient, well-trained, enthusiastic and honed to a fine cutting edge. The fact they are so immensely strong improves morale further. On top of all this is a pragmatic will to win that would seem unthinkable in the modern Western world.

Compared with NATO, the Warsaw Pact alliance demonstrates several marked differences. The most fundamental is that, while the Atlantic Alliance is an association of nations so free that it is hard to tell how many belong (France belongs in a way, but not militarily, Iceland does but never attends meetings, and Turkey and Greece hardly speak to one another), the Warsaw Pact is a matter of iron discipline which, if necessary, is imposed by the strongest member. The United States is by far the most powerful member of NATO, but has no wish to impose iron discipline; it merely believes in collective security, and is more interested in business (including arms business, for that matter) than ideology. Communist nations have a different scale of values, and we in the West do not know how far the aircraft industries of the industrially advanced WP nations – East Germany, Czechoslovakia and Poland – have fought behind locked doors to get into licence production with the latest types of Soviet combat aircraft.

Time was when licences were granted

PART TWO
The Warsaw Pact Air Forces

almost as a matter of course. Poland and Czechoslovakia, in particular, built hundreds of MiGs in the 1950s and 1960s, and have the capability to handle anything designed by that famous bureau, or Sukhoi's, today. There is not only nothing doing, but these modern warplanes have yet to appear in the markings of those Warsaw Pact air forces. The fact that the Warsaw Pact has not only had two rebellions put down by military force, but that life in the Communist countries goes on as before, speaks volumes about just what kind of "alliance" it is in comparison with NATO.

The WP countries are the buffer states, the ideological no-man's land, between West and East. With a bit of luck they may gradually develop social, commercial and even military contact between the two great European societies until the Iron Curtain has been eroded. This might even call the bluff of the Soviet Union. The Russians will increasingly have to ask themselves how far the pretence that they are threatened by the Western powers is really worth perpetuating as a belief.

BULGARIA

Land area: 43,000 square miles approx.

Population: 8,850,000 approx.

GNP: (1977 $US) 21·2 billion approx.

Defence vote: 1976 (1977 $US) 538 million.

Armed-forces manpower: about 155,000.

Compulsory service: air force 2 years.

The most southerly of the European WP nations, Bulgaria also has the smallest population, least industry, lowest GNP and a basically agrarian economy. On the other hand it has substantial manpower in its armed forces, and in fact at any one time some 9·2 per cent of all males aged 18–45 are calculated to be serving in the Bulgarian forces (mainly the large Army), compared with 6·9 per cent for the Soviet Union, 6·0 per cent for Czechoslovakia and below 5 per cent for other WP countries.

Bulgaria's recent history reflects her wish not to offend her powerful and sometimes aggressive neighbours. On 1 March 1941 the Nazi government of Germany succeeded in pressurizing the Bulgars to join the seemingly victorious Axis (the Luftwaffe promptly used Bulgarian bases in their campaign through Greece and Jugoslavia, and on via Crete to Libya). In return the BAF was built up with supplies of all kinds, including Bf 109G and other modern combat aircraft. These were not used against the Soviet Union, and by 1944 the Bulgars were trying to run with the hare and hunt with the hounds, claiming neutrality and friendship with Moscow. The Soviets refused to accept this, declared war in September 1944, and almost at once accepted Bulgaria's unconditional surrender. In 1947 harsh terms were imposed in a treaty, among other items limiting the BAF to 90 aircraft and 5,000 personnel. Today it has about 400 aircraft and at least 25,000 personnel.

Today's BAF relies almost totally on

Above: This Bulgarian MiG-19PM all-weather fighter is unusual in having no pylons for "Alkali" AAMs.

the Soviet Union and other WP members for military equipment, including combat aircraft. It has always been one of the last WP air forces to receive new types of equipment, and until the late 1960s still had a few World War II Soviet machines including the La-7 fighter and Li-2 transport. Today the bulk of the combat inventory comprises various pre-1970 MiG types, and like the Bulgarian Navy the BAF remains a small force in comparison with the numerically large Army. Geographically, Bulgaria is not thought to lie in line with any major expected thrust directed from Moscow, though it could play a role in the supply of equipment, such as tactical combat aircraft, to the Middle East, Africa and other countries. Bulgaria's long Black Sea shore is patrolled by its own Navy, which has a handful of Mil helicopters. Overall, Bulgaria is judged one of the Soviet Union's staunchest allies.

Above: All Warsaw Pact air forces naturally use absolutely standard flying clothing, most of it supplied from the Soviet Union. This Bulgarian fighter pilot is wearing the partial-pressure ventilated suit, based on the original US Air Force suit of 1952 and changed only in detail.

Above: Bulgarian pilot and crew-chief confer on the special ladder needed to clear the wing-root NR-30 of one of the oldest of all Pact aircraft, a MiG-19S. This has three hard-hitting cannon, and two UV-16-57 rocket pods on the inboard weapon pylons behind the landing-gear bays.

Most of Bulgaria's military air forces operate under direct army command, with the exception of an air-defence division—equipped with SAMs—and a few helicopters operated by the Navy for air-sea rescue and patrol in the Black Sea. The air-defence division is under the direct command of the Minister of Defence, who is the commander-in-chief of the Bulgarian armed forces.

Like many other East European air forces, the Bulgarian air arm was formed under Soviet tutelage shortly after the 1939–45 war. Although the strength of the Bulgarian air force is limited technically to 90 aircraft by the terms of the 1944 peace treaty with the Soviet Union, it was allowed to grow well beyond that figure after Bulgaria came under Soviet influence. The air arm has not been greatly expanded or modernized since the early 1960s, however.

Defence Terms

Under the terms of the Warsaw Pact the Bulgarian armed forces are independent until the Pact is faced by a collective threat. In that event the forces come under the control of the Soviet High Command. Air Units would probably be attached to the Soviet Union's 15th Air Army, normally based in the Odessa military district. Missile units are presumably integrated into the Soviet PVO defence network in any case. Bulgaria is in the first line of defence between Greece and Turkey and the Romanian oilfields, but is well away from the European central region.

About 60 Mikoyan MiG-17 "Frescos" still form the greatest part of the air force, but the balance is likely to shift in favour of the MiG-21 "Fishbed", about 50 of which are now in service in interceptor, fighter-bomber and fighter-reconnaissance roles. A single regiment flies 35 Mikoyan MiG-19s, and in 1977 a handful of Ilyushin Il-28s were reported to be still flying with a reconnaissance squadron. Training units operate the Yakovlev Yak-11, the Yak-18 and the Czech Aero L-29, with the MiG-15UTI for advanced

training. Transport aircraft include half-a-dozen Antonov An-2s, ten Ilyushin Il-14s and a few Lisunov Li-2s (Douglas C-47s). There are four Ilyushin Il-18s and a pair of Tupolev Tu-134 VIP transports. Army transport helicopters include 40 Mi-4s and a handful of Mi-6 heavy-lift helicopters. The Navy operates about six Mil Mi-4s and some WSK Mi-2s for search and rescue.

Bulgaria will probably not receive the latest generation of Soviet combat aircraft for some time to come, but will take delivery of newer versions of the MiG-21 to make good attrition in its current fleet.

Details of deployment are not available, although it is known that the headquarters of the tactical air force is located at Plovdiv. The tactical aircraft form a single com-

Right: Called, rather unkindly, "Clod" in the NATO reporting system, the Antonov An-14 is an outstanding short-field STOL utility transport. The Bulgarian and other Pact air forces use An-14s for staff transport, utility freight, front-line resupply and casualty-evacuation.

Above: Bulgarian flak troops practising with their ZPU-2, a highly mobile towed platform with two Soviet-supplied Vladimirov KPV heavy machine guns. Though the 14·5mm calibre of this gun is only a little more than that of the 0·5in Browning, its projectile energy is more than double.

Above: Simulated sea/air rescue by an Mi-4 helicopter of the Bulgarian Air Force. Like all Pact air forces this arm keeps its equipment very much longer than most units in the West, where squadron aircraft over 15 years old are comparatively few and far between.

posite division, in contrast to the practice in larger Warsaw Pact forces where each division is assigned to a specific role. The division comprises three large regiments, two of which operate in the fighter-bomber role—with an intercept capability in the case of the MiG-21s, which are likely to be based near Sofia—and one is responsible for reconnaissance.

The air-defence division operates SA-2 "Guideline" SAMs, in three zones centred on Sofia, Plovdiv and Yambol.

Training is carried out on Yak-11 and Yak-18 piston-engined trainers. Pupils proceed via the L-29 and the MiG-15UTI to operational squadrons, the only operational conversions trainers being MiG-21Us.

It is believed that the aircraft of the Bulgarian Air Force, like those of many other non-Soviet Warsaw Pact forces, are supported from the Soviet Union. Stocks of some spares are presumably held in Bulgaria, and these may include engines; Soviet military engines have notoriously short overhaul lives. However, it is unlikely that such aircraft-engineering facilities as exist in Bulgaria are capable of carrying out major overhauls of modern military aircraft, and Bulgaria is presumably dependent on the Soviet Union in this respect.

CZECHOSL

Land area:	49,000 square miles approx.
Population:	14,950,000 approx.
GNP:	(1977 $US) 47·5 billion.
Defence vote:	1976 (1977 $US) 1,805 million.
Armed-forces manpower:	180,000 approx.
Compulsory service:	air force 3 years.

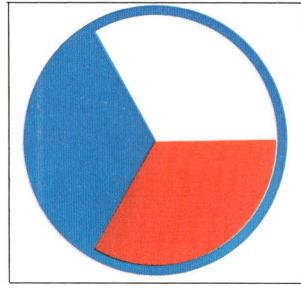 In its short 20-year period between its formation as an independent state in October 1918 and the Nazi takeover in October 1938 and March 1939, Czechoslovakia made more rapid progress towards industrialization and self-sufficient prosperity than any other country in Europe. Even today it is probably, on a per capita basis, the most industrialized of all WP countries. It still has a capable aircraft industry, and if it were independent could probably design and build all its aircraft except for large civil transports. One of the most varied and beautiful European countries, Czechoslovakia has no coastline but an extensive frontier with West Germany, a member of NATO, and Austria.

In World War II tens of thousands of Czechs served with Allied forces, notably the RAF. This, and the progressive outlook and free heritage of the Czech people, has resulted in an underlying affinity with Western culture and a liberalism in thought which has made it difficult for the Czechs to embrace wholeheartedly the restrictive and dogma-ridden Soviet culture, despite 30 years of painstaking "weeding-out" of all reactionary personnel (such as anyone who served with the RAF) and constant political indoctrination. The inner conflict broke into the open in the move towards a more liberal government in 1968, which was instantly suppressed by Soviet armoured forces deployed on a large scale which physically surrounded the Czech Parliament and

OVAKIA

brutally and effectively restored the status quo. Following this sudden clash, the Soviet Union quickly concluded a special "status of forces"

Above: A pupil pilot of the *Ceskoslovenske Letectvo* about to wave away the chocks from an L-39 Albatros. Compared with the earlier L-29 this replacement has a better crew layout, with raised instructor seat. The Soviet-designed turbofan gives it increased flight endurance.

agreement with the hapless Czechs, which makes Soviet troops in this WP central sector subordinate direct to the Soviet High Command and ignores the WP entirely.

Czech industry had previously been responsible for manufacture of the major part of the national defence needs in almost all hardware except battle tanks, transport aircraft and helicopters. Today all Czech combat aircraft are supplied by the Soviet Union—and paid for, like the support costs of the Soviet occupying forces—and the only Czech-built military aircraft is the Aero L-39 Albatros, the standard jet trainer of all WP countries except Poland. It is significant that the potentially valuable capacity of the Czech industry, which until 1968 built most MiG fighters up to the MiG-21PFM ("Fishbed F"), is not now being used. As described later, the CL (*Ceskoslovenske Letectvo*, Czech Air Force) remains formidable, and third-largest of all WP air arms, but it is denied any of the post-1970 combat types.

The Czechoslovak air airm (*Ceskoslovenske Letectvo*) is responsible for air defence and the support of Czechoslovak and allied ground forces. It is believed to be divided into two Air Armies, one of which is responsible for air defence and the other one for support of ground forces. The air-defence force, the 7th Air Army, is independent of Army command and responsible directly to the Ministry of Defence, while the 10th Air Army carries out tactical support under the direction of the local front commander.

Unlike other Warsaw Pact air forces the Czech air arm is not entirely a Soviet creation. The air force revived immediately after World War II, when the country was attempting to maintain its independence from the Soviet Union. Before the coup d'etat of 1948 aligned Czechoslovakia closely with the Soviet Union, the Czech aircraft industry had equipped its air force with Avia S-199 fighters derived from the Messerschmitt Bf 109 and had exported some of those aircraft to Israel; a programme was under way to put the Messerschmitt Me 262 jet fighter into production under the designation S-92 and new jet fighters were under development. Following the 1948 coup, however, the air force expanded under Soviet control to become the strongest of the Warsaw Pact air arms by the second half of the 1950s. Although its equipment was Soviet-designed, many aircraft were Czech-built and some Czech-produced aircraft were exported. Licence-production covered the Mikoyan MiG-15, the MiG-17, the MiG-19 and the Ilyushin Il-28 in the 1950s, and in the early 1960s the Czech industry built MiG-21F-13s for the air force.

Czechoslovakia's position in the Warsaw Pact is somewhat ambiguous following the events of 1968, when an increasing trend towards "liberal socialism" was abruptly stopped by Soviet occupation, with the assistance of other Warsaw Pact forces. The Czech air arm's pre-eminence among the Warsaw Pact forces has diminished, and it is Poland rather than Czechoslovakia which is at the forefront of modernization. Under the Warsaw Pact the Czech forces are taken under Soviet command if a collective threat faces the members of the Pact; in the case of the Czech air arm this would mean that the 10th Air Army would be attached to the Soviet Air Army based in Czechoslovakia (headquartered at Milovice, north-east of Prague) under the command of the Central Group of Soviet Forces. The 7th Air Army would fall under Soviet PVO control, and is almost certainly integrated into the PVO structure in any case.

Aircraft of the CL

Backbone of the air force is the fleet of 300 Mikoyan MiG-21s, although early Czech-built clear-weather MiG-21Fs must still form a large proportion of the 220 MiG-21s assigned to the intercept role. Forty MiG-21RF "Fishbed Hs" operate in the fighter-reconnaissance role with cameras and electronic countermeasures (ECM) equipment. Some 70 Sukhoi Su-7 "Fitter As" provide close-support strength and according to one report they are being supplemented with swing-wing Su-20 "Fitter Cs", export model of the Soviet Su-17. Older types still in service include 40 Mikoyan MiG-17s in the fighter-bomber role.

Aero L-39s are beginning to replace L-29 basic and MiG-15UTI advanced trainers. About ten Sukhoi Su-7U "Moujik" and 30-plus Mikoyan MiG-21U "Mongol" conversion trainers are included in the total operational fleet of training aircraft available to the *Ceskoslovenske Letectvo*.

About 40 transport aircraft include Antonov An-24s and older Ilyushin Il-14s, with some Il-18s. Mil Mi-4 and Mi-8 transport helicopters are operated, with a total force of about 100.

Above left: Ground crew hold the ladder and chocks as a Czech S-107 (licence-built MiG-21F) taxies out on a training sortie. The -21F is the oldest type of MiG-21 still flying with Pact air forces, and the only model still in use with the original tapered nose and small inlet. Some MiG-21s are armed with the AA-2 "Atoll"—the only-launched missile in Czech service.

Above: An S-105 version corresponding to the MiG-19PF (perekhvatchik, interceptor), with Izumrad A1 radar (called "Scan Odd" in the NATO designation system) but still retaining guns instead of AAMs. This example, looking very rough and "bitty" was on public display in Prague. Most of the Czech-built S-105s were of the earlier MiG-19SF type, without radar.

Above: This impressive row of anti-aircraft guns is of interest because the Czech M-53 (twin-30mm) usually has 10-round side clips, while these have the 50-round top-feed boxes of the semi-enclosed vehicle-mounted M-59.

Right: Photographed from an angle that makes the fin look larger than the wing, this MiG-21U trainer (probably of the type called "Mongol B" by NATO) is coupled to a ground electric power truck. It was not made in Czechoslovakia.

It is likely that more modern aircraft will be supplied to both Poland and Czechoslovakia now that the "front-line" units in East Germany have been largely re-equipped. However, even the Su-20 is not equipped to carry the latest Soviet ASMs, and the only air-launched missile in Czech service remains the AA-2 "Atoll" AAM which arms the MiG-21. The 7th Air Army is believed to command about 60 SAM batteries, probably equipped with SA-2 "Guidelines" and SA-3 "Goas".

The 7th Army comprises two regional divisions. Each of these includes three interceptor regiments with about 36 MiG-21s each, together with support aircraft, and five SAM regiments, normally of 12 batteries. One of the divisions is presumably centred on Prague. The 10th Air Army has four fighter-bomber regiments and the MiG-21RFs equip two reconnaissance regiments, but the detailed allocation of bases is not known.

Industry and Training

It is likely that the Czech aircraft industry handles a proportion of the air arm's engineering requirements. Naturally the indigenous types such as the L-39 and its Walter Titan engine (a licence-built version of the Soviet Ivchenko AI-25) are locally supported, and an industry capable of building aircraft and engines such as these should have no problems in supporting the relatively unsophisticated combat types provided to Czechoslovakia by the Soviet Union. The Soviet Union may, however, retain control over these types for political reasons, possibly by means of confining overhaul of their Tumansky and Lyulka engines to the Soviet Union. Transport aircraft are almost certainly maintained by the State airline CSA.

The Czech forces conduct their own training with the L-29, L-39 and primary trainers, and conversion trainers attached to operational units. Pardubice, Pilsen and Bratislava are among training bases.

Above: This S-107 version is the later Czech-built counterpart of the MiG-21PFM, with numerous major changes compared with the original type on p. 44. Roughly 170 are believed to be in current use with the CL. It has a side-hinged canopy and large flush aerials in the fin.

Above: Internal reflections from the long canopy of the CS-102 (Czech-built MiG-15UTI trainer) do not mar this unusual air-to-air photograph of an S-104 (Czech-built MiG-17F). About 100 of the aged MiGs are still in use with CL ground-support/attack squadrons.

Below: An excellent portrait of an L-29 Delfin of the Czech air force (CL). It is noteworthy that this example, here being flown solo, is fitted with the standard Warsaw Pact SIF/IFF equipment, whose three rod aerials (under the tail) resulted in the NATO code-name of "Odd Rods".

Land area: 41,000 square miles approx.

Population: 17,300,000 approx.

GNP: (1977 $US) 49·6 billion approx.

Defence vote: 1977 (1977 $US) 2,890 million.

Armed-forces manpower: 157,000.

Compulsory service: air force 2 years.

The DDR (German People's Republic) came into being in 1949, and was a founder-signatory of the WP in 1955, yet it is recognized only by Communist governments. For basic reasons stemming from World War II, and distrust of any wish by Germans to unite their divided country, the East German forces are the only ones in the WP having not even a pretence of national command. All are subordinate to the Moscow-administered Combined Supreme Command. Moreover, large and powerful as the DDR's forces may be, they are yet dwarfed by the immense power of the GSFG (Group of Soviet Forces in Germany), the firepower of which (measured against length of front) exceeds that of any other land force in the world.

Though it has large reserves and paramilitary forces, the DDR armed forces are modest in numerical terms. In fighting power, however, the air force, the LSK (*Luftstreitkräfte*) and LV (*Luftverteidigung*, air defence), is powerful, with more combat aircraft than the RAF despite only one-third as many personnel. Until 1968 the aircraft types included some of the latest in the Soviet inventory, despite the fact that no attempt has been made—so far as is known in the West—to utilize the large and technically skilled DDR labour force, many with aircraft experience prior to 1945, to construct aircraft either

MANY

Above: The newest combat aircraft in the LSK (East German Air Force) is the MiG-21MF, with four underwing pylons and many features not found on earlier models.

of DDR or Soviet design. All LSK/LV aircraft are of Soviet origin, except for trainers from Czechoslovakia. Today the types deployed show very little advance on ten years ago, the only significant change being the supply of later sub-types of MiG-21. This is in the sharpest contrast to the GSFG, which has the latest available equipment, some of it in use in East Germany as long as eight years but not supplied to any WP air force. Likewise, the equipment of the LV, which includes five SAM regiments armed almost entirely with V75-series (SA-2 "Guideline") missiles, has scarcely been updated at all in the past decade, while the GSFG deploys SA-4, -6, -7, -8 and -9.

This apparent decline in the relative position of the DDR's forces is the more surprising when it is noted that, in the Soviet view, the "Northern Tier" WP nations—DDR, Poland and Czechoslovakia—receive priority over the less-important and poorer "Southern Tier". The DDR probably has more links of a cultural and economic nature with the West than other WP countries, and as part of former Nazi Germany it has every reason to be closely watched for any sign of reaction or counter-revolution. Yet its vital geographic location, and industrial strength, puts it ostensibly in the No 2 slot among WP nations, preceded only by Poland.

East Germany's air force, the *Luftstreitkräfte* (LSK), forms—together with the Soviet Union's 16th Air Army—the first line of the Warsaw Pact's European air strength. Apart from a small force of East German Navy helicopters responsible for search and rescue in the Baltic Sea, it has a monopoly of East German air power. Its commander-in-chief is usually a first deputy in the Ministry of National Defence.

The Soviet Union started to build up the nucleus of the LSK before either of the Germanies was permitted to have an air force under international treaty. Initially known as the VP-L (*Volkspolizei-Luft*, or Air Police) the force was formed in the early 1950s and in late 1956 became the LSK. Single-seat and two-seat MiG-15s were delivered in the following year, and the LSK has now built up to become one of the largest forces of all those aligned with the USSR in the Warsaw Pact.

The 16th Air Army

Uniquely among Pact nations, East Germany has placed its armed forces under the peacetime command of the Soviet Union. (Other non-Soviet Pact forces only come under Soviet command in case of a collective threat to Pact security, and revert to national control when the threat recedes.) Powerful as the LSK is, it is only half the size of the 16th Air Army, which controls it. The LSK is in fact virtually an extension of the 16th Air Army, using different bases (only Parchim seems to be shared) and German personnel.

The Mikoyan MiG-21 "Fishbed" in its various forms is the most numerous type in the LSK inventory. About 200 are in service in the fighter-bomber and reconnaissance roles, and the remaining MiG-21F clear-weather fighters are likely to be replaced by newer types such as the MiG-21SMT "Fishbed K, L and N" used by the 16th Air Army. Next in num-

Above: This frame from a ciné film shows a pupil pilot in the LSK bringing in an L-29 Delfin trainer to a nicely judged landing. Tanks are carried instead of weapons.

Above right: Two MiGs in loose echelon formation over the DDR (East Germany). The fighter is an early MiG-21F, while the trainer is a MiG-21UTI of the "Mongol B" type.

Below: Called V750VK, and with the NATO designation SA-2 "Guideline", this obsolescent SAM is still widely used by all Pact anti-aircraft troops, including the LSK.

Below right: Primary training in the LSK is not normally done from ploughed fields; this Yak-18A was flown to the Danish island of Bornholm by a defecting LSK captain.

LSK deployment				
Division	**Regiment**	**Type**	**Base**	**Number**
3rd Air Defence (Neubranden-burg)	2nd Fighter	MiG-21	Neubrandenburg	36
	9th Fighter	Su-7	Peenemünde	36
	13th SAM	SA-2	Parchim	12 batteries
	17th SAM	SA-3	Uhlenkrug	12 batteries
	18th SAM		Sanitz	12 batteries
1st Air Defence (Cottbus)	1st Fighter	MiG-21	Cottbus	36
	3rd Fighter	Su-7	Preschen	36
	7th Fighter		Drewitz	36
	8th Fighter		Marxwalde	36
	14th SAM	SA-2	Steuergraebchen	12 batteries
	16th SAM	SA-3	Ladeburg	12 batteries
	31st Helicopter		Brandenburg-Briesen	
	27th Transport		Dresden-Klotsche	

erical importance is the Sukhoi Su-7 "Fitter A", about 90 of which equip two regiments in the close-support role. The proportion of obsolescent types in the LSK is the lowest in the Pact outside the Soviet Union; some 50 MiG-17 "Frescos" remained in service at the end of 1976, but the force was recently reported to be growing smaller.

Replacing the MiG-17

More advanced strike and close-support types are believed to be replacing the MiG-17s. According to one source the very advanced Mikoyan MiG-27 "Flogger D" is being supplied to LSK units as well as to the 16th Air Army, and the Sukhoi Su-20 "Fitter C" may also be adopted.

The LSK transport force operates mainly in support of the fighter and strike units, as well as running a few aircraft in the service of the government. The most numerous type is the Ilyushin Il-14; about 20 are in service and, judging from the pattern in other forces, they are likely to be replaced by Antonov An-26s or the new An-32. A few An-2 and An-14 light transports operate in the communications role. In early 1977 it was reported that some of the Il-14s were in service as electronic intelligence (Elint) platforms.

The East German Government fleet—now diminished by the sale of an Antonov An-24 to Vietnam—may be an extension of the national airline Interflug rather than an LSK operation. Two Il-18s, three Tupolev Tu-124s and a pair of Tu-134s are operated, but the Tu-124s are probably due for retirement.

The LSK has about 80 transport and training helicopters, with WSK Mi-2s and Mil Mi-4s now being replaced by the Mi-8. The East German Navy flies about eight Mi-4s from Baltic bases for search and rescue duties.

A variety of training aircraft are operated. At present Yakovlev Yak-11s, Aero L-29 Delfins and MiG-15UTIs are operated, together with MiG-21Us and Su-7Us attached to operational units for conversion training. The LSK has about eight Su-7Us and 20-plus MiG-21Us. There is no trainer version of the MiG-27, and any LSK units operating this type may have MiG-23U "Flogger Cs" for training and ECM duties.

In structure and deployment the LSK follows the pattern of a Soviet Air Army, with combat units grouped in divisions and separate support regiments; fighter units, for instance, are grouped in divisions, as are the SAM units which are integrated with the Soviet PVO defence network. LSK headquarters is at Strausberg-Eggersdorf. The SAM units operate some 60 batteries of SA-2 "Guideline" and SA-3 "Goa" missiles.

LSK Training

The training structure of the LSK appears to be mostly independent of the Soviet Air Forces now, although Frontal Aviation still exerts a greater influence over LSK training than it does over that of the other Warsaw Pact air forces. Like its neighbours, East Germany appears to be moving from a three-tier training system to a two-level structure. The present three training aircraft—Yak-11, L-29 and MiG-15UTI—seem likely to be replaced by the Zlin Z-42 and the Aero L-39 Albatros; no direct advanced-trainer replacement for the MiG-15UTI seems to be emerging.

Maintenance and support for the LSK is likely to be integrated with the support for the 16th Air Army of Frontal Aviation, apart from Government transport aircraft maintained and overhauled by State airline Interflug. East Germany abandoned its attempts to set up an aircraft industry in the late 1950s, and it is unlikely that any East German organisation would be able to maintain modern aircraft. All LSK overhaul is carried out by Soviet Air Force engineering units and by the Soviet aircraft industry, in Germany and in the Soviet Union.

Above: Changing oxygen bottles between flights by an LSK MiG-21UM, the latest (R-13-powered) trainer version.

Above right: A busy scene at an East German airfield occupied by a MiG-23S fighter regiment of the GSFG. These versatile swing-wing aircraft have been stationed in the DDR for seven years, as have units equipped with the MiG-27, but neither has been permitted to the host air force.

Below: LSK recruits being given basic instruction in how a turbojet works, with the aid of a Klimov VK-1 in a part-dismantled MiG-15 single-seater. In the background, an An-2TD. Far more than in Western countries, Warsaw Pact nations impart technical training via the armed forces.

Below right: Night flying by an LSK MiG-21FL. Note the runway lights, and "Odd Rods" IFF aerials under the nose.

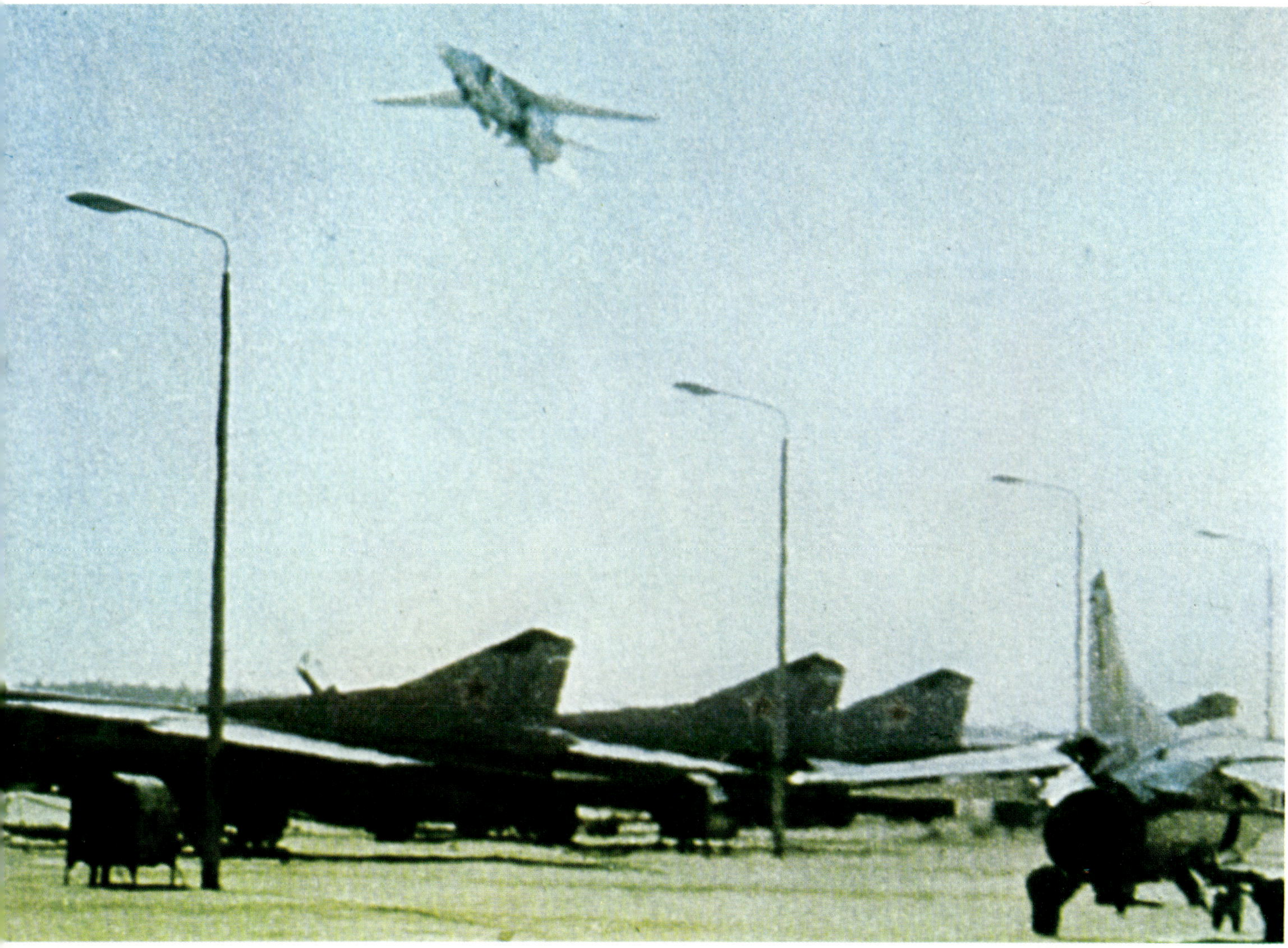

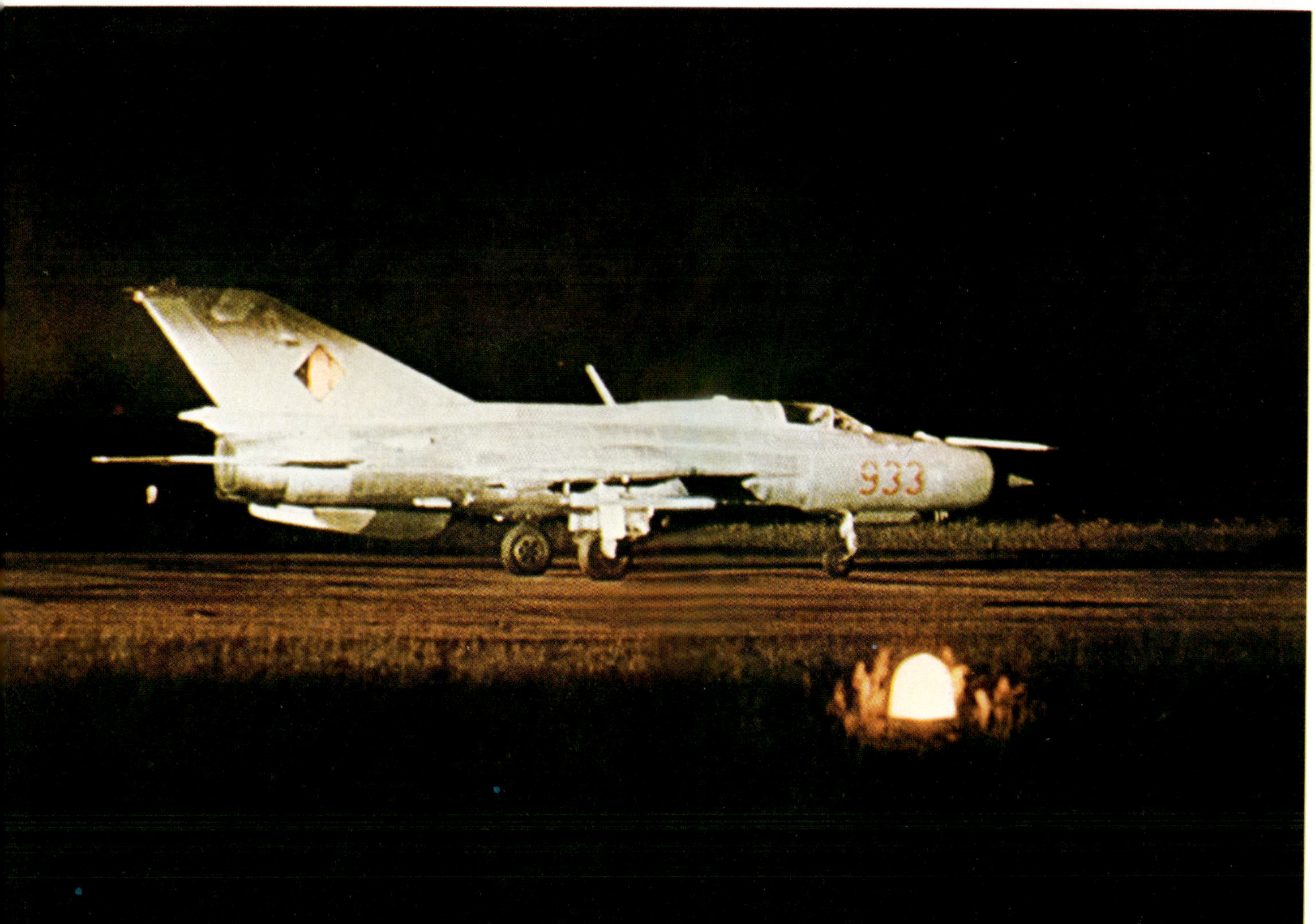
933

HUNGARY

Land area: 36,000 square miles approx.

Population: 10,600,000 approx.

GNP: (1977 $US) 23·0 billion approx.

Defence vote: 1977 (1977 $US) 590 million.

Armed-forces manpower: 101,000.

Compulsory service: air force 2 years (technicians 3 years).

In World War II Hungary did not have much choice; though not actually occupied or annexed by Hitler, it played along with Nazi Germany, signed the anti-Comintern Pact in 1939 and in July 1940, with Italy, signed the Axis Tripartite Pact and entered World War II. A substantial aircraft industry grew up by licence-production of mainly Italian and German combat aircraft, with one versatile locally designed machine. But by 1944 the disenchanted and frightened Hungarians had had enough, and late that year they set up a new Provisional Government that signed an armistice with the Allies. Like other signatories of the WP, post-war Hungary elected a Communist government and was allowed by its Soviet masters to possess small national armed forces. In the 1950s these forces were allowed to grow far beyond the stipulated limit, but in 1956 came the sudden counter-revolution, the bloody insurrection against dull and oppressive Soviet rule that (apart from the 1968 Soviet invasion of Czechoslovakia) remains unique in post-war Europe. Following the suppression of this uprising, the Hungarian forces were reduced in size.

Today they have grown slightly once more, but are still small and relatively ill-equipped compared with the Northern Tier WP nations. Hungary has a GNP second from the bottom of the WP league, and has found it very difficult to meet the planned schedule for expanding and modernizing its forces and at the same time pay the substantial costs of supporting the occupying Soviet forces.

Above: The omnipresent L-29 Delfin is standard advanced trainer of the Hungarian air force.

The financial problem hits advanced-technology forces hardest, and the Hungarian air force is the smallest in the WP. Like all WP countries except Bulgaria and the DDR, Hungary has a frontier with the Soviet Union, and is in no position to argue with "Big Brother".

Yet the consistently low defence expenditure, at a regular 2·4 per cent of GNP, is lowest in the WP apart from Romania, and the surfacing of the simmering resentment at the size of Soviet support costs, shows that all is not entirely well in the Hungarian camp.

The smallest of the Warsaw Pact air arms, the Hungarian Air Force is subordinate to the command of the Hungarian Army. Its main role is tactical support of the army, but its interceptor and SAM squadrons form part of the Warsaw Pact air-defence system and defend major targets in Hungary itself. Apart from the air force itself, the only paramilitary air activity consists of a few helicopters attached to the Danube river patrol force.

Like most of the Warsaw Pact forces, the Hungarian air arm is a post-war Soviet creation, the wartime force having been totally defeated and dismantled by the Soviet Union after the 1939–45 war. The final 1947 peace treaty between Hungary and the Soviet Union set a technical limit to the strength of the air force, but this limit has been disregarded since the air force expanded under Soviet control. By the mid-1950s Hungary had the strongest air force in the Balkans.

Some Hungarian air force units took part in the 1956 rebellion against Soviet occupation forces, and following the suppression of the revolt the air force was demobilized. Its restoration started in 1957, but since that time the Soviet Union has maintained a close control over the Hungarian armed forces.

Defence Terms

Under the Warsaw Pact the Hungarian Government retains nominal control over its armed forces in peacetime. However, control would revert to the Soviet Union in the event of a collective threat to the Pact. The Hungarian air force is probably outnumbered by the Soviet Air Army based in Hungary, which is believed to have some 200 combat types in addition to support aircraft. The Soviet Air Army, with its headquarters at Tokol south of Budapest, would take over control of the Hungarian Air Force in wartime and both forces would operate under a Soviet front commander. As in Czechoslovakia the Soviet forces have the dual role of allies and occupying forces.

The Mikoyan MiG-21 "Fishbed" is the most important

Above: Quick departure from an Mi-8 of the Hungarian air force during assault exercises. Note weapon pylon.

Below: Though it is the smallest Pact air force, the Hungarian AF has the reasonably modern MiG-21SMT of 1971.

type in the inventory, with a total force of about 80 aircraft including perhaps eight MiG-21U "Mongol" two-seaters. A single regiment operates 35 Sukhoi Su-7s in the close-support role.

Antonov An-26 "Curl" freighters have recently been delivered to replace some of the older aircraft—Lisunov Li-2s and Ilyushin Il-14s—in service with the single transport regiment. A total of 25–30 transports include An-2s and An-24s as well as the types previously mentioned. A small number of Mil Mi-8s have been delivered to supplement the older Mi-4s.

The Training Fleet

Training types include Yakovlev Yak-11s and Yak-18s, as well as the standard Aero L-29 Delfin. The MiG-21Us are presumably attached to operational units. Some MiG-15UTIs may be retained as intermediate trainers.

Hungary's military aircraft constitute a single Air

Above: Called "Curl" by NATO, the An-26 short-range transport is seen here with the Hungarian air force.

Right: The Hungarians still do nearly all their advanced pilot-training on the MiG-15UTI. They are probably Czech-built CS-102 versions, and are kept immaculate.

Division, with two fighter regiments, the Su-7s in a fighter-bomber regiment, and a single transport regiment. The other component of the Hungarian air forces is an Air Defence Division, which commands two battalions of SA-2 "Guideline" missiles.

Hungary is presumably far from independent in terms of engineering support for its air forces, although training is likely to be autonomous. Basic maintenance is probably carried out on the local base, but it is not likely that local facilities can handle major periodic overhauls, and these are carried·out in the Soviet Union itself. Like many of the smaller non-Soviet Warsaw Pact forces, the Hungarian Air Force would not be able to operate effectively without the active support of the Soviet Union.

POLAND

Land area: 120,000 square miles approx.

Population: 34,600,000 approx.

GNP: (1977 $US) 72·7 billion.

Defence vote: 1977 (1977 $US) 2,440 million.

Armed-forces manpower: 307,000.

Compulsory service: air force 3 years (AA, rocket, electronic, 3 years).

During World War II the Soviet Union displayed a strange ambivalence towards Poland. Though Poland was the victim of the Nazi aggression that started the war, the Soviet Union invaded Poland also, with army and air units, on 16 September 1939, and occupied half the country up to a frontier agreed with the Nazis until the latter invaded eastwards on 22 June 1941. During this occupation period there occurred the notorious massacre in the Katyn Wood which resulted in the near-elimination of the Polish officer corps at the hands of the Russians. Throughout the war the Soviets refused to collaborate with the Poles in the RAF, even in the long-range missions to help the Warsaw uprising in 1944. In 1943 a complete Polish air force was formed in the Soviet Union from personnel who had managed to escape from Poland, and this became the nucleus of the post-war Polish Air Force (at first PLW, *Polskie Lotnictwo Wojskowe*; now PWL, *Polskie Wojska Lotnicze*). Yet the even greater numbers of Poles who flew with the RAF, manning 14 combat squadrons in mid-1944, were refused admission to the post-war Polish Air Force, and most of those that did return to their homeland were imprisoned. They had, presumably, been tainted by association with Imperialists.

Despite its brief period of independence—20 years, the same as Czechoslovakia—Poland had acquired a reputation second-to-none for military capability and efficiency, and the native courage and skill has been abundantly in evidence even under the rigid WP yoke. As the biggest and most important member of the WP after the Soviet Union, Poland has consistently ranked No 1 in priority for military equipment. At the same time it has, like the other Satellites, been denied any arms that might conceivably pose a threat to the Soviet Union. The PWL has no strategic aircraft, no long-range attack machines and, so far as is known in the West in early 1978, no modern Soviet aircraft other than the Su-20 which, though a poor performer compared with the Su-19, and not even the equal of the Soviet Su-17, is at least better than anything in any other WP air force.

Compared with all other WP countries Poland has potentially the largest and most broadly based aircraft industry. In 1955, when it signed the Warsaw Pact, Poland received several major programmes transferred from the Soviet Union, the chief aviation transfer being the An-2 biplane, closely followed by the Mil Mi-1 helicopter. The An-2 has remained in production almost up to the present time, and has led to the WSK-PZL-Mielec and CNPSL-PZL-Warsaw factories becoming the centre for utility/agricultural aircraft throughout the Communist Bloc. The little Mi-1, designated SM-1 in its Polish version, led in turn to the WSK-PZL-Swidnik factory becoming the Communist centre

Above: Most of the aircraft in this line-up are MiG-21 MF fighters, but nearest the camera is a tandem-seat trainer. It has the external attitude sensor on the left side of the nose, but only two underwing pylons; it thus appears to be intermediate between the MiG-21U "Mongol B" and the later MiG-21UM. Poland has never made the MiG-21.

for light helicopters. The Mi-2 turbine-engined light helicopter has been mass-produced and further developed in Poland, and later light helicopters are in the design stage. Poland is also a major centre for light aeroplanes and gliders, as well as all piston engines of Soviet origin and various other aircraft engines. But the strategically important licence-production of combat aircraft has, as in Czechoslovakia, been terminated. Poland built various types of MiG-15 and MiG-17 in 1953–63, and even developed advanced ground-attack versions superior to the Soviet original, but none of the later Soviet combat types has gone into production in Poland. It is not obvious whether this is in accord with Polish wishes and financial capability, or whether it is a situation imposed by the Soviet Union. In other weapon fields, including light naval craft, armour and most infantry weapons Poland maintains flourishing production lines. It also, contrary to the spirit of uniform standardization implicit in the Pact, refused the Czech L-39 trainer and produced its own TS-11 Iskra, complete with its own turbojet engine, as standard advanced jet and weapons trainer of the PWL.

Poland's is the largest air force in the Warsaw Pact outside the Soviet Union, forming the second line of defence in Europe together with the Soviet 37th Air Army. Interceptor, SAM and fighter-bomber divisions are responsible to the Command of Aviation Forces, which in turn is subordinate to the Ministry of Defence in peacetime. Poland is also the only Warsaw Pact member outside the Soviet Union to have a fixed-wing naval air force. The Polish Air Force (Polish initials PWL) is the only Warsaw Pact air force to be larger than the Soviet Air Army stationed in its home country, and in recent years has emerged as the most technically advanced of the non-Soviet forces.

Origins of the PWL

The PWL originated in the Soviet 6th Air Army, formed with Polish and Polish-Russian personnel in 1944 to take part in the offensive into Germany. The 6th Air Army was completely modelled on the Soviet pattern in concept, organisation and structure; following the March 1946 Russo-Polish Air Agreement it started to expand, but under very close Soviet control. Mikoyan MiG-15s were delivered in the early 1950s and Ilyushin Il-28 light bombers followed in 1955. The MiG-15 and MiG-17 were placed in production in Poland under the designations LiM-2 and LiM-5. After the events in Hungary of 1956 the Polish Air Force was granted rather more independence from deeply resented Soviet control, but at the same time its expansion was slowed down and later aircraft in the MiG series were not licence-built. During the early 1960s the Soviet Union attempted to discourage the manufacture of military aircraft in Poland and gave priority to the Czech air force and industry. The emphasis has reversed since the Czech attempt at independence and the invasion of 1968.

Poland is a signatory of the Warsaw Pact, and in time of a threat to the Pact its forces would fall under the supreme command of the Soviet Union. In that event the PWL's fighter-bomber divisions would be assigned to the 37th Air Army of Soviet Frontal Aviation, with its headquarters at Legnica. The interceptor divisions are in any case integrated into the Soviet PVO network of air-defence zones. The 37th Air Army is part of the Northern Group of Soviet Forces.

Deployment of the Su-20

Poland is the only non-Soviet Warsaw Pact force confirmed to have taken delivery of aircraft more modern than the MiG-21/Su-7 generation. (The Soviet Union has been surprisingly reluctant about supplying new-type aircraft to the Warsaw Pact, particularly in comparison with the massive deliveries of the MiG-23/27 family to the Middle East). At least one regiment of 35 swing-wing Su-20 "Fitter Cs" has been delivered to replace LiM-5 fighter-bombers, and deliveries of this quasi-new-generation variant of the standard Su-7 are continuing, probably to replace the second LiM-5 regiment. Ilyushin Il-28 light bombers still equipped one small unit in 1976.

The MiG "Fishbed" and the standard fixed-wing Su-7 "Fitter A" still form the greatest part of the PWL front-line strength. Upwards of 300 MiG-21s of all marks equip nine fighter regiments forming three divisions; these include some 30 MiG-21U "Mongol" conversion trainers, and in addition the PWL has a few MiG-21RF "Fishbed H" reconnaissance fighters. All MiG-21s carry the AA-2 "Atoll" and AA-22 "Advanced Atoll" AAMs. About 180 Sukhoi Su-7 "Fitter As" equip five fighter-bomber regiments, with a proportion (15–20 aircraft) of Su-7U "Moujik" trainers. At the time of writing one regiment still operated 35–40 LiM-5s (Polish-built MiG-17s), but these are likely to be replaced by Su-20s.

Other combat aircraft equip Poland's Naval Air Division,

Above: Standard tactical helicopter of the PWL is the PZL-Swidnik Mi-2 with lateral weapon pylons. The latter can carry rocket or gun pods, but in this case the load comprises four "Sagger" wire-guided anti-tank missiles. The "Swatter" missile is also used in this role.

Above right: Once extremely numerous, the pleasant Il-28 twin-jet tactical bomber is still used by several Warsaw Pact air forces including the Soviet Union. This Polish example is used in various utility and training roles.

Right: The An-12 is the Polish PWL's largest airlift transport. Like the strictly comparable C-130 Hercules, the speedy Antonov is characterised by four diagonal pencils of exhaust smoke at take-off or landing power.

Below right: Manufactured under licence in Poland as the SBLim-1, the MiG-15UTI serves widely throughout all the Warsaw Pact air forces. This PWL example has the usual underslung drop tank, though the slipper type is still seen.

Below: Polish airborne troops leap from a Russian-built Mi-4 helicopter of the PWL during Warsaw Pact exercises. Though designed 25 years ago, the Mi-4 is extremely useful and can carry 14 equipped troops. Note the inevitable SIF/IFF ("Odd Rods") aerials ahead of the windscreen.

which is still responsible to the Command of Aviation Forces and is thus part of the PWL. The LiM-5 "Fresco" remains in service at regiment strength, but there is just one squadron of 12 MiG-21F "Fishbed C" day fighters. A few Ilyushin Il-28 "Beagles" remain in service for coastal strike and similar duties.

The Training Fleet

The training fleet is largely equipped with Polish-designed aircraft. These include the WSK-Mielec TS-11 Iskra jet trainer, developed in the early 1960s in competition with the Czech Aero L-29, and the WSK TS-8 Bies primary trainer. Some Yak-18s are operated and the ubiquitous MiG-15UTIs used for advanced training. WSK has not developed an aircraft in the class of the Aero L-39 Albatros and the new Czech trainer will probably be acquired to replace the TS-11 and MiG-15UTI.

Tactical transport and logistic support of combat units is provided by a mixed transport regiment of about 45 aircraft, including Antonov An-12s and An-26s. A few An-24s and An-2 biplanes are also operated, as are six Ilyushin Il-14s. A single Tu-134 is operated by state airline LOT on behalf of the Polish Government, together with three Yakovlev Yak-40 trijets. Some Polish PZL Wilgas serve in the utility/liaison role.

Helicopter forces include a substantial number of WSK Mi-2s produced in Poland; the Mil-designed Mi-2 was never placed in production in the Soviet Union and WSK has delivered aircraft to the USSR as well as other nations. Mi-4s and Mi-8s, the latter armed with unguided rockets for fire suppression, form the transport force. The Naval Air Division has a similar but smaller helicopter transport force, with some Mi-2s and Mi-4s serving in the air-sea rescue role.

PWL missile forces, integrated into the Soviet PVO network, comprise 30 SA-2 "Guideline" sites protecting

Above: As far as is known, the Polish PWL is the only air force in any Warsaw Pact satellite country to have swing-wing aircraft. But they are hardly the latest type, for the Su-20 has even less power and equipment than the Su-17. At least one regiment of 35 aircraft has been delivered.

Below: A suited-up Polish fighter pilot in the cockpit of his MiG-21 (probably an MF or SMT). The rather clumsy radar scope with viewing hood (not needed with bright daylight displays) and optical sight combine to make the forward view inadequate by Western standards.

Below: This An-2M is a rather rare bird, a float-seaplane version of the An-2T multi-role STOL transport roughly equivalent to the Soviet An-2V. Built by WSK-PZL-Mielec, the An-2M is one of several versions used by the PWL, the total amounting to at least 100 aircraft.

Above: Polish MiG-21PF fighters, one of the older sub-types of the most numerous of all Warsaw Pact aircraft, share the apron at a PWL airbase with at least one old LIM-5P (licence-built MiG-17) which appears to be in storage. The MiG-21 is easy to keep serviceable.

strategic targets against medium-altitude intruders. The Polish Navy is the only non-Soviet Warsaw Pact navy to possess SAMs; a single SAM Kotlin destroyer is fitted with the SA-N-1 missile system, using the "Goa" missile.

Details of PWL deployment are not available, but it is believed that there are some 35–40 military airfields active in Poland. Some of these are used by Soviet Frontal Aviation units. In addition to permanent bases there is a considerable number of dispersal strips in the forward area, often using hardened stretches of road and equipped to receive control and support facilities.

Training was the responsibility of the Aviation Inspector's Office until 1967, when the AIO was merged into the Command of Aviation Forces. Primary training is carried out on piston-engined aircraft, with basic training on the TS-11. Pilots proceed to the squadrons after advanced training on the MiG-15UTI. Normally, one squadron in each regiment is assigned the training role, four of its complement of 12 aircraft being two-seaters.

Poland's aircraft industry, centred on PZL-WSK-Mielec, WSK-Swidnik and CNPSL-PZL-Warszawa, is one of the most technically capable in the non-Soviet Warsaw Pact countries. It has designed and manufactured the M-15 agricultural aircraft and is a major partner in production of the Ilyushin Il-86 airliner. However, it is not clear to what extent it acts as a support organisation for the PWL, and the Soviet Union may prefer to ensure that its satellite air forces remain dependent upon it for engineering services and major overhaul work. Probably airframes manufactured in Poland will be maintained there, but it is likely that the engines of combat types at least are overhauled in the Soviet Union.

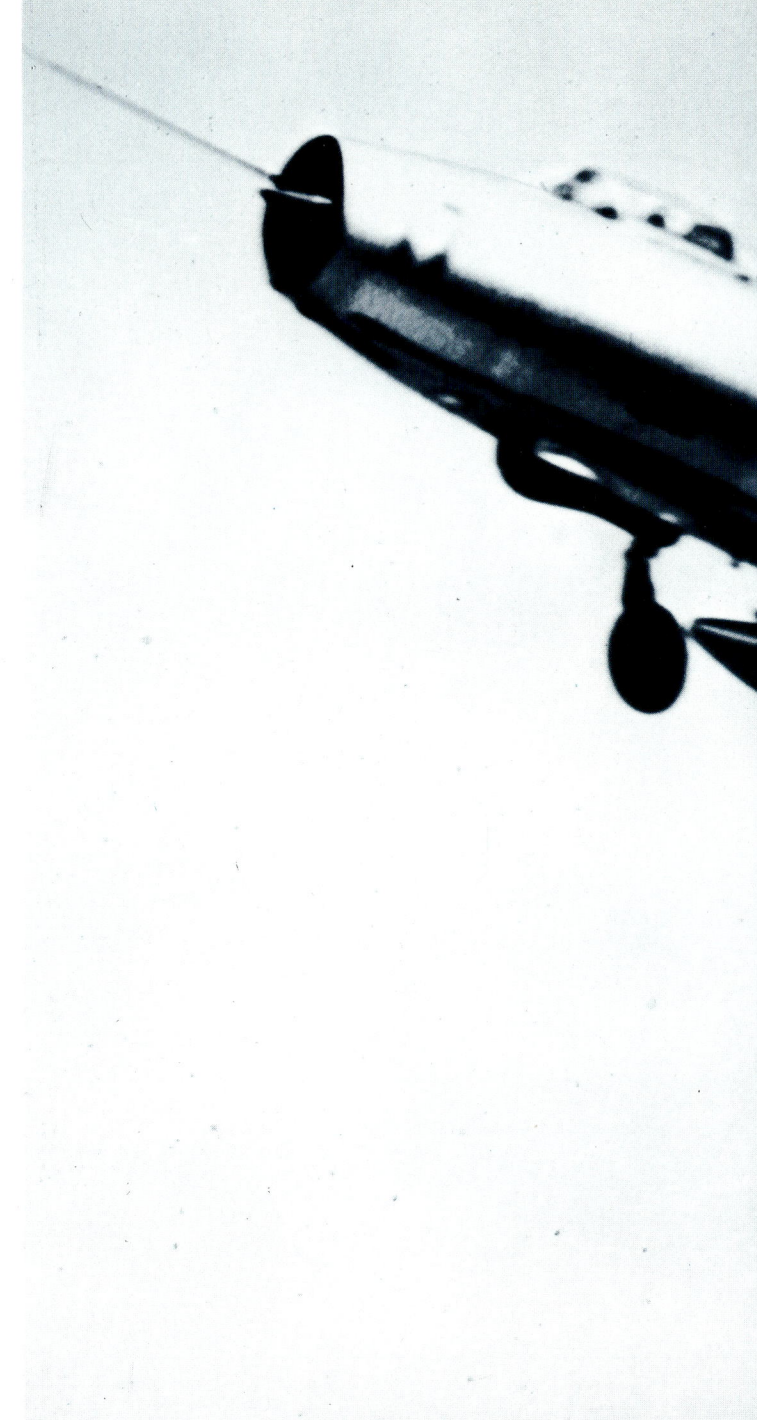

Above: This PWL Mi-8 helicopter is not the usual military multi-role model but the passenger transport with large rectangular windows. It is used as a VIP and staff transport. The Mi-8 has not been manufactured in Poland.

Below: One of the lesser-known types used in Warsaw Pact air forces is Poland's TS-8 Bies basic trainer, powered by the 330hp WN-3 radial. Several hundred Bies were built by WSK-Mielec in 1956–59, and a few are still used.

Above: Take-off by a pair of Su-7B close-support aircraft of the PWL. Now supplemented by the greatly superior Su-20, these extremely limited but large and thirsty aircraft must be on the brink of retirement.

Below: Though it lost to Czechoslovakia's Albatros as a standard Warsaw Pact trainer, the slim TS-11 Iskra is used by the PWL as the Bies replacement. At least 300 of three versions are in use, one being a single-seat attack model.

ROMANIA

Land area: 91,700 square miles approx.

Population: 21,700,000 approx.

GNP: (1977 $US) 45·3 billion approx.

Defence vote: 1977 (1977 $US) 824 million.

Armed-forces manpower: 182,000.

Compulsory service: air force 2 years.

Between the world wars this considerable country, second only to Poland among the WP Satellites in size, had a powerful national aircraft industry which designed and produced all types of military and most civil aircraft. In particular the IAR.80 series were stressed-skin fighters worthy to rank with the other single-seat fighters of World War II, and used in appreciable numbers on the Eastern Front. Romania had tried to avoid becoming drawn into the war, and Britain and France had freely supplied modern bomber and fighter/attack aircraft to try to prevent the country throwing in its lot with the Axis, but to no avail. Romania joined the Axis and declared war on the Soviet Union on 22 June 1941, with Germany. In 1942 Romanian industry, led by the IAR company, went into licence-production with the Bf 109G, but Romanian forces—especially air groups—on the Eastern Front suffered severe losses, and in August 1944 a coup d'état overthrew the government and opened the country to the advancing Red Army, thereby avoiding bloodshed.

Though it had fought the Soviet Union, Romania was allowed a rather larger air force than its neighbours, and in any case by 1950 the Soviet occupying forces were actively building up the Romanian air force to considerably greater strength than ostensibly allowed. Until 1960 Romania played ball and received advanced Soviet equipment including the MiG-15, -17, -19 and -21, as well as a broad spread of other combat and utility aircraft. But since 1960 Romania has increasingly been the unruly miscreant in the WP line-up, consistently and openly refusing to fulfil its requirements. Though its armed forces are far from negligible, they are smaller than they are supposed to be, and the defence vote represents the smallest percentage of GNP (a fairly steady 1·8 per cent) of any member of the WP. The Soviet insistence on Russianization, Russian language and Soviet methods in every detail has been openly flouted. Even more remarkably, Western military equipment has been

Above: So far as is known, the latest combat aircraft in Romania is the primitive MiG-21PF.

bought, including French missile-armed Alouette III helicopters, and Soviet attempts at basing troops in Romania, and moving those already there, have met with a stubborn lack of co-operation.

Romania also has a small coastal navy and a large army, the largest of all Satellites except Poland; but again, modernization and integration with Soviet forces are far behind schedule. A further straw in the wind is the fact that, instead of building Soviet types, the capable Romanian aircraft industry builds indigenous designs and the British One-Eleven and Islander civil transports.

Romania's position, isolated in the centre of the Eastern Bloc, has not encouraged it to give high priority to defence. A home-defence/close-support/SAM force comprising three divisions is commanded by the Ministry of Defence, and in addition the Romanian Navy operates a small number of helicopters for search-and-rescue duties in the Black Sea.

The Romanian Air Force is a post-war Soviet creation, having started as a Romanian-manned division of the Soviet air force. Modernization and increasing independence followed in the mid-1950s when the first MiG-15 jet fighters were delivered.

Romania is a member of the Warsaw Pact, and is pledged to put its forces under Soviet control in the event of a collective threat to the Pact nations. There are no Soviet forces stationed in Romania; in wartime the Romanian air divisions could either be attached to the 15th Air Army in the Odessa military district or to the Southern Group of Soviet Forces based in Hungary.

In recent years Romania has moved to reduce its dependence on the Soviet Union, developing close links outside the Warsaw Pact with Jugoslavia, and producing an increasing amount of military equipment.

Typifying and leading this trend is the air force, which is due in 1978 to start taking delivery of some 80 IAR.93 Orao strike fighters, developed in collaboration with Soko in Jugoslavia and incorporating a considerable amount of Western equipment including Rolls-Royce Viper engines. The Orao will replace 80 obsolescent MiG-17s now in service with two fighter-bomber regiments.

Two regiments fly about 80 MiG-21F "Fishbed Cs" and MiG-21PF "Fishbed Ds", the latter having limited all-weather capability, in the interceptor role. A single air-defence division backs up the fighters with SA-2 "Guideline" medium-range SAMs. The fighters themselves carry AA-2 "Atoll" IR-homing missiles. A single regiment of Sukhoi Su-7 "Fitter As" provides close support.

The combat aircraft form two mixed air divisions, the small size of the air force ruling out the usual practice of assigning specific roles to each division. The two air divisions probably correspond to the two Romanian military districts, centred on Cluj and Bucharest.

The transport force operates some 30 Il-14s, ten Antonov An-2s and an Ilyushin Il-18 in a single independent regiment. Fifty Aérospatiale Alouette IIIs have been built under licence for the helicopter force, which also operates WSK Mi-2s and a smaller number of Mil Mi-4s and Mi-8s. The Romanian Navy SAR fleet comprises four Mi-4s. Some Czech L-200 Morava light twins are flown for liaison.

Training and Industry

Training follows the standard Warsaw Pact pattern, and the Romanian Air Force is also likely to move from a three-level to a two-level structure. Primary training is currently carried out on piston-engined Yak-18s, with basic training on L-29 Delfins and advanced instruction on MiG-15UTIs before conversion. The more capable L-39 Albatros is however expected to replace the L-29 and the MiG-15UTI, with the Jugoslav UTVA-75 being the most likely replacement for the Yak-18.

Although Romania is planning to expand its aircraft industry, and at the time of writing is negotiating to produce BAC One-Eleven airliners for export within the Eastern bloc, it probably remains dependent on the Soviet Union for most of its engineering support; there is no sign that the Soviet Union intends to adopt the "sister factory" concept of US manufacturers, whereby all engineering work is contracted out to local companies. Such types as the Orao, however, are likely to be locally maintained, with Western support for the Orao's Viper engine.

Above: Though it is hard to tell it apart from the near-identical helicopter in Polish use (p. 60), this Mi-4 is serving with the Romanian Air Force. About ten are in use, together with modest numbers of Polish Mi-2s and the much larger Soviet-built Mi-8, as well as 47 French Alouettes.

Left: The Romanian air force *(Fortele Aeriene ale Republicii Socialiste Romania)* still uses a few Li-2 Soviet-built DC-3 versions for paratroop training. They have Shvetsov M-63 engines and an entry door on the right side. The main Romanian transport is the Il-14, about 30 being in use.

Below: A remarkable example of self-sufficiency, which in a way is a startling defiance of Pact doctrine, the Orao tactical attack aircraft is a joint programme with Jugoslavia. Powered by twin British Viper turbojets, this neat aircraft has a high-altitude speed of Mach 1·6.

SOVIET UN

Land area: 8,648,000 square miles approx.	
Population: 258 million approx.	
GNP: (1977 $US) 650 billion approx.	
Defence vote: 1977 (1977 $US) est. 125 billion.	
Armed forces manpower: 3,700,000 approx.	
Compulsory service: air force 3 years (coast defence 4 years, navy 5).	

The giant size, strength and attitude of the Soviet Union distorts the Warsaw Pact, in that it is hardly a free collaborative grouping of sovereign nations enjoying collective defence but a master and what from the start have often been called the "Satellite countries". Though the United States is by far the largest and most powerful member of NATO, it has neither the authority nor the wish to give commands to the other partners, whose total freedom to take their own decisions is jealously guarded to the point where it frequently and dangerously damages military effectiveness. The WP Satellites, on the other hand, have twice been kept in line at the point of the gun (Hungary in 1956, Czechoslovakia in 1968).

As spelt out in the companion book *The Soviet War Machine*, the Soviet Union finds it difficult, or impossible, to live with the rest of the world in a state of impartial objectivity. From the bloody formation of the country almost 60 years ago (one cannot take November 1917 as a starting date because for years the outcome of the civil war was far from

obvious) the Soviet Union has believed that what it calls "the Capitalist Nations" or "the Imperialists" wish to attack it and see it overthrown. The violent aggression by Nazi Germany in June 1941 is held to reinforce this view. Soviet history books do not mention the fact that, to throw back the Nazi invader, the capitalist Allies in 1941–45 provided all the help they could muster to the Soviets until the Allied forces met on the Elbe. The school textbooks also omit to mention that, after World War II when the USA alone possessed nuclear weapons and the means to deliver them, this gigantic and unrepeatable imbalance of power was not used to destroy the Soviet Union in the way that the Soviet leaders would have their population believe is forever sought by the Western world.

There has to be a threat before massive defence funding can be justified, and—though any citizen of any NATO country knows all too well that the idea is ludicrous—the Soviet Government continues to build up enormous forces by land, sea, air and space on the basic premise that these forces are needed to resist attack by the Capitalists. So successful has the unrelenting campaign against NATO been that, in the Soviet Union especially, the armed forces are among the most important and popular sectors of society. One has only to imagine the impact (or lack of it) in Western media of photographs captioned "Our Heroes" or "On guard" to recognize the gulf between the Communist and Capitalist society. The giant paradox is, of course, that the Soviet Union does have the capability and, if need be, the motivation, to take over by force the whole of Europe,

Above: The latest night and all-weather interceptor of the Soviet IA-PVO is the MiG-23S.

while the supposed aggressive European NATO countries lack the means and the motivation to invade anyone, let alone the Soviet Union!

Unlike those of NATO, or any other Western-style society, all WP troops are subjected to continual political indoctrination. This is all part of the centrally controlled political and economic infrastructure that pervades every aspect of Soviet life, and of which military affairs are an integral and central part. Without any overt wish to oppress, the fact remains that the entire WP population is subjected to totally managed media, centralized ideology and an overall pressure for

standardization. This is manifest in such end-results as suppression of minorities, harsh treatment of "dissidents", and universal teaching of the Russian language, Communist Party beliefs and ideology (especially among the military) and Soviet military organization and doctrine, down to the finest points of detail. Of course, this makes for maximum military efficiency, which is tested rigorously in large-scale exercises involving several WP countries at a time.

Of all the WP countries, the Soviet Union is the only one to possess strategic weapons, major offensive weapon-systems, large naval units and, in particular, nuclear weapons. Only the Soviet Union has the industrial and financial strength to create the full range of modern weapon-systems. The WP Satellites have extremely limited potential to create weapons, and in the field of air power it is limited to helicopters in the small to medium size (Poland), jet trainers (Czechoslovakia and Poland), light general-aviation aircraft such as utility transports and agricultural machines (Poland, Romania and, to a lesser degree, Czechoslovakia) and sailplanes (Poland, Czechoslovakia and Romania). Special mention must be made of the unique Jurom (Jugoslavia/ Romania) twin-jet tactical attack aircraft designed and built jointly by Romania and a non-member of the WP, Jugoslavia. This is discussed in the entry on Romania.

While Soviet aircrew eventually graduate to a position of trust, flying long transport, reconnaissance and electronic-warfare missions thousands of kilometres from Communist territory, other WP aircrew are rigorously prohibited from crossing their own frontiers. No other WP country but the Soviet Union has any counterpart to the Strategic Rocket Troops (the élite of all Soviet armed forces) nor the Zenith Rocket Troops, the SAM element of the PVO, the air defence of the homeland. Soviet fighter and interceptor squadrons of the IA-PVO (air defence) and FA (frontal aviation, ie tactical multi-role) have since 1971 been almost wholly re-equipped with new and extremely advanced types of aircraft, a high proportion of them with variable-geometry "swing wings", of which only the Sukhoi Su-20 has been supplied to Poland. This appears to be a distinct change in policy, and may reflect either a lack of trust of its Satellites on the part of the Soviet Union or retaliation at the former's small defence vote, expressed as a percentage of GNP, compared with that of the Soviet Union.

The aviation and missile forces of the Soviet Union are numerically the largest in the world, not only meeting the needs of one of the world's two superpowers but also giving the Soviet Union military domination over an organisation of secondary industrial powers in the Warsaw Pact. In recent years the rapid expansion and modernisation of Soviet military aviation has given rise to increasing concern in the West.

There is no single "Soviet Air Force", comprising all military aviation under one command. The armed forces of the Soviet Union are integrated beneath a single General Staff. Three main aviation contingents report directly to the General Staff and another is under naval control.

Of the three main elements one—the Strategic Rocket Forces (Russian initials RVSN)—has no combat aircraft at all. The Air Defence Forces (designated the PVO, from their Russian initials) command extensive surface-to-air and anti-ballistic missile defences (ZA-PVO) as well as what is by far the largest manned interceptor force in the world (IA-PVO). Other aviation activities are the responsibility of the Air Force (VVS) in its three operating sections: these are Frontal Aviation (FA), which provides tactical support to the Ground Forces; Long-Range Aviation (DA), which constitutes the Soviet Union's strategic bomber force, and Military Transport Aviation (VTA). The VTA fleet is backed up by the civil freighters of the Soviet Union's state airline, Aeroflot.

Below left: The SAM called by NATO SA-3 "Goa" is extremely widely used both by Pact countries and friendly nations. Radars are "Flat Face" (acquisition) and "Low Blow".

Below: IA-PVO interceptors practise formation flying for display and propaganda purposes. These are Su-15s of the original "Flagon A" type, with delta wing. It is not known if the new-wing D/E/F models are rebuilds.

The fourth aviation element of the Soviet forces is Naval Aviation (AV-MF). It is subordinate to the Soviet naval command rather than directly to the General Staff as are the RVSN, VVS and PVO. Its historical role can be loosely described as "support of the fleet" and its importance has expanded dramatically in the last two decades with the growth of the Soviet Fleet.

In the Soviet Union it is difficult to say where civilian government ends and military command begins. Communist Party Secretary Leonid Brezhnev chairs the Council of Defence, composed of high-level military and political officials including Defence Minister Dmitry Ustinov. In wartime the Council of Defence would probably assume the government of the Soviet Union; in times of peace it ensures the country's industrial and political readiness for war. Between the Council of Defence and the General Staff is the Main Military Council, which in peacetime is responsible for the strategic direction of the armed forces. It is thought to be chaired by Defence Minister Ustinov. Ustinov and Brezhnev were awarded high honorary military rank in 1976.

Command Structure

Both the General Staff and the Main Military Council have responsibilities reaching higher and lower than those of Western military commands, which delegate more of their work to departments of the civilian government. The Soviet high command is responsible for long-range planning and the analysis of both military and political situations, as well as the administration of training and support services.

The close links between military and civil administration have in the past led to sweeping political decisions which have had profound effects on the air services. The strategic bomber force was regarded as an élite in the

1930s; it declined during World War II, but came back into the limelight once nuclear weapons were available. Under Krushchev in the late 1950s and early 1960s, however, it lost all priority in favour of the RVSN, and is only now showing signs of catching up in terms of importance with the USAF Strategic Air Command. Another decision with long-term consequences was Krushchev's dictum in the mid-1950s that there should be no more specialised ground-attack aircraft; it was to be 20 years before Frontal Aviation could field a specialised strike fighter in the shape of the Mikoyan MiG-27.

RVSN is the youngest of the services. Soviet experiments with long-range military rockets started after 1945 with captured German equipment and engineers, and by the second half of the 1950s had reached the stage where Krushchev could found the RVSN and order the development of an intercontinental ballistic missile (ICBM) force. This proved more difficult than anticipated and it was not until 1962 that an effective ICBM entered service. In the same year an attempt to locate medium-range missiles in Cuba, within range of the United States, led to the Cuba missile crisis. The RVSN is reported to be responsible for anti-satellite systems, and its activities are now covered by the Vladivostok agreement of November 1974 on control of strategic weapons.

Origins of the VVS

VVS has its origins in the Revolution, when some units of the former Imperial Russian forces took part in the Civil War. Post-revolutionary development was hampered by the destruction of the Civil War and the loss of some leading designers who emigrated to the West. By the 1930s the VVS had been built up into a large and powerful force, but the battles between VVS detachments and the German Condor Legion in the Spanish Civil War showed that technologically it was in the second rank at best.

Stalin's purges swept away many VVS leaders and effectively prevented the force from modernising itself after the Spanish Civil War. The VVS was heavily defeated in the early days of the German invasion in the second half of 1941 and early 1942, and the force which emerged from battle experience was very different from the pre-war VVS. By 1945 the VVS had become a higher command level as far as the tactical combat forces were concerned, and the next few years saw the same development in the strategic bombing and transport arms.

The tactical combat force, FA, dates its status as the "first among equals" of the three VVS commands back to 1942. In that year the Soviet tactical forces were formed into Air Armies charged with support of the front line and subordinated to the commander-in-chief for a particular military front. By the war's end there were some 17 Air Armies. Armies were assigned to a specific area; the next largest unit was the division, normally assigned to a specific role. The division comprised three or four regiments, each operating some 50 aircraft of a single type. This pattern of organisation remains in force.

FA fielded 12,000 combat aircraft in the early 1950s, but many of these were wartime types or their developments. Priority was given to strategic arms—bombers and interceptors rather than strike aircraft—and right up to the late 1960s FA was equipped with aircraft not well suited to the close-support role. But the end of the Krushchev era, and the replacement of the "nuclear tripwire" strategy with "flexible response", meant that the FA had to be re-armed for its new role. Now an increasing number of FA's 4600 aircraft are the new types which were designed and developed in the late 1960s and early 1970s.

The strategic bomber component of the VVS—designated DA since 1946—has suffered more than most from the fluctuations in Soviet policy. Russia pioneered the heavy bomber in the 1914–18 war, with Sikorsky's *Ilya Mourometz* class of bombers. Some fought briefly for the

Above: The two known sub-types of MiG-25R reconnaissance aircraft. Left: "Foxbat B" with cameras and SLAR, and, on the right, "Foxbat D" with no cameras but a larger SLAR and various electronic changes. The two black blobs on the D-model are members of a servicing crew.

Bolsheviks in the Civil War, but the heavy bomber element disappeared by 1923.

The VVS formed a new bomber force in the early 1930s, equipped with the TB-1 and the then advanced TB-3. They had been mainly replaced by more modern types by the outbreak of war in 1941, but the force was virtually annihilated during suicidal unescorted daylight raids on tactical targets. Reformed in March 1942 under the designation ADD, the bombers, mainly Pe-8s and Il-4s, carried out a number of attacking raids on German targets before being placed under direct VVS control as the 18th

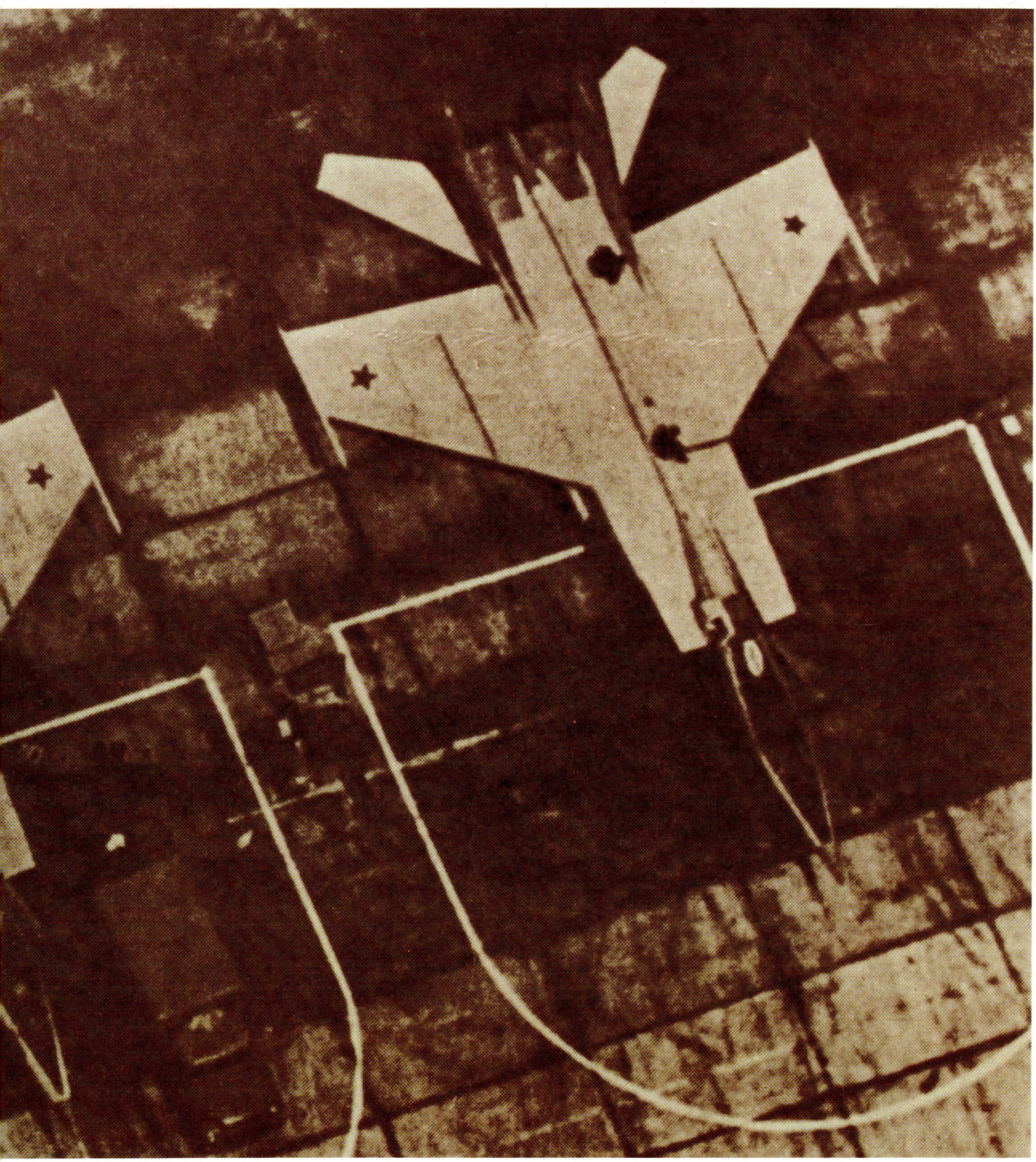

Air Army in December 1944.

Two events led to the reconstitution of the independent strategic bombing force as the DA in 1946. The first was the internment in 1944 of three USAAF Boeing B-29 Superfortresses which force-landed in Soviet territory after raids on Japan. The second was the development of nuclear weapons. Copied in every detail as the Tupolev Tu-4, the B-29 became the carrier of the Soviet fission bomb.

DA, VTA and PVO

The new DA was responsible for diverting a great deal of US military effort into strategic defence after the US "bomber scare" of the 1950s. But by the time the first Soviet intercontinental bombers entered service it was realised that the subsonic medium-altitude bomber was a sitting duck. The supersonic Myasishchev Mya-52 was the DA's last hope to hold its own against the rising RVSN, but it failed dismally to achieve its design range. Krushchev was disgusted and the programme was cancelled in 1960. Since that time DA has been predominantly a medium-range force, and only now, with the "Backfire" bomber and a new tanker fleet, is it showing signs of recovering its strength.

The youngest VVS command is the VTA freighter fleet, with its origins in the late 1920s. Closely associated with paratroop forces up to the mid-1950s, the VTA began to increase in size and effectiveness with the delivery of specialised Antonov freighters from 1957. The big Mil Mi-6 helicopter also flew in that year. In the late 1960s VTA took delivery of the very large and extremely long-range Antonov An-22 Antei, giving it a new global airlift mobility. The smaller Antonovs are now being replaced by the Ilyushin Il-76, which can carry twice the payload twice as far.

Represented on the General Staff with the VVS and RVSN is the air defence organisation, the PVO. Created in early 1941, as the alliance between the Soviet Union and Germany became more strained, the PVO started life as an organisation of district commanders who co-ordinated interceptor and anti-aircraft artillery forces on a regional basis. Its autonomy within the VVS increased throughout the war, and it became wholly independent in the immediate post-war years.

PVO Planning and the AV-MF

The PVO forces and particularly the independent Moscow PVO District were the priority units in the 1950s as the bomber threat grew, and most research and development efforts were biased to its needs. With the advent of the surface-to-air missile in the late 1950s the PVO forces split into two subdivisions: the IA-PVO manned intercepter force and the ZA-PVO in command of strategic SAMs (not including the tactical SAMs attached to Ground Forces).

PVO planning in the late 1950s and early 1960s assumed that the bomber threat would continue to expand, but the expansion and modernisation of the interceptor force were slowed down slightly when Western planners seemed to abandon the manned bomber. In the 1970s IA-PVO has started a new re-equipment programme, and ZA-PVO has acquired a new role with the development of the Soviet anti-ballistic missile (ABM) system.

In recent years the AV-MF has grown as fast as the surface fleet it supports. Its force of flying boats and fighters for coastal defence expanded rapidly during the war, but in 1953 the fighter squadrons were taken over by the local PVO commands and Air Armies as part of a general downgrading of the surface fleet. The AV-MF was a small but enterprising force, armed with twin-jet Tu-14 torpedo-bombers and pioneering the use of shore-based Mi-4 helicopters for anti-submarine warfare (ASW).

AV-MF's current growth followed Admiral Gorshkov's revival of the surface fleet. With the need to support a

Right: Do the Russians really make aircrew parade for a lecture, or last-minute briefing, after they have got out to their aircraft? With up to two pilots and a flight engineer each, the six men in this night-time line-up could be the crews of the two pylon-equipped Mi-8s.

Below: Several years ago there were more than 200 MiG-27 attack aircraft serving with the GSFG, and this photograph was taken near an East German airfield. When this book went to press the MiG-27 had been in service seven years, but was still not used by any Satellite air force.

worldwide fleet, AV-MF acquired long-range aircraft surplus to the requirements of the unfavoured DA, and built up a powerful maritime strike, reconnaissance and electronic intelligence (Elint) force. In 1962 AV-MF deployed its first shipboard helicopters for ASW. In 1967 the specialised helicopter carrier *Moskva* was commissioned. Towards the end of the same decade the first specialised Soviet ASW aeroplane, the Ilyushin Il-38, entered service. In 1976 the AV-MF was sharing first deliveries of the swing-wing "Backfire" with DA and, even more significantly, carried out open-sea trials with "Forger" vertical-take-off-and-landing (VTOL) light attack aircraft on the carrier *Kiev,* adding a new dimension to the fastest-expanding of all the Soviet air arms.

The Warsaw Pact Alliance

The Soviet Union's main alliance is the Warsaw Pact, on which its security against attack from the West is based. The other Pact countries are Poland, Czechoslovakia, Hungary, East Germany, Romania and Bulgaria. The armed forces of these countries are under Soviet command and their role is mainly defensive. Their aircraft industries are confined to the development of smaller types.

Signature of the Pact in May 1955 confirmed the Soviet Union's hegemony over Eastern Europe, established in fact between 1945 and 1950. The Soviet Union has been ready in the past to use force if any of the Pact countries steps out of line.

Three Eastern European nations are members neither of the Warsaw Pact nor of Nato. One, Albania, has no links at all with the Soviet Union. Finland and Jugoslavia, however, have a looser relationship with the Soviet Union than the other Warsaw Pact countries. Neither state abuts on to the central NATO area, so they do not present a severe security risk. The air forces of

Above: Still little-known in the West, SA-9 "Gaskin" is thought to be an up-rated and improved SA-7 "Grail" SAM, for close-range air defence. This amphibious BRDM-2, the usual carrier vehicle, has only the outer pair of missile launcher boxes fitted. Both crew-men are standing.

both rely on the Soviet Union for first-line aircraft, but Finland buys some equipment in the West and Jugoslavia is developing its own aircraft. Close co-operation between Jugoslavia and Romania has led to the development of a joint combat aircraft, the Orao.

Outside Eastern Europe, the Soviet Union buys influence through military and civil aid programmes. Beneficiaries of "MiG diplomacy" in the Middle East have included Libya, Syria and Iraq. That there is another side to the coin is demonstrated by the example of Egypt, where the supply of spares for Soviet-built aircraft has fluctuated with changes in international relationships. Cuba is an important ally and outpost in Central and South America, and Peru has already added Soviet aircraft to its combat fleet—Su-22s being now in service.

The Soviet Union's two main potential enemies are NATO and China. Conscious efforts have been made to reduce the tension between the Soviet Union and its allies and NATO, and it is still not clear what the attitude of the new ruling group in China will be to the Soviet Union.

SALT I and II

The first round of Strategic Arms Limitation Talks between the Soviet Union and the USA reached an accord at the end of 1974, and the Salt II series is under way as these words are written. So far efforts to achieve a similar agreement on tactical arms in the European theatre (Mutual and Balanced Force Reduction, or MBFR) have been to no avail, mainly because of Western disquiet at the rapidly increasing strength of the Soviet conventional

Above: Unlike the Satellite members of the Warsaw Pact, politically important export customers have been allowed to buy both the MiG-23S fighter and MiG-27 attack aircraft. The latter is seen here in a fly-past over Cairo; large numbers of the export version are also flying in Libya.

forces which would operate in the European theatre.

Another possible area of tension is the Iranian border, where the Imperial Iranian Air Force is massing in increasing strength. It is unlikely that any move would be made, however, unless the Soviet Union were to become acutely short of petroleum reserves.

Inventory

The Soviet forces are expanding at an unprecedented rate, and older weapon systems which were clearly inferior to their Western contemporaries are being replaced by new weapons which match the best Western products.

Strategic Rocket Forces

The RVSN (Strategic Rocket Forces) typifies this trend, sharing as it does the task of strategic deterrence with the sea-launched ballistic missiles of the Soviet Navy and, to a lesser extent, the bombers and air-launched cruise missiles of DA. The total number of intercontinental delivery vehicles is limited by international agreement, but current second-generation missiles are now being replaced by new, more accurate weapons and even these will be replaced by fourth-generation weapons now under development and likely to start test launchings soon.

The oldest missiles in the RVSN inventory are 500 SS-4 "Sandal" intermediate-range ballistic missiles (IRBMs). These missiles and 100 slightly longer-range SS-5 "Skeans" are not subject to the Salt agreement. Some SS-5s are launched from underground silos, but most of the IRBMs

Above: Photographs inside Soviet aircraft factories are rare, and usually carefully arranged. Several have been permitted in the Perm engine plant, which among other things makes Soloviev helicopter engines. These are main gearboxes for Mi-8 helicopters.

are fired from "soft", above-ground sites. A major exception is the other current IRBM, the land-mobile SS-15 "Scrooge".

The latest IRBM is the SS-20 (formerly SS-X-20) which is now deployed. It is reported that the normal SS-20 warhead, comprising three multiple re-entry vehicles (MRVs), can be replaced by a single warhead and an extra stage to turn the SS-20 into an intercontinental ballistic missile (ICBM).

ICBM Systems

Some of the earlier ICBM systems in the RVSN order of battle are now being dismantled to make way for new weapons within the SALT ceilings. Among these are the SS-7 "Saddler" (the first Soviet ICBM to become fully operational, in 1962), the SS-8 "Sasin" and the SS-9 "Scarp". Numbers in service were put in late 1976 as 90 SS-7s, 200 SS-8s and 210 SS-9s.

Numerically the most important ICBM in RVSN service is the SS-11 "Sego", with a total of nearly 1,000 missiles in service, all in hardened silo installations. Some 850 SS-11 Mod 1s are being gradually replaced by Mod 3 weapons with MRVs. Together with the solid-propellant SS-13 "Savage"—which has not proved a success, with only 60 missiles in service—the SS-11 constitutes the second-generation of Soviet ICBMs.

The first of the third-generation missiles, the solid-propellant SS-X-16, had not entered service by late 1976, but is likely to replace the SS-13. It has twice the throw weight and better accuracy than the SS-13, and it can be land-mobile like the SS-15 IRBM. It has been preceded into service by the SS-17, which is an evolutionary development of the SS-11 "Sego" and uses the same silos. Like SS-11, the SS-17 is a liquid-propellant missile, but unlike the older weapon it carries multiple, independently targeted re-entry vehicles (MIRVs), four in number and

suitable for counter-force strikes on enemy ICBM silos. Forty SS-17s are in service. Also in service is the SS-19, developed as a back-up to the SS-17 and broadly similar in throw weight and accuracy; some 140 SS-19s are operational.

Much larger and more powerful than the SS-17 and SS-19 is the intended replacement for the SS-9 "Scarp", the SS-18. The Mod 1 version now in service carries a single warhead, but the Mod 2 under development carries eight MIRVs. The Mod 3 will carry a single, more accurate warhead. Fifty SS-18s have been deployed, in silos better protected than any others in the RVSN.

At least three "fourth-generation" ICBMs are reported to be under development, for service in the mid-1980s. Other developments include still more accurate re-entry vehicles and the MARV (manoeuvring re-entry vehicle) which is designed to evade defensive systems.

Sea-launched ballistic missile forces are also being modernised, with greater accuracy and MRVs. There are still a few obsolete SS-N-4 "Sark" SLBMs in service, representing the first SLBM to go into service, more than 20 years ago. About half the Sark-firing submarines were converted in the mid-1960s to fire the SS-N-5 "Serb", which now arms eight Hotel II and eleven Golf II boats.

SLBM Development

Numerically the most important SLBM in Soviet service is the SS-N-6 "Sawfly", which started to close the technological gap between US and Soviet systems in 1967. More than 1,000 missiles now arm 34 Yankee-class boats, each with 16 launch tubes, and the SS-N-6 Mod 3 with three MRVs is beginning to replace earlier versions.

The Soviet Union has now taken the lead in SLBM development with the entry into service of the 8000km-range SS-N-8, fitted as standard with MRVs and arming Delta submarines. Eight twelve-round Delta Is are being

Above: Longest-ranged of the mass-produced battlefield SAMs, SA-4 "Ganef" rides in pairs on a specially designed launch/transporter. Once used by Egypt, this big weapon has recently also entered service in the East German Army. Each Soviet field army has nine batteries of SA-4s.

Above: Though it has considerable slant range and ceiling, the V750-series SAM (SA-2 "Guideline") is totally outmoded, and costly and clumsy compared with modern weapons. This Polish missile is one of many thousands used for training; most will probably eventually be fired.

Left: Pre-flight work on a MiG-25U "Foxbat C" trainer. This has a stepped-up instructor cockpit, no radar or sensors but the complete air-data and navigation system. The truck is probably for ground electric power.

Below: Among the many features of the so-called MiG-21 "bis" or "Fishbed N" are an enlarged dorsal spine fairing and a fat pitot boom carrying air-data transducers. The fundamental obsolescence of the wing remains, however.

joined by a rapidly expanding force of 16-round Delta IIs, and a completely new 20-missile boat is under development. New-generation missiles with 8000km-plus ranges—the solid-propellant SS-XN-17 and liquid-fuel SS-XN-18—are undergoing trials.

Of the three combat elements in the VVS it is the tactical FA which has been most modernised and re-equipped over the past ten years. FA is estimated to take more than half the 1000 high-performance combat aircraft which Soviet aircraft factories produce every year. Moreover, these new aircraft are much more suited to the tactical support role than the MiG-21 and Su-7 which formed the backbone of the FA throughout the 1960s after being developed to meet air-defence-orientated requirements. The 1970s have also seen the Soviet Union attempting to catch up with the West in development of guided air-to-surface missiles (ASMs) and weapon-aiming systems, with new weapons beginning to reach front-line regiments in 1977.

FA Deployment

Exact estimates of the composition of the FA are hard to come by, particularly in view of the rapid introduction of the latest types of aircraft and the difficulty of telling whether older aircraft have been retired or placed in reserve. But it is currently estimated that FA deploys some 4600 first-line combat aircraft, split roughly equally among three groups: new-technology aircraft introduced since 1971; relatively modern types; and aircraft which by Western standards are obsolescent. The last group is already being taken out of service in front-line areas, although the Soviet Union tends to keep aircraft in service for some years after their Western contemporaries have been declared obsolete. A corollary of this policy is that Soviet aircraft fly fewer hours per year, extending their airframe lives.

A Frontal Aviation Army's largest sub-unit is the division, which is assigned to a specific role. (All units are, however, trained to some extent in the delivery of tactical nuclear free-fall weapons.) The main equipment of fighter divisions is still the Mikoyan MiG-21 "Fishbed" series, flown in the early 1950s in prototype form and in service since the later years of the decade. More than 1000 of the 1500-plus MiG-21s in first-line Soviet service fly with FA fighter, fighter-bomber and reconnaissance units, and an increasing proportion are the latest third-generation versions ("Fishbed H/J/K/L/N") with increased payload and an internal gun. They are regarded as true multi-role aircraft, albeit with a limited range. Later MiG-21s can carry a mix of up to four AA-2-2 "Advanced Atoll" radar homing and "Atoll" infra-red homing air-to-air missiles (AAMs), or bombs and unguided rockets for ground attack.

Introduction of the MiG-23MS

Since 1971, however, FA fighter divisions have been phasing in the much more capable MiG-23MS "Flogger B" variable-sweep air-superiority fighter. Its useful combat radius is far greater than that of the MiG-21—some 500nm compared with 150nm for the smaller fighter—and it carries a heavier armament, comprising a pair of medium-range AA-7 "Apex" AAMs (usually, one IR-homing and one semi-active homing) and two IR dogfight missiles known as AA-8 "Aphid". Like the later MiG-21s it has an internal GSh-23 twin-barrel cannon of 23mm calibre. More than 500 MiG-23MS fighters are in service, and production is estimated to be running at almost 150 aircraft a year, for the Soviet Union and for export.

The MiG-23MS has a secondary ground-attack capability superior to that of the MiG-21 or even the Sukhoi Su-7, the standard Soviet strike fighter of the 1960s. The roles of the fighter and fighter-bomber divisions are, however, diverging. The considerable expansion of the

Above: What appears to be a weapon pylon is in fact the skis of a Polish soldier boarding an Mi-4 for a winter assault. Pact forces constantly practise such missions.

Right: Since 1960 Soviet aircraft designers have raised their sights and given even tactical aircraft trans-Europe range. The big Tupolevs reach the Azores.

Ground Forces' surface-to-air missile formations has reduced the need for fighters over the battlefield, so aircraft like the MiG-23MS would be used to carry the air war outside SAM range. Fighter-bomber units similarly are equipping with more specialised and longer-range aircraft.

The MiG-27 and Su-19

Probably the most important of the new ground-attack types is the MiG-27 "Flogger D", derived from the MiG-23MS but with a new nose section, a modified engine and completely different armament and weapon-aiming systems. The high commonality of the MiG-27 with the MiG-23 allowed a rapid build-up of production and more than 250 have been deployed since early 1974. Under development to arm the MiG-27 are television-guided, laser-guided and anti-radiation ASMs and "smart bombs" and some of these at least are already operational. The new weapons include the 6nm-range AS-7, thought to be command-guided, and the AS-X-10 of similar range but with TV guidance.

The MiG-27 could probably attack targets in Eastern England at full load, but is more suited to operations within continental Europe. FA is introducing a deep-penetration strike aircraft, however, in the shape of the Sukhoi Su-19 "Fencer", and deployment of this aircraft in East Germany has considerably reduced the dependence of forward commanders on the long-range strike aircraft of the DA.

"Fencer" flew in 1970 and was reported operational in regiment strength towards the end of 1976, production having taken some time to build up. It is a two-seater, nearly twice as heavy as the MiG-27, and can reach most

Right: There are several thousand MiG-21s of various types in Warsaw Pact squadrons. This appears to be a rather old PF, with "Atoll" AAM shoes. The navigation lights are on, but a ground-crewman is still busy above the left wing, on which is spread a protective sheet.

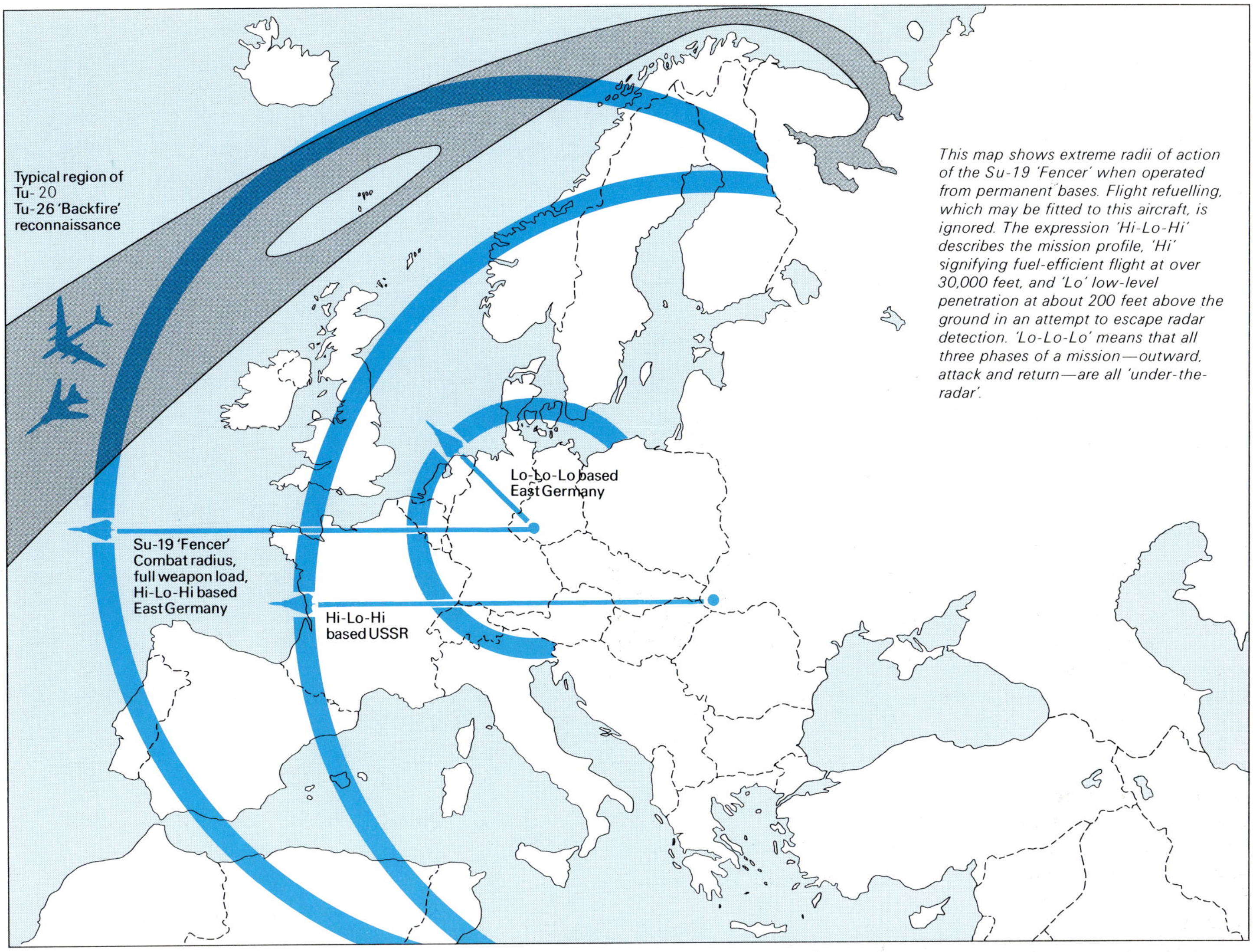

Typical region of
Tu-20
Tu-26 'Backfire'
reconnaissance

Lo-Lo-Lo based
East Germany

Su-19 'Fencer'
Combat radius,
full weapon load,
Hi-Lo-Hi based
East Germany

Hi-Lo-Hi
based USSR

This map shows extreme radii of action of the Su-19 'Fencer' when operated from permanent bases. Flight refuelling, which may be fitted to this aircraft, is ignored. The expression 'Hi-Lo-Hi' describes the mission profile, 'Hi' signifying fuel-efficient flight at over 30,000 feet, and 'Lo' low-level penetration at about 200 feet above the ground in an attempt to escape radar detection. 'Lo-Lo-Lo' means that all three phases of a mission—outward, attack and return—are all 'under-the-radar'.

important European targets from East German bases. Later versions may have a multi-mode attack radar, but early aircraft have the same avionics fit as the MiG-27. Armament includes the GSh-23 rather than the six-barrel 30mm "Gatling" gun of the MiG-27, but the Su-19 will add a pair of 50nm-range AS-X-9 anti-radar missiles to the array of ASMs carried by the smaller aircraft.

The third basic type of variable-sweep combat aircraft in FA service is the Sukhoi Su-17 "Fitter C, D/E", derived from the Su-7 via what was intended to be a purely experimental variable-sweep "Fitter B" test-bed flown in 1967. It offered a considerable improvement in field/payload/range performance over the "Fitter A", however, and could be placed in production fairly rapidly. Compared with the experimental "Fitter B" the Su-17 has an uprated engine, and it has eight stores pylons as against six on later "Fitter As". It has not been seen with the sensors associated with the new generation of Soviet ASMs, however, and is clearly an interim type. Over 250 Su-17s have been delivered to FA.

The new strike aircraft are replacing some of the older FA types such as the 1951-vintage MiG-17—only withdrawn from FA units in East Germany in late 1976—and the Yak-28 "Brewer" light bomber. About 1,000 of these types remain in service. The 500-plus Sukhoi Su-7s are likely to stay in service for some time, despite their limited range and weapon load.

Tactical Reconnaissance

Tactical reconnaissance for FA is mainly provided by MiG-21RF "Fishbed Hs", with wingtip electronic countermeasures pods and a reconnaissance pack replacing the GSh-23 cannon. Perhaps 300 are in service. Since 1971 FA has operated the Mach 3 MiG-25R "Foxbat B" for optical and electronic reconnaissance, but so far this type has

been used only in small numbers and it is doubtful whether there are as many as 100 aircraft of this type attached to FA. The two-seater MiG-23U "Flogger C", basically a conversion trainer variant of the MiG-23MS, has also been reported in the electronic countermeasures (ECM) role, with external ECM pods replacing missiles. But Frontal Aviation is also converting Yakovlev Yak-28 "Brewer" light bombers to the "Brewer E" ECM configuration, because its internal weapons bay offers more space for electronics than is available in the MiG-23 airframe.

The Mi-24 "Hind" Gunship

FA acquired a new capability in 1973 with the introduction of its first "gunship" helicopters. About 250 Mil Mi-24 "Hind" helicopters are in service, and progressive improvements in armament and weapon aiming have now led to the definitive "Hind D" variant, with sophisticated sighting systems and a multi-barrel machine gun in a nose turret. Unguided rockets and, it is believed, a new type of anti-tank missile are carried on stub wings. The new missile may be TV-command guided with IR terminal homing. Some sources say that there is a completely new anti-tank helicopter under development, but these reports may have arisen from early accounts of "Hind D".

The Mi-24 is a squad carrier as well as a gunship, with a cabin for 8–12 troops. The primary FA transport helicopter, however, is the Mil Mi-8 "Hip", a twin-turbine type with 35 seats. Some 600 Mi-8s are in service, and most can be armed with unguided rockets for fire suppression in combat. Sources differ on the division of the VVS helicopter fleet between FA and VTA, but it is not likely that the larger Mi-6 "Hook" and Mi-10K "Harke" would be used by FA in forward areas because of their size and vulnerability to small SAMs.

Support for FA divisions is organic, each having a

Above: By mid-1978 the most numerous type in the Soviet Air Force may no longer be the MiG-21 but the MiG-23, which is used by both IA-PVO and the FA. A multi-role aircraft, the MiG-23S is primarily an all-weather interceptor, with a rapid-fire cannon and two types of AAM. Soviet swing-wing aircraft appear often to be parked with wings folded.

Above left: Lowering a test missile of the SS-5 "Skean" family into a silo, probably about 1962. Powered by a twin-chamber first-stage engine burning storable liquids, this led to an operational IRBM in the 2,000-mile (3200-km) range class, since superseded by SS-14 and -20.

transport squadron and a communications flight. The twin-turboprop-plus-jet-booster Antonov An-26 "Curl" is used by FA, as are the An-14 and the An-2 biplane. The Czech Aero 45 is used for liaison.

Predictions of future FA equipment must be strictly speculative. The development of a canard fighter as a MiG-21 replacement has been reported, and it is certainly possible that FA would have a requirement for an air-superiority fighter more agile than the MiG-23MS. Deployment of a V/STOL tactical fighter is also a possibility, although Warsaw Pact forces, like the Swedish Air Force, make extensive use of road bases.

The Strategic Bomber Arm

The strategic bomber arm of the VVS, the DA, fielded a relatively modest force throughout the 1960s and early 1970s. Its intercontinental strike force now comprises about 50 subsonic Tupolev Tu-95 "Bear Bs", armed with turbojet-powered AS-3 "Kangaroo" cruise missiles. For strike and reconnaissance within the European theatre DA continues to operate some 170 medium-range Tu-22 "Blinder As and Bs", the latter being in the majority and

armed with the 750km-range AS-4 "Kitchen" missile. AS-3 and AS-4 are both large weapons, carried singly. Tanker support for the DA has up to now been provided by some 85 Myasishchev Mya-4 "Bison As", converted from the bomber role after the type failed to achieve its design range.

"Backfire" and SALT

DA is however now being re-equipped with the Tupolev "Backfire" swing-wing bomber, first flown in 1969 and reported as fully operational, after a fairly protracted development, in 1977. Western intelligence sources estimate that some 350 of the definitive version of "Backfire", the refined and improved "Backfire B", will enter DA service.

"Backfire's" main purpose is to replace the Tu-22 fleet in the intermediate-range strike role. Compared with the Tu-22 it can fly a much greater proportion of its mission at low level, substantially enhancing DA's ability to survive Nato air defences. Now that the AS-6 "Kingfish" ASM is fully developed, "Backfire" will carry one of these weapons, but in early 1977 the AS-6 was not in service and "Backfires" were carrying a single AS-4 "Kitchen" as an interim weapon to serve until the "Kingfish" became operational.

The flexibility of the turbofan-powered, variable-sweep "Backfire" allows it to present the same sort of long-range threat to the USA as is now posed by the ageing Tu-95s, because it can cover a considerable proportion of the USA on high-altitude, subsonic missions with flight refuelling.

Efforts have been made by the USA to have "Backfire" included among the weapons controlled by the SALT agreements, but the Soviet Union has insisted that it should be excluded, as a medium-range system. The balance of argument may shift if DA puts into service the tanker version of the Ilyushin Il-76 freighter to support the "Backfire" fleet, as the US Department of Defense expects.

Some US sources maintain that a new, longer-range bomber is under development as a direct replacement for the Tu-95. These reports may, however, be references to the canard delta bomber developed as a back-up to the Tupolev bomber by the Sukhoi bureau and test-flown in the early 1970s. It is not thought to have advanced beyond the flight-test stage.

VTA Aircraft

VTA, the transport and airlift command of the VVS, is a respectably sized force in its own right, but is backed up by the considerable resources of Aeroflot, particularly for strategic airlift and the movement of troops within the Soviet Union. Some 40 of the Soviet Union's 50 Antonov An-22 freighters are Aeroflot aircraft, and all of them appear to be equipped to full military standard with mapping radar and paradropping sights. VTA has some 600 Antonov An-12 tactical transports which differ from Aeroflot's 250 aircraft only in possession of a tail gun turret with two 23mm guns. Reports indicate that a new turbofan-powered transport, the An-40, is being designed to replace the An-22.

The An-12s are likely to be replaced by the new Ilyushin Il-76. This four-jet freighter flew in March 1971 and joined service test units in late 1974. It is designed to have twice the payload and twice the range of the An-12 while using the same airfields. VTA aircraft have a tail turret similar to that of the An-12.

Smaller Transports

Smaller fixed-wing transports include the Antonov An-26 and the older An-2 and An-14. Some An-8s—the twin-engine, unpressurised ancestor of the An-12—may remain in service, probably in the training role. Some 500 Mil Mi-6 heavy-lift helicopters are probably under VTA command, and it is possible that the vast Mi-12 is in limited service. Smaller transport helicopters are likely to be under FA control.

VVS training bases are estimated to have nearly 2000 Czech-designed Aero L-29s in service. These aircraft and the remaining MiG-15UTI advanced trainers are likely to be replaced by another Czech design, the Aero L-39 all-through trainer, which was being phased into VVS service in 1975. All combat units have two-seater aircraft attached for conversion training; typically, one squadron per regiment has four two-seaters out of 12 aircraft. The MiG-23U, MiG-25U and the trainer versions of the third-generation MiG-21s lack the full avionic equipment of the single-seaters; only the Su-7U "Moujik" of FA types is a fully operational combat aircraft. Another important trainer is the Mil Mi-2 helicopter, a Soviet design built in Poland and which is the main VVS rotary-wing trainer.

Re-equipment of the PVO

The thawing of the Cold War and the recession of the US bomber threat led to a slowdown in the modernisation of the air-defence forces of the PVO. Re-equipment is now gathering momentum, however, to meet the threat posed by US cruise missiles and the increasing numbers of long-range strike aircraft (F-111 and Tornado) in the Nato inventory.

The Sukhoi Su-15 "Flagon" is probably the most numerous interceptor in the IA-PVO, more than 700 being in service. Some of these are early-production "Flagon As", with the same "Skip Spin" radar and AA-3-2 "Advanced Anab" missiles as the 1961-vintage Yakovlev Yak-28P "Firebar" (some 200 in IA-PVO service), but an increasing number are of the later "Flagon D and E" variants. "Flagon E"—which may well have a different bureau designation from the earlier aircraft—has a modified wing, more power-

ful engines and better avionics than "Flagon A", and may carry the AA-7 "Apex" missile fitted to the MiG-23MS.

There are only some 280 MiG-25 "Foxbat A" interceptors in PVO service because the high-flying supersonic bombers (US XB-70 Valkyrie) which the type was designed to intercept failed to materialise. Unlike the initial "Foxbat A", the new aircraft is designed to operate outside direct ground control, and its range is much increased. It can carry two of the very large AA-6 "Acrid" missiles which arm some "Foxbat As" plus four AA-7 "Apex", and has an internal gun. It has a new radar which can detect and guide missiles on to lower-flying targets.

The PVO's current standard long-range interceptor is the Tupolev Tu-28P "Fiddler". Some 200 of these very large two-seat fighters, carrying four AA-5 "Ash" AAMs, remain in service to defend vast areas of the Soviet periphery where the SAM screen is thin.

Older, less effective types are deployed in the interior air-defence zones. They include some 600 Sukhoi Su-9s and Su-11s, similar to the FA's Su-7 but of tailed-delta layout. They carry the same armament as "Firebar" and "Flagon

A"—radar. Other units operate a total of around 250 older interceptors with limited all-weather capability—probably MiG-17s.

One very important type in the IA-PVO inventory is the Tu-126 "Moss" airborne warning and control system, derived from the Tu-114 airliner with a "mushroom" radar on top. A small force of these aircraft—reported at no more than 20—provides early warning and control of interceptors outside the range of ground controllers. Unlike the USAF Boeing E-3A, the Tu-126 is an overwater-only system, but it was in service eight years ahead of the E-3 and is expected to be replaced in the 1980s by a more advanced system which would presumably match the E-3's operational capability.

SAM Training

Training in the IA-PVO is separate from VVS but follows a similar pattern, with L-29s being replaced by L-39s for basic and intermediate training, pilots converting via the Su-11U "Maiden" or Su-15U "Flagon" C. IA-PVO

Above: Though totally outmoded as an air-portable weapon, the "Scud A" tactical missile on IS-3 (JS-3) chassis weighs well over 40 tonnes and demonstrates An-22 capability. Other loads shown in public include three "Frog 5" rockets on their PT-76 chassis, or two complete SA-4 "Ganef" SAM systems.

PVO units have An-2s and An-26s for support purposes.

The main strategic SAM in ZA-PVO is the SA-5 "Gammon", a high-altitude, long-range weapon which started to replace the SA-2 "Guideline" in the mid-1960s. Some 1100 SA-5s are reported to be in service, and a general upgrading of the SAM system is in prospect. A hypersonic SAM designed to intercept AGM-69 SRAM missiles carried by USAF strategic bombers is under development.

Remotely piloted vehicles used for SAM training and development include conversions of obsolete combat types such as the Yakovlev Yak-25RD "Mandrake" strategic reconnaissance aircraft and the MiG-19 interceptor. Purpose-built drones include the Lavochkin La-17 and a high-altitude, supersonic-cruise RPV with a single Tumansky R-266 engine.

ZA-PVO is also responsible for the anti-ballistic-missile (ABM) system, based on the "Galosh" and "Improved Galosh" interceptor missiles. There are four 16-missile sites around Moscow, with "Hen House" radars on the Soviet periphery for target acquisition and tracking. A new ABM, designated SH-4, and a high-acceleration missile similar to the US Martin Orlando Sprint are reported under development.

The development of mobile surface-to-air missiles has been very important to Soviet tactics, effectively freeing Frontal Aviation for the strike and longer-range air-superiority roles. Each Soviet Army Group—of which there are five permanently deployed in East Germany, for example, with a sixth acting as back-up in time of war—is responsible for an area measuring 50km along the battle front and 100km deep. Every Group has five batteries of SA-6 "Gainful" medium-range SAMs powered by integral rocket/ramjets, nine batteries of the longer-range SA-4 "Ganef" and three of the SA-2 "Guideline".

SA Batteries

An SA-6 battery comprises a "Straight Flush" radar vehicle, using the same PT-76 light-tank chassis as the missile vehicles; three of the latter, carrying three rounds each; and a reloading vehicle. Three of the batteries travel with the ground forces about 5km back from the forward edge of the battle area and the remaining two are deployed some 10km further back in the gaps between the forward systems. An SA-4 battery consists of an H-band "Pat Hand" acquisition and fire-control radar, three twin-launcher tracked vehicles and a reloader. Surveillance and initial target acquisition for both the SA-4 and SA-6 are the responsibility of E-band "Long Track" radars. The leading three SA-4 batteries travel some 10km behind the Army's forward forces with the other six moving in a belt 25km back from the front.

Defence of rear areas is provided by the SA-2, each battery containing six launchers, a loading vehicle and a Fan Song van-mounted fire-control radar. The Army also has SA-3 "Goa" SAMs, together with SA-7 "Grail" shoulder-launched weapons, the SA-9 "Gaskin" development using uprated missiles fired from four-round launchers on BRDM wheeled vehicles, and the new SA-8 "Gecko". The last-named is roughly equivalent to the West's Euromissile Roland and carries a four-round launcher, surveillance radar, tracking radar, low-light television camera and command links on one six-wheeled amphibious vehicle.

The Naval Air Arm

Naval SAMs are closely related to land-based weapons. Widely used on earlier ship classes is the SA-N-1 system, which uses the same missile as the land-based SA-3 "Goa". Standard area-defence system on the more modern large ships is the SA-N-3, which is believed to use the rocket/ramjet missile of the SA-6 system, on automatic twin launchers fed from below decks. The close-range SA-N-4, discreetly concealed in a flush "silo" installation, is thought to use the SA-8 missile. The shipboard "Guideline", the SA-N-2, has on the other hand not been successful, and only one installation has been commissioned.

The naval air arm, AV-MF, is perhaps the most diverse of all the Soviet air forces and one of the fastest expanding. As the Soviet surface fleet has grown and expanded its area of influence the AV-MF has followed it with a fleet of missile carriers, Elint, ECM and maritime reconnaissance aircraft, and now VTOL aircraft have gone to sea.

The bulk of the AV-MF anti-shipping strike force is still composed of 290 elderly Tupolev Tu-16 "Badgers" delivered in the early 1960s as the DA phased the type out of its inventory. Most of the Tu-16s are "Badger Gs", carrying a pair of 320km-range AS-5 "Kelt" ASMs, but there are still

Above: A Soviet soldier, wearing the collar insignia of the artillery, standing guard over a pontoon bridge with the original pattern of SA-7 "Grail" shoulder-fired SAM. A new model has much improved IR guidance.

some "Badger Cs" in service with a single 200km-range AS-2 "Kipper". About 50 Tu-22 "Blinder Cs" serve in the reconnaissance/Elint role with a free-fall strike capability.

These aircraft and missiles are likely to be replaced in the anti-surface-shipping role by the vastly more capable Tupolev "Backfire B" now completing work-up with AV-MF units, and the 220km-range AS-6 "Kingfish" missile. "Backfire" versions are likely to be configured for Elint, ECM and reconnaissance, and an eventual AV-MF force of 100 mooted in the West may be on the low side. The 75 "Badgers" serving in the tanker role with AV-MF may be replaced by the Ilyushin Il-76 tanker.

AV-MF's coastal-defence strike units still retain about 20 Ilyushin Il-28T "Beagles" armed with torpedoes. According to some sources the Il-28Ts are being replaced by Yak-28 "Brewers" retired from FA, but it is now reported that Sukhoi Su-17 "Fitter C" variable-sweep strike fighters are being delivered.

Maritime Reconnaissance

For wide-ranging maritime reconnaissance the AV-MF relies on the Tu-95 "Bear" now that the M-4 "Bison C" is being retired. There are rather more than 50 Tu-95s in AV-MF service, although some have been lost, and their long range and endurance are invaluable. "Bear Cs and Fs" are in service in the maritime reconnaissance role and "Bear Es" carry cameras for photo-reconnaissance and mapping. Some "Bear Ds", with a ventral radar for mid-course guidance of SS-N-3 "Shaddock" surface-to-surface missiles, may have been converted to "Bear F" configuration. There are also about 50 maritime reconnaissance/ ECM/Elint "Badger Ds and Fs" in service, and these have recently been joined by Antonov An-12 "Cub C" ECM air-

Above: One of thousands of SA-2 type SAMs on its operational launcher, with the articulated loader transporter (not the handling trolly seen on page 81) on the right. Ground equipment is incompatible with later SAMs.

Below: According to the US Defense Department, Tu-126 ("Moss") has limited effectiveness over water and is "ineffective" over land. Common sense suggests that this is not so; Soviet hardware is designed to be effective.

No visible vernier or
attitude-control jets

Ablative
protected nose

Warhead

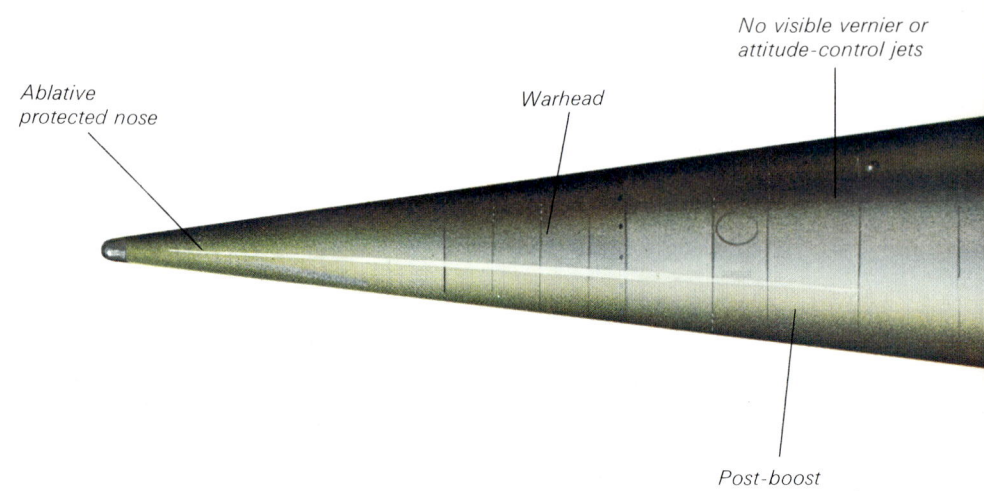

Post-boost
propulsion and
guidance bay

Weatherproof
fabric shroud

Possibly sprung
mounting boxes

ABM-1 "Galosh" Anti-Ballistic Missile

Type: Strategic anti-ballistic-missile missile (ABM).

Propulsion: High-energy solid rocket propulsion, almost certainly three tandem stages.

Missile Data: Overall length estimated at 65ft (19·8m); diameter (fins folded) about 101in (2·57m); launch weight estimated at 72,000lb (32,660kg).

Operation: "Galosh" is launched from a transport container mounted in an underground emplacement at a near-vertical angle. The launch complex of the 64 launchers near Moscow is each equipped with the "Try Add" radar installation comprising a "Chekhov" target-tracking radar and two guidance radars, all linked by computer and alerted by remote "Hen Housed" PAR (phased-array radar) in frontier areas—(100 such launchers were permitted under the SALT I agreement). Ultimate range is estimated at 186 miles (311km) and the thermonuclear warhead at 2—3 megatons. The missile has acutely sloping cone angles to facilitate climb through the atmosphere at hypersonic speed.

Four first-stage nozzles

Fixed first-stage stabilizer fins

MAZ-543 tug. Same tug used for SS-5 "Skean", SS-8 "Sasin", SS-9 "Scarp", SS-11 "Sego", SS-N-6 "Sawfly" and other missiles

Open (rear) end of container (travels rear-end first) revealing four first-stage motor nozzles

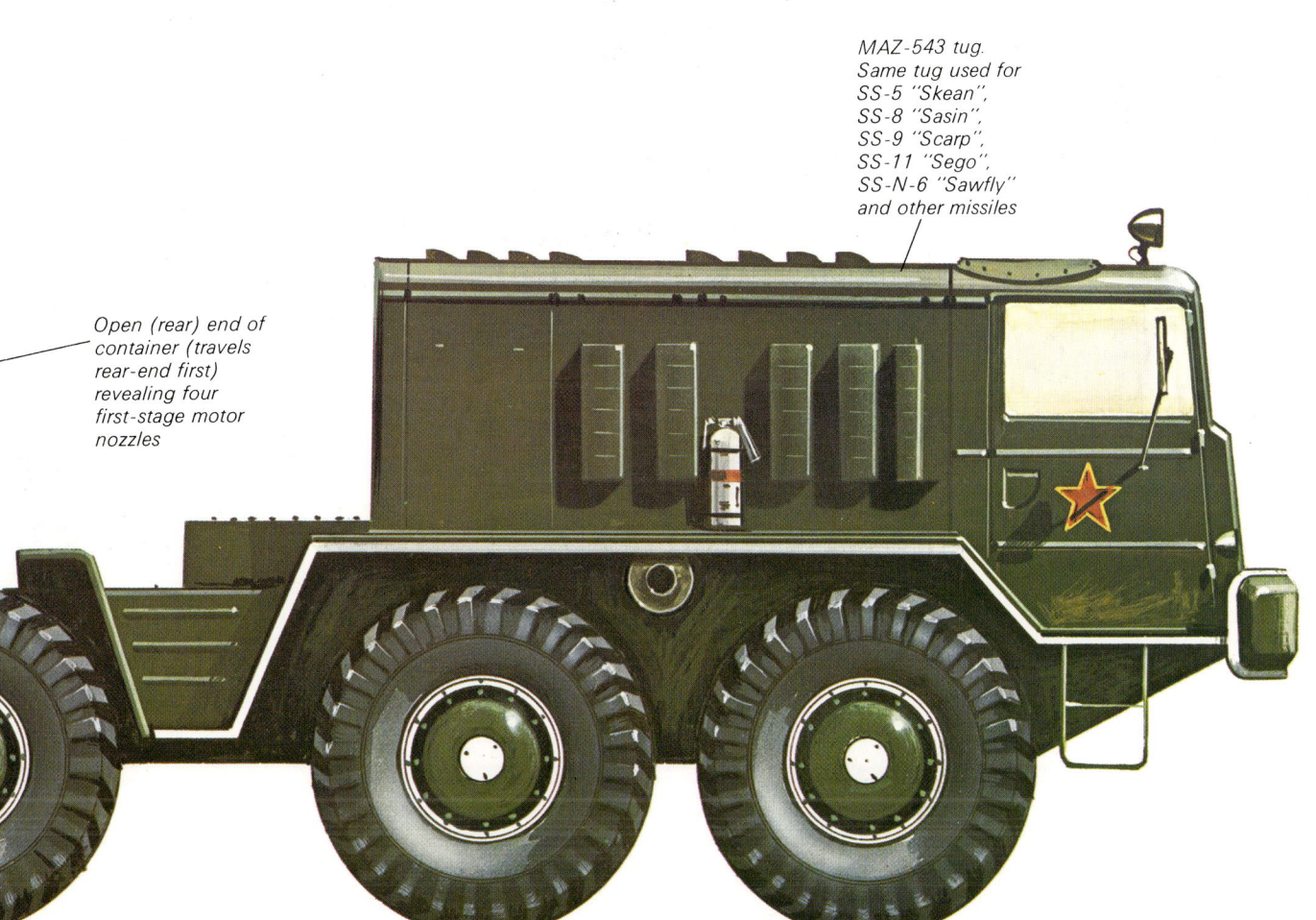

Base for
communications and
azimuth aerial

Cantilevered
frame supports
launcher

Forward-
folding front
frame

Transverse pivot
for rear of
launchers

Pow
slew
pre-
to co

Box over
final drives

Tow hooks o
used to carry
power cables

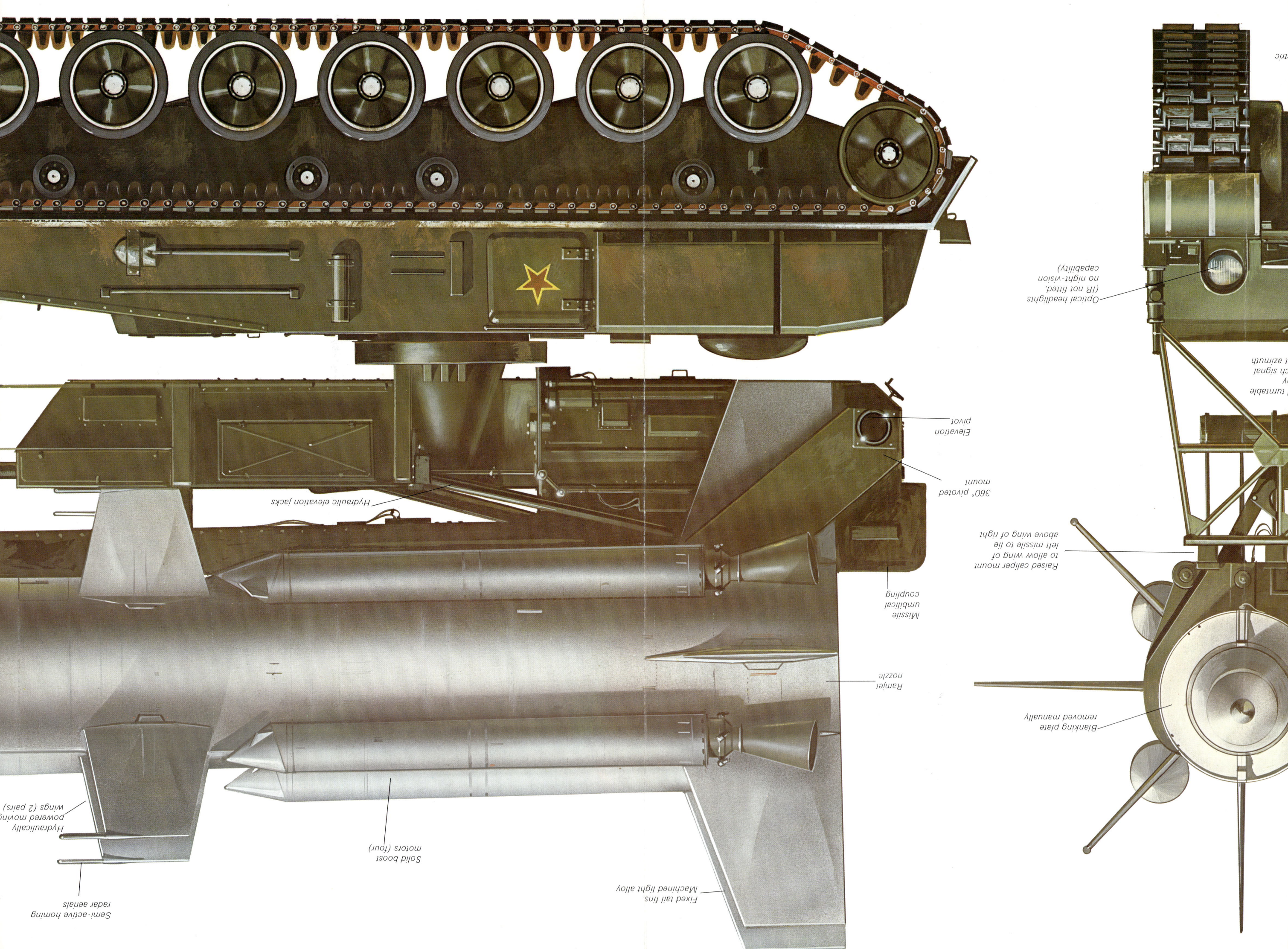

Optical headlights (IR not fitted, no night-vision capability)

Elevation pivot

360° pivoted mount

Hydraulic elevation jacks

Missile umbilical coupling

Ramjet nozzle

Raised caliper mount to allow wing of left missile to lie above wing of right

Blanking plate removed manually

Solid boost motors (four)

Fixed tail fins. Machined light alloy

Hydraulically powered moving wings (2 pairs)

Semi-active homing radar aerials

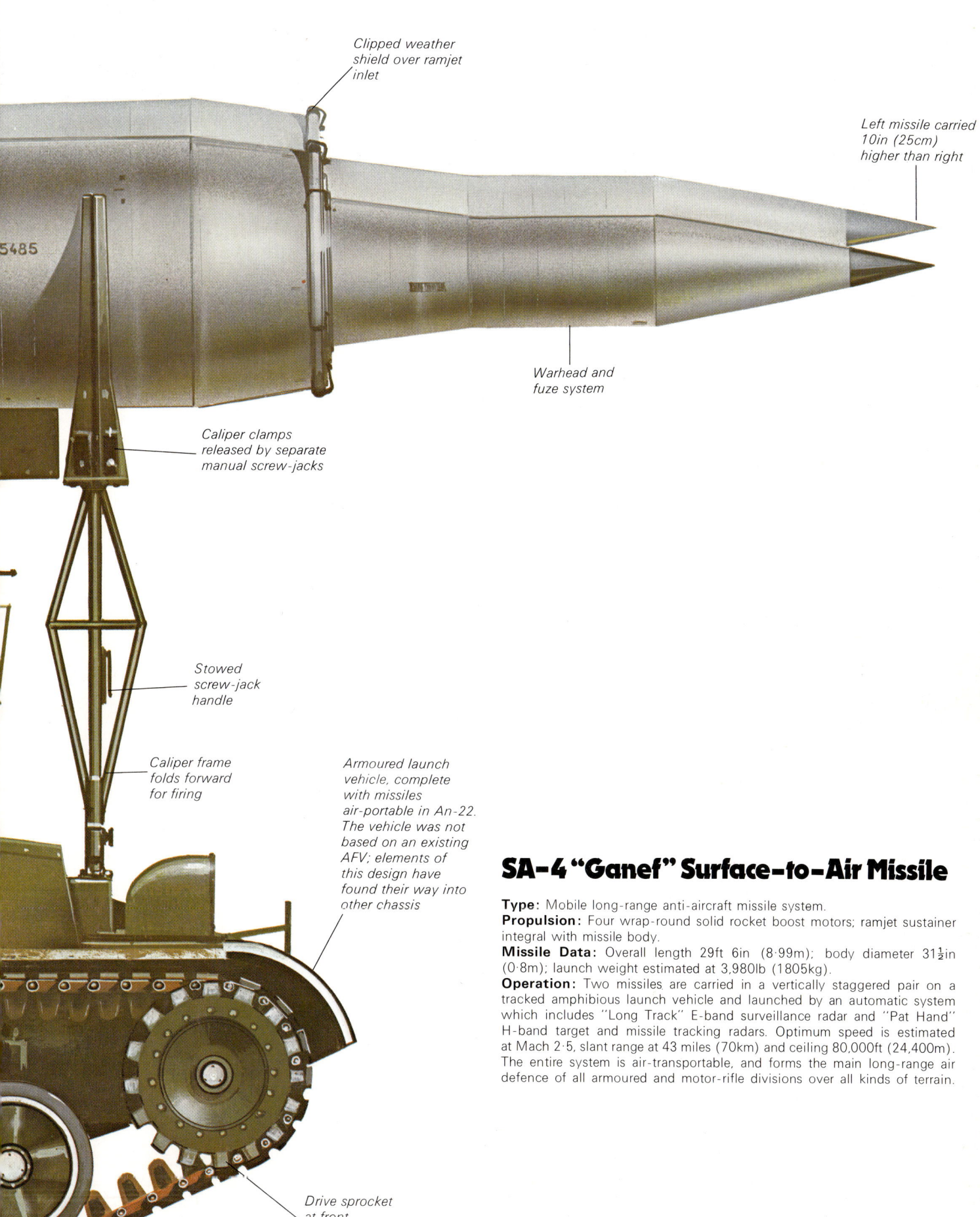

Clipped weather shield over ramjet inlet

Left missile carried 10in (25cm) higher than right

5485

Warhead and fuze system

Caliper clamps released by separate manual screw-jacks

Stowed screw-jack handle

Caliper frame folds forward for firing

Armoured launch vehicle, complete with missiles air-portable in An-22. The vehicle was not based on an existing AFV; elements of this design have found their way into other chassis

Drive sprocket at front

SA-4 "Ganef" Surface-to-Air Missile

Type: Mobile long-range anti-aircraft missile system.
Propulsion: Four wrap-round solid rocket boost motors; ramjet sustainer integral with missile body.
Missile Data: Overall length 29ft 6in (8·99m); body diameter 31½in (0·8m); launch weight estimated at 3,980lb (1805kg).
Operation: Two missiles are carried in a vertically staggered pair on a tracked amphibious launch vehicle and launched by an automatic system which includes "Long Track" E-band surveillance radar and "Pat Hand" H-band target and missile tracking radars. Optimum speed is estimated at Mach 2·5, slant range at 43 miles (70km) and ceiling 80,000ft (24,400m). The entire system is air-transportable, and forms the main long-range air defence of all armoured and motor-rifle divisions over all kinds of terrain.

craft converted from VTA or Aeroflot freighters.

AV-MF has always flown flying boats for anti-submarine warfare (ASW) and currently has some 75 Beriev Be-12 "Mail" amphibians armed with rockets and free-fall weapons. Since 1970, however, it has been phasing in its first specialised land-based ASW system, the Ilyushin Il-38 "May", and more than 55 are in service. Like the very similar Lockheed Orion the Il-38 was adapted from an airliner, the Ilyushin Il-18.

The AV-MF shore-based ASW helicopter units are also being upgraded with the introduction of the Mil Mi-14 "Haze", an amphibious ASW helicopter based on the Mi-8 "Hip" (a few of which equip specialised AV-MF minesweeping units). First flown in 1973, the Mi-14 started to replace Mi-4 "Hounds" in AV-MF service in early 1977.

"Hormone" and "Forger"

Shipboard helicopter units are mainly equipped with the Kamov Ka-25 "Hormone", a less than elegant but very compact twin-turbine co-axial ASW helicopter. Some 160 have entered service since the mid-1960s, including some "Hormone Bs", which provide over-the-horizon missile guidance associated with the SS-N-3 "Shaddock", and a few transport versions. Ka-25s are carried on the helicopter carriers *Moskva* and *Leningrad* as well as by the aircraft carrier *Kiev*. Some sources expect the Ka-25 to be replaced by a new helicopter on the larger ships, possibly related to a new gunship for FA, and it is possible that the *Kiev* class will deploy Mi-24s in support of amphibious operations or that the Mi-14 will go to sea.

Perhaps the biggest single advance in AV-MF equipment however, is the deployment of the "Forger" VTOL light attack aircraft, believed to be a product of the Yakovlev design team. As few as 30 "Forgers" may be in service and the aircraft on *Kiev* form a trials unit of perhaps a dozen single-seat "Forger As" and a pair of "Forger B" two-seat conversion trainers. Forger can carry AA-2 "Atoll" or AA-8 "Aphid" missiles, but has not yet been seen with advanced ASMs or associated avionics. This and the fact that "Forger" is a purely VTOL type, which cannot make rolling take-offs and take advantage of the angled decks of the new carriers, support the contention that "Forger" is mainly an experimental aircraft and that a truly V/STOL follow-on will appear by the time the second carrier, *Minsk*, is commissioned in 1979.

Deployment

Details of the deployment of the Soviet forces are even more scarce than information about the total inventory. The strict "need-to-know" security policy operated by the Soviet Union, under which virtually all information is classified to some degree, combines with the natural fluidity of military deployments to produce a near-impenetrable security blanket.

Soviet sea-launched strategic missiles are of course highly mobile, most of the Soviet missile submarines ranging widely from their bases with the Northern Fleet in the Murmansk region and the Pacific Fleet at Vladivostok. Land-based ICBMs of the RVSN are siloed in a belt 500km long and 400km wide, stretching from a point east of Moscow to the Lake Baikal region. Mobile and fixed IRBMs are deployed in European and Asian regions, threatening China and Europe.

Deployment of VVS Forces

Rather more may be said about the deployment of the VVS forces. Frontal Aviation is divided into at least 15 Air Armies, all except four being attached to the Military Districts within the Soviet Union. The four exceptions are attached to the Groups of Soviet Forces in the Warsaw Pact countries: the mighty 16th in East Germany; the 37th,

headquartered at Legnice in Poland; one Air Army centred on Milovice in Czechoslovakia; and a fourth headquartered at Tokol, near Budapest in Hungary.

The Air Army's largest sub-unit is the division, assigned to a specific role. A division will usually operate a number of different types in three regiments. Each regiment operates a single combat type from a single base, although units of a division will normally be grouped closely together within the Air Army's district. The 16th (see table) is fairly typical in structure, although it fields more than 1,000 combat aircraft compared with 250–300 in other Air Armies.

Transport and reconnaissance are the responsibility of individual regiments attached directly to the Army, rather than being organised into divisions. This system has flexibility in some cases: the MiG-25R regiment deployed with the 37th Air Army in Poland has detached squadrons to East Germany under 16th Air Army command.

Regiments comprise three squadrons of 12 aircraft each, and one of these usually operates about four two-seater aircraft for conversion training.

The long-range bomber force of the DA is not numerically larger than an FA Army, and the largest sub-unit of DA is the division. There are three DA divisions, one in the Far East district, based on the coast of the Bering Sea; one in the Murmansk area; and one in European Russia. Each comprises three regiments of three ten-aircraft squadrons. The bulk of the Tu-22 medium-range bomber force is European-based, although some aircraft face

Right: Despite the impression given by this unusual (dusk?) picture, the "Hind D" does not have Buddy inflight-refuelling capability. Soviet tactical forces are all night-equipped.

Below: A monster Antei (An-22) comes in to a tactical airstrip already occupied by a row of ASU-85 amphibious assault guns flown in by An-12 transports.

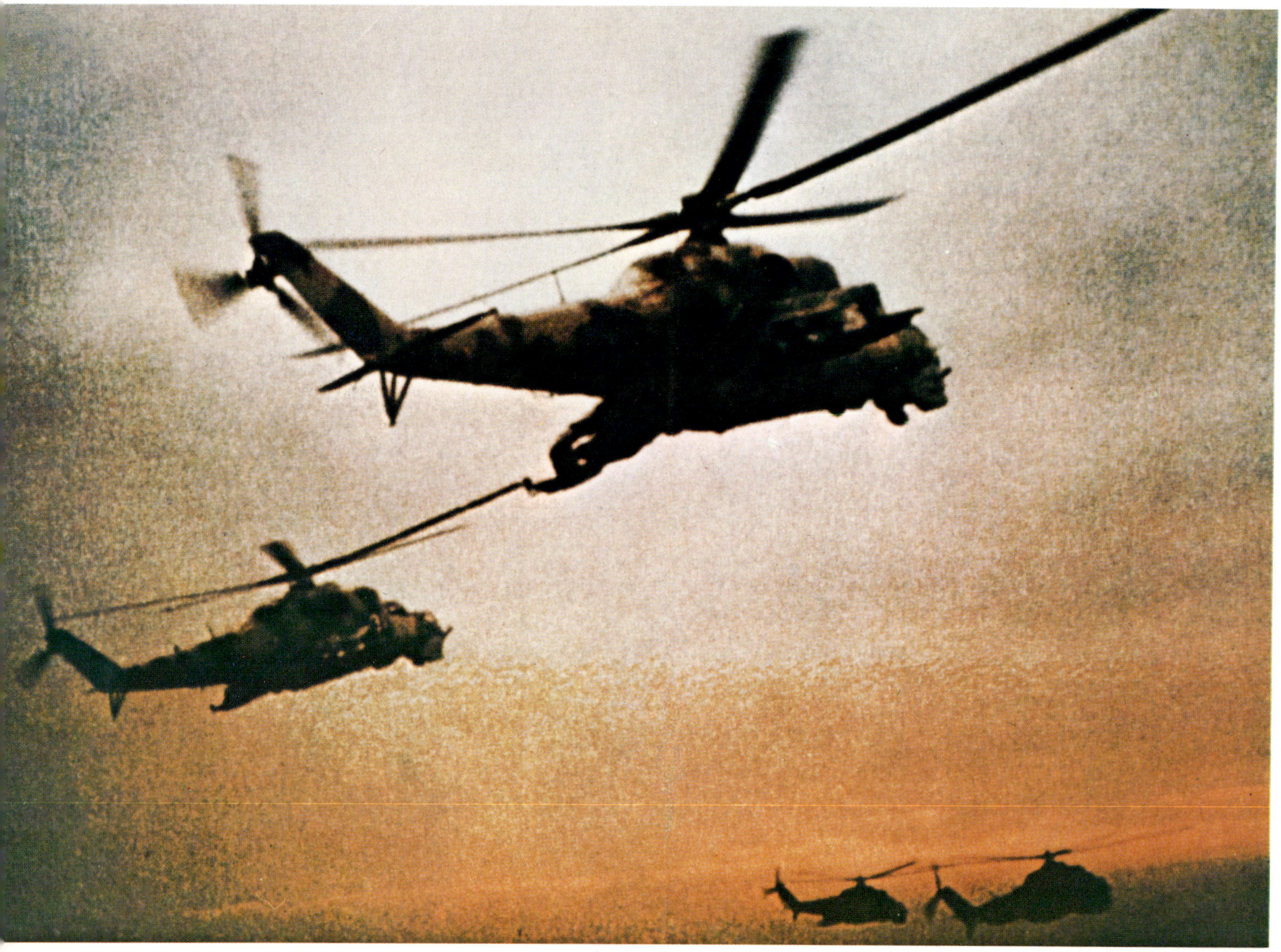

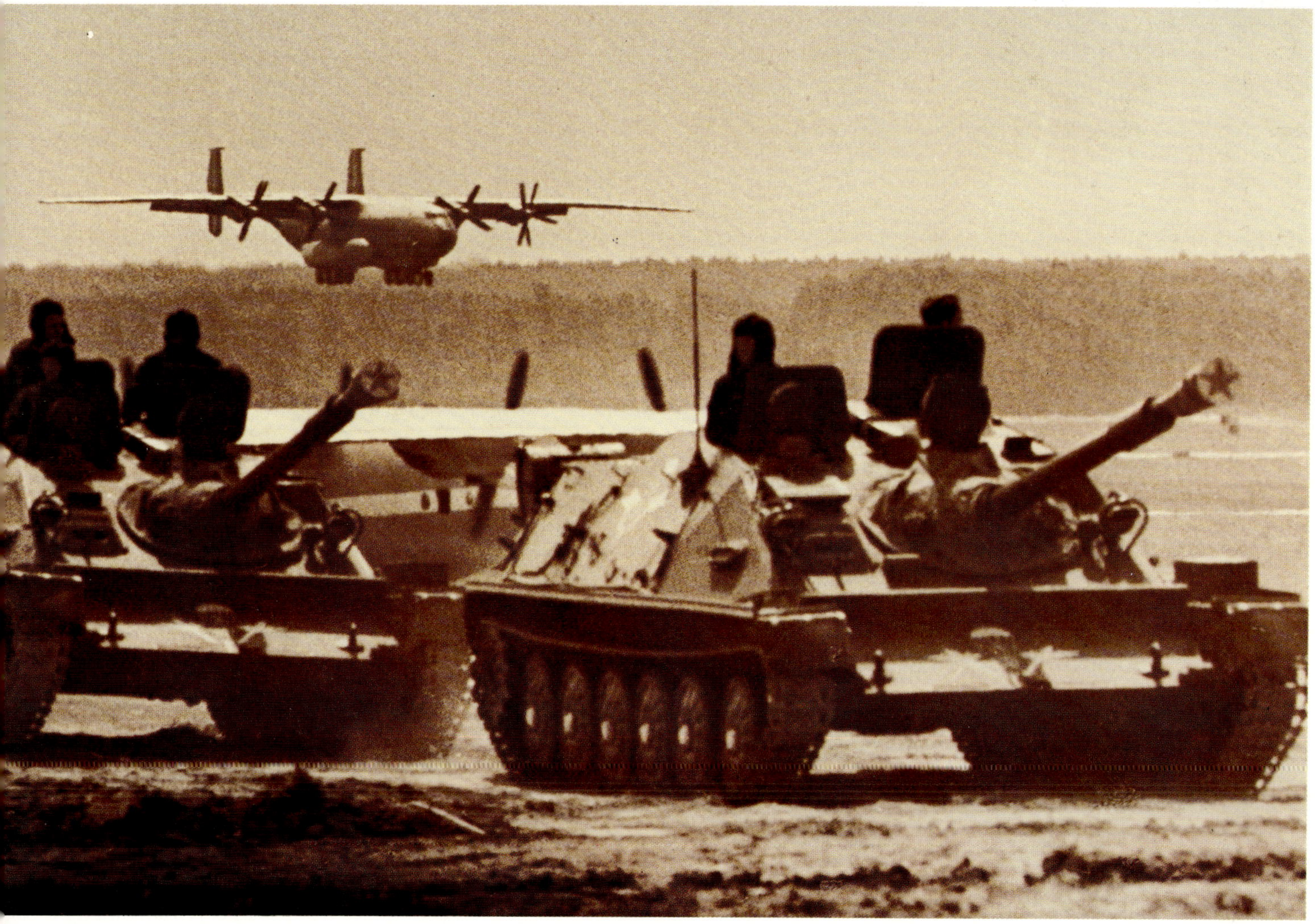

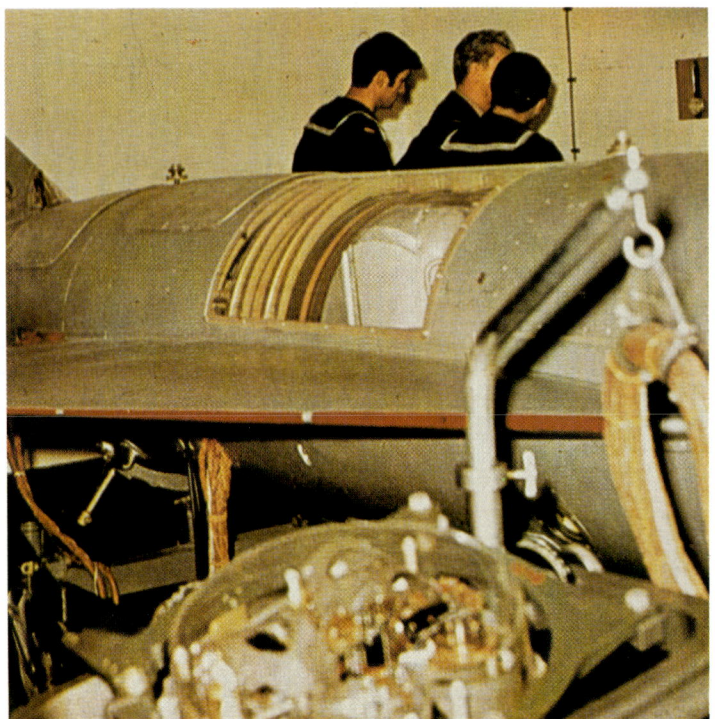

Left: A wintry scene at an IA-PVO base showing servicing of an Su-9 interceptor. Now relegated to operational training, this has less power and older missiles than the Su-11, which in turn has now been largely replaced by the twin-engined Su-15. The Su-9 is larger than a MiG-21.

Below: A fascinating photograph taken inside a classroom of the Soviet naval air arm (AV-MF) occupied by an early subsonic ASM. The weapon is probably an AS-2 "Kipper", and an inspection plate has been removed to reveal part of the fuel tankage. In the foreground is what appears to be a shock-mounted twin-gyro guidance platform.

China in the Far East, and the new "Backfire" started to join the European units first. The long-range Tu-95s are concentrated in the Northern and Siberian Divisions, the latter now receiving "Backfires", and all units include M-4 "Bison" tankers.

VTA is so closely associated with Aeroflot, presumably using the same training and support facilities, that it is virtually impossible to separate VTA deployment from Aeroflot's vast network.

Deployment of IA-PVO Forces

The manned interceptors of the IA-PVO are deployed in two types of organisation. First there are two PVO Districts, Baku and Moscow, which between them protect the central industrial regions of the Soviet Union. About half the IA-PVO interceptors, predominantly the more modern types, are assigned to the PVO districts, the division being the largest unit. The other half of the PVO divisions are attached to the other Soviet Union Military Districts, and some are reported to be under the command of the Groups of Soviet Forces in Germany, Czechoslovakia and Hungary.

The PVO divisions attached to the Military Districts mainly operate the Su-15 and older, less capable types of aircraft. Exceptions are the Tupolev Tu-28P long-range fighters based in Northern and Eastern Siberia to counter over-the-pole strikes by USAF B-52s, and the MiG-25s and Su-15s now being deployed in the Far East against a growing Chinese bomber threat.

ZA-PVO missiles are deployed in belts around the main industrial areas of the Soviet Union, as well as in target-defence installations protecting major cities such as Moscow and Sverdlovsk. So far only Moscow is defended by an ABM system.

AV-MF deployment follows the organisation of the surface fleet, in four main groups: the Baltic fleet head-quartered at Kaliningrad; the Northern fleet based around Murmansk; the Black Sea fleet at Sevastopol and the Pacific fleet at Vladivostok.

The Baltic AV-MF units operate mainly the shorter-range types, including probably the greater part of the Tu-22s, Be-12 amphibians and Su-17 strike fighters. The Mi-4P anti-submarine helicopters are being replaced by the new Mi-14 "Haze".

Atlantic surveillance and strike is the responsibility of the Northern AV-MF units, ranging all the way down to the Azores after flying around the North Cape of Norway. Some of the AV-MF "Backfires", Tu-95s and Tu-16 missile

16th Air Army deployment

Division	Regiments	Type	Base	No	Notes
Light bomb /Recce	3	Yak-28	Grossenhain Furstenwalde Juterbog	100	Being replaced by Su-19 "Fencer"
Trans*	3	An-26 An-14 An-2	Furstenwalde Oranienburg Spremberg	100	*Regiments attached to Air Army; no divisional command
Fighter	3	MiG-23MS MiG-21	Putznitz Gross-Dolln Wittstock	120	Northern group
Fighter/GA	3	MiG-27 Su-7 Su-17	Neuruppin Rechlin Parchim	120	Northern group
Armed helo	up to 3	Mi-24	Stendal Parchim ?	100+	Northern group Building up early 1977
Fighter	3	MiG-23MS MiG-21	Juterbog Kothen Zerbst	120	Southern group
Fighter	3	MiG-23MS MiG-21	Merseburg Altenburg Alt-Lonnewitz	120	Southern group
Fighter/GA	3	MiG-27 Su-7 Su-17	Brusin Finow Werneuchen	120	Southern group
Recce/ECM*	3	MiG-21R Yak-28 some An-12	Altenburg Stendal Welzow	120	*Regiments attached to Air Army; no divisional command

Disposition of 200+ Mi-8 transport helicopters not known

carriers are based in the Northern region, together with An-12 "Cub C" Elint aircraft and Ilyushin Il-38s. Tu-16 tankers provide support.

Support for the Soviet fleet in the Mediterranean and the Indian Ocean is provided by AV-MF aircraft attached to the Black Sea fleet: it is reported that Tu-95s have over-flown Iran on their way down to the Indian Ocean, and Mozambique is reported to be allowing the construction of an AV-MF base on the island of Bazaroto. Il-38s and "Cub Cs" have been reported in the Indian Ocean as well as in the Mediterranean, and have operated in Egyptian markings from Egyptian bases. Be-12s mainly confine their activities to the Black Sea region itself, but Tu-16s range over the entire Mediterranean in the reconnaissance role. Lastly, the Pacific fleet uses the Tu-95 predominantly, because of its great range and endurance.

Above: This Lightning F.6 may have been long in the tooth, but the Tu-95 (Tu-20) "Bear D" is undoubtedly older. Like most Soviet aircraft, these giant turboprop aircraft have been rebuilt and re-equipped for new roles.

All the Soviet fleets presumably possess land bases to support the helicopters (and now fixed-wing VTOL aircraft) deployed aboard surface ships (see table).

The Soviet air forces have had no direct combat experience since the 1941–45 war, although the Soviet Union was closely involved in the Vietnam war. Where Soviet material has seen action, as in Vietnam and the Middle East, the capture of Soviet pilots or rocket crews would have been highly embarrassing and they have not directly engaged in hostilities. However, MiG-25Rs based at Cairo West made some overflights of Israeli-held territory in late 1971.

Training in the Soviet aerospace forces is extremely basic and very formal, giving little encouragement to the development of individual initiative. The VVS and PVO operate separate basic training systems; only the PVO has an advanced school, at Armavir. The Soviet air forces rely on regiment training; pilots stay with their regiments much longer than is usual in Western forces, and each regiment has a group of two-seater aircraft with training as their primary role. Even the Tu-22 exists in a conversion-trainer version, assigned to DA regiments.

Engineering support for the Soviet air forces is presumably the responsibility of the Ministry of Aircraft Production plants which manufacture all combat aircraft. Soviet aircraft are designed on the assumption that a defective item can always be removed, replaced from stock and returned to the factory for overhaul, this philosophy extending to engines as well as to avionics. The main function of the organic light transport groups within Frontal Aviation is probably spares supply and the ferrying of components for overhaul.

AV-MF shipboard power				
Class (number+ in build)	Aircraft	No	SAMs	Notes
Kiev (1+2)	"Forger"	12	SA-N-3	SS-N-12 cruise missiles may have strategic role. New V/STOL aircraft, Mi-14 "Haze" and new light helicopter may be embarked on later ships
	Ka-25	20	SA-N-4	
Moskva (2)	Ka-25	18	SA-N-3	Moskva has ferried Mi-8 minesweepers. Used for "Forger" sea trials
Sverdlov (1)			SA-N-2	One conversion only
Sverdlov (2)	Ka-25	2	SA-N-4	Two command ships
Kara (4+1)	Ka-25	2	SA-N-3	Most modern Soviet cruiser class
			SA-N-4	
Kresta I (4)	Ka-25	2	SA-N-1	"Hormone B" for missile guidance
Kresta II (9+)	Ka-25	2	SA-N-3	"Hormone A"
Krivak (11)			SA-N-4	
Kynda (4)			SA-N-1	
Kashin (19)	Ka-25	2	SA-N-4?	In process of modernisation
Kanin (7)	Ka-25	2	SA-N-1	
Kotlin SAM (8)			SA-N-1	
Grisha (21+)			SA-N-4	Corvette
Nanuchka (16+)			SA-N-4	Corvette
Ugra (9)	Ka-25K	2		Submarine support
Don Helo (2)	Ka-25K	2		

Western observers, often almost unconsciously, tend to under-rate the technical capability of the Soviet Union. This in turn warps judgement. It is when one evaluates Soviet hardware, and especially military hardware, against the likely operating environment that one comes up with a different set of answers. Every item in the entire war inventory of the Warsaw Pact countries is designed exactly to meet a need, and to fulfil its function in an environment that is usually harsh, mobile and likely to be characterized by improvisation and intense action round the clock. How many Western air forces would be perfectly happy on a snowy night if you took away their air bases? Many Western aircraft are supposed to be able to operate from unpaved surfaces, but how many actually do it? Apart from the unique Harrier, to which an airfield is a luxury, most Western (NATO) tactical air power is based on 10,000-foot concrete runways. A Jaguar has, it is true, landed on a British motorway and

PART THREE

Technical Directory

taken off again, and on grass at a Ministry test base, but how many Jaguar squadrons have operated for weeks at a time far from the nearest airfield? Hitler's Luftwaffe operated for years moving from field to field, and so do the Warsaw Pact tactical regiments with their supersonic jets. This is the biggest single plus they can chalk up over the supposedly superior NATO squadrons.

The second factor where WP tactical air power is second to none is in the vital and central matter of electronics. Communications, IFF, all-weather navigation and landing aids, all-weather weapon delivery and all forms of countermeasures are built into the latest Soviet warplanes in a most impressive way. Truly, the West has to run to stay in the same place.

Aero L-29

L-29 Delfin ("Maya")

Origin: Aero Vodochody national corporation, Czechoslovakia.
Type: Basic trainer.
Engine: One 1,960lb (890kg) thrust M-701 single-shaft turbojet.
Dimensions: Span 33ft 9in (10·29m); length 35ft 5½in (10·81m); height 10ft 3in (3·13m).
Weights: Empty 5,027lb (2280kg); maximum loaded 7,804lb (3540kg).
Performance: Maximum speed at 16,400ft (5000m) 407mph (655km/h); initial climb 2,755ft (840m)/min; service ceiling 36,090ft (11,000m); maximum range on internal fuel 397 miles (640km).
Armament: Two wing hardpoints on which can be attached two 7·62mm guns, small tanks, or various other loads including bombs of up to 220lb (100kg).
History: First flight 5 April 1959; service delivery 1963; final delivery 1974.
Users: Bulgaria, Czechoslovakia, Egypt, E Germany, Guinea, Hungary, Indonesia, Iraq, Nigeria, Romania, Soviet Union, Syria, Uganda.

Development: Designed by a team led by K. Tomas and the late Z. Rublic, the L-29 was Czecholsovakia's submission in 1960 as the standard Warsaw

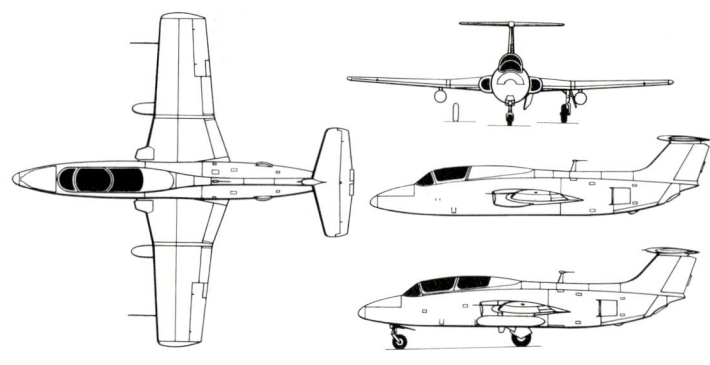

Above: Three-view of L-29 (plus side view of L-29A Akrobat single-seat version for aerobatic demonstration).

Pact trainer. It won, and though disgruntled Poland went ahead with the TS-11 Iskra, other Communist countries and several other air forces adopted this trainer and more than 3,000 were delivered. Two variants, not built in quantity, were the L-29A single-seat aerobatic version and the L-29R for counter-insurgency operations with nose cameras and underwing stores.

Above: The build-standard (the precise schedule of equipment and other customer-choice items) varies slightly between different Warsaw Pact air forces. This L-29, serving with the Soviet VVS Military Schools organization, has no ejection-seat warning (red triangle) for the rear cockpit. Most L-29 trainers are wired and stressed for underwing loads, but seldom carry them.

Above: The L-29 is entirely of stressed-skin construction, has two light-alloy fuel tanks in the fuselage, and mainly hydraulic systems. The Motorlet M-701c engine is all-Czech.

Below: A test flight with an L-29 Delfin development aircraft, probably the second prototype in 1960.

Aero L-39 Albatros

L-39, L-39Z

Origin: Aero Vodochody national corporation, Czechoslovakia.
Type: Basic and advanced trainer.
Engine: One 3,792lb (1720kg) thrust Walter Titan two-shaft turbofan (licence-built Ivchenko AI-25-TL).
Dimensions: Span 31ft 0½in (9·46m); length 40ft 5in (12·32m); height 15ft 5½in (4·72m).
Weights: Empty 7,341lb (3330kg); maximum loaded 10,141lb (4600kg).
Performance: Maximum speed at 16,400ft (5000m) 466mph (750km/h); Mach limit in dive 0·80; cruising speed at 5000m, up to 423mph (700km/h); initial climb 4,330ft (1320m)/min; service ceiling 37,075ft (11,300m); max range at 5000m on internal fuel 565 miles (910km).
Armament: Provision for light external load of tanks, bombs, rockets or 7·62mm gun pods (weight unstated) on two hardpoints under wings; internal fittings confined to gun-camera and sight.
History: First flight 4 November 1968; service delivery late 1973.
Users: Czechoslovakia, Iraq, Soviet Union (other Warsaw Pact countries in due course).

Development: Designed by a team led by Jan Vlcek, the L-39 is succeeding well in its task of replacing the L-29, and in 1972 it was accepted in principle as the future trainer of all Warsaw Pact countries except Poland. It forms part of an integrated pilot-training system which includes a flight simulator, ejection-seat trainer and mobile automatic test equipment. The L-39Z was under development in 1973 as a light attack version which, like all L 39s, can be operated from unpaved surfaces. Iraq is believed to have ordered both models.

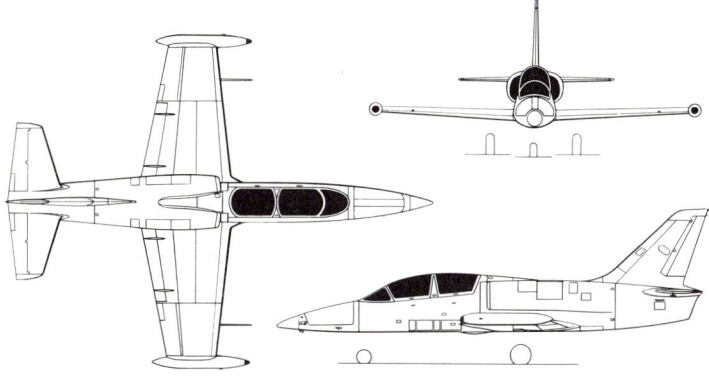

Above: Three-view of L-39 Albatros.

Above: From this angle the Albatros looks strangely hump-backed, partly because of the broad inlet ducts. These ducts feed air to a highly developed small turbofan of Soviet origin which is also used in the Yak-40 STOL transport and the Polish M-15 agricultural biplane. The ejection seats can be used at ground level, but not at speeds below 94mph (150km/h).

Below: The shapely turbofan-powered Albatros marks a great advance over the mass-produced Delfin. It will be interesting to see how well it does in the world trainer market.

Antonov (WSK) An-2

An-2 (many variants) and WSK-Mielec An-2; ("Colt")

Origin: The bureau of Oleg K. Antonov, Soviet Union; today made only by WSK-Mielec, Poland, and State Industry of China.
Type: STOL transport.
Engine: One 1,000hp Shvetsov ASh-62IR nine-cylinder radial; (since 1960) one 1,000hp WSK-Kalisz ASz-62IR.
Dimensions: Span 59ft 8½in (18·18m) (lower wing 46ft 8½in, 14·24m); length 41ft 9½in (12·74m); height 13ft 1½in (4·00m).
Weights: (2P): Empty 7,605lb (3450kg); maximum loaded 12,125lb (5500kg).
Performance: Maximum speed (P, 11,574lb, 5250kg) 160mph (258 km/h); typical cruise 115mph (185km/h), min safe speed 56mph (90km/h); service ceiling 14,425ft (4400m); typical takeoff or landing over 35ft (10·7m) on grass 1,050ft (320m); range with 1,102lb (500kg) payload 560 miles (900km).
History: First flight 31 August 1947; service delivery (An-2) July 1948, (Fong Chou) December 1957, (WSK) 1960.
Users: 44 countries including the following air forces or other military operators: Afghanistan, Algeria, Bulgaria, China, Cuba, Egypt, Ethiopia, E Germany, Hungary, Iraq, N Korea, Mali, Mongolia, Poland, Romania, Somalia, Soviet Union, Sudan, Syria, Tanzania, Tunisia, Vietnam.

Development: When this bulky biplane appeared in 1947 it appeared to be an obsolete mistake. So unmistaken was it that it has been manufactured in larger quantities than any other single type of aircraft since World War II: Soviet production had topped 5,000 when responsibility was passed to Poland in 1960, and a few hundred additional aircraft with angular tails were made in the Soviet Union in 1964–70; Polish output was continuing in 1977 with the nation's total well over 7,500, and the Chinese Fong Chou output is thought to exceed 5,000, making a combined figure of something over 18,000. Of these perhaps one-quarter are military, and many serve in para-military roles. Versions are numerous, and have different designations in the Soviet Union and Poland, but the chief military roles are paratroop and aircrew training, supply of frontier posts and general transport/casevac duties.

Below: Probably built in the Soviet Union, this is another TD model in service with the VVS. Many hundreds of similar aircraft are used by the DOSAAF para-military training organization.

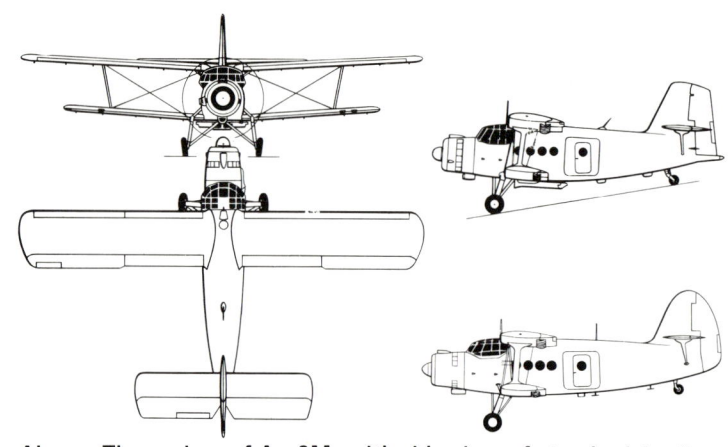

Above: Three-view of An-2M, with side view of standard An-2.

Above: Despite its antiquated appearance the An-2 remains ideal for many duties. This is an An-2TD paratroop trainer of the *Polskie Wojska Lotnicze*, made in Poland by WSK-PZL-Mielec.

Antonov An-12

An-12 ("Cub")

Origin: Design bureau of Oleg K. Antonov, Kiev, Soviet Union.
Type: Paratroop, passenger and freight transport.
Engines: Four 4,000ehp Ivchenko AI-20K single-shaft turboprops.
Dimensions: Span 124ft 8in (38m); length 121ft 4½in (37m); height 32ft 3in (9·83m).
Weights: Empty 61,730lb (28,000kg); loaded 121,475lb (55,100kg).
Performance: Maximum speed 482mph (777km/h); maximum cruising speed 416mph (670km/h); maximum rate of climb 1,970ft (600m)/min; service ceiling 33,500ft (10,200m); range with full payload 2,236 miles (3600km).
Armament: Powered tail turret with two 23mm NR-23 cannon.
History: First flight (civil An-10) 1957; (An-12) believed 1958.
Users: Algeria, Bangladesh, Egypt, India, Indonesia, Iraq, Jugoslavia, Poland, Soviet Union, Sudan.

Development: In 1958 Antonov flew a large twin-turboprop which owed something to German designs of World War II and the C-130. From this evolved the An-10 airliner and the An-12, which since 1960 has been a standard transport with many air forces. Fully pressurised, the An-12 has an exceptionally high performance yet can operate from unpaved surfaces. At least one was fitted with large skis with shallow V planing surfaces equipped with heating (to prevent sticking to ice or snow) and brakes. Nearly all have the tail turret, and under the transparent nose is a weather and mapping radar, which in most Soviet Air Force An-12s has been changed to a more powerful and larger design. The rear ramp door is made in left and right halves which can be folded upwards inside the fuselage, either for loading heavy freight with the aid of a built-in gantry or for the dispatch of 100

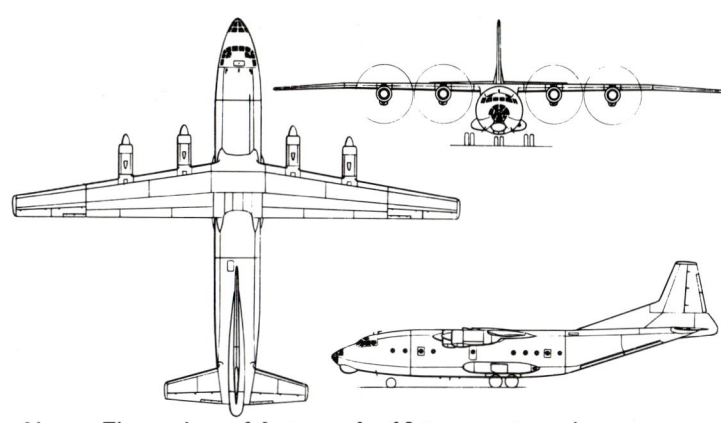

Above: Three-view of Antonov An-12 transport version.

paratroops in less than one minute. Typical freight load is 44,090lb (20,000kg), and the An-12 can carry all Soviet APCs, the ASU-85 SP-gun and such anti-aircraft vehicles as the ZSU-23-4 and SA-6 missile carrier. In manoeuvres of Warsaw Pact forces as many as 30 of these capable aircraft have landed at one airstrip in simulated battle conditions.

continued on page 108▶

Below: A typical An-12 as used in large numbers by the Soviet VVS and many other air forces. Many An-12s are now serving as Elint (electronic intelligence) platforms ("Cub Cs").

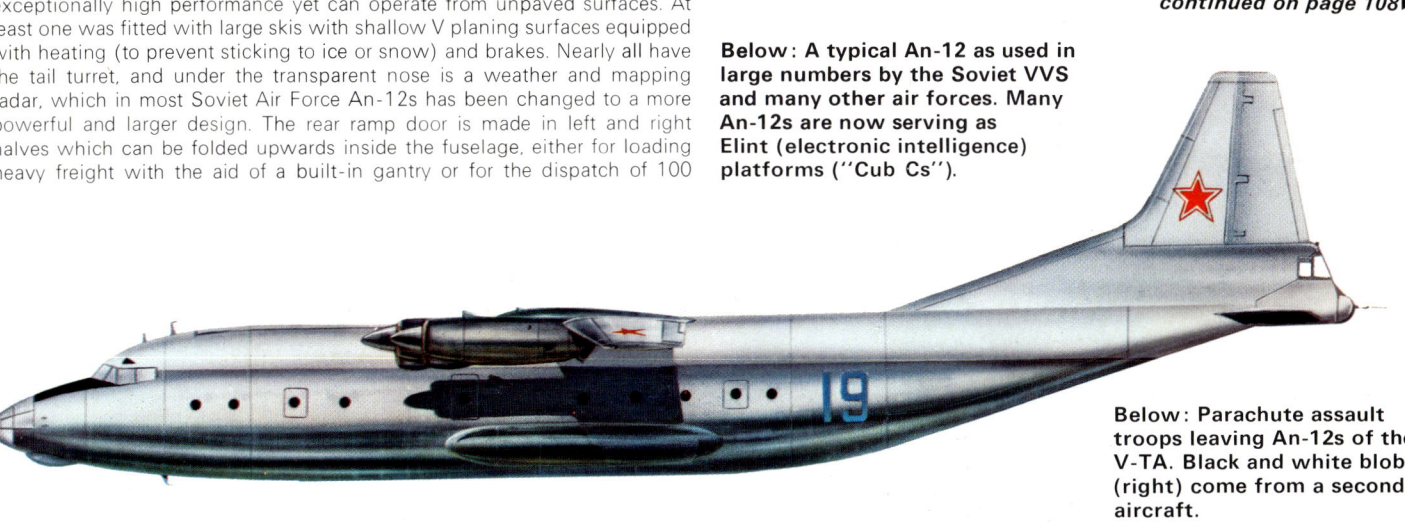

Below: Parachute assault troops leaving An-12s of the V-TA. Black and white blobs (right) come from a second aircraft.

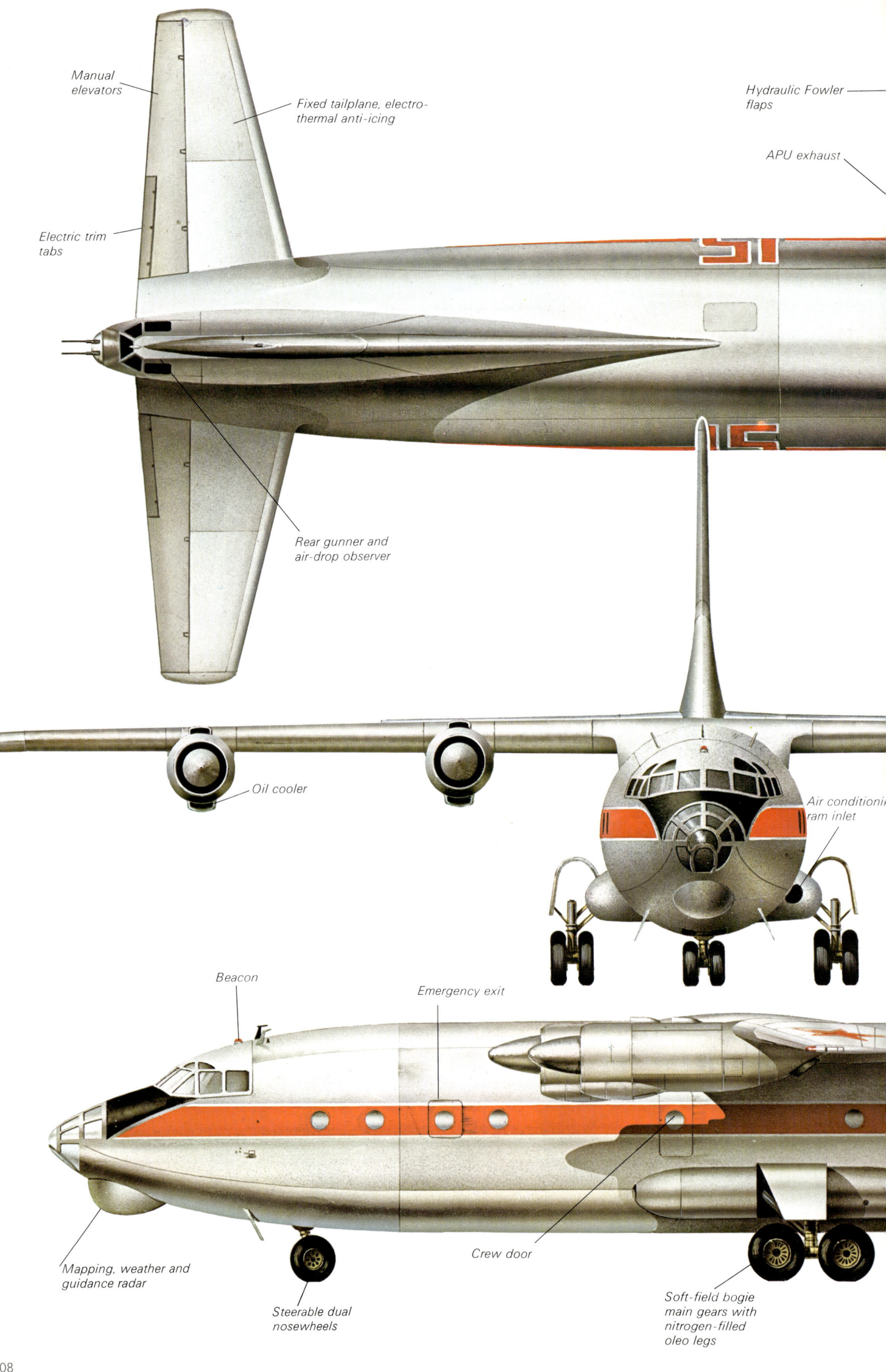

Manual
elevators

Fixed tailplane, electro-
thermal anti-icing

Hydraulic Fowler
flaps

APU exhaust

Electric trim
tabs

Rear gunner and
air-drop observer

Oil cooler

Air conditioning
ram inlet

Beacon

Emergency exit

Crew door

Mapping, weather and
guidance radar

Steerable dual
nosewheels

Soft-field bogie
main gears with
nitrogen-filled
oleo legs

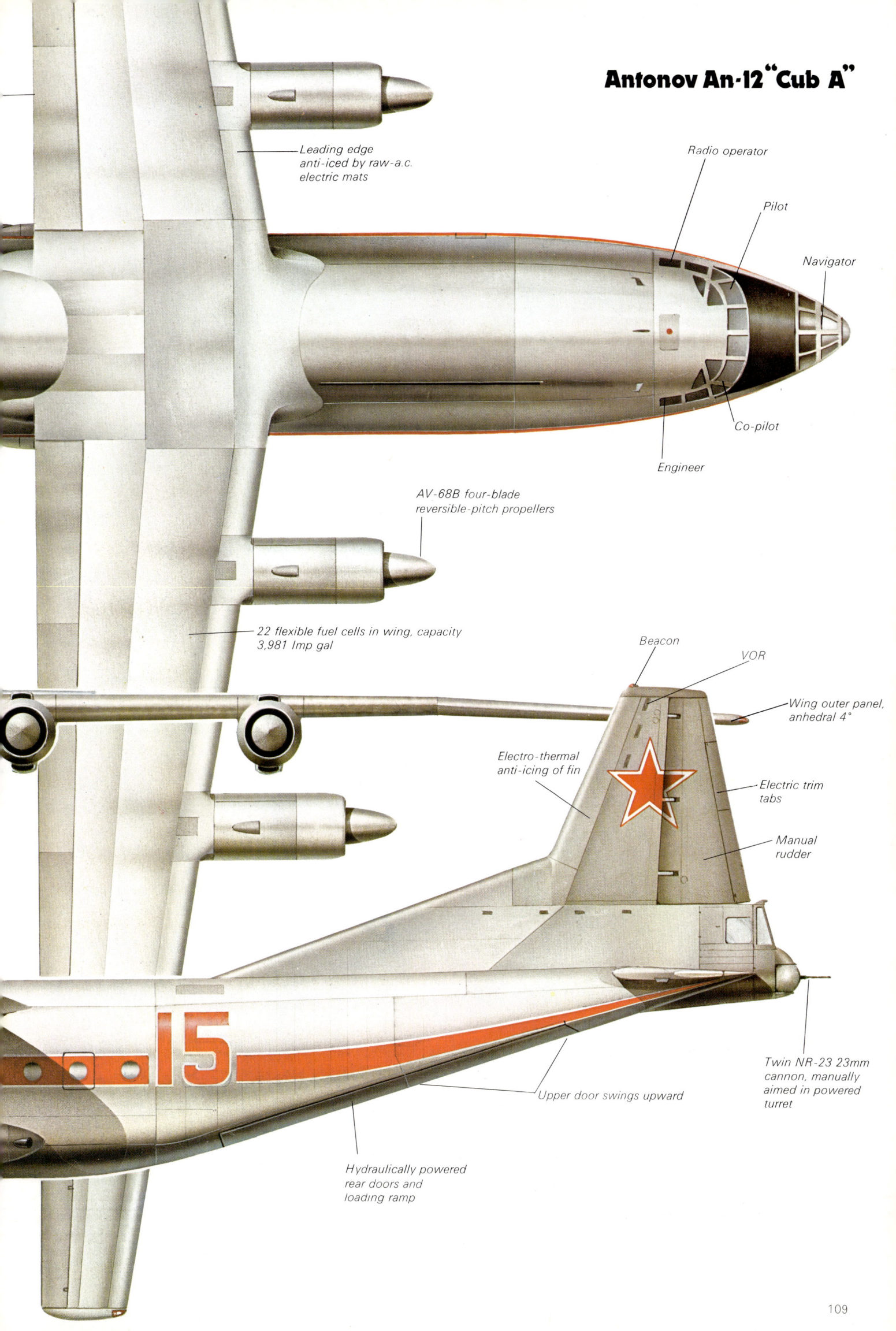

Antonov An-12 "Cub A"

Leading edge anti-iced by raw-a.c. electric mats

Radio operator

Pilot

Navigator

Co-pilot

Engineer

AV-68B four-blade reversible-pitch propellers

22 flexible fuel cells in wing, capacity 3,981 Imp gal

Beacon

VOR

Wing outer panel, anhedral 4°

Electro-thermal anti-icing of fin

Electric trim tabs

Manual rudder

Twin NR-23 23mm cannon, manually aimed in powered turret

Upper door swings upward

Hydraulically powered rear doors and loading ramp

Antonov An-22

An-22 Antei (Antheus) ("Cock")

Origin: The design bureau of Oleg K. Antonov, Soviet Union.
Type: Heavy logistic transport.
Engines: Four 15,000shp Kuznetsov NK-12MA single-shaft turboprops.
Dimensions: Span 211ft 4in (64·40m); length overall (prototype) 189ft 7in (57·80m); height overall 41ft 1½in (12·53m).
Weights: Empty, equipped 251,325lb (114,000kg); maximum loaded 551,160lb (250,000kg).
Performance: Maximum cruise 422mph (679km/h); range with max payload of 176,350lb (80,000kg) 3,100 miles (5000km), range with max fuel and payload of 99,200lb (45,000kg) 6,800 miles (10,950km).
History: First flight 27 February 1965; final delivery, believed 1974.
User: Soviet Union.

Development: Largest aircraft in the world apart from the 747 and C-5A, the An-22 is the result of a surprisingly late decision to mate the great NK-12M engine/propeller combination with a capacious freight fuselage. As early as July 1967 three Soviet air force Anteis took part in an air display in the assault role, and since then an unknown number have operated with both the civil operator, Aeroflot, and the air force. Anteis carried almost all the war material supplied to the MPLA in Angola, and have made many other long overseas flights besides setting various world records for payload/height and speed/payload, the speeds all being in the region of 370mph (596km/h). The nose does not open but houses two large radars, for navigation, mapping, weather and airdropping, as well as several other avionic aids. There are seats for about 29 passengers aft of the flight deck, while at the lower level is a hold 14ft 5in (4·40m) square in section, with beaver-tail rear doors.

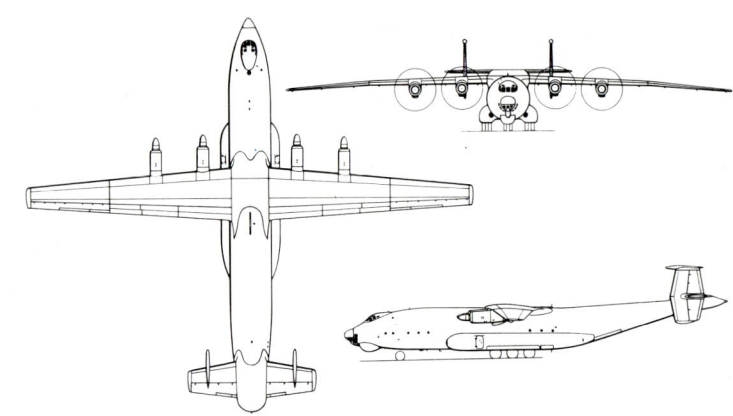

Above: Three-view of An-22 (note wing anhedral).

Above: Antei with civil registration SSSR-67691, landing.

Below: An-22 in service with V-TA of Soviet Air Force. Few military Anteis have been seen; those that carried weapons to the MPLA in Angola belonged to Aeroflot.

Below: Close-up of Antei nose showing the two large radomes.

Antonov An-26

An-24V, 24RV, 24T, 26 and 30, 24 ("Coke"), 26 ("Curl"), 30 ("Clank")

Origin: The design bureau of Oleg K. Antonov, Soviet Union.

Type: (24V and RV) passenger and troop transport, (24T and 26) freight transport, (30) aerial survey and mapping.

Engines: (24V and T) two Ivchenko AI-24A single-shaft turboprops, shaft power not disclosed but 2,550ehp; (24RV) same, plus one 1,985lb (900kg) thrust RU-19-300 auxiliary turbojet in right nacelle; (26 and 30) two AI-24T each rated at 2,820ehp plus (26) one RU-19-300, or (30) one 1,765lb thrust (800kg) RU-19A-300.

Dimensions: Span 95ft 9½in (29·20m); length overall (24) 77ft 2½in (23·53m), (26) 78ft 1in (23·80m), (30) 79ft 7in (24·26m); height (24, 30) 27ft 3½in (8·32m), (26) 28ft 1½in (8·575m).

Weights: Empty (24V) 29,320lb (13,300kg), (26) 33,113lb (15,020kg); maximum loaded (24V, T) 46,300lb (21,000kg), (24RV) 48,060lb (21,800 kg), (26) 52,911lb (24,000kg), (30) 50,706lb (23,000kg).

Performance: Typical cruising speed 267mph (430km/h); range with max payload of 12,125lb (5500kg), no reserves, (24V) 341 miles (550km), (24T) 397 miles (640km), (26) about 400 miles (645km).

History: First flight (24) April 1960, (26) late 1960s.

Users: (Mainly 24) Bangladesh, Congo, Czechoslovakia, Egypt, E Germany, Hungary, Iraq, Jugoslavia, Laos, Mongolia, Poland, Romania, Somalia, Soviet Union, Sudan, Vietnam, S. Yemen.

Development: One of the world's most numerous turboprop transports, the An-24 is primarily civil but small numbers of several versions have been

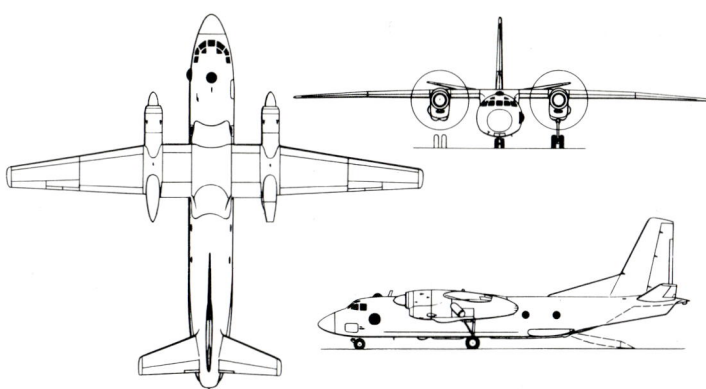

Above: Three-view of An-26; note engine nacelles in plan view.

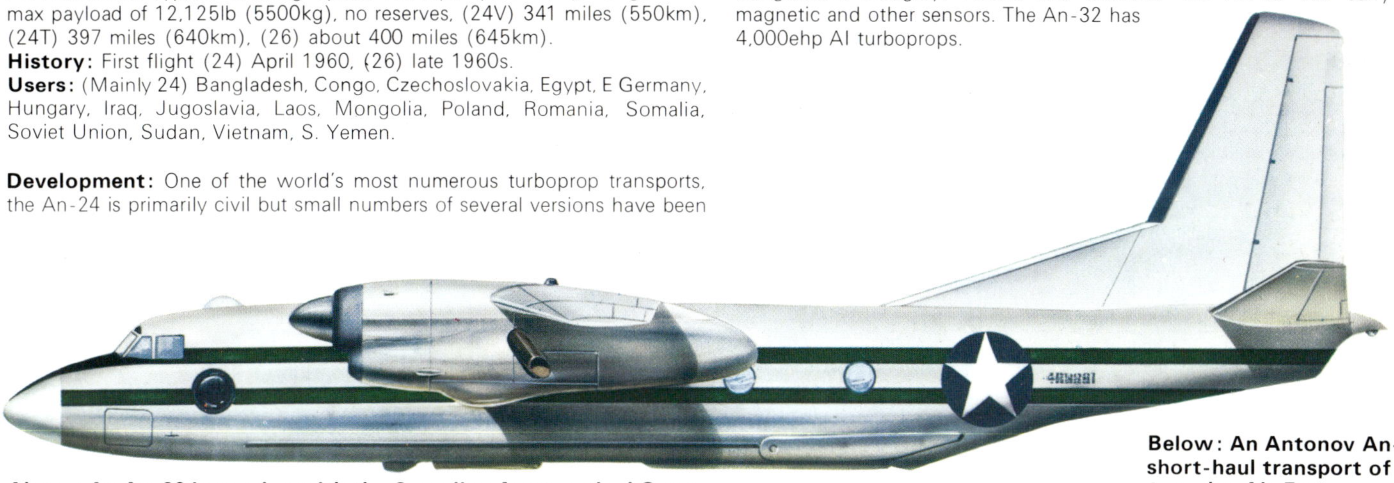

supplied to the air forces listed above. The more powerful An-26 has a beaver-tail rear door for loading or airdropping bulky loads; it serves with Bangladesh, Hungary, Poland and Somalia. The An-30 can carry IR, magnetic and other sensors. The An-32 has 4,000ehp AI turboprops.

Above: An An-26 in service with the Somalian Aeronautical Corps.

Below: An Antonov An-26 short-haul transport of the Jugoslav Air Force.

Beriev M-12

Be-12 Tchaika ("Mail")

Origin: Design bureau of Georgi Mikhailovich Beriev, Taganrog, Soviet Union.
Type: Ocean reconnaissance and utility amphibian.
Engines: Two 4,190ehp Ivchenko AI-20D single-shaft turboprops.
Dimensions: Span 97ft 6in (29·7m); length overall 99ft (30·2m); height on land 22ft 11½in (7m).
Weights: Empty approximately 48,000lb (21,772kg); maximum approximately 66,140lb (30,000kg).
Performance: Maximum speed about 380mph (612km/h); cruising speed 199mph (320km/h); service ceiling 38,000ft (11,582m); range with full equipment 2,485 miles (4000km).
Armament: At least 6,600lb (3000kg) sonobuoys and AS bombs in internal weapon bay; one to three external hard points for stores under each outer wing.
History: First flight 1960 or earlier; combat service probably about 1962; set many world records in 1964, 1968, 1972 and 1973.
User: Soviet Union (possibly also Egypt and/or Syria).

Development: The bureau of Georgi M. Beriev, at Taganrog on the Azov Sea, is the centre for Soviet marine aircraft. The Be-6, powered by two 2,300hp ASh-73TK radial engines and in the class of the Martin PBM or P5M, served as the standard long-range ocean patrol flying boat from 1949 until about 1967. In 1961 Beriev flew a remarkable large flying boat, the Be-10, powered by two Lyulka AL-7PB turbojets, but though this set world records it never entered major operational service. Instead a more pedestrian turboprop aircraft, first seen at the 1961 Moscow Aviation Day at the same time as the swept-wing Be-10, has fast become the Soviet Union's standard large marine aircraft. The Be-12 Tchaika (Seagull) is an amphibian, with retractable tailwheel-type landing gear. Its twin fins are typical of older aircraft, and the gull wing, which puts the engines high above the spray, gives an air of gracefulness. The Be-12 is extremely versatile. The search and mapping radar projects far ahead of the glazed nose, and a MAD (magnetic anomaly detector) extends 15ft behind the tail. Much of the hull is filled with equipment and there is a weapon and sonobuoy bay aft of the wing with watertight doors in the bottom aft of the step. Be-12s, known as M-12s in service with the Soviet naval air fleets, have set many class records for speed, height and load-carrying. They are based all around the Soviet shores, mainly with the Northern and Black Sea fleets.

Above: An M-12 Tchaika takes off from an AV-MF base (note the Tu-22 "Blinder C" in the distance).

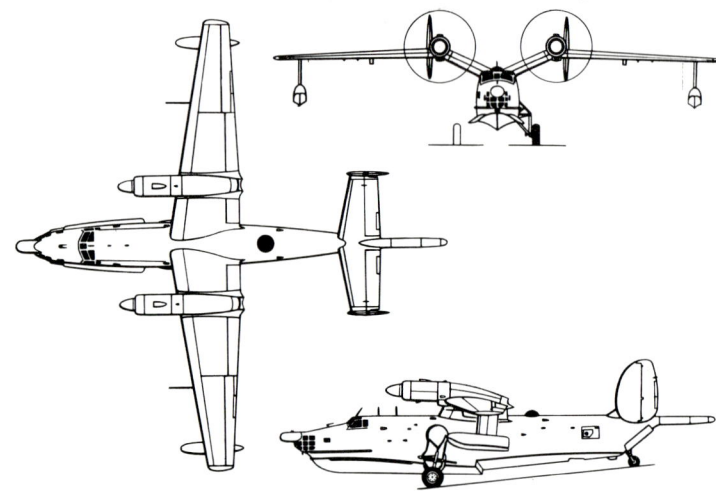

Above: Three-view of M-12 with landing gear extended.

Below: The Soviet Union has always built precisely the aircraft it wanted. Like the An-2, the Be-12 has perfect fitness for purpose; again, like the An-2, it is getting long in the tooth.

Ilyushin Il-28

Il-28, 28R, 28T ("Beagle"), 28U ("Mascot")

Origin: Design bureau of Sergei V. Ilyushin, Soviet Union; also built in Czechoslovakia (as B-228) and China.
Type: Three-seat bomber and ground attack; (28R) reconnaissance; (28T) torpedo carrier; (28U) dual trainer.
Engines: (Pre-1950) two 5,005lb (2270kg) thrust Klimov RD-45F; (post-1950) two 5,952lb (2700kg) thrust Klimov VK-1 single-shaft centrifugal turbojets.
Dimensions: Span (without tip tanks) 70ft 4¾in (21·45m); length 57ft 10¾in (17·65m); height 22ft (6·7m).
Weights: Empty 28,417lb (12,890kg); maximum loaded 46,297lb (21,000kg).
Performance: Maximum speed 559mph (900km/h); initial climb 2,953ft (900m)/min; service ceiling 40,355ft (12,300m); range with bomb load 684 miles (1100km).
Armament: (Il-28, typical) two 23mm NR-23 cannon fixed in nose and two NR-23 in powered tail turret; internal bomb capacity of 2,205lb (1000kg), with option of carrying double this load or external load (such as two 400mm light torpedoes).
History: First flight (prototype) 8 August 1948; (production Il-28) early 1950; service-delivery 1950; final delivery (USSR) about 1960, (China) after 1968.
Users: Afghanistan, Algeria, Bulgaria, China, Cuba (not operational), Czechoslovakia (-28U), Egypt, Finland (target tugs), E Germany (U), Indonesia, Iraq, N Korea, Nigeria, Poland (U), Romania (U), Somalia, Soviet Union, S Yemen, Syria, Vietnam, Yemen Arab.

Development: After World War II the popular media in the West published a succession of indistinct photographs, drawings and other pictures purporting to show Soviet jet aircraft. Apart from the MiG-9 and Yak-15 (and, after 1951, MiG-15) all were fictitious and by chance none happened to bear much resemblance to aircraft that actually existed. Thus, whereas the 1950 *Jane's* published a drawing and "details" of an Ilyushin four-jet bomber, it knew nothing of the extremely important Il-28 programme then coming to the production stage. Roughly in the class of the Canberra, the Il-28 prototype flew on two RD-10 (Jumo 004 development) turbojets, but the much superior British Nene was quickly substituted and, in VK-1 form, remained standard in the 10,000 or more subsequent examples. Unusual features are the sharply swept tail surfaces, the single-wheel main gears retracting in bulges under the jetpipes, the fixed nose cannon and the rear turret manned by the radio operator. Known to NATO as "Beagle", it equipped all the Warsaw Pact light bomber units in 1955-70 and was also adopted by the AV-MF as the Il-28T torpedo bomber (that service having originally chosen the rival Tu-14T). The Il-28U dual trainer has distinctive stepped cockpits, and the 28R reconnaissance version (many probably converted bombers) carry a wide range of electronics and sensors. No longer a front-line type in the Soviet Union, the Il-28 remains in service with some 12 air forces outside Europe, the most important being that of China where some hundreds were built under a licence granted before 1960.

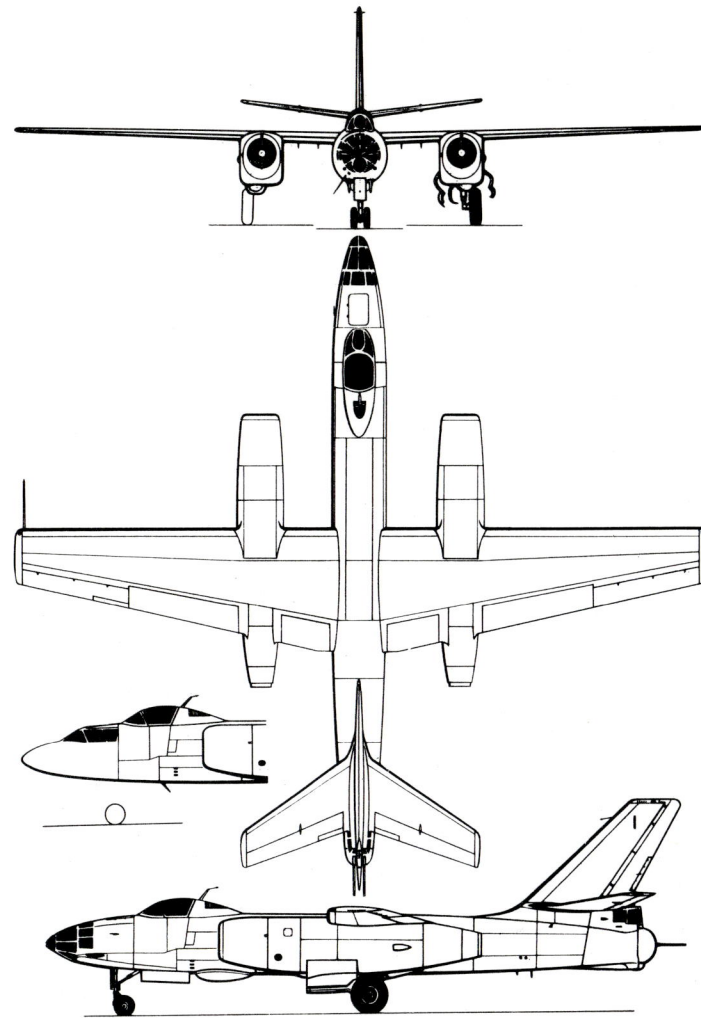

Above: Three-view of Il-28 with inset showing -28U. Many examples in second-line service with Warsaw Pact air forces now carry additional electronics aerials.

Below: The Il-28U conversion trainer is still standard equipment with the Air Force of the People's Liberation Army of China. The bomber version is used by the Navy.

Above: Il-28T of Navy of Chinese People's Republic.

Ilyushin Il-38

Il-38 ("May")

Origin: Bureau named for Ilyushin, Soviet Union.
Type: Maritime patrol and anti-submarine.
Engines: Four Ivchenko AI-20 single-shaft turboprops, probably rated at about 5,000shp each.
Dimensions: Span 122ft 8½in (37·4m); length 129ft 10in (39·6m); height about 35ft (10·7m).
Weights: Empty, approximately 90,000lb (40,820kg); maximum loaded, approximately 180,000lb (81,650kg).
Performance: Maximum speed, about 450mph (724km/h); maximum cruising speed, about 400mph (644km/h); range with typical mission load, about 4,500 miles (7240km); endurance, about 15hr.
Armament: Internal weapon bay ahead of and behind wing accommodating full range of anti-submarine torpedoes, bombs, mines and other stores; possibly external racks for stores such as guided missiles between weapon-bay doors under wing and beneath outer wings (but not yet seen).
History: First flight (Il-18 transport) July 1957; first disclosure of Il-38, 1974, by which time it was well established in operational service.
Users: Egypt (or Soviet detachments in Egypt) until 1976, India, Soviet Union (AV-MF).

Development: Following the example of the US Navy and Lockheed with the Electra/P-3 Orion transformation, the Soviet Naval Air Arm (AV-MF) used the Il-18 transport as the basis for the considerably changed Il-38, known to NATO by the code-name of "May". Compared with the transport it has a wing moved forward and a considerably longer rear fuselage, showing the gross shift in centre of gravity resulting from the changed role. Whereas in the transport the payload is distributed evenly ahead of and behind the wing, the rear fuselage of the Il-38 contains only sensors, sonobuoy launchers of several kinds and a galley, with the main tactical compartment just behind and above the wing, with a probable tactical crew of eight. Most of the heavy stores and consoles are ahead of the wing, together with the search radar. The only added item at the rear is the MAD

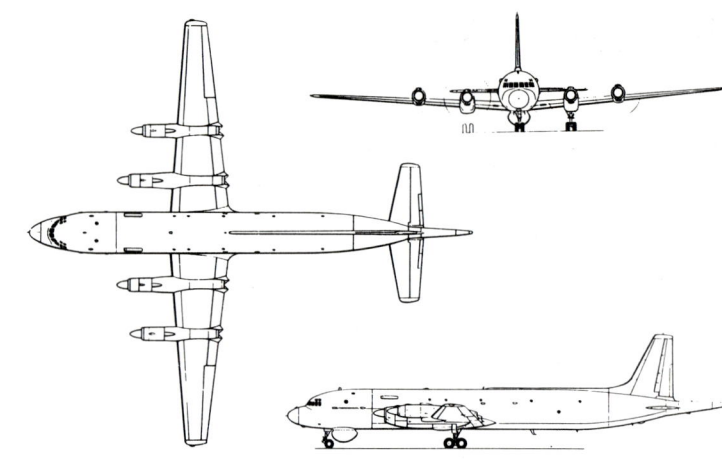

Above: Three-view of Il-38 (NATO name "May").

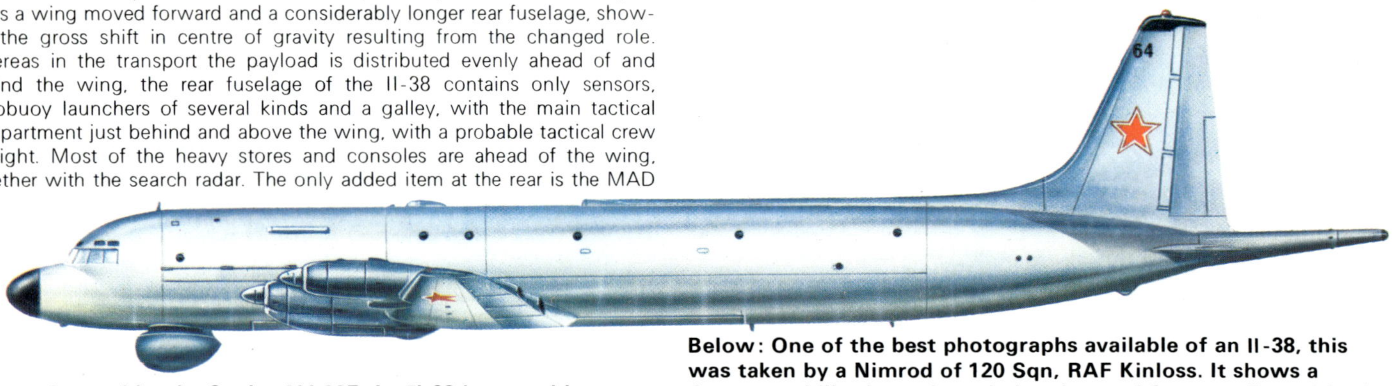

(magnetic anomaly detector) sting, not a heavy item. So far little is known of the Il-38 and photographs show few of the items one would expect to see. There is no weapon bay below the wing and pressurized fuselage, as in the Nimrod and P-3, no major sensor outlets and aerials and no apparent external stores pylons. On the other hand the Il-38 is potentially as good as a P-3, though probably not up to the sensor and computer standard of the P-3C.

Above: As used by the Soviet AV-MF the Il-38 is a notably clean aircraft.

Below: One of the best photographs available of an Il-38, this was taken by a Nimrod of 120 Sqn, RAF Kinloss. It shows a drogue-stabilized sonobuoy being dropped from medium altitude by an Il-38 taking part in Atlantic exercises.

Ilyushin Il-76

Il-76 ("Candid")

Origin: Bureau named for Ilyushin, Soviet Union.
Type: Heavy freight transport.
Engines: Four 26,455lb (12,000kg) thrust Soloviev D-30KP two-shaft turbofans.
Dimensions: Span 165ft 8in (50·5m); length 152ft 10½in (46·59m); height 48ft 5in (14·76m).
Weights: Empty, about 159,000lb (72,000kg); maximum loaded 346,125lb (157,000kg).
Performance: Maximum speed, about 560mph (900km/h); maximum cruising speed 528mph (850km/h); normal long-range cruising height 42,650ft (13,000m); range with maximum payload of 88,185lb (40,000kg) 3,100 miles (5000km).
Armament: Military version has rear turret (twin NR-23?).
History: First flight 25 March 1971; production deliveries 1973.
User: Soviet Union (V-TA).

Development: First seen in the West at the 1971 Paris Salon, the Il-76 created a most favourable impression. Though superficially seeming to be another Ilyushin copy of a Lockheed design, in this case the C-141, in fact the resemblance is coincidental. The design was prepared to meet a basic need in the Soviet Union for a really capable freighter which, while carrying large indivisible loads, with a high cruising speed and intercontinental range, could operate from relatively poor airstrips. The result is a very useful aircraft which, though initially being used by Aeroflot in the 1971-75 and 1976-80 plans for opening up Siberia, the far north and far east of the Soviet Union, is obviously a first-class strategic and tactical transport for military use. It has very powerful engines, all fitted with reversers, a high-lift wing for good STOL performance and a high-flotation landing gear with 20 wheels. The nose is typical of modern Soviet aircraft for "outback" operation, and closely resembles that of the An-22. The big fuselage, usefully larger in cross-section than that of the C-141, is fully pressurized and incorporates a powerful auxiliary power unit and freight handling systems. There seems no reason why the rear clamshell doors should not be opened in flight to permit heavy dropping. In 1977 deliveries appeared to have swung in favour of the military, and a special tanker version was reported to be under development to support the Tupolev "Backfire". NATO code-name of the Il-76 is "Candid".

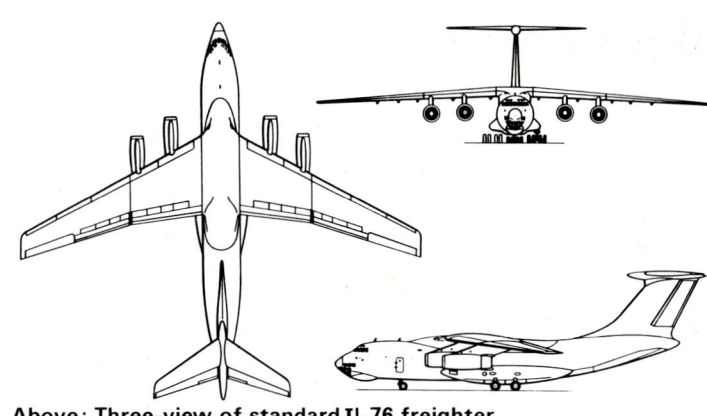

Above: Three-view of standard Il-76 freighter.

Above: This US Navy photograph shows several of the Il-76's good qualities, among them large body cross-section, STOL wing and "high flotation" multi-wheel landing gear. These are assets for military use.

Below: Civil Il-76 photographed at Moscow during proving flights to Tyumen natural-gas and oil fields in remote Siberia.

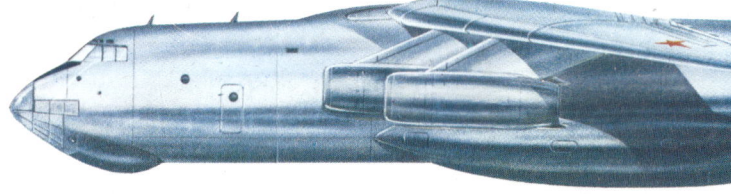

Above: Il-76 as used by V-TA and AV-MF; tanker may be similar.

115

Kamov Ka-25

Ka-25 ("Hormone")
(several versions, designations unknown)

Origin: Design bureau named for Nikolai I. Kamov, Soviet Union.
Type: Ship-based ASW, search/rescue and missile-guidance helicopter.
Engines: Two 900hp Glushenkov GTD-3 free-turbine turboshafts.
Dimensions: Main rotor diameter (both) 51ft 8in (15·75m); fuselage length, about 34ft (10·36m); height 17ft 8in (5·4m).
Weights: Empty, about 11,023lb (5000kg); maximum loaded 16,535lb (7500kg).
Performance: Maximum speed 120mph (193km/h); service ceiling, about 11,000ft (3350m); range, about 400 miles (650km).
Armament: One or two 400mm AS torpedoes, nuclear or conventional depth charges or other stores, carried in internal weapon bay.
History: First flight (Ka-20) probably 1960; service delivery of initial production version, probably 1965.
Users: India, Soviet Union (AV-MF), Syria.

Development: Nikolai Kamov, who died in 1973, was one of the leaders of rotorcraft design in the Soviet Union, a characteristic of nearly all his designs being the use of superimposed co-axial rotors to give greater lift in a vehicle of smaller overall size. Large numbers of Ka-15 and -18 piston-engined machines were used by Soviet armed forces, but in 1961 the Aviation Day fly-past at Tushino included a completely new machine designated Ka-20 and carrying a guided missile on each side. It was allotted the NATO code-name of "Harp". Clearly powered by gas turbines, it looked formidable. Later in the 1960s it became clear that from this helicopter Kamov's bureau, under chief engineer Barshevsky, had developed the standard ship-based machine of the Soviet fleets, replacing the Mi-4. Designated the Ka-25 and allotted the new Western code name of "Hormone", it is in service in at least five major versions, with numerous sub-types. Whereas the "missiles" displayed in 1961 have never been seen since, and are thought to have been dummies, the Ka-25 is extremely fully equipped with all-weather anti-submarine sensing and attack equipment. The four landing wheels are each surrounded by a buoyancy bag ring which can be swiftly inflated by the gas bottles just above it. Ka-25s are used aboard the carriers (ASW cruisers) *Minsk, Kiev, Moskva* and *Leningrad, Kresta* and *Kara* class cruisers and from shore bases.

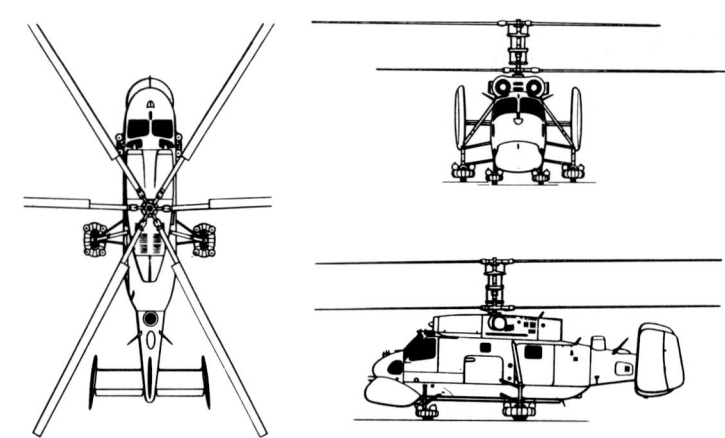

Above: Three-view of Ka-25 "Hormone A" with emergency flotation system.

Above and below: Two examples of the basic ASW version of the Ka-25, called "Hormone A" by NATO. Fitness for harsh service is demonstrated by the long production life of the Ka-25 and the profusion of re-equipped versions.

Mikoyan/Gurevich MiG-15 UTI

MiG-15 and -15bis ("Fagot"), MiG-15UTI ("Midget")

Origin: Design, the Mikoyan/Gurevich bureau, Soviet Union; licence production as described in text.

Type: (-15) single-seat fighter; (-15UTI) dual-control trainer.

Engine: (-15) one 5,005lb (2270kg) thrust RD-45F single-shaft centrifugal turbojet; (-15bis and most -15UTI) one 5,952lb (2700kg) VK-1 of same layout; (later -15bis) 6,990lb (3170kg) (wet rating) VK-1A.

Dimensions: Span 33ft 0¾in (10·08m); length (-15, -15bis) 36ft 3¼in (11·05m); (-15UTI) 32ft 11¼in (10·04m); height (-15, -15bis) 11ft 1¾in (3·4m); (-15UTI) 12ft 1½in (3·7m).

Weights: Empty (all) close to 8,820lb (4000kg); maximum loaded (-15) 12,566lb (5700kg), (11,270lb clean); (-15UTI) 11,905lb (5400kg), (10,692lb clean).

Performance: Maximum speed (-15) 668mph (1075km/h); (-15bis) 684mph (1100km/h); (-15UTI) 630mph (1015km/h); initial climb (-15, -15UTI) 10,500ft (3200m)/min; (-15bis) 11,480ft (3500m)/min; service ceiling (-15, -15bis) 51,000ft (15,545m); (-15UTI) 47,980ft (14,625m); range (at height, with slipper tanks) 885 miles (1424km).

Armament: (-15, as first issued) one 37mm N cannon under right side of nose and one 23mm NS under left side; (-15, -15bis and variants) one 37mm with 40 rounds under right and two 23mm each with 80 rounds under left, with two underwing hard-points for slipper tanks or stores of up to 1,102lb (500kg); (-15UTI) single 23mm with 80 rounds or 12·7mm UBK-E with 150 rounds under left side, plus same underwing options.

History: First flight 30 December 1947; (MiG-15UTI) 1948; service delivery August 1948; final delivery, probably 1953 (USSR) and about 1954 in Poland and Czechoslovakia.

Users: Afghanistan, Albania, Algeria, Angola, Bulgaria, China, Cuba, Czechoslovakia, Egypt, Finland, E Germany, Guinea, Hungary, Indonesia (in storage), Iraq, N Korea, Mali, Mongolia, Morocco (in storage), Nigeria, Poland (?), Romania, Somalia, Soviet Union, S Yemen, Sri Lanka, Syria, Tanzania, Uganda, Vietnam.

Development: No combat aircraft in history has had a bigger impact on the world scene than the MiG-15. Its existence was unsuspected in the West until American fighter pilots suddenly found themselves confronted by all-swept silver fighters which could fly faster, climb and dive faster and turn more tightly. Gradually the whole story, and the start of the world pre-eminence of the Mikoyan-Gurevich bureau, could be traced back to the decision of the British government to send to the Soviet Union the latest British turbojet, the Rolls-Royce Nene (long before the Nene was used in any British service aircraft). At one stroke this removed the very serious lack of a suitable engine for the advanced fighter the bureau were planning, and within eight months the prototype MiG-15 had flown and the Nene was frantically being put into production (without a licence) in slightly modified form as the RD-45. The original MiG-15 owed a lot to the Ta-183 and other German designs, but the production machine had a lower tailplane, anhedral, wing fences, and other changes. Notable features were the extensive use of high-quality welding and the quick-detach package housing the two (later three) heavy cannon. Production rapidly outstripped that of any other aircraft at that time, at least 8,000 being built in the Soviet Union in about five years, plus a further substantial number at Mielec, Poland, as the Lim-2, and at the newly established Vodochody works near Prague as the S-103 (S = stihac, fighter). The two satellite countries also made the UTI trainer under an extension of their original licences, finally producing several thousand trainers by rebuilding MiG-15 fighters phased out of front-line service after 1954. In 1958 the Chinese plant at Shenyang began licence-production of the MiG-15UTI as the F-2. Most MiG-15 fighters were of the more powerful 15bis type with perforated flaps and redesigned rear-fuselage airbrakes; small numbers were made of a night fighter version with simple AI radar and of a ground-attack version with large ordnance carriers inboard of the drop tanks (the latter being originally of the slipper type but after 1952 often being carried below the wing on braced pylons). Known to NATO as "Fagot" (the trainer being "Midget"), the MiG-15 saw considerable combat in Korea but suffered from the inexperience of its hastily trained Chinese and Korean pilots. As late as 1960 it was still used as a fighter by 15 countries and in 1977 the UTI trainer was still a standard type in the Soviet Union, and in all the countries listed earlier. Very few air forces today use the single-seater.

Above: A MiG-15UTI of the Ilmavoimat (Finnish Air Force) No 31 Sqn gets rolling on hard-packed snow.
Below: A MiG-15UTI of the Polish Air Force (PWL). Probably built in about 1959 as an SBLim-1 by the WSK-Mielec in Poland, it is one of a considerable number of trainer versions still in intensive use (where are the West's T-33s, Meteors and Vampires?). UTI means Uchebno-Trenirovochny Istrebitel, training fighter.

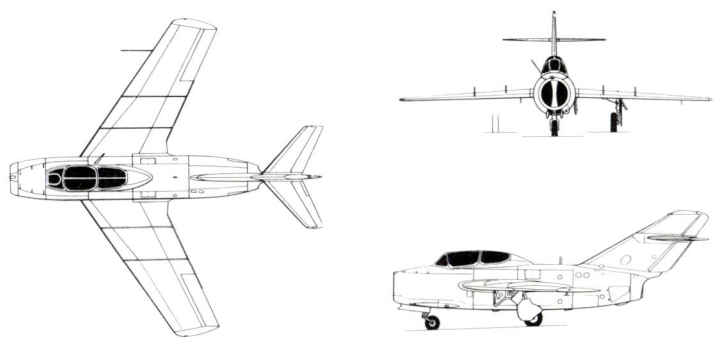

Above: Three-view of MiG-15UTI (without tanks).

Mikoyan/Gurevich MiG-17

MiG-17, -17P, -17F (Lim-5P and -5M, S-104, F-4), -17PF and -17PFU ("Fresco")

Origin: The design bureau of Mikoyan and Gurevich, Soviet Union; licence-production as described in the text.

Type: Single-seat fighter; (PF, PFU) limited all-weather interceptor.

Engine: (-17, -17P) one 5,952lb (2700kg) thrust Klimov VK-1 single-shaft centrifugal turbojet; (later versions) one 4,732/7,452lb (3380kg) VK-1F with afterburner.

Dimensions: Span 31ft (9·45m); length (all) 36ft 3in (11·05m); height 11ft (3·35m).

Weights: Empty (all) about 9,040lb (4100kg); loaded (F, clean) 11,773lb (5340kg); maximum (all) 14,770lb (6700kg).

Performance: Maximum speed (F, clean at best height of 9,840ft) 711mph (1145km/h); initial climb 12,795ft (3900m)/min; service ceiling 54,460ft (16,600m); range (high, two drop tanks) 913 miles (1470km).

Armament: (-17) as MiG-15, one 37mm and two 23mm NS-23; (all later versions) three 23mm Nudelmann-Rikter NR-23 cannon, one under right side of nose and two under left; four wing hardpoints for tanks, total of 1,102lb (500kg) of bombs, packs of eight 55mm air-to-air rockets or various air-to-ground missiles.

History: First flight (prototype) January 1950; service delivery, 1952; service delivery (F-4) January 1956; final delivery (Soviet Union) probably 1959.

Users: Afghanistan, Albania, Algeria, Angola, Bulgaria, China, Cuba, Czechoslovakia, Egypt, E Germany, Guinea, Hungary, Indonesia (in storage), Iraq, Kampuchea, N Korea, Mali, Morocco (in storage), Nigeria, Poland, Romania, Somalia, S Yemen, Soviet Union, Sri Lanka, Sudan, Syria, Tanzania, Uganda, Vietnam, Yemen Arab.

Development: Only gradually did Western observers recognise the MiG-17 as not merely a slightly modified MiG-15 but a completely different aircraft. Even then it was generally believed it had been hastily designed to rectify deficiencies shown in the MiG-15's performance in Korea, but in fact the design began in about January 1949, long before the Korean war. This was because from the first the MiG-15 had shown bad behaviour at high speeds, and though the earlier fighter was eventually made completely safe (partly by arranging for the air brakes to open automatically at Mach 0·92) it was still a difficult gun platform due to its tendency to snake and pitch. The MiG-17 — which was probably the last fighter in which Gurevich played a direct personal role — had a new wing with thickness reduced from 11 per cent to about 9 per cent, a different section and planform and no fewer than

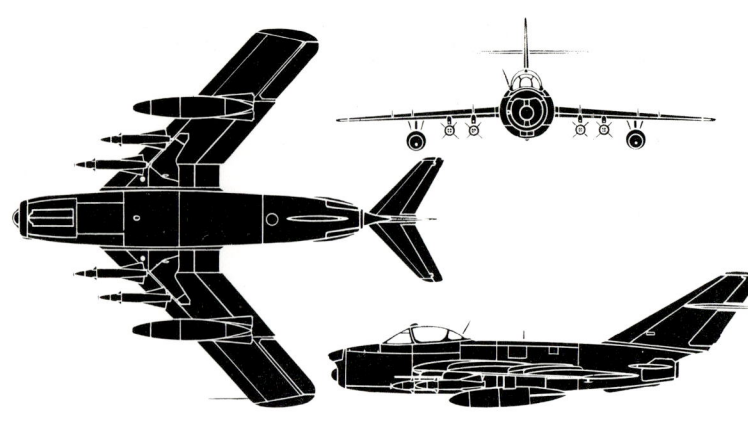

Above: Three-view of typical MiG-17F (NATO name, "Fresco C").

three fences. Without taper and with inboard sweep of 47° this made a big difference to high-Mach behaviour, and in fact there are reasons to believe the MiG-17 can be dived to make a sonic bang. With a new tail on a longer rear fuselage the transformation was completed by considerable revision of systems and equipment, though at first the VK-1 engine was unchanged. In 1958 the first limited all-weather version, the -17P, went into modest production with longer nose housing the same Izumrud ("Scan Odd") AI radar and ranging avionics as was also in production for the MiG-19. With the introduction of an afterburning engine the airbrakes were moved aft of the wing, away from the hot back end, but this was not a good position and they were returned (in enlarged rectangular form) to the tail in the most important sub-type the -17F. This was made in Poland as the Lim-5P (the -5M being a rough-field close-support version with larger tyres and drag chute), in Czechoslovakia as the S-104 and in China as the F-4. The PF was the afterburning all-weather version, and the final model was the PFU with guns removed and wing pylons for four beam-riding "Alkali" air-to-air missiles. Total production for at least 22 air forces must have considerably exceeded 5,000, exports from China alone exceeding 1,000. Many 17F remained in use in the mid-1970s.

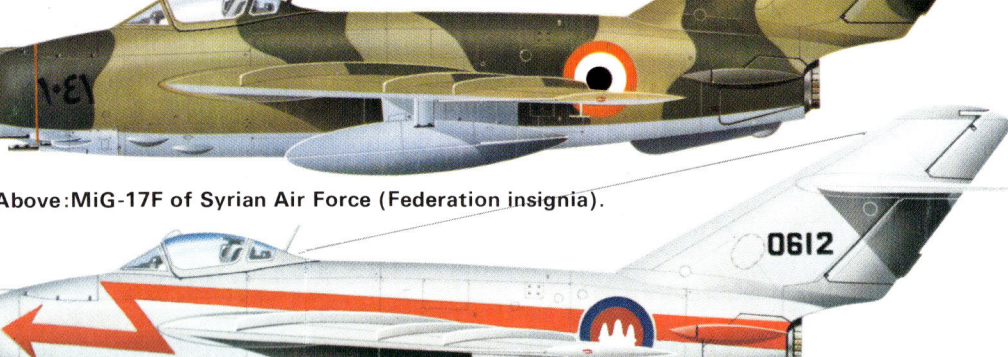

Above:MiG-17F of Syrian Air Force (Federation insignia).

Above: Chinese-built F-4 of Kampuchea (formerly Cambodia) Air Force.

Bottom left: Early MiG-17 fighters in service with the AV-MF (Soviet naval air force) Black Sea Fleet, around 1953. At first Western intelligence mistakenly thought the MiG-17 merely a modified -15, the pioneer swept-wing MiG that was such a shock when encountered by Allied pilots over Korea in 1950–51. The MiG-17 did not participate in the Korean war.

Below: A dramatic picture, taken by the combat camera of a USAF F-4 Phantom, showing the last moment of a MiG-17F of the Vietnam People's Air Force. The white shape near the left tailplane is a Sidewinder missile. The MiG is in a tight turn at about 400 knots at low/medium level, typical dogfight conditions.

Mikoyan/Gurevich MiG-19

MiG-19, -19S, -19SF (Lim-7, S-105, F-6), -19PF and -19PM ("Farmer")

Origin: The design bureau named for Mikoyan and Gurevich, Soviet Union; licence-production as described in the text.

Type: Single-seat fighter (PF, PM, all-weather interceptor).

Engines: (-19, -19S) two 6,700lb (3,040kg) thrust (afterburner rating) Mikulin AM-5 single-shaft afterburning turbojets; (-19SF, PF, PM) two 7,165lb (3250kg) thrust (afterburner) Klimov RD-9B afterburning turbojets.

Dimensions: Span 29ft 6½in (9m); length (S, SF, excluding pitot boom) 42ft 11¼in (13·08m); (-19PF, PM) 44ft 7in (13·59m); height 13ft 2¼in (4·02m).

Weights: Empty (SF) 12,698lb (5760kg); loaded (SF, clean) 16,755lb (7600kg); (maximum, SF) 19,180lb (8700kg); (PM) 20,944lb (9500kg).

Performance: Maximum speed (typical) 920mph at 20,000ft (1480km/h, Mach 1·3); initial climb (SF) 22,640ft (6900m)/min; service ceiling (SF) 58,725ft (17,900m); maximum range (high, with two drop tanks) 1,367 miles (2200km).

Armament: See text.

History: First flight, September 1953; service delivery early 1955; first flight (F-6) December 1961.

Users: Afghanistan, Albania, Bulgaria, China, Cuba, Czechoslovakia, E Germany (not operational), Hungary, Indonesia (in storage), Iraq, N Korea, Pakistan, Poland, Romania, Soviet Union, Tanzania, Uganda (ex-Iraq), Vietnam.

Development: With the MiG-19 the Mikoyan-Gurevich bureau established itself right in the front rank of the world's fighter design teams. The new fighter was on the drawing board as the I-350 before even the MiG-15 had been encountered in Korea, the five prototypes being ordered on 30 July 1951. Maj. Grigori Sedov flew the first aircraft on 18 September 1953 on the power of two non-afterburning AM-5 engines giving only 4,410lb thrust each. Nevertheless, despite the high wing loading and bold sweep angle of

continued on page 120▶

Above: The first intimate contact Western pilots had with the MiG-19 was in 1961 when Pakistan bought the F-6 (Chinese-built version). It made a most favourable impression.

Below: The MiG-19F is still flying in numbers with many countries (this one is Russian). It has "Scan Odd" search/ranging radar for all-weather fighting, but still retains the punchy NR-30 guns.

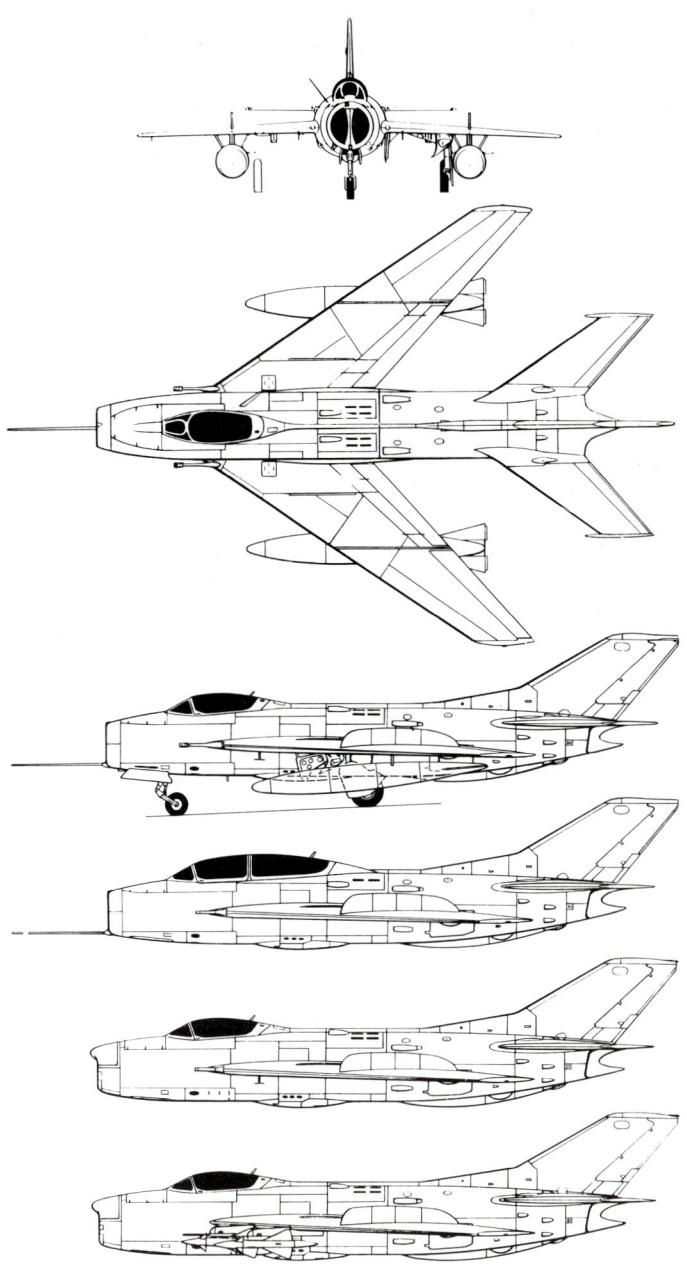

MiG-19 variants: top three views, F-6 (-19SF); then (top to bottom) MiG-19U, -19PF and -19PM with missiles.

►55° (at 25% chord), the MiG-19 handled well, large fences and Fowler flaps giving satisfactory low-speed control. With afterburning engines the MiG-19 became the first Russian supersonic fighter and it was put into production on a very large scale, rivalling that of the MiG-15 and -17, despite a 100 per cent increase in price. After about 500 had been delivered the MiG-19S (*stabilizator*) supplanted the early model with the fixed tail-plane and manual elevators replaced by a fully powered slab. At the same time the old armament (unchanged since MiG-15 and -17) was replaced by three of the new 30mm NR-30 guns, one in each wing root and one under the right side of the nose. A large ventral airbrake was also added. In 1956 the AM-5 engine was replaced by the newer and more powerful RD-9, increasing peak Mach number from 1·1 to 1·3. The new fighter was desig-nated MiG-19SF (*forsirovanni*, increased power), and has been built in very large numbers. Total production possibly exceeds 10,000, including licence-manufacture as the Lim-7 in Poland, S-105 in Czechoslovakia and F-6 in China. The corresponding MiG-19PF (*perekhvatchik*, interceptor) has an Izumrud AI radar (called "Scan Odd" by NATO) in a bullet carried on the inlet duct splitter, with the ranging unit in the upper inlet lip, changing the nose shape and adding 22in to the aircraft length. The final production version was the MiG-19PM (*modifikatsirovanni*), with guns removed and pylons for four early beam-rider air-to-air missiles (called "Alkali" by NATO). All MiG-19s can carry the simple K-13A missile (the copy of Side-winder, called "Atoll" by NATO) and underwing pylons can carry two 176 gal drop tanks plus two 551lb weapons or dispensers. Perhaps sur-prisingly, there has been no evidence of a two-seat trainer version of this fine fighter, which in 1960 was judged obsolescent and in 1970 was fast being reappraised as an extremely potent dogfighter. Part of the understand-ing of the MiG-19's qualities has resulted from its purchase in large numbers by Pakistan as the F-6 from the Chinese factory at Shenyang. The notable features of the F-6 were its superb finish, outstanding dogfight man-oeuvrability and tremendous hitting power of the NR-30 guns, each projectile having more than twice the kinetic energy of those of the Aden or DEFA of similar calibre. Though China soon ceased making the MiG-21 the F-6 remains in production, and has even been developed into the F-9.

1 Rear navigation light
2 Amplifier for rear-warning radar
3 Access panels
4 Fin structure
5 Rudder
6 Pen-nib exhaust fairing
7 Slab tailplane
8 Anti-flutter weights
9 Afterburners
10 Tail bumper
11 Afterburner cooling air intakes
12 Fin fillet
13 Braking parachute packing panel
14 Ventral strake
15 Aft fuel tanks
16 Starboard airbrake
17 Fuel filler cap
18 Oil tanks
19 Fuselage break point
20 Fuel dump vents
21 Port auxiliary tank (176 gal/ 800 litres)
22 Port navigation lamp
23 Port wing fence (full chord)
24 Wing structure
25 Dorsal spine (control rod tunnel)
26 Ram air intake
27 Air conditioning system
28 Klimov RD-9B turbojets 7,165 lb/3,250 kg with afterburner)
29 Main tanks
30 VHF aerial
31 Rear-sliding canopy
32 Ejection seat
33 Optical gunsight
34 Instrument panel
35 Pilot's controls
36 Control column
37 Foot pedals
38 Accumulator
39 Radio altimeter transmitter receiver
40 VHF transmitter
41 VHF receiver
42 Starboard inlet duct
43 Combat camera
44 Bifurcated intake
45 Pitot head (hinged)
46 Nosewheel retraction cylinder
47 Landing light (port side)
48 Forward-retracting nose-wheel
49 Cannon muzzle-brake
50 Taxi-ing light
51 Nosewheel doors
52 30mm NR-30 cannon
53 Case chute
54 Starboard 30mm NR-30 cannon
55 Compressed air bottle
56 Ammunition feed
57 Radio altimeter dipole
58 Perforated ventral airbrake
59 Main undercarriage door
60 Mainwheel retraction cylinder
61 Levered-suspension main landing-gear
62 Starboard mainwheel
63 Auxiliary tank pylon
64 Starboard auxiliary tank (176 gal/800 litres)
65 Starboard navigation lamp

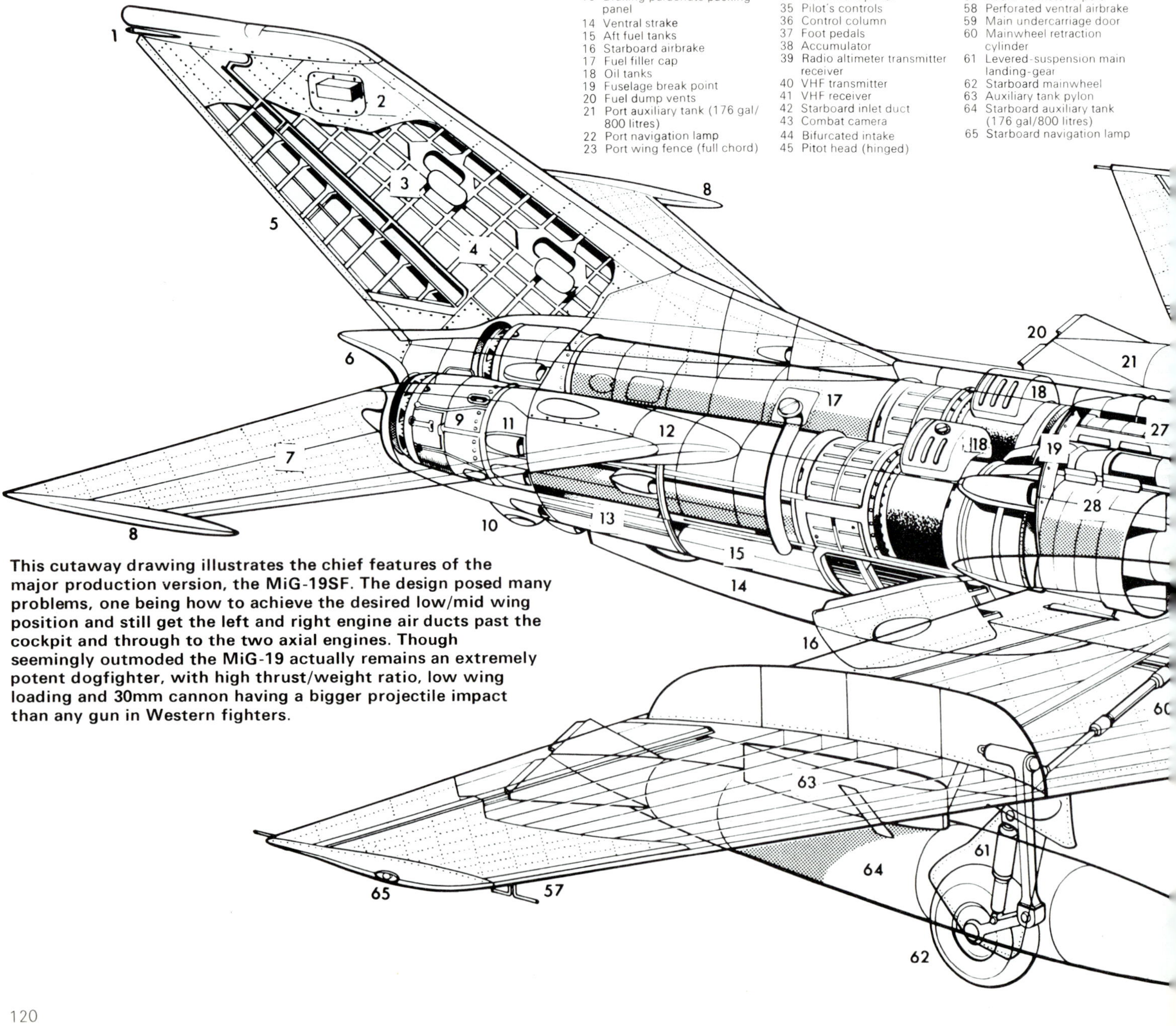

This cutaway drawing illustrates the chief features of the major production version, the MiG-19SF. The design posed many problems, one being how to achieve the desired low/mid wing position and still get the left and right engine air ducts past the cockpit and through to the two axial engines. Though seemingly outmoded the MiG-19 actually remains an extremely potent dogfighter, with high thrust/weight ratio, low wing loading and 30mm cannon having a bigger projectile impact than any gun in Western fighters.

Above: A Chinese-built F-6 of the Pakistan Air Force, photographed by hand-held camera from the cockpit of an aircraft in loose formation. The F-6 gave a creditable account of itself in the warfare with India.

Left, above: One of the few good air-to-air photographs of a MiG-19 in Soviet IA-PVO service, this shows the PM interceptor with beam-riding "Alkali" missiles.

Above: An F-6 (Chinese-built MiG-19SF) of the Peoples' Republic of China Air Force.

Above: An F-6 of the Pakistan Air Force in camouflage finish.

Above: A MiG-19PM of the Polish Air Force, showing nose radar and "Alkali" air-to-air missiles.

Mikoyan/Gurevich MiG-21

MiG-21, 21F (S-107), 21FA, 21PF, 21FL, 21PFS, 21PFM, 21PFMA, 21M, 21R, 21MF, 21SMT, 21bis, 21U, 21US and 21UM plus numerous special versions. ("Fishbed"), 21U ("Mongol")

Origin: The design bureau named for Mikoyan and Gurevich; Soviet Union; licence-production as described in the text.
Type: Single-seat fighter; (PFMA and MF) limited all-weather multi-role; (R) reconnaissance; (U) two-seat trainer.
Engine: In all versions, one Tumansky single-shaft turbojet with afterburner; (-21) R-11 rated at 11,240lb (5100kg) with afterburner; (-21F) R-11-F2-300 rated at 13,120lb (5950kg); (-21FL, PFS, PFM and PFMA) R-11-G2S-300 rated at 13,668lb (6200kg); (-21MF and derivatives) R-13-300 rated at 14,500lb (6600kg).
Dimensions: Span 23ft 5½in (7·15m); length (excluding probe) (-21) 46ft 11in (14·3m); (-21MF) 48ft 0½in (14·6m); height (little variation, but figure for MF) 14ft 9in (4·5m).
Weights: Empty (-21) 11,464lb (5200kg); (-21MF) 12,346lb (5600kg); maximum loaded (-21) 18,740lb (8500kg); (-21MF) 21,605lb (9800kg) (weight with three tanks and two K-13A, 20,725lb, 9400kg).
Performance: Maximum speed (MF, but typical of all) 1,285mph (2070km/h, Mach 2·1); initial climb (MF, clean) 36,090ft (11,000m)/min; service ceiling 59,050ft (18,000m); range (high, internal fuel) 683 miles (1100km); maximum range (MF, high, three tanks) 1,118 miles (1800km).
Armament: See text.
History: First flight (E-5 prototype) late 1955; (production -21F) late 1957; service delivery early 1958.

Users: Afghanistan, Albania, Algeria, Angola, Bangladesh, Bulgaria, China, Cuba, Czechoslovakia, Egypt, Finland, E Germany, India, Indonesia (in storage), Iraq, Jugoslavia, Nigeria, N Korea, Poland, Romania, Somalia, Soviet Union, Sudan, S Yemen, Syria, Tanzania, Uganda, Vietnam, Yemen Arab.

Development: Undoubtedly the most widely used combat aircraft in the world in the 1970s, this trim little delta has established a reputation for cost effectiveness and in its later versions it also packs a more adequate multi-role punch. It was designed in the 18 months following the Korean War. While Sukhoi developed large supersonic fighters to rival the American F-100, the Mikoyan-Gurevich bureau, by now led only by Col-Gen Mikoyan (who died in 1970), concentrated on a small day interceptor of the highest possible performance. Prototypes were built with both swept and delta wings, both having powered slab tailplanes, and the delta was chosen for production. At least 30 pre-production aircraft had flown by the time service delivery started and the development effort was obviously considerable. The initial MiG-21 abounded in interesting features including Fowler flaps, fully powered controls, upward ejection seat fixed to the rear of the front-hinged canopy (which incorporated the whole front of the cockpit enclosure except the bullet-proof windshield) to act as a pilot blast-shield, and internal fuel capacity of only 410 gal. Armament was two 30mm NR-30 in long fairings under the fuselage, the left gun usually being replaced by avionics. Part of these avionics serve the two K-13 ("Atoll") missiles carried on wing pylons on the slightly more powerful 21F. This had radar ranging, 515 gal fuel, broader fin, upward-hinged pitot boom attached under the nose (to prevent people walking into it) and two dorsal blade aerials. Czech-built

Above: HAL Type 77 (licence-built MiG-21PF) of Indian Air Force, with GP-9 gun pack and K-13A.

Above: An early version, the MiG-21F, as serving with the Romanian Air Force.

Above: MiG-21MF as supplied to Egyptian Air Force.

Right: The cutaway drawing depicts one of the later MiG-21 sub-types, the MF. This is believed to have been the first production model with the Tumansky R-13 series engine, giving increased performance. This may be the variant which is thought to be going into production in North Korea.

aircraft (still called 21F) did not have the rear-view windows in the front of the dorsal spine. The F was called "Fishbed C" by NATO and Type 74 by the Indian Air Force; it was also the type supplied to China in 1959 and used as the pattern for the Chinese-built F-8. As the oldest active variant it was also the first exported or seen in the West, the Finnish AF receiving the 21F-12 in April 1963.

At Tushino in 1961 the prototype was displayed of what became the 21PF, with inlet diameter increased from 27in to 36in, completely changing the nose shape and providing room for a large movable centre-body housing **continued on page 126▶**

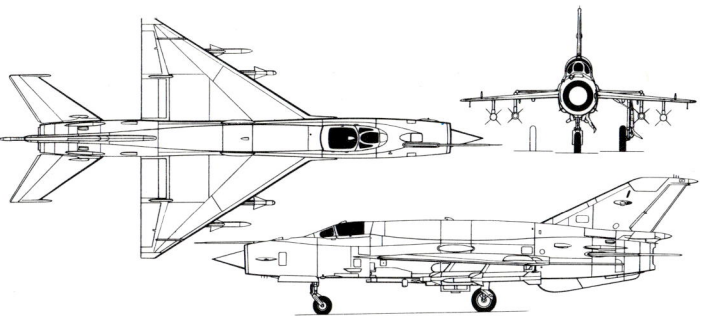

Above: Three-view of MiG-21SMT ("Fishbed K") with four K-13A missiles.

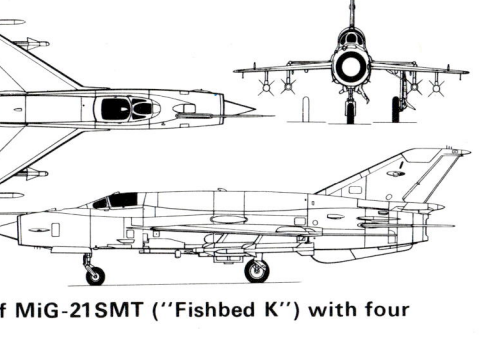

Above: The chief sub-type of the MiG-21 in service with the Soviet IA-PVO is called "Fishbed L" by NATO, its exact Soviet designation being unknown. It is essentially an MF with a Tacan-type navigation/homing system.

1 Pitot-static boom
2 Pitch vanes
3 Yaw vanes
4 Conical three-position intake centrebody
5 "Spin Scan" search-and-track radar scanner
6 Boundary layer slot
7 Engine air intake
8 Radar ("Spin Scan")
9 Lower boundary layer exit
10 Aerials
11 Nosewheel doors
12 Nosewheel leg and shock absorbers
13 Castoring nosewheel
14 Anti-shimmy damper
15 Avionics bay access
16 Attitude sensor
17 Nosewheel well
18 Spill door
19 Nosewheel retraction pivot
20 Bifurcated inlet duct
21 Avionics bay
22 Electronics equipment
23 Inlet duct
24 Upper boundary layer exit
25 Dynamic pressure probe for q-feel
26 Semi-elliptical armour-glass windscreen
27 Gunsight mounting
28 Fixed quarterlight

29 Radar scope
30 Control column (with tailplane trim switch and two firing buttons)
31 Rudder pedals
32 Underfloor control runs
33 KM-1 two-position zero-level ejection seat
34 Port instrument console
35 Undercarriage handle
36 Seat harness
37 Canopy release/lock
38 Starboard wall switch panel
39 Rear-view mirror fairing
40 Starboard-hinged canopy
41 Ejection-seat headrest
42 Avionics bay
43 Control rods
44 Air-conditioning plant
45 Suction relief door
46 Inlet duct
47 Wing root attachment fairing
48 Wing/fuselage spar-lug attachments (four)
49 Fuselage ring frames
50 Intermediate frames
51 Main fuselage fuel tank
52 RSIU radio bay
53 Auxiliary intake

54 Leading-edge integral fuel tank
55 Starboard outer weapons pylon
56 Outboard wing construction
57 Starboard navigation light
58 Leading-edge suppressed aerial
59 Wing fence
60 Aileron control jack
61 Starboard aileron
62 Flap actuator fairing
63 Starboard blown flap — SPS (sduva pogranichnovo sloya)
64 Multi-spar wing structure
65 Main integral wing fuel tank
66 Undercarriage mounting/pivot point
67 Starboard mainwheel leg
68 Auxiliaries compartment
69 Fuselage fuel tanks Nos 2 and 3
70 Mainwheel well external fairing
71 Mainwheel (retracted)
72 Single inlet duct
73 Control rods in dorsal spine
74 Compressor face

75 Oil tank
76 Avionics pack
77 Engine accessories
78 Tumansky R-13 turbojet (rated at 14,550 lb/6,600 kg with afterburner)
79 Fuselage break/transport joint
80 Intake
81 Tail surface control linkage
82 Artificial-feel unit
83 Tailplane power unit
84 Hydraulic accumulator
85 Tailplane trim motor
86 Fin-spar attachment plate
87 Rudder power unit
88 Rudder control linkage
89 Fin structure

90 Leading-edge panel
91 Radio cable access
92 Magnetic detector
93 Fin mainspar
94 RSIU (radio-stantsiya istrebitelnaya ultrakorotkykh vol'n — very-shortwave fighter radio) aerial plate
95 VHF/UHF aerials
96 IFF aerial
97 Formation light
98 Tail warning radar
99 Rear navigation light
100 Fuel vent
101 Rudder construction
102 Rudder hinge
103 Braking-parachute hinged fairing
104 Braking parachute stowage
105 Tailpipe (variable convergent nozzle)
106 Afterburner installation
107 Afterburner bay cooling intake
108 Tailplane linkage fairing
109 Nozzle actuating cylinders
110 Tailplane torque tube
111 All-moving tailplane
112 Anti-flutter weight
113 Intake
114 Afterburner mounting
115 Fixed tailplane root fairing
116 Longitudinal lap joint
117 External duct (nozzle hydraulics)
118 Ventral fin
119 Engine guide rail
120 JATO rocket canted nozzle

121 JATO rocket thrust plate forks (rear mounting)
122 JATO pack
123 Ventral airbrake (retracted)
124 Trestle point
125 JATO release solenoid (front mounting)
126 Underwing landing light
127 Ventral stores pylon
128 Mainwheel inboard door
129 Splayed link chute
130 Twin 23mm GSh-23 cannon installation
131 Cannon muzzle fairing
132 Debris deflector plate
133 Auxiliary ventral drop tank
134 Port forward air brake (extended)
135 Leading-edge integral fuel tank
136 Undercarriage retraction strut
137 Aileron control rods in leading edge
138 Port inboard weapons pylon
139 UV-16-57 rocket pod
140 Port mainwheel
141 Mainwheel leg
142 Mainwheel leg
143 Aileron control linkage
144 Mainwheel leg pivot point
145 Main integral wing fuel tank
146 Flap actuator fairing
147 Port aileron
148 Aileron control jack
149 Outboard wing construction
150 Port navigation light
151 Port outboard weapons pylon
152 "Advanced Atoll" infrared-guided AAM
153 Wing fence
154 Radio altimeter aerial

Mikoyan/Gurevich MiG-21SMT "Fishbed K"

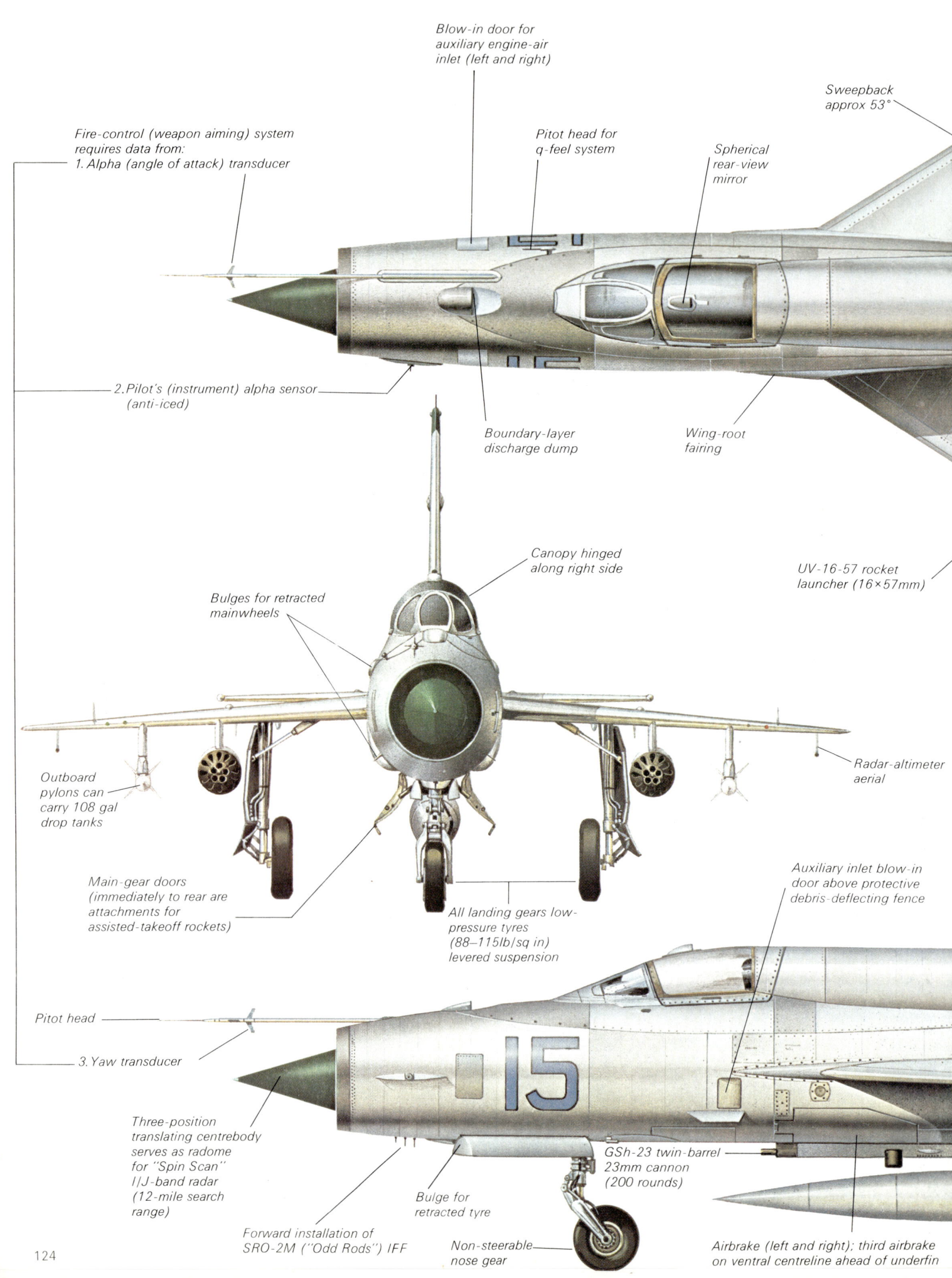

Fire-control (weapon aiming) system requires data from:
1. Alpha (angle of attack) transducer

2. Pilot's (instrument) alpha sensor (anti-iced)

Blow-in door for auxiliary engine-air inlet (left and right)

Pitot head for q-feel system

Spherical rear-view mirror

Sweepback approx 53°

Boundary-layer discharge dump

Wing-root fairing

Bulges for retracted mainwheels

Canopy hinged along right side

UV-16-57 rocket launcher (16×57mm)

Outboard pylons can carry 108 gal drop tanks

Radar-altimeter aerial

Main-gear doors (immediately to rear are attachments for assisted-takeoff rockets)

All landing gears low-pressure tyres (88–115lb/sq in) levered suspension

Auxiliary inlet blow-in door above protective debris-deflecting fence

Pitot head

3. Yaw transducer

Three-position translating centrebody serves as radome for "Spin Scan" I/J-band radar (12-mile search range)

Forward installation of SRO-2M ("Odd Rods") IFF

Bulge for retracted tyre

Non-steerable nose gear

GSh-23 twin-barrel 23mm cannon (200 rounds)

Airbrake (left and right); third airbrake on ventral centreline ahead of underfin

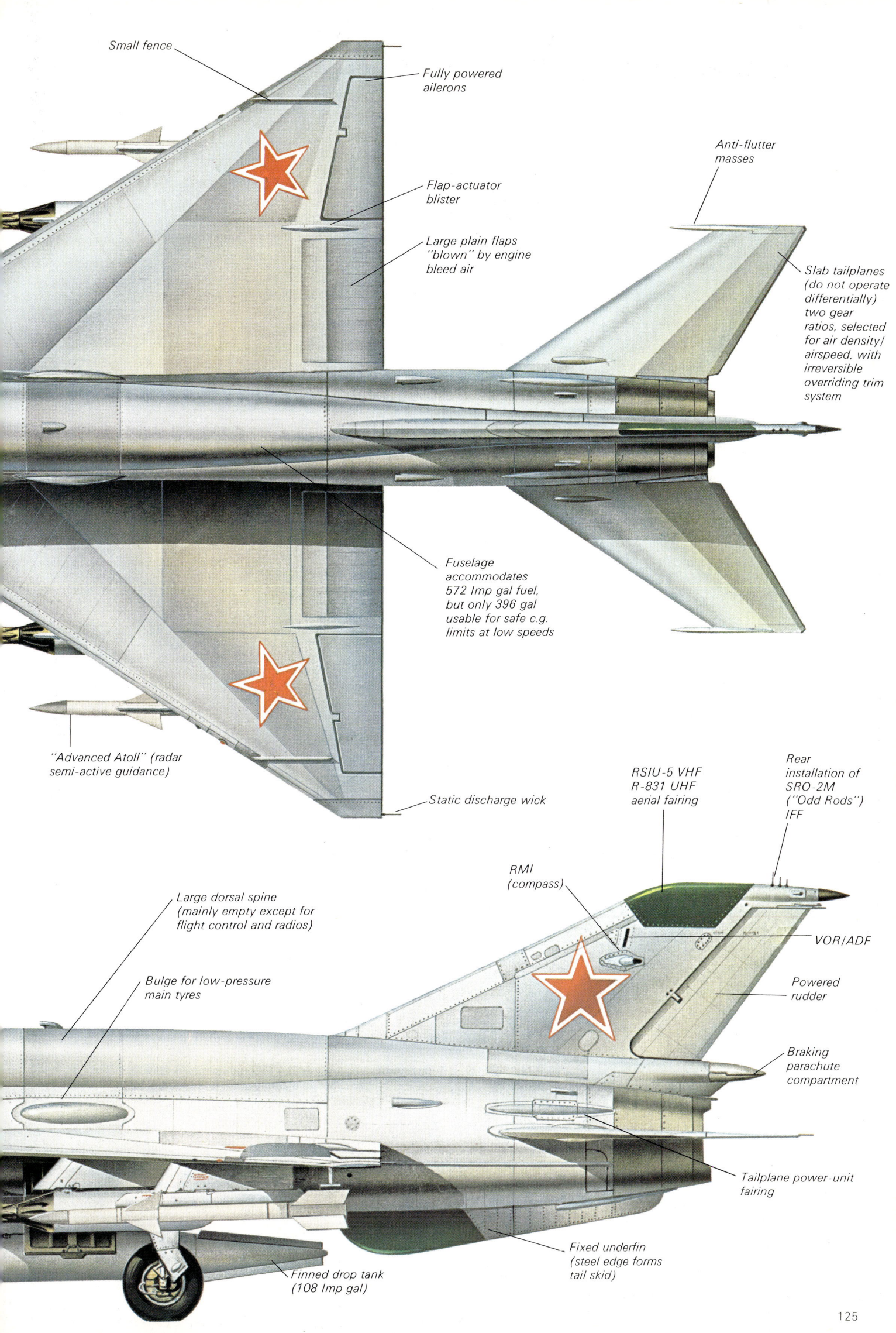

Small fence

Fully powered ailerons

Flap-actuator blister

Large plain flaps "blown" by engine bleed air

Anti-flutter masses

Slab tailplanes (do not operate differentially) two gear ratios, selected for air density/airspeed, with irreversible overriding trim system

Fuselage accommodates 572 Imp gal fuel, but only 396 gal usable for safe c.g. limits at low speeds

"Advanced Atoll" (radar semi-active guidance)

Static discharge wick

RSIU-5 VHF R-831 UHF aerial fairing

Rear installation of SRO-2M ("Odd Rods") IFF

RMI (compass)

VOR/ADF

Large dorsal spine (mainly empty except for flight control and radios)

Bulge for low-pressure main tyres

Powered rudder

Braking parachute compartment

Tailplane power-unit fairing

Finned drop tank (108 Imp gal)

Fixed underfin (steel edge forms tail skid)

►the scanner of the R1L (NATO "Spin Scan") AI radar. Other changes include deletion of guns (allowing simpler forward airbrakes), bigger main-wheels (causing large fuselage bulges above the wing), pitot boom moved above the inlet, fatter dorsal spine (partly responsible for fuel capacity of 627gal) and many electronic changes. All PF had an uprated engine, late models had take-off rocket latches and final batches had completely new blown flaps (SPS) which cut landing speed by 25mph and reduced nose-up attitude for better pilot view. The FL was the export PF (L = *lokator*, denoting R2L radar) with even more powerful engine. Like the F models rebuilt in 1963-64, this can carry the GP-9 gunpack housing the excellent GSh-23 23mm twin-barrel gun, has a still further broadened vertical tail and drag-chute repositioned above the jetpipe. The PFS was the PF with SPS blown flaps, while the PFM was a definitive improved version with another 19in added to the fin (final fillet eliminated), a conventional seat and side-hinged canopy, and large flush aerials in the fin. One-off versions were built to prove STOL with lift jets and to fly a scaled "analogue" of the wing of the Tu-144 SST. The very important PFMA, made in huge numbers, was the first multi-role version, with straight top line from much deeper spine (housing equipment and not fuel and holding tankage to 572gal), and four pylons for two 1,100lb and two 551lb bombs, four S-24 missiles and/or tanks or K-13A missiles. The 21M has an internal GSh-23 and since 1973 has been built in India as Type 88. The 21R has multi-sensor reconnaissance internally and in pods and wing-tip ECM fairings, as do late models of the 21MF, the first to have the new R-13 engine. The RF is the R-13-powered reconnaissance version. One of the few variants still in production is the SMT, with fuel restored to the spine and more comprehensive avionics including tail-warning radar.

Code-named "Mongol" and called Type 66 in India, the U is the tandem trainer, the US has SPS flaps and UM the R-13 engine and four pylons. Many other versions have been used to set world records. About 10,000 of all sub-types have been built, and in 1977 output was continuing at perhaps three per week in the Soviet Union, with a much lower rate in India; in early 1976 N Korea was said to be also in production. Many of the early models of this neat fighter were sweet to handle and quite effective day dogfighters, but the majority of the subtypes in use have many adverse characteristics and severe limitations.

In late 1976 a new version appeared, the MiG-21bis (Fishbed L); this is a cleaned-up and refined MiG-21MF with Tacan-type navigation and other improvements.

Top: This frame from a Soviet motion picture shows a MiG-21, probably a PFM, blasting off with the aid of two large JATO (jet-assisted takeoff) boost rockets, used by many versions.

Above: Hardware counts for more than paint, and the variable (and crude) paintwork on these HAL-built Type 77 (MiG-21 FL) does no harm. This was the first model made in India.

Mikoyan/Gurevich MiG-23

MiG-23, -23S and -23U ("Flogger")

Origin: The design bureau named for Mikoyan and Gurevich, Soviet Union; no production outside the Soviet Union yet reported.

Type: (-23S, "Flogger B") single-seat all-weather interceptor with "Flogger E" export variant of unknown designation; (-23U, "Flogger C") dual-control trainer and ECM platform.

Engine: One Tumansky afterburning turbofan of unknown type, rated at about 14,500lb (6577kg) dry and 20,500lb (9300kg) with maximum after-burner.

Dimensions: (Estimated) Span (72° sweep) 28ft 7in (8·7m), (16°) 47ft 3in (14·4m); length (export) 53ft (16·15m), (S, U) 55ft 1½in (16·80m); height 13ft (3·96m).

Weights: (Estimated) empty 17,500lb (7940kg); loaded (clean or fighter mission) 30,000lb (13,600kg); maximum permissible 33,000lb (15,000kg).

Performance: Maximum speed, clean, 840mph (1350km/h, Mach 1·1) at sea level; maximum speed, clean, at altitude, 1,520mph (2445km/h, Mach 2·2); maximum Mach number with missiles (MiG-23S) about 2; service ceiling about 55,000ft (16,765m); combat radius (hi-lo-hi) about 400 miles (640km).

Armament: (-23S) one 23mm GSh-23 twin-barrel gun on ventral centreline, plus various mixes of air/air missiles which usually include one or two infra-red or radar-homing AA-7 "Apex" and/or infra-red or radar-homing AA-8 "Aphid", the latter for close combat; (-23U) none reported.

History: First flight, probably 1965; (first production aircraft) believed 1970; service delivery, believed 1971.

Users: Iraq, Libya, Soviet Union, Syria (and almost certainly other countries in 1977).

Development: Revealed at the 1967 Moscow Aviation Day, the prototype swing-wing MiG-23 was at first thought to be a Yakovlev design, though it appeared in company with a jet-lift STOL fighter having an identical rear fuselage and tail and strong MiG-21-like features (though much bigger

than a MiG-21). Over the next four years the Mikoyan bureau greatly developed this aircraft, which originally owed something to the F-111 and Mirage G. By 1971 the radically different production versions, the -23S fighter and -23U trainer, were entering service in quantity, and by 1975 several hundred had been delivered to Warsaw Pact air forces and also to Egypt. Today Egypt is believed no longer to operate the type, but large deliveries have been made to other countries. The MiG-27 attack version is described separately.

There are three main versions. The first to enter service was the MiG-23S all-weather interceptor, with powerful highly-afterburning engine, "High Lark" nose radar (said in 1973 by the then Secretary of the USAF to be "comparable with that of the latest Phantom") and, almost certainly, a laser ranger and doppler navigator. ECM and other EW equipment is markedly superior to anything fitted in previous Soviet aircraft, and apparently as good as comparable installations in Western fighters (other than the F-15).

Several hundred S models are currently in service with the Soviet IA-PVO air forces, and they are replacing the Su-9 and -11 and Yak-28P. Missiles are carried on a centreline pylon (which often carries a drop-tank instead), on pylons under the inlet ducts and under the fixed wing gloves (centre section). For overseas customers a simplified sub-type is in production, with the same high-Mach airframe and systems as the -23S fighter but lacking the latter's radar (NATO calls this model "Flogger E" but the Soviet designation was unknown as this book went to press). The third MiG-23 so far seen is the tandem two-seat -23U, used for conversion training and as an ECM and reconnaissance platform. This again has the fighter's high-speed airframe and systems, but has not been seen with any weapons or delivery systems.

continued on page 128▶

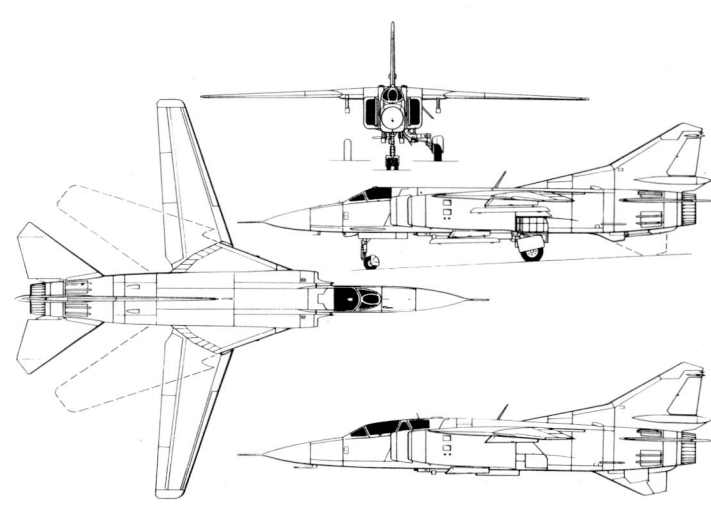

Above: Three-view of MiG-23S, with side view of MiG-23U trainer (lower right).

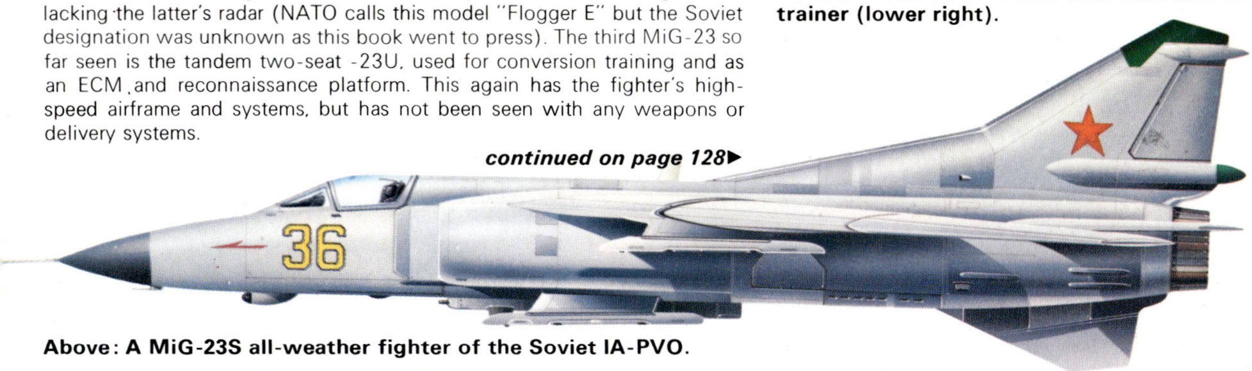

Above: A MiG-23S all-weather fighter of the Soviet IA-PVO.

Below: Called "Flogger E" by NATO, this export version of the MiG-23B is fitted with a radar of lower power, with a smaller radome. This one belongs to the Libyan Air Force, which also has the MiG-23U trainer.

Mikoyan/Gurevich MiG-23S "Flogger B"

Sirena 3 forward-facing radar-warning aerials (left and right)

High Lark air-intercept radar

Spherical rear-view dogfight mirror

Boundary-layer ejectors

Steel wing carry-through box

Pylons for AA-7 "Apex", AA-8 "Aphid" or 1,000kg tanks (wing 16° or 45° only)

Main-gear doors

Anti-skid brake system

Folded fin

Anti-iced hinged ramp

Perforated splitter-plate

Triple unit SRO-2 ("Odd Rods") IFF aerials

Alpha (angle of attack) sensor vane

Zero/zero seat

SP-50 ILS ("Swift Rod") forward-facing aerial

Main doppler radar aerial (type unknown)

Laser rangefinder

Cable conduit and ARL data-link

GSh-23 twin-23mm cannon

Pylons (3) for: AA-7 "Apex" AA-8 "Aphid" AS-7 "Kerry" or 1,000kg tanks

Twin-wheel steerable nose gear

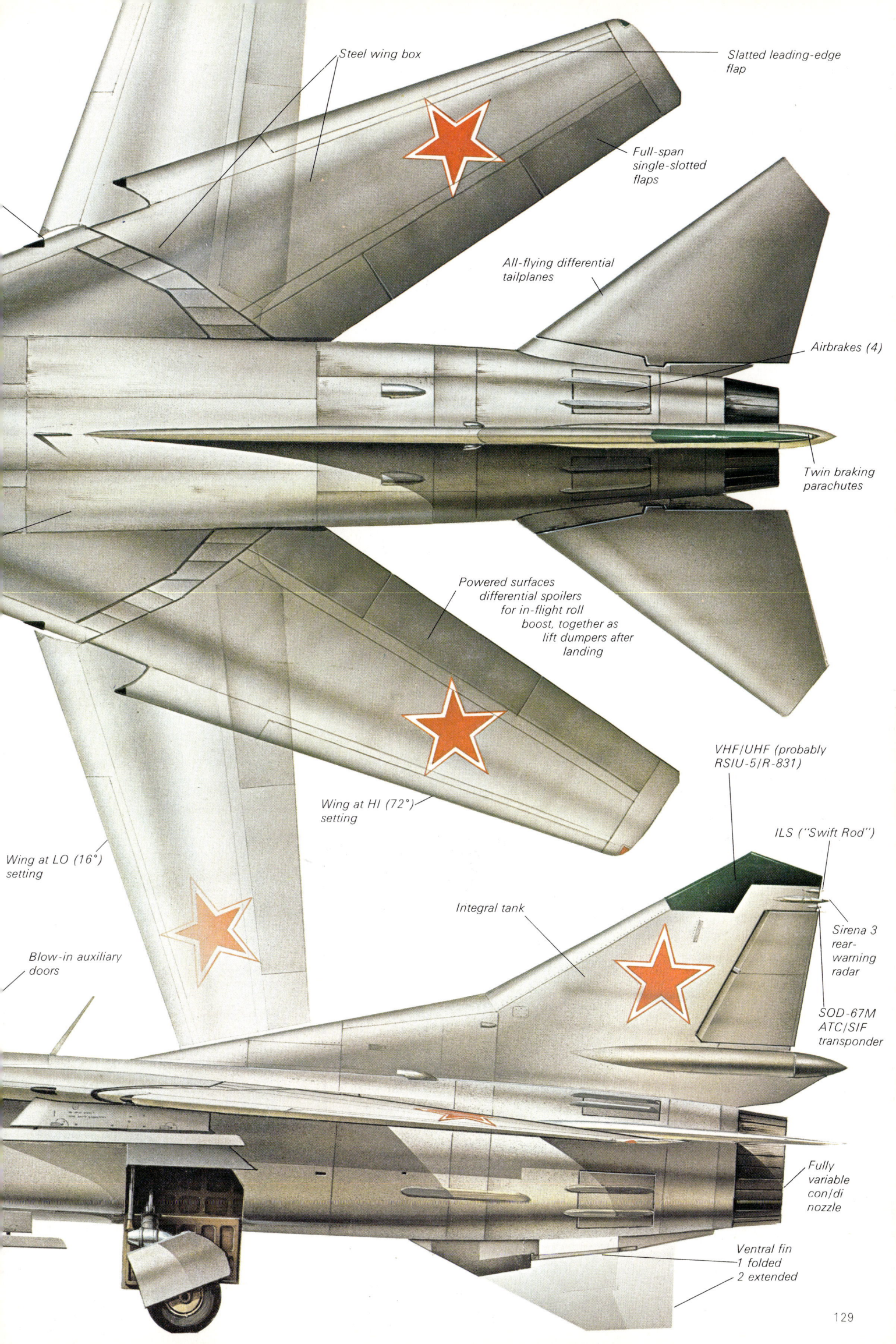

Steel wing box

Slatted leading-edge flap

Full-span single-slotted flaps

All-flying differential tailplanes

Airbrakes (4)

Twin braking parachutes

Powered surfaces differential spoilers for in-flight roll boost, together as lift dumpers after landing

VHF/UHF (probably RSIU-5/R-831)

Wing at HI (72°) setting

ILS ("Swift Rod")

Wing at LO (16°) setting

Integral tank

Sirena 3 rear-warning radar

SOD-67M ATC/SIF transponder

Blow-in auxiliary doors

Fully variable con/di nozzle

Ventral fin 1 folded 2 extended

Mikoyan/Gurevich MiG-25

MiG-25, -25R and -25U ("Foxbat")

Origin: The design bureau named for Mikoyan and Gurevich, Soviet Union.
Type: "Foxbat A" (believed to be MiG-25S), all-weather long-range interceptor; MiG-25R, reconnaissance; MiG-25U, tandem-seat dual trainer with stepped cockpits.
Engines: Two Tumansky R-266 afterburning turbojets each rated at 24,500lb (11,110kg) with full augmentation.
Dimensions: Span 46ft (14·0m); (R) c 44ft (13·4m); length ("A") 73ft 2in (22·3m), (R) 74ft 6in (22·7m), (U) about 76ft (23·16m); height 18ft 6in (5·63m).
Weights: (Fighter) empty 44,000lb (19,960kg); normal loaded 68,350lb (31,000kg); maximum loaded with external missiles or tanks 77,000lb (34,930kg).
Performance: (Estimated) maximum speed at altitude 2,100mph. (3380km/h, Mach 3·2); initial climb, about 50,000ft (15,240m)/min;

continued on page 132 ▶

Mikoyan/Gurevich MiG-25 "Foxbat A"

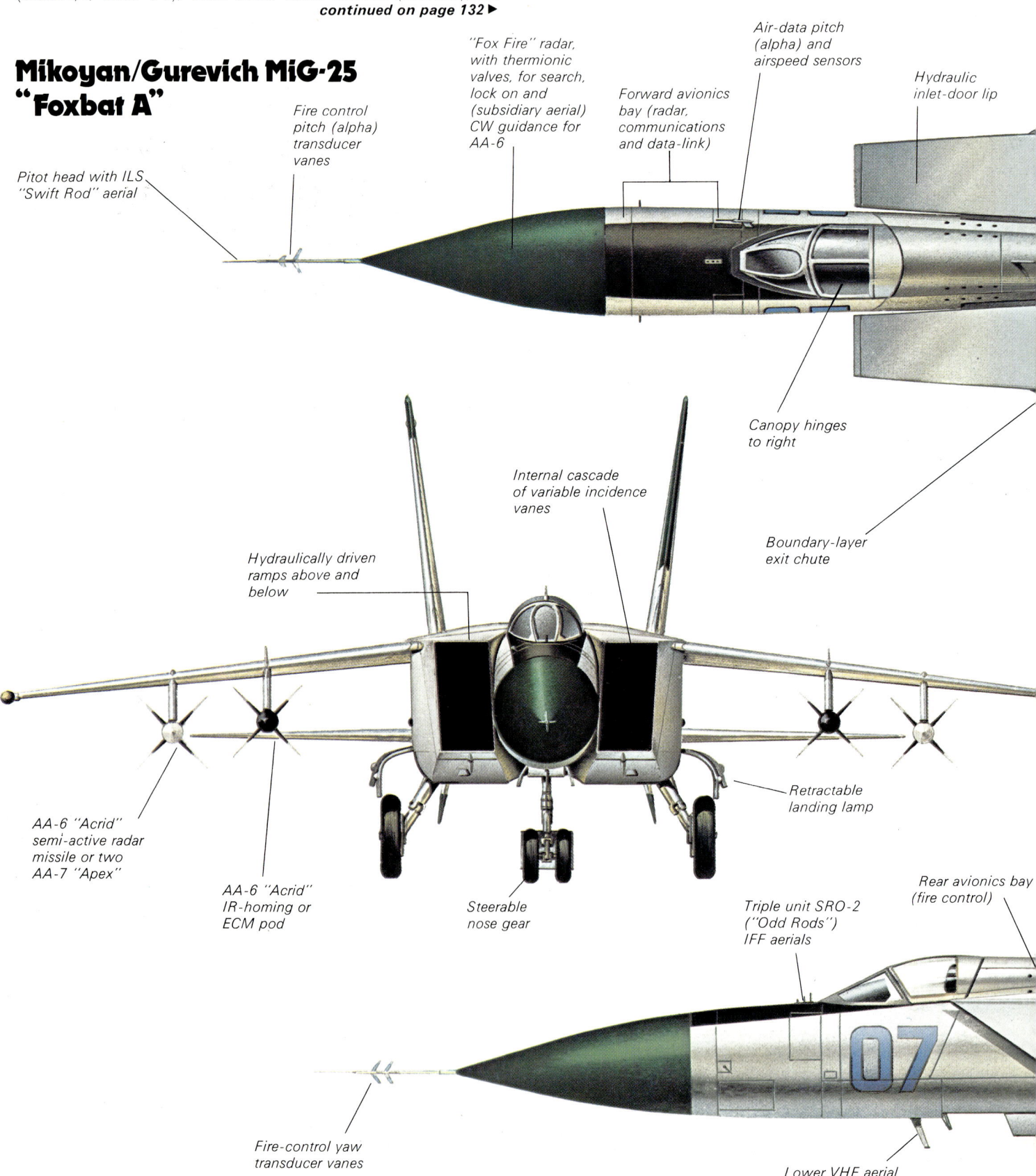

Pitot head with ILS "Swift Rod" aerial

Fire control pitch (alpha) transducer vanes

"Fox Fire" radar, with thermionic valves, for search, lock on and (subsidiary aerial) CW guidance for AA-6

Forward avionics bay (radar, communications and data-link)

Air-data pitch (alpha) and airspeed sensors

Hydraulic inlet-door lip

Canopy hinges to right

Boundary-layer exit chute

Internal cascade of variable incidence vanes

Hydraulically driven ramps above and below

AA-6 "Acrid" semi-active radar missile or two AA-7 "Apex"

AA-6 "Acrid" IR-homing or ECM pod

Steerable nose gear

Retractable landing lamp

Triple unit SRO-2 ("Odd Rods") IFF aerials

Rear avionics bay (fire control)

Fire-control yaw transducer vanes

Lower VHF aerial

130

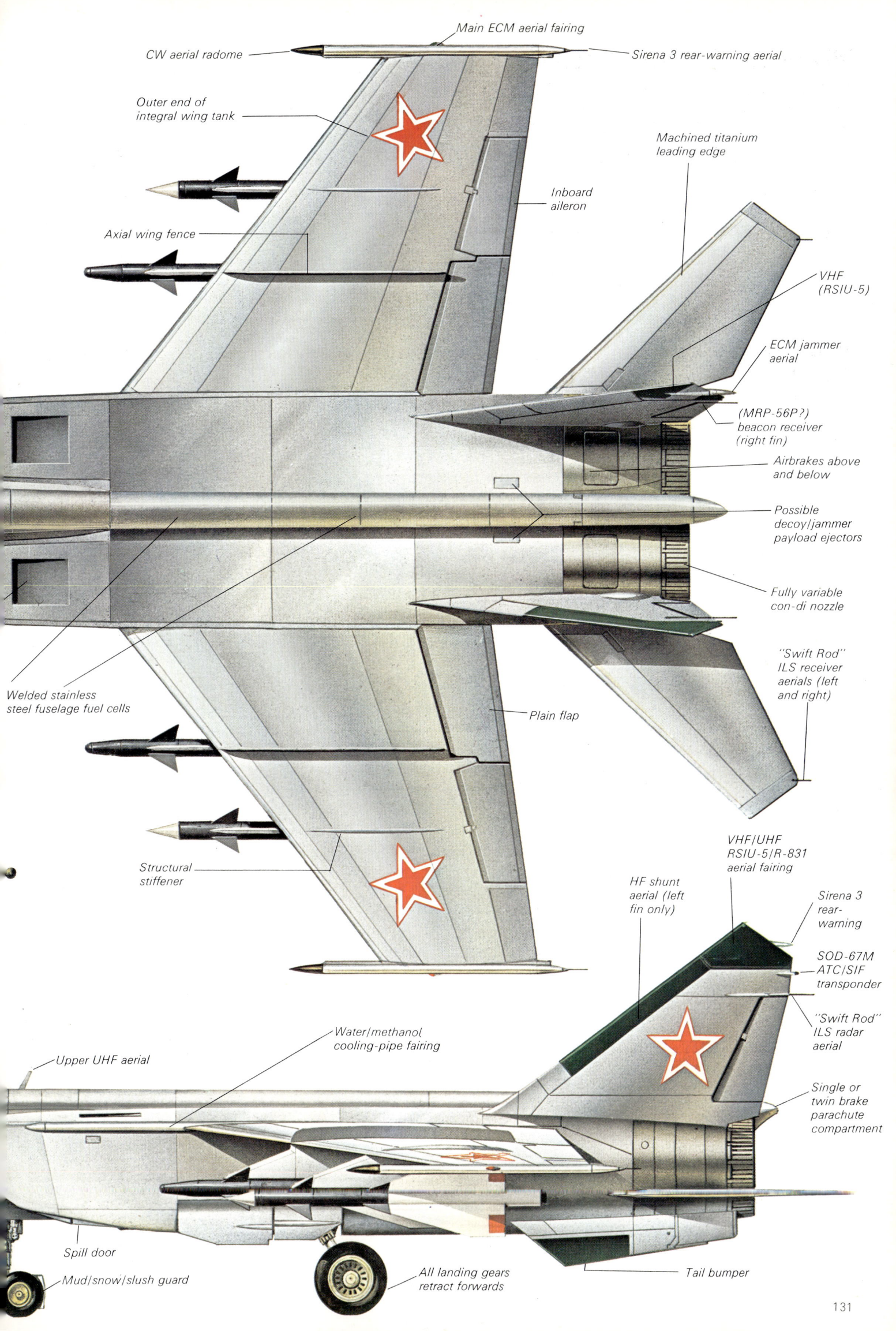

CW aerial radome

Main ECM aerial fairing

Sirena 3 rear-warning aerial

Outer end of integral wing tank

Machined titanium leading edge

VHF (RSIU-5)

Axial wing fence

Inboard aileron

ECM jammer aerial

(MRP-56P?) beacon receiver (right fin)

Airbrakes above and below

Possible decoy/jammer payload ejectors

Fully variable con-di nozzle

"Swift Rod" ILS receiver aerials (left and right)

Welded stainless steel fuselage fuel cells

Plain flap

Structural stiffener

VHF/UHF RSIU-5/R-831 aerial fairing

HF shunt aerial (left fin only)

Sirena 3 rear-warning

SOD-67M ATC/SIF transponder

"Swift Rod" ILS radar aerial

Water/methanol cooling-pipe fairing

Upper UHF aerial

Single or twin brake parachute compartment

Spill door

Mud/snow/slush guard

All landing gears retract forwards

Tail bumper

▶service ceiling 73,000ft (22,250m); high-altitude combat radius without external fuel, 700 miles (1130km).

Armament: ("A") four underwing pylons each carrying one AA-6 air-to-air missile (two radar, two infra-red), or other store; no guns; ("B") none.

History: First flight (E-266 prototype) probably 1964; (production reconnaissance version) before 1969; (production interceptor) probably 1969; service delivery (both) 1970 or earlier.

User: Soviet Union.

Development: This large and powerful aircraft set a totally new level in combat-aircraft performance. The prototypes blazed a trail of world records in 1965–67 including closed-circuit speeds, payload-to-height and rate of climb records. The impact of what NATO quickly christened "Foxbat" was unprecedented. Especially in the Pentagon, Western policymakers recognised that here was a combat aircraft that outclassed everything else, and urgent studies were put in hand for a new US Air Force fighter (F-15 Eagle) to counter it. By 1971 at least two pairs of reconnaissance aircraft were flying with impunity over Israel, too high and fast for Phantoms to catch, while others have made overflights deep into Iran. This version is different in many respects, the nose having cameras instead of a "Fox Fire" radar, and other sensors being carried under the large body. Both versions have twin outward-sloping vertical tails, single mainwheels and a flush canopy shaped for speed rather than pilot view. From the start the main development effort has been applied to the basic MiG-25 (so-called "Foxbat A") interceptor, which has been developed in structure, systems and armament since first entering service with the PVO. In 1975 the original AA-5 missiles were supplemented, and later replaced, by the monster AA-6 "Acrid", which is easily the biggest air/air missile in service in the world. The radar-homing version has a length of about 20ft 2in (6·15m) and effective range of 28 miles (45km); the infra-red missiles have a length of just over 19ft (5·8m) and range of some 12·5 miles (20km). Another major improvement since entering service is flight-refuelling capability, not yet fitted to all MiG-25 versions. The detailed inspection of an interceptor version landed at Hakodate AB, Japan, on 6 September 1976, showed that in service pilots are forbidden to use the limits of the available flight performance, presumably to avoid thermal fatigue of the airframe; it also showed this particular machine to have early "Fox Fire" radar comparable in basic technology with the AWG-10 Phantom radar (as would be expected). Radars in current production are unquestionably solid-state pulse-doppler types able to look down and track low-flying aircraft against ground clutter. Several MiG-25s, most of them MiG-25R models on ELINT missions, have been plotted by Western radars at Mach 2·8. It should be emphasized that at this speed the MiG-25 — and any other aircraft — flies in a straight line. The MiG-25 was not designed for air combat, and if it became involved in a dogfight its speed would — like most other aircraft — soon be subsonic. The MiG-25U trainer carries neither weapons nor sensors, but is needed to convert pilots to what is still, 18 years after design, a very advanced and demanding aircraft.

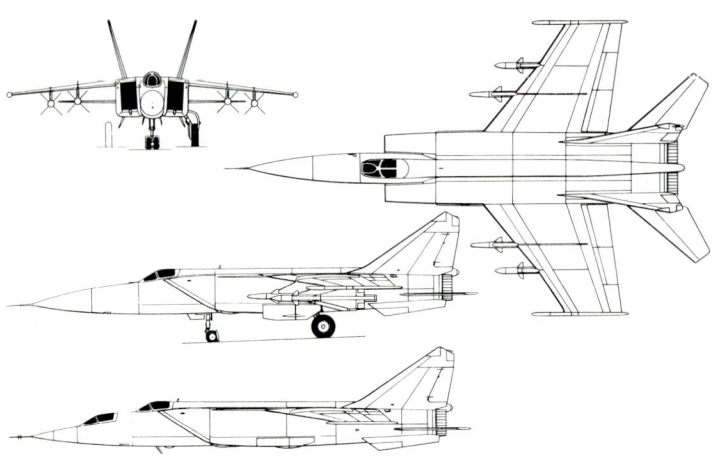

Above: Three-view of MiG-25 ("Foxbat A") with side view (bottom) of -25U.

Though today an 18-year-old design, the MiG-25 is still the world's fastest combat aircraft. This fighter version appears to be streaming fuel from near the outboard leading edges.

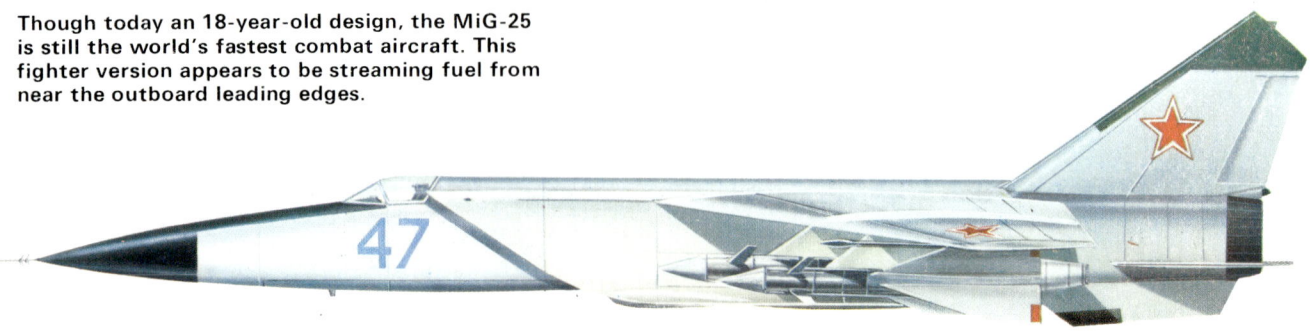

Above: Side elevation of MiG-25 interceptor, with 20ft AA-6 missiles.

Mikoyan/Gurevich MiG-27

MiG-27 ("Flogger D") and ("Flogger F")

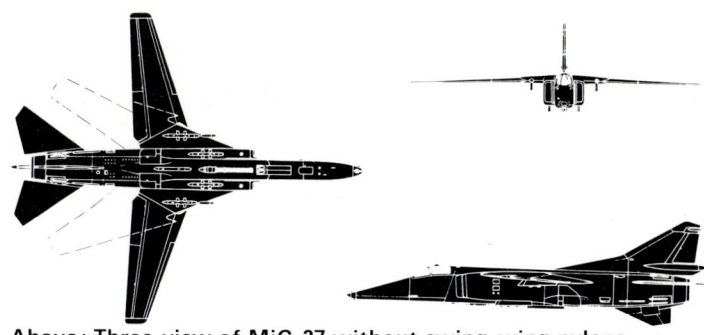

Origin: The design bureau named for Mikoyan and Gurevich, Soviet Union; no production outside the Soviet Union yet reported.

Type: Single-seat tactical attack, probably with reconnaissance capability.

Engine: One afterburning turbofan of unknown type (probably Tumansky, related to that of MiG-23) rated at about 13,500lb (6125kg) dry and 24,250lb (11,000kg) with maximum afterburner.

Dimensions: Similar to MiG-23 except fuselage nose is longer but pitot head shorter giving fractionally shorter overall length; height about 15ft (4·6m).

Weights (estimated): Empty 17,300lb (7850kg); maximum loaded 39,130lb (17,750kg).

Performance: Maximum speed at low level (clean) about Mach 1·2, (maximum weight) subsonic; maximum speed at high altitude (clean) about 1,055mph (1700km/h, Mach 1·6); take-off to 50ft (15m) at 34,600lb (15,700kg) 2,625ft (800m); service ceiling (clean) about 50,000ft (15,250m); combat radius with bombs and one tank (hi-lo-hi) 600 miles (960km); ferry range (wings spread with three tanks) over 2,000 miles (3200km).

Armament: One 23mm six-barrel Gatling-type gun in belly fairing; seven external pylons (centreline, fuselage flanks under inlet ducts, fixed wing gloves and swing-wings) for wide range of ordnance including guided missiles (AS-7 "Kerry") and tactical nuclear weapons to total weight of 4,200lb (1900kg). All ECM are internal and all pylons are thus usable by weapons or tanks. Those on the outer wings are not always fitted; they are piped for drop tanks, but do not pivot and thus may be loaded only when the wings remain unswept.

History: First flight, possibly about 1970; service delivery, before 1974.

Users: Egypt, Libya, Soviet Union (FA) and Syria (and almost certainly other countries in 1977).

Development: Derived from the same variable-geometry prototype flown by the MiG bureau at the 1967 Aviation Day, this aircraft was at first called "MiG-23B" in the West but is now known to have a different Soviet service designation that is almost certainly MiG-27. Bureau numbers are generally unknown for the MiG series; Mikoyan himself died in December 1970 and Gurevich in November 1976, and recent designs are known only by their service numbers. Compared with the MiG-23 this attack version carries heavier loads and is simpler and optimised for low-level operation. The airframe differs in having a shallower nose with a flat pointed profile housing mapping/terrain-following radar, laser ranger, doppler radar and radio altimeter, with good pilot view ahead and downward. The cockpit is heavily armoured. The engine is more powerful than that of the MiG-23 but is fed by fixed inlets and has a shorter and simpler nozzle. Main wheels are fitted with

Above: Three-view of MiG-27 without swing-wing pylons.

Above: An extremely revealing photograph showing one of the latest MiG-27 sub-types festooned with mission equipment.

large low-pressure tyres, and special provision is made for rough-field operation. Internal ECM equipment is extensive, and pods on the wing-glove leading edges appear to contain an opto-electronic seeker (left) and passive radar receiver (right). Internal fuel capacity is estimated at 1,183 Imp gallons (5380lit) including fuel in the fin; no provision for flight refuelling has been noted. The "Flogger F" has the engine installation and gun of the MiG-23, with variable inlets, and lacks the comprehensive MiG-27 avionics. These are thought to be development aircraft or an export version. Possible problems with the basic aircraft are suggested by reports that in a few months the Syrian AF has written off 13 out of 50 supplied.

continued on page 134▶

Below: The MiG variable-geometry attack aircraft—almost certainly MiG-27 in FA service—is an extremely refined and cost/effective aircraft. This picture shows an unusual sub-type with variable inlets.

Mikoyan/Gurevich MiG-27 "Flogger D"

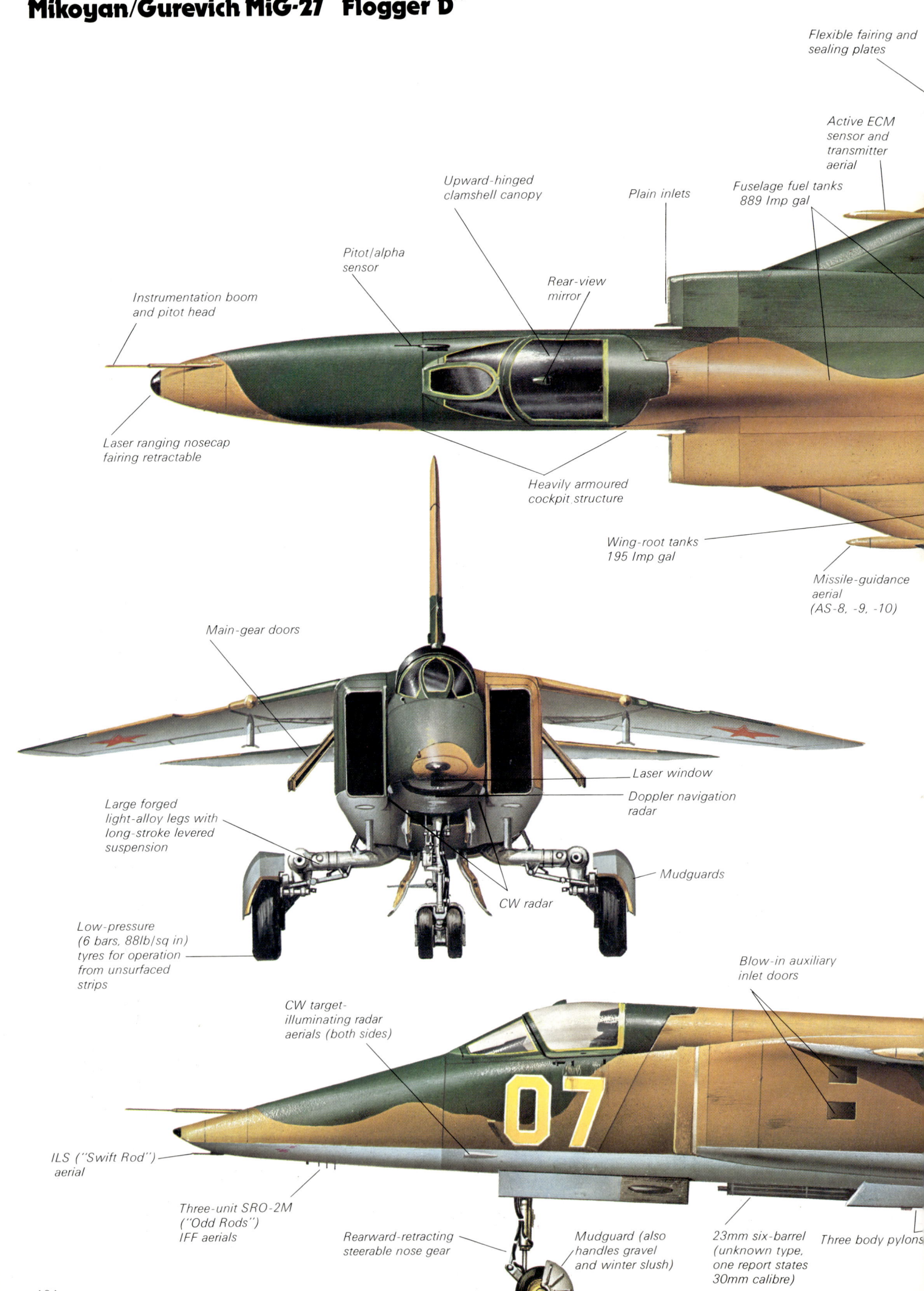

Flexible fairing and sealing plates

Active ECM sensor and transmitter aerial

Upward-hinged clamshell canopy

Plain inlets

Fuselage fuel tanks 889 Imp gal

Pitot/alpha sensor

Rear-view mirror

Instrumentation boom and pitot head

Laser ranging nosecap fairing retractable

Heavily armoured cockpit structure

Wing-root tanks 195 Imp gal

Missile-guidance aerial (AS-8, -9, -10)

Main-gear doors

Large forged light-alloy legs with long-stroke levered suspension

Laser window

Doppler navigation radar

Mudguards

CW radar

Low-pressure (6 bars, 88lb/sq in) tyres for operation from unsurfaced strips

Blow-in auxiliary inlet doors

CW target-illuminating radar aerials (both sides)

ILS ("Swift Rod") aerial

Three-unit SRO-2M ("Odd Rods") IFF aerials

Rearward-retracting steerable nose gear

Mudguard (also handles gravel and winter slush)

23mm six-barrel (unknown type, one report states 30mm calibre)

Three body pylons

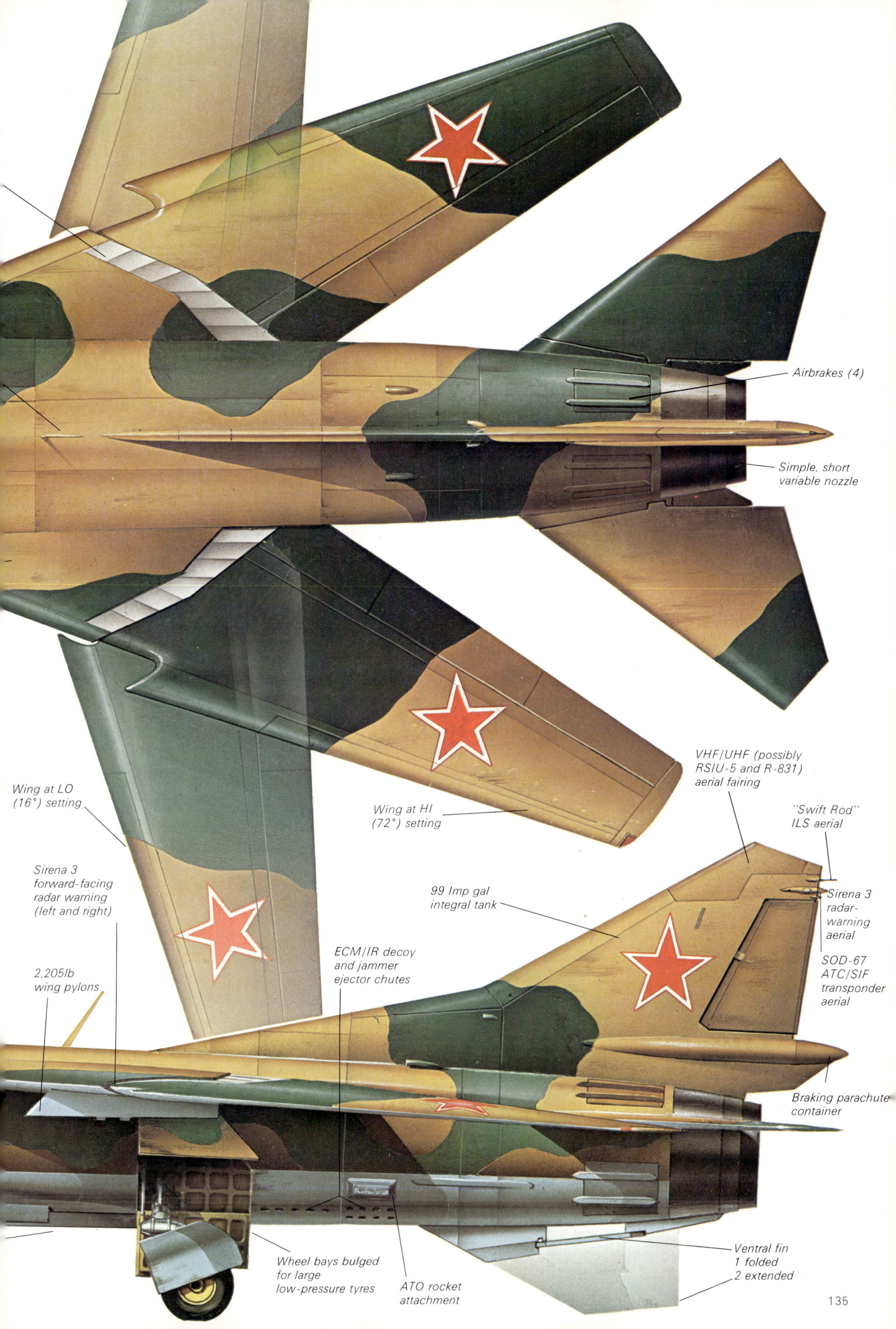

Airbrakes (4)

Simple, short
variable nozzle

Wing at LO
(16°) setting

Wing at HI
(72°) setting

VHF/UHF (possibly
RSIU-5 and R-831)
aerial fairing

"Swift Rod"
ILS aerial

Sirena 3
forward-facing
radar warning
(left and right)

Sirena 3
radar-
warning
aerial

99 Imp gal
integral tank

SOD-67
ATC/SIF
transponder
aerial

2,205lb
wing pylons

ECM/IR decoy
and jammer
ejector chutes

Braking parachute
container

Wheel bays bulged
for large
low-pressure tyres

ATO rocket
attachment

Ventral fin
1 folded
2 extended

Mil Mi-1

Mil Mi-1, WSK-Swidnik SM-1 and variants ("Hare")

Origin: The design bureau of Mikhail L.Mil, Soviet Union; later transferred entirely to WSK-Swidnik, Poland.
Type: Utility helicopter.
Engine: 575hp Ivchenko AI-26V (PZL-Kalisz AI-26V) seven-cylinder radial.
Dimensions: Main rotor diameter 46ft 11in (14·35m); length of fuselage (ignoring rotors) 39ft 4¾in (12·10m); height overall (rotors turning) 10ft 10in (3·31m).
Weights: Empty (typical) 4,145lb (1880kg); maximum loaded 5,291lb (2400 kg).
Performance: Maximum speed 105mph (170km/h); typical cruise 90mph (145km/h); range 360 miles (580km).
Armament: None.
History: First flight (prototype) 1950 (also reported as September 1948); service delivery 1951; final delivery (SM-2) about 1963.
Users: Albania, Bangladesh, Bulgaria, China, Cuba, Czechoslovakia, East Germany, Egypt, Iraq, Kampuchea, North Korea, Mongolia, Poland, Romania, Somalia, Soviet Union (various military arms, DOSAAF and Aeroflot), Sudan, Syria, Vietnam and possibly Yemen.

Development: Mikhail Mil began work on rotary-winged aircraft before 1930, but the Mi-1, his first production helicopter, was begun in 1948. Its design owed much to the Sikorsky S-51 and Bristol 171, with almost identical main rotor to the British machine and similar shafting and clutch. The basic Mi-1 seated four, two-by-two, in a comfortable cabin. The Mi-1T dispensed with one seat and carried extra operational equipment including full radio, blind-flying instruments and a winch, with provision for two 33 gal external fuel tanks. Well over 1,000 were built, including a proportion of dual-control Mi-1U trainers. In 1955 licence-production of the four-seat model began at WSK-Swidnik (now WSK-Zygmunta Pulaskiego, named

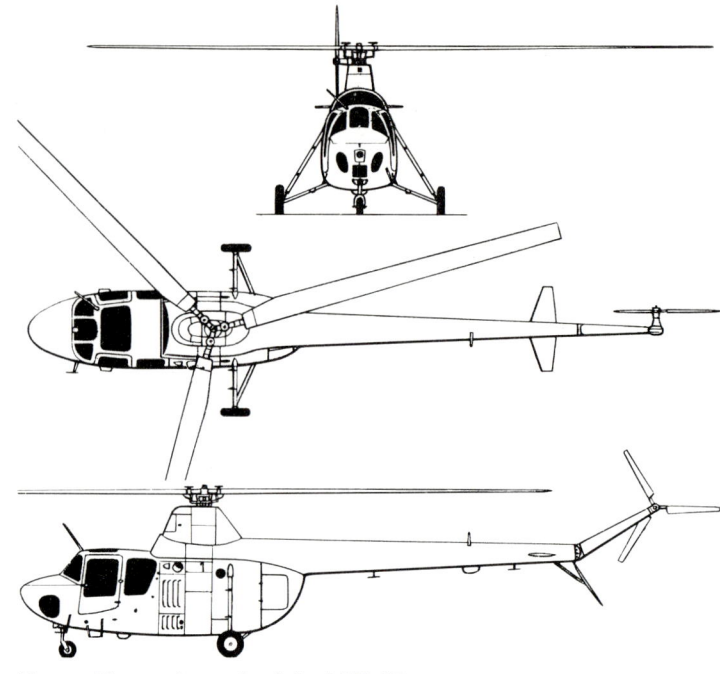

Above: Three-view of original Mi-1T.

after the famed pre-war Polish aircraft designer), where at least 1,000 were built in about ten years. Several new versions were developed at Swidnik, including the SM-2 five-seater.

Below: Military Mi-1 serving in the general utility role, with 33-gal (150-litre) auxiliary fuel tanks. Large numbers are still in use, whereas there are few contemporary Western helicopters.

Mil Mi-2

Mil Mi-2 (V-2) and Mi-2M ("Hoplite")

Origin: WSK-PZL-Swidnik, near Lublin, Poland; original design by Mil bureau, Soviet Union.
Type: Multi-role utility.
Engines: Two WSK-Rzeszów (Isotov licence) GTD-350P turboshafts, each with contingency rating of 431shp.
Dimensions: Diameter of three-blade main rotor 47ft 6¾in (14·50m); length overall (rotors turning) 57ft 2in (17·42m); height overall 12ft 3½in (3·75m).
Weights: Empty (2) 5,213lb (2365kg); maximum loaded 8,157lb (3700kg).
Performance: Max cruise 124mph (200km/h); range with max payload of 1,763lb (800kg) and 5 per cent reserve 105 miles (170km).
History: First flight (Mil) 1961, (WSK) November 1963, (2M) 1 July 1974.
Users: (Military) include Bulgaria, Czechoslovakia, Hungary, Poland, Romania, Soviet Union.

Development: The first production helicopter in the Soviet Union was the Mi-1, modelled along the lines of the S-51 and Sycamore and flown by Mikhail Mil's bureau in September 1948. During the 1950s it became evident, and confirmed by American and French development, that helicopters could be greatly improved with turbine engines. S. P. Isotov

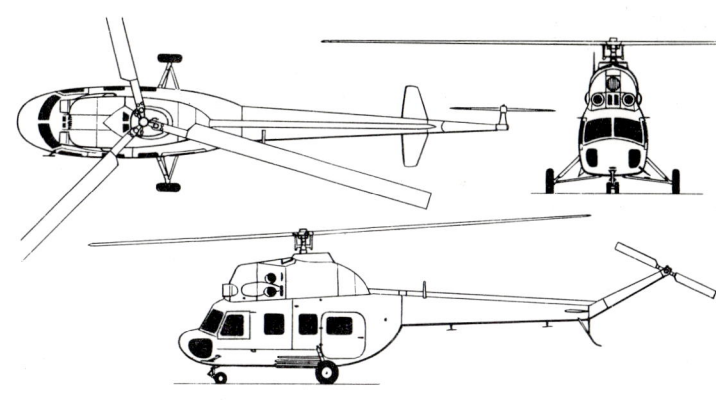

Three-view of WSK-Swidnik Mi-2 without special role equipment.

developed the GTD-350 engine and Mil used two of these in the far superior Mi-2. After initial development at the Mil bureau (Soviet designation V-2) this was transferred to Poland in 1964, after the first Swidnik-built example had flown. WSK-Swidnik has since delivered many hundreds, possibly one-third of them to military customers, and developed plastic rotor blades and the wide-body Mi-2M seating 10 passengers instead of eight. Role kits include two rocket or gun-pod pylons or four stretchers.

Above: A WSK-Swidnik Mi-2 of the Polish Air Force (skis often added round wheels).

Below: This WSK-Swidnik Mi-2 is armed with four AT-3 "Sagger" missiles, the chief helicopter missile of the Warsaw Pact.

Mil Mi-4

Mi-4 (sub-designations unknown) ("Hound")

Origin: The design bureau of Mikhail L. Mil, Soviet Union.
Type: Multi-role transport and ASW helicopter.
Engine: One 1,700hp Shvetsov ASh-82V 18-cylinder two-row radial.
Dimensions: Diameter of four-blade main rotor 68ft 11in (21·00m); length of fuselage (ignoring rotors) 55ft 1in (16·80m); height overall 17ft 0in (5·18m).
Weights: Empty (typical, not ASW) 11,650lb (5268kg); maximum loaded 17,200lb (7800kg).
Performance: Economical cruise 99mph (160km/h); range 250 miles (400km) with 8 passengers or equivalent, 155 miles (250km) with 11.
Armament: (Most) none; (army assault) fixed or movable machine gun or cannon in front of ventral gondola, optional weapon pylons for rocket or gun pods; (ASW) nose radar, towed MAD bird, sonobuoys, marker flares and other search gear, and torpedo or depth bombs.
History: First flight (prototype) 1951, (production) 1952; service delivery 1953; final delivery after 1961.
Users: (Military) Afghanistan, Albania, Algeria, Bulgaria, China, Cuba, Czechoslovakia, Egypt, Finland, E Germany, Hungary, India, Indonesia, Iraq, Jugoslavia, Kampuchea, N Korea, Mali, Mongolia, Poland, Romania, Somalia, Soviet Union, Syria, Vietnam, Yemen.

Development: Produced in a frantic·hurry on Stalin's direct order, this helicopter looked very like a Sikorsky S-55 when it appeared, but was gradually recognised in the West as considerably bigger and more capable

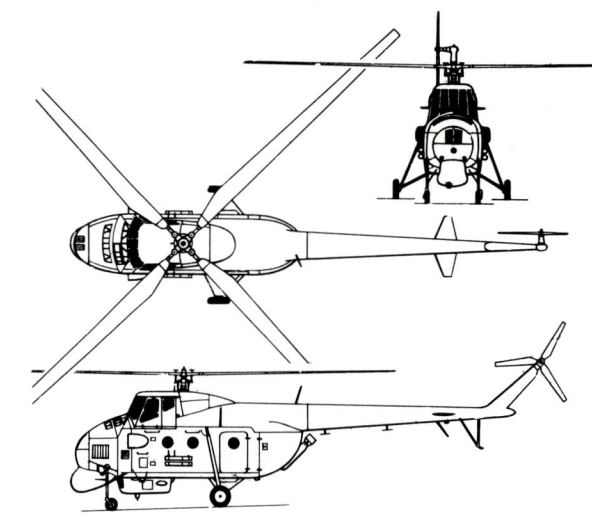

Three-view of Mi-4 ASW version (Soviet designation unknown).

even than the S-58. Among its many versions are assault, ambulance and naval ASW variants, the normal transports having large rear doors for artillery, missiles and small vehicles, and seats for 14 equipped troops. Several thousand were built, and nearly all remain in service, except that some of those exported (to Cuba and Egypt, especially) are no longer operational.

Right: Basic transport Mi-4, Czech Air Force.

Below: An impressive "assault"—but why should each of these Mi-4 "Hound" helicopters have delivered only six men?

Mil Mi-6

Mi-6 ("Hook")

Origin: The design bureau of Mikhail L.Mil, Soviet Union.
Type: Heavy transport helicopter.
Engines: Two 5,500shp Soloviev D-25V (TV-2BM) single-shaft free-turbine engines geared to common R-7 gearbox.
Dimensions: Main rotor diameter 114ft 10in (35·00m); length overall, rotors turning 136ft 11½in (41·74m); fuselage length 108ft 10½in (33·18m); height 32ft 4in (9·86m).
Weights: Empty 60,055lb (27,240kg); maximum loaded (limit for VTO) 93,700lb (42,500kg).
Performance: Maximum speed at max weight 186mph (300km/h); cruising speed 155mph (250km/h); service ceiling 14,750ft (4500m); range with 13,228lb (6000kg) payload 404 miles (650km); max ferry range 900 miles (1450km).
Armament: Most Mi-6 helicopters used for tactical roles have a gun, probably of 13·2mm calibre, manually aimed from the nose compartment.
History: First flight probably early 1957; service delivery 1959.
Users: Algeria, Bulgaria, Egypt, Ethiopia, Iraq, Libya, Peru, Soviet Union (several arms including V-TA and also Aeroflot), Syria and Vietnam.

Development: When this monster helicopter was designed in 1954–56 it was by far the largest in the world, and even today its dynamic components of engines, gearbox, rotors and drive shafts have no rival. In its early days this helicopter set many world records, including one for sheer circuit speed at over 211mph (340km/h). In 1959–72 a total production run of at least 500 was built for various general transport, utility, firefighting and flying-crane duties, the last two sub-types not being fitted with the large fixed wings (span 50ft 2½in, 15·30m) which in other versions bear part of the lift in cruising flight and thus enable higher speeds to be attained. Surprisingly, the twin nosewheels and large low-pressure main wheels do not retract. Normally flown by a crew of no fewer than five, the Mi-6 seats 65 armed troops or can alternatively carry 41 stretcher (litter) patients and two attendants, or a wide range of bulky loads, including vehicles, loaded through rear clamshell doors. In exercises fleets of these impressive aircraft have airlifted many kinds of weapons, including Frog rockets on their PT-76 tracked chassis, as well as large radars and heavy artillery. All Soviet APCs (armoured personnel carriers), armoured cars and light MICVs (mechanised infantry combat vehicles) can be carried.

continued on page 140▶

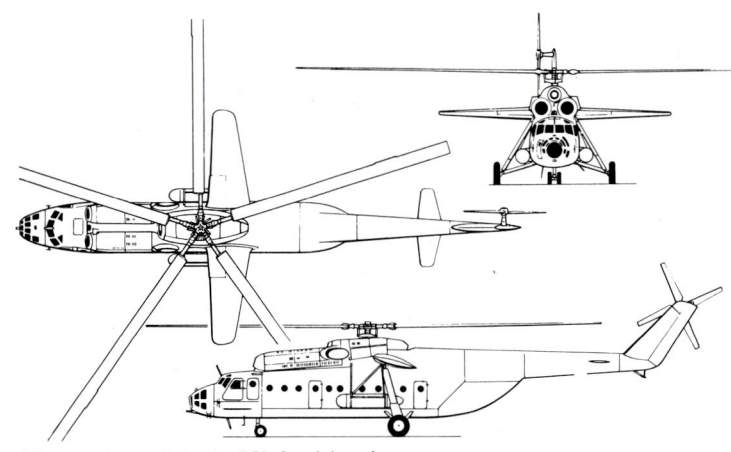

Three-view of basic Mi-6 with wings.

Above: Despite its size and fixed landing gear the Mi-6 is a very fast helicopter. Two can carry the payload of an An-12.

Below: A civil Mi-6 fitted with wings and the external long-range tanks, 164 gal (745 litres) on left and 150 gal on right.

Mil Mi-6 "Hook"

Trimming tailplane, worked by irreversible screwjack

Geared cooling fan for oil-system radiator

Low pressure oleo strut

Wings are removed for operation in flying-crane role

High pressure oleo strut

Hydraulically powered controls

Door for pilots

Door for navigator, flight engineer and radio operator

50

Optically flat sighting panel

Steerable twin-wheel nose gear

External tanks for 7,695lb fuel (35% of total)

Fixed (ground-adjustable) tab

Electro-thermal rubber-potted anti-icing strip

Hydraulically actuated engine cowls serve as inspection and maintenance platforms

Electrically anti-iced glass sandwich

All metal rotor blades built up on tapered steel-tube spar

Wing has high angle of attack

Tail bumper

Full-section hydraulically powered doors and loading ramp

Passenger doors

Mil Mi-8

Mi-8, Mi-8T ("Hip", "Haze")

Origin: The design bureau named for Mikhail Mil, Soviet Union.
Type: General utility helicopter for internal loads and externally mounted weapons; "Haze", ASW.
Engines: Two 1,500shp Isotov TV2-117A single-shaft free-turbine engines driving common VR-8A gearbox.
Dimensions: Main rotor diameter 69ft $10\frac{1}{2}$in (21·29m); overall length, rotors turning, 82ft $9\frac{3}{4}$in (25·24m); fuselage length 60ft $0\frac{3}{4}$in (18·31m); height 18ft $6\frac{1}{2}$in (5·65m).
Weights: Empty (-8T) 15,026lb (6816kg); maximum loaded (all) 26,455lb (12,000kg) (heavier weights for non-VTO operation).
Performance: Maximum speed 161mph (260km/h); service ceiling 14,760ft (4500m); range (-8T, full payload, 5 per cent reserve at 3,280ft) 298 miles (480km).
Armament: Optional fitting for external pylons for up to eight stores carried outboard of fuel tanks (always fitted); typical loads eight pods of 57mm rockets, or mix of gun pods and anti-tank missiles (Mi-8 not normally used in anti-tank role).
History: First flight 1960 or earlier; service delivery of military versions, before 1967.
Users: Afghanistan, Bangladesh, Czechoslovakia, Egypt, Ethiopia, Finland, E Germany, Hungary, India, Iraq, Jugoslavia, N Korea, Libya, Pakistan, Peru, Poland, Romania, Somalia, Soviet Union, S Yemen, Sudan, Syria, Vietnam.

Development: Originally powered by a single 2,700shp Soloviev engine, the Mi-8 soon appeared with its present engines and in 1964 added a fifth blade to its main rotor. It has since been the chief general utility helicopter of the Warsaw Pact powers and many other nations. By mid-1974 it was announced that more than 1,000 had been built, the majority for military purposes and with about 300 having been exported. Since then the Mi-8 has continued in production. The basic version is a passenger and troop carrier normally furnished with quickly removable seats for 28 in the main cabin. The -8T is the utility version without furnishing and with circular windows, weapon pylons, cargo rings, a winch/pulley block system for loading and optional electric hoist by the front doorway. All versions have

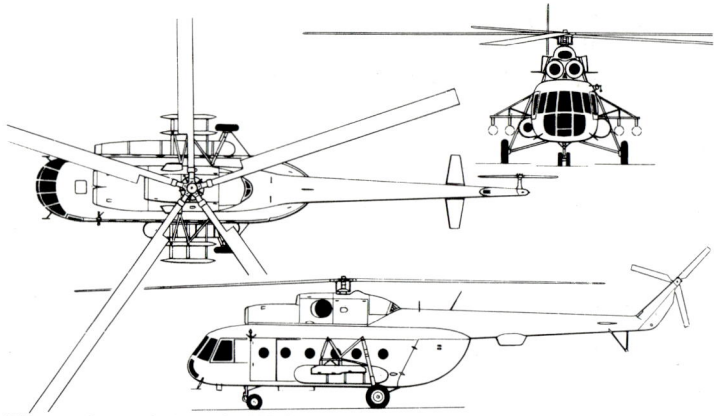

Three-view of assault Mi-8 with weapon pylons and tailboom radar.

large rear clamshell doors (the passenger version having airstairs incorporated) through which a BRDM and other small vehicles can be loaded. "Haze" has AS radar, MAD bird and weapons.

Above: "Haze" is the NATO name for this anti-submarine version of the Mi-8, first seen in 1976. Features include retractable land wheels, amphibious boat hull with rear sponsons, large search radar and towed MAD bird (seen stowed against rear of fuselage pod). Bureau designation is believed to be Mi-14.

An Mi-8 serving with the Egyptian Air Force (no radar or weapons).

Below: A civil Mi-8 serving with Aeroflot. There is also a passenger version with large square windows, and some have spats.

Mil Mi-10

Mi-10 (V-10) and Mi-10K (V-10K) ("Harke")

Origin: The design bureau named for Mikhail Mil, Soviet Union.
Type: Heavy-lift crane helicopter.
Engines: Two 5,500shp Soloviev D-25V free-turbine engines driving common R-7 gearbox (late-model Mi-10K believed to have 6,500shp D-25VF engines).
Dimensions: Main rotor diameter 114ft 10in (35·00m); overall length, rotors turning, 137ft 5½in (41·90m); fuselage length 107ft 9¾in (32·86m); height (Mi-10) 32ft 2in (9·80m), (Mi-10K) 25ft 7in (7·80m).
Weights: Empty (-10) 60,185lb (27,300kg), (-10K) 54,410lb (24,680kg); maximum loaded (-10) 96,340lb (43,700kg), (-10K) 83,776lb (38,000kg) (-10K with VF engines, unknown heavier weight).
Performance: Maximum speed at max weight (both) about 124mph (200km/h), cruising speed (-10, max wt) 112mph (180km/h), (-10K, max wt) 124mph (200km/h), (-10K, unladen) 155mph (250km/h); range (-10 with 26,455lb/12,000kg slung load) 155 miles (250km), (-10K ferry without load) 494 miles (795km).
Armament: None seen.
History: First flight (-10) 1960, (-10K) probably 1965; service delivery of military -10 probably 1962.
Users: Soviet Union (Aeroflot and several branches of armed forces).

Development: These crane-type helicopters use the dynamic parts developed for the Mi-6. The original Mi-10 was designed, like the much smaller Sikorsky Skycrane (CH-54 Tarhe) with tall landing legs so that it can straddle its load. The slim fuselage has the upper section similar to that of the Mi-6, but with no wings. The flight deck is arranged for two pilots and a flight engineer, and TV cameras under the nose and tail are used to watch the slung load and the touch-down of the eight landing wheels. The main cabin can be used for freight but is usually fitted with 14 tip-up seats along each side (28 in all). The Mi-10 can be landed on to its load, taxi over it or pick it up whilst hovering, the maximum size of load being 65ft 7in (20·0m) long and 32ft 9½in (10·0m) wide. Maximum slung load is 17,635lb (8000kg) but if a hydraulically gripped platform is used it can be 33,070lb (15,000kg). The Mi-10K has shorter landing gears, slimmer tailfin and a different flight deck with one pilot facing forward and the second facing down and aft in a ventral gondola (there is no engineer). The K can carry a slung load as heavy as 30,865lb (14,000kg).
Note: the entry "Origin" above, as in the description of all later Mil helicopters, reflects the fact that Mil himself died in early 1970. The new head of the bureau is Marat N. Tishchenko.

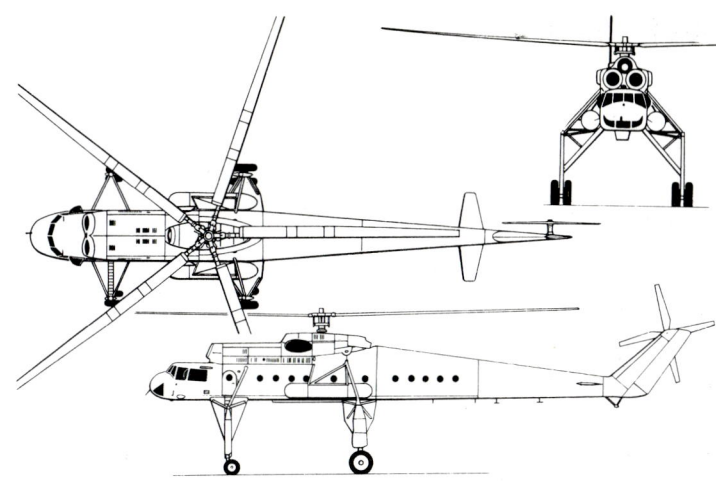

Above: Three-view of the original Mi-10 version.

Above: The Mi-10K is by far the most capable flying-crane (heavy lift) helicopter in the world, except for the seldom-seen V-12. This close-up shows the small landing wheels and the useful inbuilt airstairs; the extra pilot's door is unusual.

Below: The original long-legged version of Mi-10 is pictured here. The lofty landing gears enable it to straddle a load such as a bus or prefabricated building.

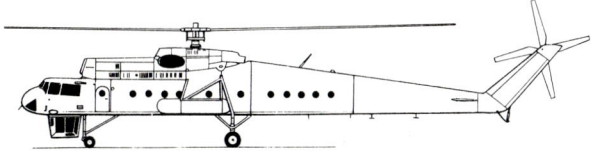

Above: Side elevation of Mi-10K (also code-named "Harke").

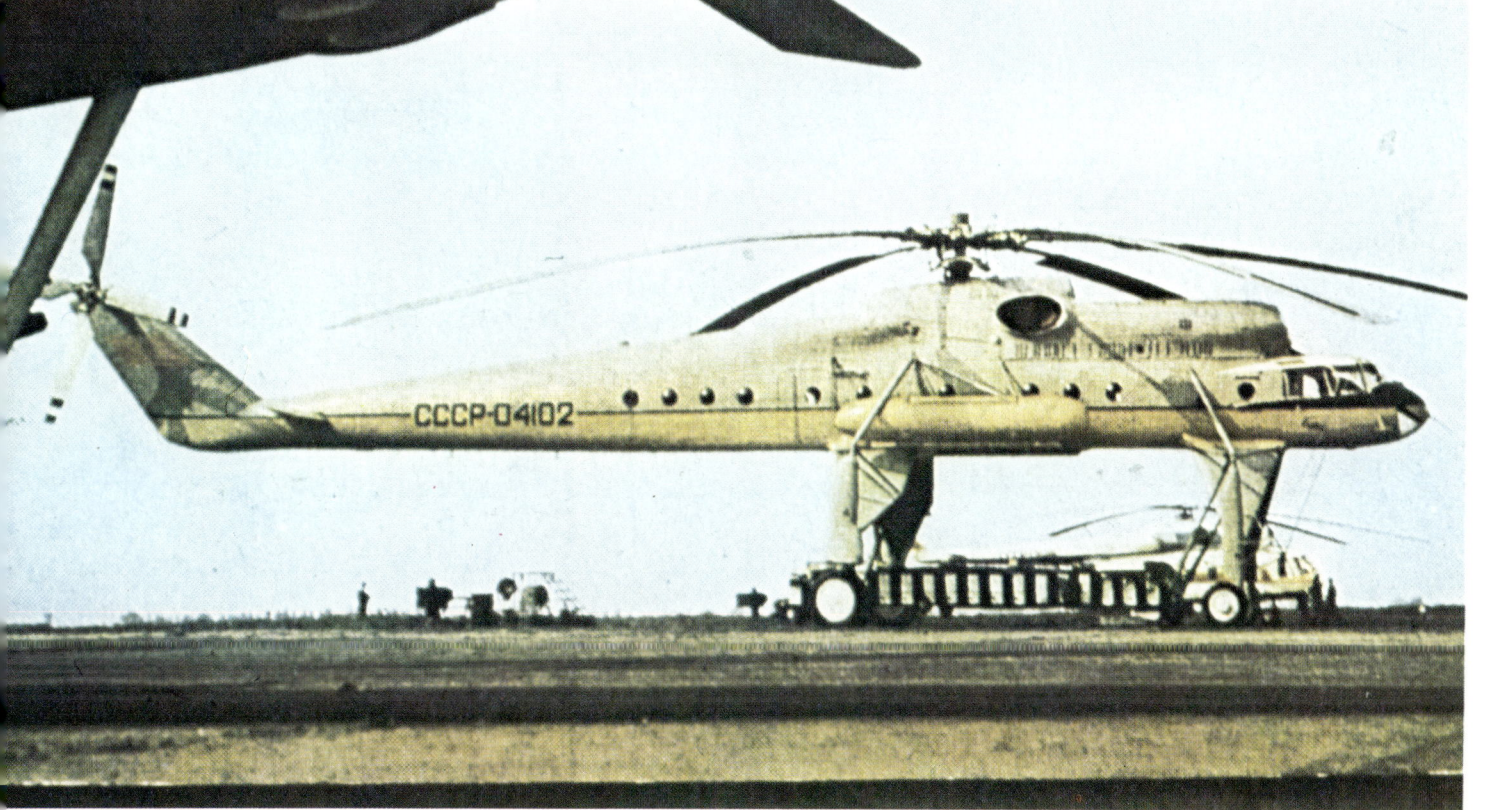

Mil Mi-12

V-12 (Mi-12) ("Homer")

Origin: The design bureau named for Mikhail Mil, Soviet Union.
Type: Large transport helicopter.
Engines: Four 6,500shp Soloviev D-25VF free-turbine engines mounted in two pairs, each geared to a common R-7 gearbox and driving one Mi-6 rotor.
Dimensions: Main rotor diameter (each) 114ft 10in (35·00m); length overall, rotors turning 130ft (39·62m); width overall, rotors turning 219ft 10in (67·00m); height 41ft 0in (12·50m).
Weights: Empty (estimated) 140,000lb (63,500kg); maximum loaded (VTO) 231,500lb (105,000kg).
Performance: Maximum speed 161mph (260km/h); cruising speed 150mph (240km/h); range with 78,000lb (35,400kg) payload 311 miles (500km).
Armament: None seen.
History: First flight (prototype) probably late 1968; service delivery not known.
User: Soviet Union (Aeroflot and V-TA).

Development: Conceived as the VTOL partner to the Antonov An-22 as the chief air freight vehicles of the Soviet Union, the V-12 is by far the largest helicopter in the world. It uses two complete Mi-6 main rotors and drive systems, uprated to late Mi-10K power, carried on the ends of a slender reverse-taper strut-braced high wing. Cross-shafts inside the wing enable flight to be maintained after loss of any engine, or even one complete left or right twin-engine package. There is a conventional aeroplane tail with tabbed rudder and elevators, but primary control is exercised by the left and right opposite-handed rotors. The gigantic fuselage has two flight decks, the main one for the pilots, engineer and electrician (systems operator) and the upper one having tandem seats for the navigator and radio operator. The cavernous cargo hold has full-section rear doors for vehicles or other bulky loads, with electric travelling crane handling systems capable of a direct lift of 22,050lb (10,000kg). Seats can be folded down around the walls for about 50 work-crew accompanying cargo. Like the An-22 a mapping and navigation radar is fitted, and provision is made for all-weather operation. Since record-breaking flights by the prototype, when a payload of 88,636lb (40,205kg) was carried, little has been heard of the V-12 but it is reported to have been in service since 1973.

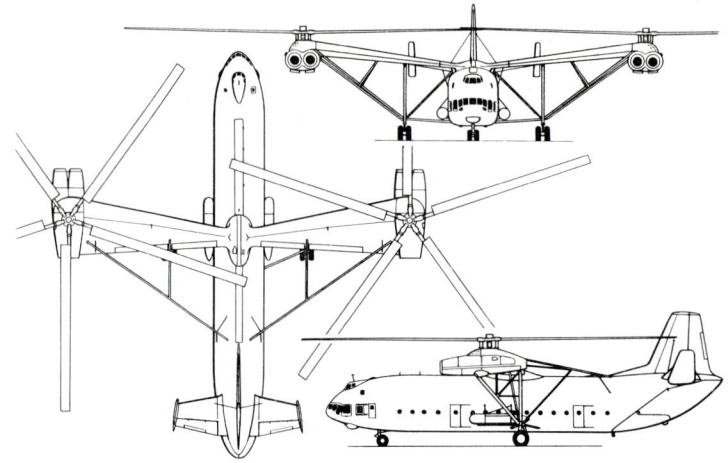

Above: Three-view of Mi-12.

Above: N-833 (in the Cyrillic alphabet N looks like H) was the V-12 development aircraft demonstrated at Paris in 1971.

Below: Undeniably impressive, and a working answer to severe problems, the V-12 has nevertheless been absent from Soviet publicity since this example visited the West in 1971.

Mil Mi-24

Mi-24 versions with NATO names ("Hind A") to ("Hind D")

Origin: The design bureau named for Mikhail Mil, Soviet Union.
Type: Tactical multi-role helicopter; (Hind D) gunship.
Engines: Almost certainly two 1,500shp Isotov TV2-117A free-turbine turboshafts.
Dimensions: (Estimated) diameter of five-blade main rotor 55ft 9in (17m); length overall (ignoring rotors) 55ft 9in (17m); height overall 14ft (4·25m).
Weights: (Estimated) empty 14,300lb (6500kg); maximum loaded 25,400lb (11,500kg).
Performance: Maximum speed 170mph (275km/h); general performance, higher than Mi-8.
Armament: (Hind A) usually one 12·7mm gun aimed from nose; two stub wings providing rails for four guided anti-tank missiles and four other stores (bombs, missiles, rocket or gun pods). (Hind B) two stub wings of different type with four weapon pylons; (Hind D) see overleaf.
History: First flight, before 1972; service delivery, before 1974.
Users: Soviet Union (probably with other Warsaw Pact forces, but not reported by early 1978).

Development: Few details are yet known of this attractive-looking battle-field helicopter, though in 1974 many were seen in service in East Germany and two versions were disclosed to the West in photographs. It appears to be based on the Mi-8, though the engines look smaller and the main rotor has blades of considerably shorter length but increased chord. The nose-wheel-type landing gear is fully retractable, and the cabin is large enough

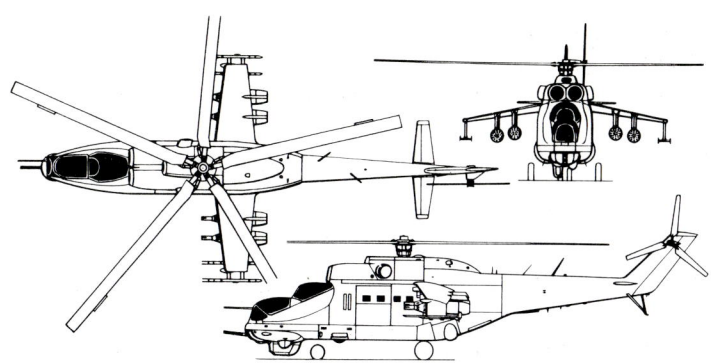

Above: "Hind D", the gunship first seen in May 1977 with new sensors and four-barrel gun.

for a crew of two and eight troops. The exterior is well streamlined, broken only by avionic aerials and the prominent weapon stub-wings. The Mi-24 is much larger than the British Lynx, yet smaller than the Mi-8. One reason may be that it is the smallest machine capable of using the well-tried Mi-8 dynamic components, and in the anti-tank role the surplus payload could be used for spare missiles or infantry teams that could be dropped and then recovered later. Maximum slung load is estimated at 8,000lb (3630kg).

continued on page 146▶

Above: "Hind A" sub-type (landing gear extended).

Below: Mi-24 of the "Hind A" sub-type, serving with the GSFG (Group of Soviet Forces in Germany).

Mil (Mi-24?) "Hind D"

Rotating beacon

VHF/ADF

Powered slab tailplane

Bulletproof windscreens with wipers

Laser ranger

UB-32 pod 32 57mm S-5 rockets

Twin launcher for AT-2 "Swatter" anti-tank missiles

Raised cockpit for pilot

Weapon operator

Kick-steps

Low-speed precision air-data boom

High-speed pitot tube

Sensor installation (FLIR, LLTV)

Thick titanium armour skin

Steerable twin-wheel nose gear (semi-exposed when retracted)

Sliding cabin door

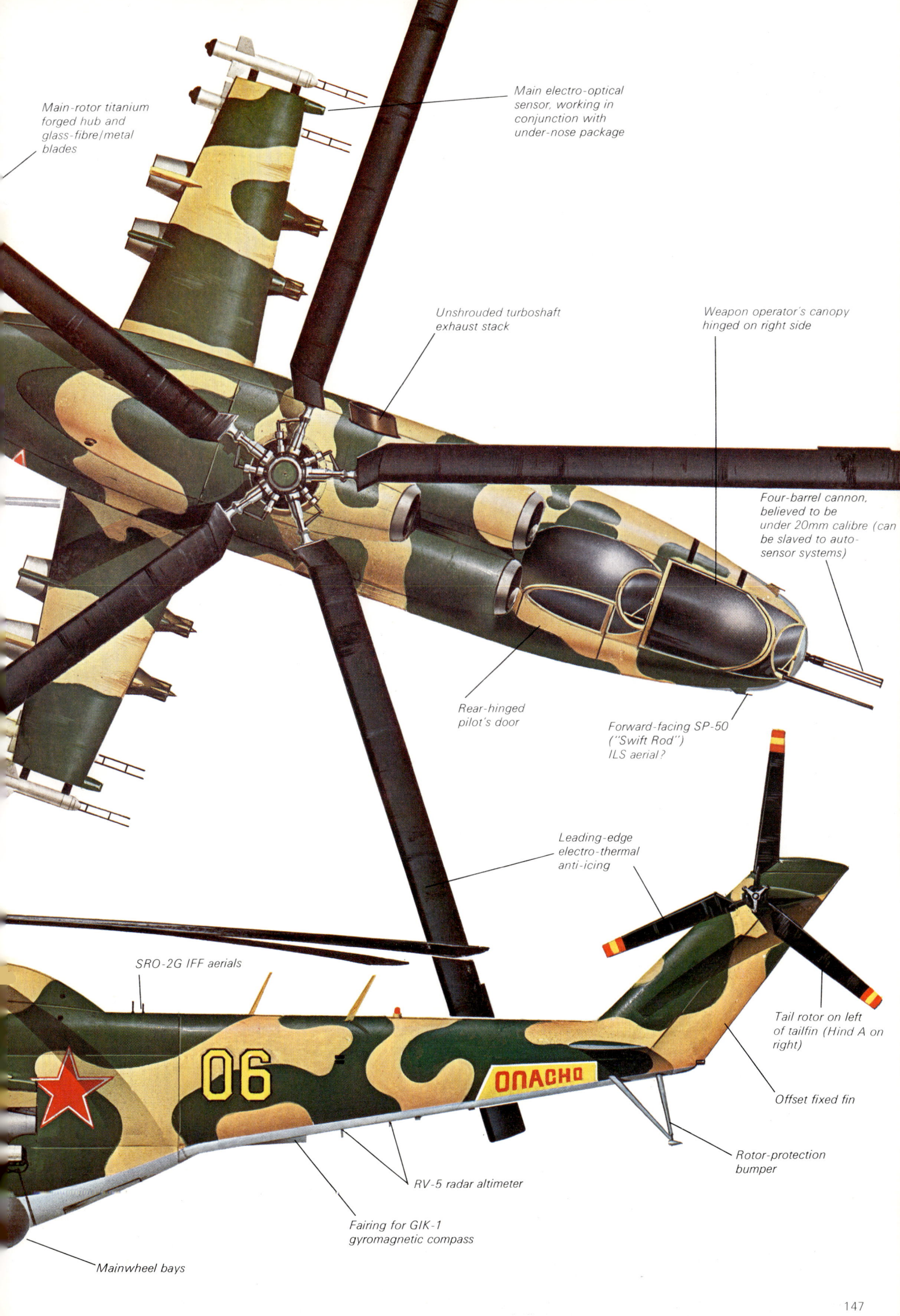

Main-rotor titanium
forged hub and
glass-fibre/metal
blades

Main electro-optical
sensor, working in
conjunction with
under-nose package

Unshrouded turboshaft
exhaust stack

Weapon operator's canopy
hinged on right side

Four-barrel cannon,
believed to be
under 20mm calibre (can
be slaved to auto-
sensor systems)

Rear-hinged
pilot's door

Forward-facing SP-50
("Swift Rod")
ILS aerial?

Leading-edge
electro-thermal
anti-icing

Tail rotor on left
of tailfin (Hind A on
right)

Offset fixed fin

Rotor-protection
bumper

SRO-2G IFF aerials

06

ОПАСНО

RV-5 radar altimeter

Fairing for GIK-1
gyromagnetic compass

Mainwheel bays

Myasishchev M-4

M-4 three versions, known to West as ("Bison A, B and C")

Origin: The design bureau of Vladimir M. Myasishchev, Soviet Union.
Type: (A) heavy bomber; (B) strategic reconnaissance and ECM; (C) multi-role reconnaissance bomber.
Engines: (A) four 19,180lb (8700kg) Mikulin AM-3D single-shaft turbojets; (B and C) four 28,660lb (13,000kg) Soloviev D-15 two-shaft turbojets.
Dimensions: (A) estimated, span 165ft 7½in (50·48m); length 154ft 10in (47·2m); height 46ft (14·1m).
Weights: Estimated, empty (A) 154,000lb (70,000kg); (B, C) 176,400lb (80,000kg); maximum loaded (A) 352,740lb (160,000kg); (B, C) 375,000lb (170,000kg).
Performance: (Estimated) maximum speed (all) 560mph (900km/h); service ceiling (A) 42,650ft (13,000m); (B, C) 49,200ft (15,000m); range (all) 6,835 miles (11,000km) with 9,920lb (4500kg) of bombs or electronic equipment.
Armament: (A) ten 23mm NR-23 cannon in manned turret in tail and four remotely controlled turrets above and below front and rear fuselage (two guns in each turret); internal bomb bays in tandem for at least 22,050lb (10,000kg) stores; (B, C) six 23mm cannon in two forward turrets and tail turret; internal bay for at least 10,000lb (4500kg) stores. In many versions a single 23mm gun is fixed on the right side of the nose, firing ahead.
History: First flight, probably 1953; service delivery, probably 1955; final delivery, probably about 1958.
User: Soviet Union (DDA, AV-MF).

Development: A single example of this large aircraft took part in the 1954 May Day parade fly past over Moscow, its size being gauged from the escorting MiG fighters. It was expected to appear in large numbers, but

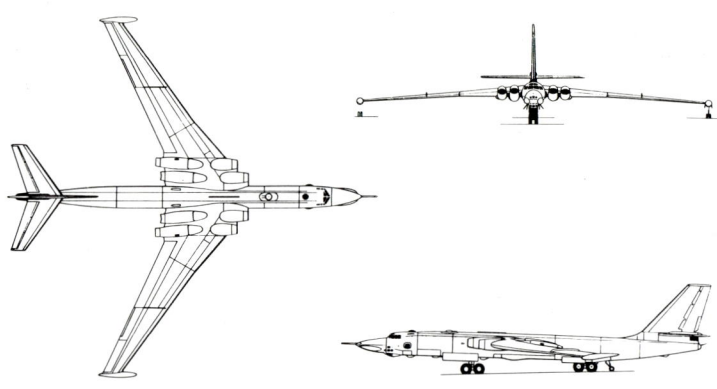

Above: Three-view of M-4 of "Bison C" sub-type.

little was heard of it for years. In fact a useful run of about 150 had been delivered, at first being used as bombers ("Bison A"). In 1959 a re-engined aircraft, called Type 201-M, set up world records by lifting a payload of 10,000kg (22,046lb) to 50,253ft (15,317m) and the formidable weight of 55,220kg (121,480lb) to 2000m (6,561ft). By this time the M-4 bombers were being likewise fitted with more powerful engines, and their role changed from bomber to long-range oversea reconnaissance, ECM and, in some cases, flight-refuelling tanker. All aircraft were given large fixed FR probes, the rear turrets were removed and a vast amount of special reconnaissance equipment fitted, with from five to 17 aerials visible all over the aircraft. In the "Bison C" sub-type a large search radar fills the entire nose, lengthening the nose by about 6ft and changing its shape. Since 1967 these now obsolescent aircraft have been frequently encountered on probing missions far over the Arctic, Atlantic, Pacific and elsewhere, at both high and low levels, the C-model having been seen most frequently.

Left: An M-4 of the sub-type called "Bison B" by NATO, photographed by an RAF Lightning over solid overcast. Most of these aircraft have been in service over 20 years.

Below: A frame from a Soviet film showing the British type of probe/drogue refuelling system used by the Soviet air forces. The receiver is an M-4 of the "Bison C" type.

Sukhoi Su-7

Su-7B, -7BM, -7BMK and -7U ("Fitter") 7U ("Moujik")

Origin: The design bureau of Pavel A. Sukhoi, Soviet Union.
Type: Single-seat close-support and interdiction; (-7U) dual-control trainer.
Engine: One Lyulka AL-7F turbojet rated at 15,430lb (7000kg) dry or 22,046lb (10,000kg) with maximum afterburner.
Dimensions: Span 29ft 3½in (8·93m), length (all, incl probe) 57ft (17·37m); height (all) 15ft 5in (4·70m).
Weights: Empty (typical -7) 19,000lb (8620kg), maximum loaded (typical -7) 30,000lb (13,610kg).
Performance: Maximum speed, clean, at altitude, (all) 1,055mph (1700km/h, Mach 1·6), initial climb (-7BM) 29,000ft (9120m)/min; service ceiling (-7BM) 49,700ft (15,150m); range with twin drop tanks (all) 900 miles (1450km).
Armament: (-7) two 30mm NR-30 cannon, each with 70 rounds, in wing roots; four wing pylons, inners rated at 1,653lb (750kg) and outers at 1,102lb (500kg), but when two tanks are carried on fuselage pylons total external weapon load is reduced to 2,205lb (1000kg).
History: First flight (-7 prototype) not later than 1955; service delivery (-7B) 1959.
Users: (-7) Afghanistan, Algeria, Czechoslovakia, Egypt, Hungary, India, Iraq, N Korea, Poland, Romania, Soviet Union, Syria, Vietnam.

Development: Two of the wealth of previously unknown Soviet aircraft revealed at the 1956 Aviation Day at Tushino were large Sukhoi fighters, one with a swept wing (called "Fitter" by NATO) and the other a tailed delta (called "Fishpot"). Both were refined into operational types, losing some of their commonality in the process. The delta entered service as the Su-9 and -11, described separately. The highly-swept Su-7 was likewise built in very large numbers, optimised not for air superiority but for ground attack. As such it has found a worldwide market, and despite severe shortcomings has been exported in numbers which exceed 700. All Sukhoi combat aircraft have been made within the Soviet Union. The good points of the Su-7 family are robust structure, reasonable reliability and low cost; drawbacks are vulnerability to small-calibre fire and the impossibility of getting adequate field length, weapon load and radius of action all together. There are many variants. The original -7B was quickly superseded by the more powerful -7BM, with twin ribbon tail chutes. The most common export model is the -7BMK with low-pressure tyres and other changes to improve behaviour from short unpaved strips. The -7U is the tandem dual trainer. Since 1964 many BMK have been seen with take-off rockets and four wing pylons.

continued on page 150▶

Above: Flame envelops the leading edge as an Su-7B fires its cannon.

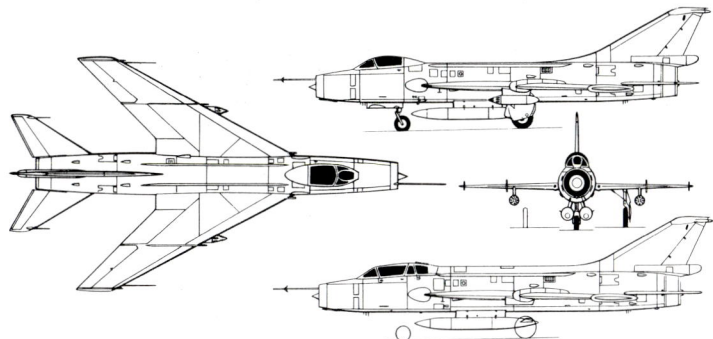

Above: Three-view of Su-7BMK, with side view (bottom) of -7U "Moujik".

Above: Well-worn Su-7B of Indian Air Force.

The -7BM has a number of detail differences, and in late sub-types has a low-pressure nosewheel tyre for soft fields, needing bulged doors (BMK)

Above: Su-7BM of Egyptian AF.

Above: Su-7B (early sub-type) of Czech Air Force.

Sukhoi Su-7BMK "Fitter A"

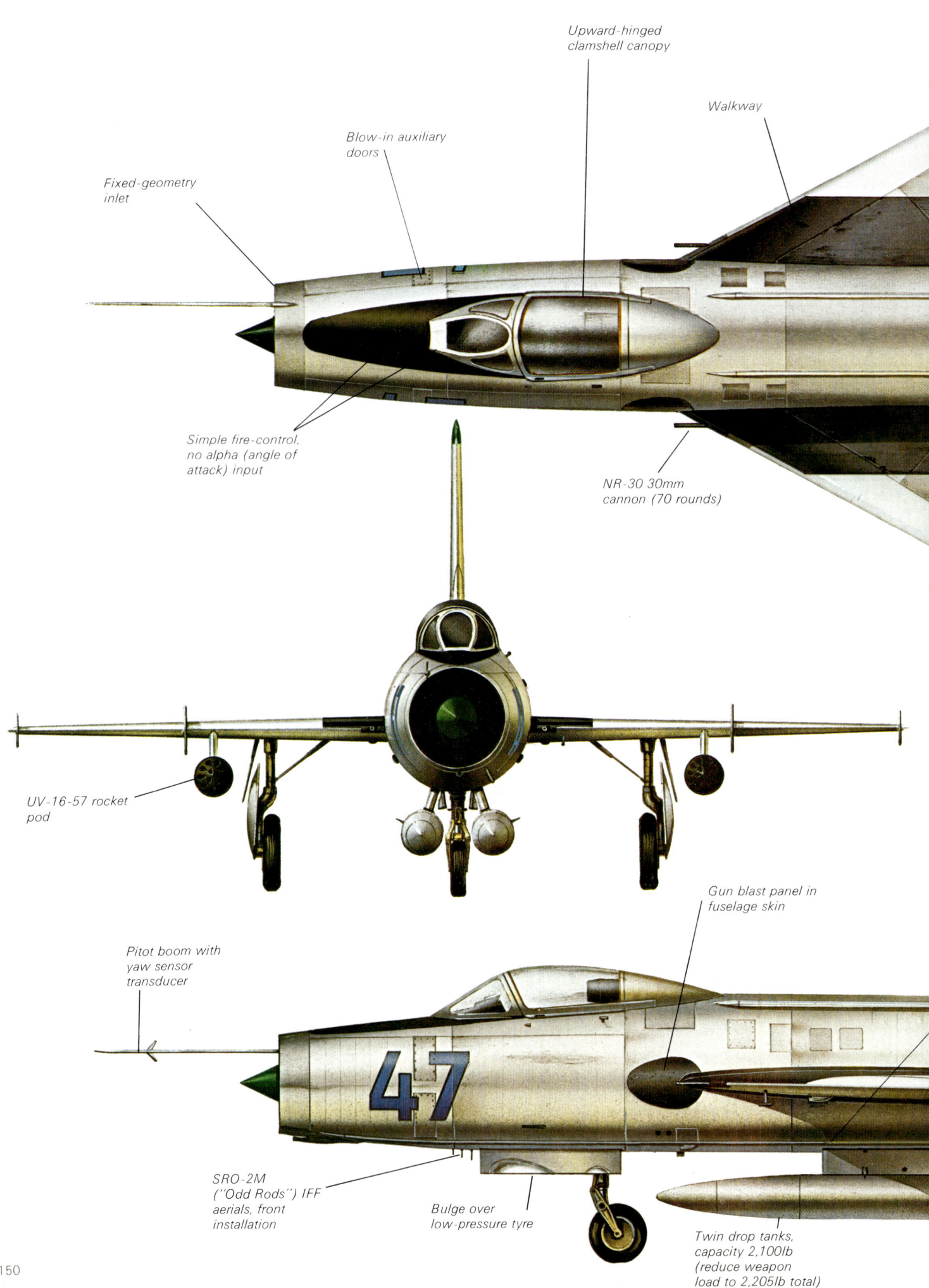

Fixed-geometry inlet

Blow-in auxiliary doors

Upward-hinged clamshell canopy

Walkway

Simple fire-control, no alpha (angle of attack) input

NR-30 30mm cannon (70 rounds)

UV-16-57 rocket pod

Gun blast panel in fuselage skin

Pitot boom with yaw sensor transducer

SRO-2M ("Odd Rods") IFF aerials, front installation

Bulge over low-pressure tyre

Twin drop tanks, capacity 2,100lb (reduce weapon load to 2,205lb total)

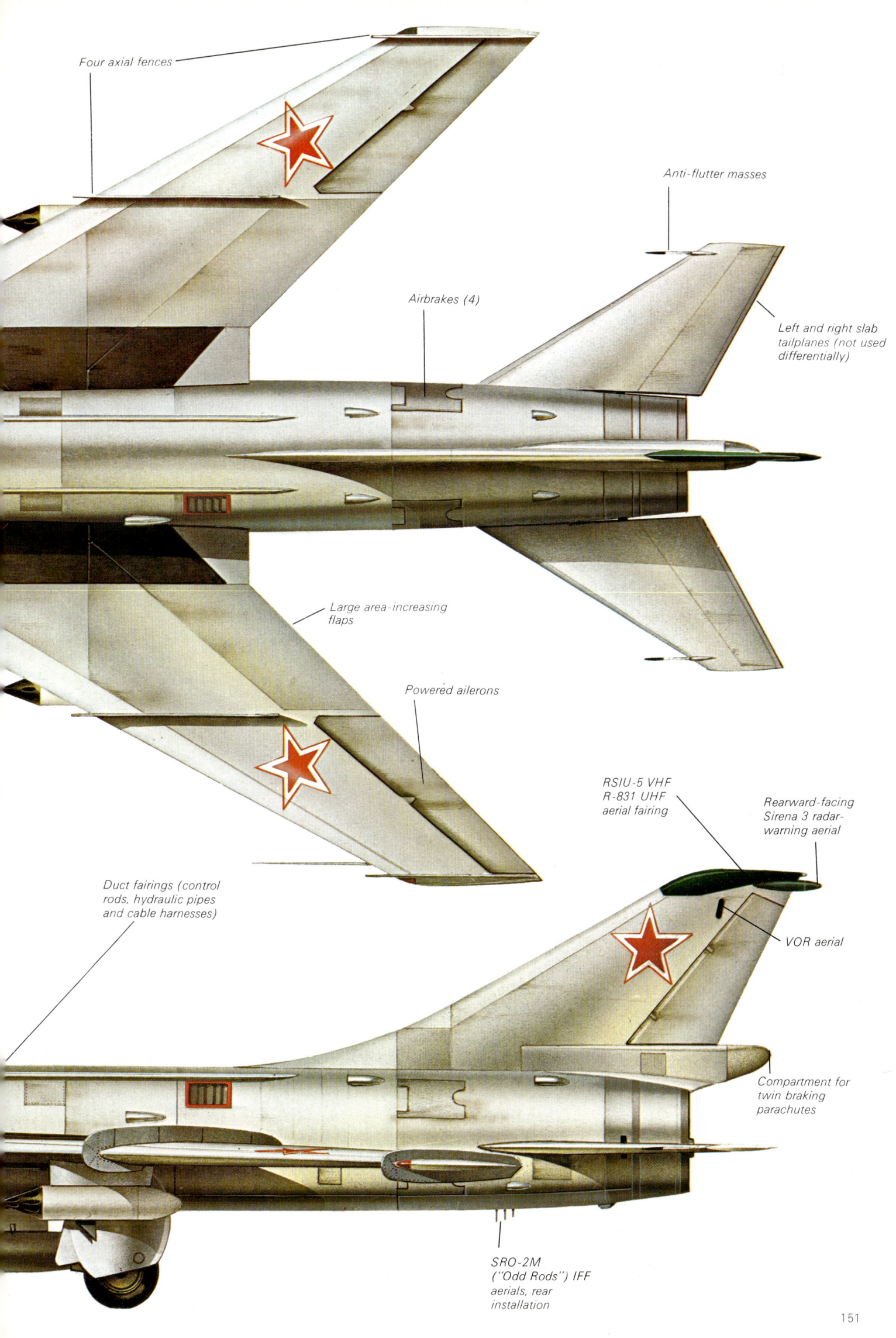

Four axial fences

Anti-flutter masses

Airbrakes (4)

Left and right slab
tailplanes (not used
differentially)

Large area-increasing
flaps

Powered ailerons

RSIU-5 VHF
R-831 UHF
aerial fairing

Rearward-facing
Sirena 3 radar-
warning aerial

VOR aerial

Duct fairings (control
rods, hydraulic pipes
and cable harnesses)

Compartment for
twin braking
parachutes

SRO-2M
("Odd Rods") IFF
aerials, rear
installation

151

Sukhoi Su-9 and Su-11

Su-9 ''Fishpot B'', Su-9U ''Maiden'' and Su-11 ''Fishpot C''.

Origin: The design bureau named for Pavel O. Sukhoi, Soviet Union.
Type: Single-seat all-weather interceptor (Su-9U, two-seat trainer).
Engine: One Lyulka single-shaft turbojet with afterburner; (Su-9 and -9U) AL-7F rated at 19,840lb (9000kg) thrust with maximum afterburner, (Su-11) AL-7F-1 rated at 22,046lb (10,000kg).
Dimensions: Span 27ft 8in (8·43m); length (-9, -9U) about 54ft (16·5m),
(-11) 57ft (17·4m); height 16ft (4·9m).
Weights: (All, estimated) empty 20,000lb (9070kg); loaded (typical mission) 27,000lb (12,250kg), (maximum) 30,000lb (13,610kg).
Performance: (-11, estimated) maximum speed (clean, sea level) 720mph (1160km/h, Mach 0·95), (clean, optimum height) 1,190mph (1910km/h, Mach 1·8), (two missiles and two tanks at optimum height) 790mph (1270km/h, Mach 1·2); initial climb 27,000ft (8230m)/min; service ceiling (clean) 55,700ft (17,000m); range (two missiles, two tanks) about 700 miles (1125km).
Armament: (-9) four AA-1 ''Alkali'' air-to-air missiles; (-9U) same as -9, or not fitted; (-11) two AA-3 ''Anab'' air-to-air missiles, one radar and the other IR.

continued on page 154 ▶

Sukhoi Su-11 "Fishpot C"

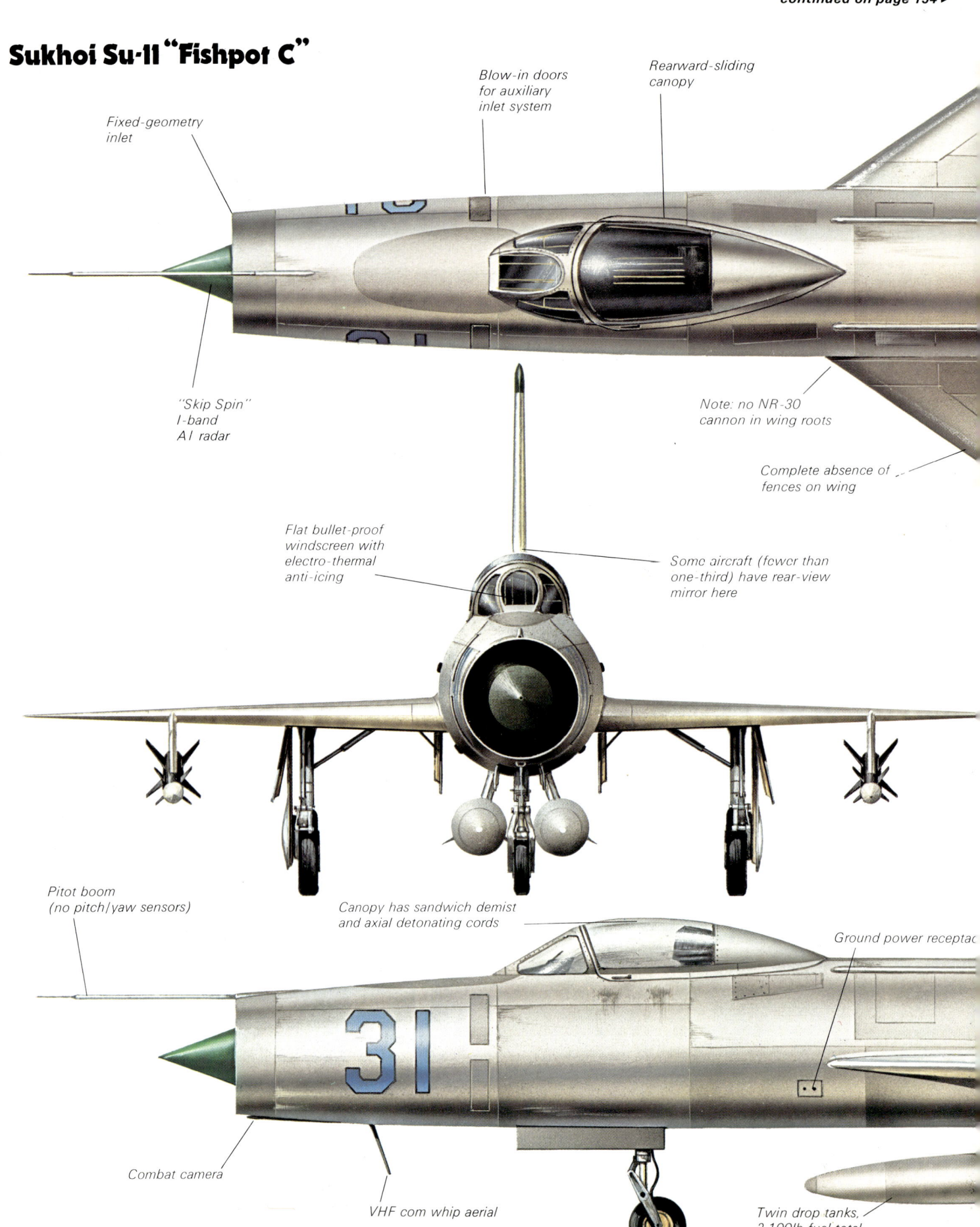

Fixed-geometry inlet

Blow-in doors for auxiliary inlet system

Rearward-sliding canopy

''Skip Spin'' I-band AI radar

Note: no NR-30 cannon in wing roots

Complete absence of fences on wing

Flat bullet-proof windscreen with electro-thermal anti-icing

Some aircraft (fewer than one-third) have rear-view mirror here

Pitot boom (no pitch/yaw sensors)

Canopy has sandwich demist and axial detonating cords

Ground power receptac

Combat camera

VHF com whip aerial

Twin drop tanks, 2,100lb fuel total

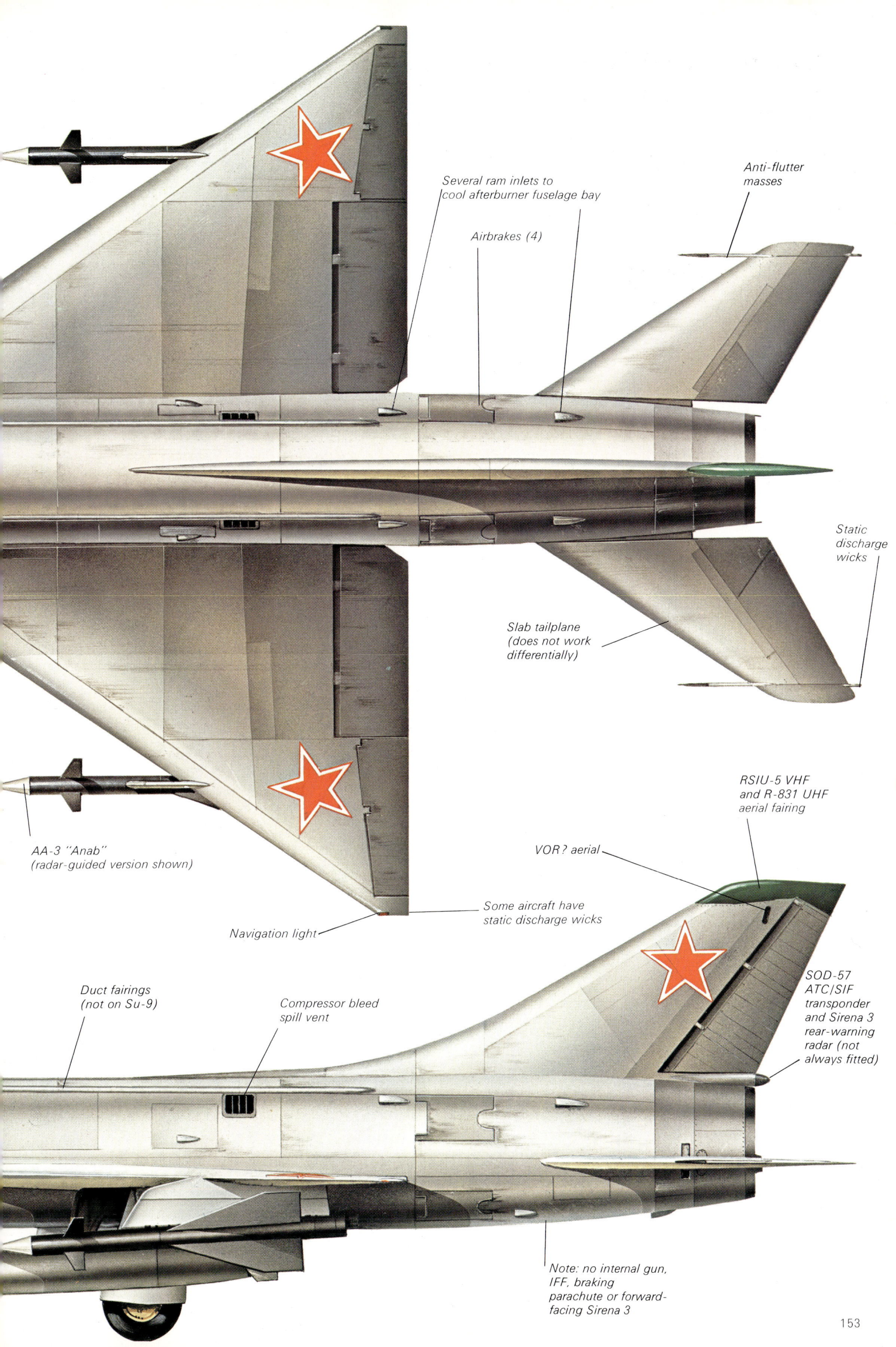

Several ram inlets to
cool afterburner fuselage bay

Airbrakes (4)

Anti-flutter
masses

Static
discharge
wicks

Slab tailplane
(does not work
differentially)

AA-3 "Anab"
(radar-guided version shown)

Some aircraft have
static discharge wicks

Navigation light

RSIU-5 VHF
and R-831 UHF
aerial fairing

VOR? aerial

Duct fairings
(not on Su-9)

Compressor bleed
spill vent

SOD-57
ATC/SIF
transponder
and Sirena 3
rear-warning
radar (not
always fitted)

Note: no internal gun,
IFF, braking
parachute or forward-
facing Sirena 3

History: First flight (-9) before 1956; (-11) probably 1966; service delivery (-9) probably 1959, (-11) 1967.
User: Soviet Union (IA-PVO).

Development: When first seen, at the 1956 Tushino display, one prototype delta-winged Sukhoi fighter had a small conical radome above the plain nose inlet, while a second had a conical centrebody. The latter arrangement was chosen for production as the Su-9, though development was rather protracted. At first sharing the same engine installation, rear fuselage and tail as the original Su-7, the Su-9 eventually came to have no parts exactly common. No gun was ever seen on an Su-9 by Western intelligence, the primitive missiles being the only armament. At least 2,000 were built, an additional number, probably supplemented by conversions, being tandem-seat dual trainers with a cockpit slightly different from that of the Su-7U. The Su-11 is cleaned up in every part of the airframe, has a longer and less-tapered nose with larger radar centrebody, completely different armament (still without guns) and a fuselage similar to the Su-7B with external duct fairings along the top on each side. Though much larger and more powerful than the MiG-21, these interceptors have an almost identical tailed-delta configuration. Unlike the MiG-21 they have all-weather capability (interpreted as "night and rain" rather than true all-weather), but are still limited in radius, endurance and armament. In 1976 they were together judged to equip one-quarter of the 2,500-strong interceptor force of the IA-PVO, but were being replaced by the Su-15 and MiG-23S.

Above: Suited-up IA-PVO pilots followed by ground staff scramble a section of Su-9 interceptors on a practice mission.

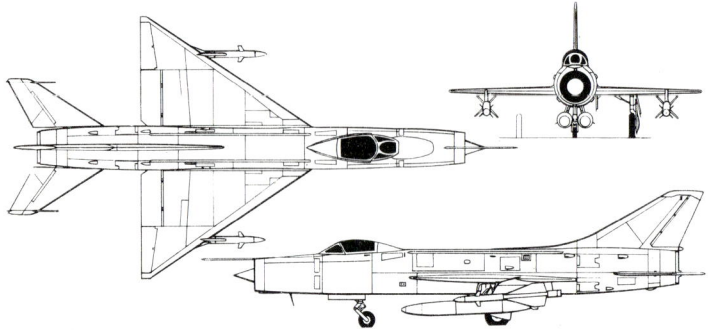

Above: Three-view of Su-11 with "Anab" missiles.

Above: Launch of an AA-3 "Alkali" air-to-air missile from No 2 pylon of an Su-9 of the IA-PVO.

Below: The Su-9 has a shorter and more tapered nose than the later Su-11. Like all Sukhoi aircraft of this generation, the Su-9 and -11 have limited internal fuel capacity and a large Lyulka afterburning engine.

Sukhoi Su-15

Versions known to the West are ("Flagon A") to ("Flagon F")

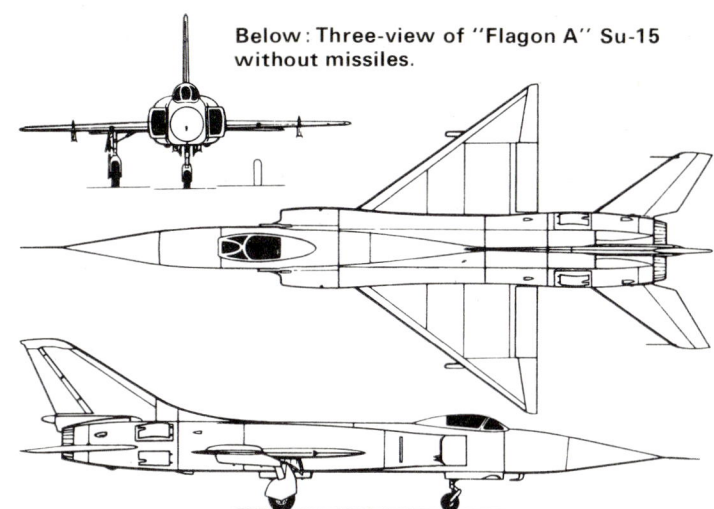

Below: Three-view of "Flagon A" Su-15 without missiles.

Origin: The design bureau of Pavel O. Sukhoi, Soviet Union.
Type: Most versions, all-weather interceptor.
Engines: Two afterburning engines, believed to be 22,046lb (10,000kg) Lyulka AL-7F single-shaft turbojets.
Dimensions: Span (A) 31ft 3in (9·50m), (D) about 36ft (11·0m); length (all) 70ft 6in (21·50m); height 16ft 6in (5·0m).
Weights: (Estimated) empty (A) 24,000lb (10,900kg), (D) 26,000lb (11,800kg); normal loaded (A) 35,275lb (16,000kg); maximum loaded (D) 46,000lb (21,000kg).
Performance: (Estimated) maximum speed at altitude, with two missiles, 1,520mph (2445km/h, Mach 2·3); initial climb 35,000ft (10,670m)/min; service ceiling 65,000ft (19,800m)· combat radius 450 miles (725km); ferry range about 1,400 miles (2250km).
Armament: Two underwing pylons normally carry one radar "Anab" and one infra-red "Anab"; two fuselage pylons normally carry drop tanks, often with a 23mm GSh-23 two-barrel cannon between them; other missiles such as AA-6 or AA-7 are probably now being carried (but not yet seen by the West).
History: First flight (Su-15 prototype) probably 1964; (production Su-15) probably 1967.
User: Soviet Union (PVO).

Development: Following naturally on from the Su-11, and strongly resembling earlier aircraft in wings and tail, the Su-15 has two engines which not only confer increased performance but also leave the nose free for a large AI radar. The initial "Flagon A" version entered IA-PVO Strany service in 1969. "Flagon B" is a STOL rough-field version with three lift jets in the fuselage and a revised "double delta" wing. "Flagon C" is the Su-15U dual trainer. "D" is basically a "B" without lift jets, "E" has new electronics and more powerful engines and "F" an ogival radome. In 1971 a US official estimated that 400 Su-15 were in service, with production at about 15 monthly. In early 1976 an estimate of PVO establishment gave the number of all Su-15 versions in combat service as 600. Though small numbers have served in Warsaw Pact countries and, in 1973, in Egypt, all Su-15s are at present believed to serve with the IA-PVO. There has been speculation in the West that later models could carry the "Fox Fire" radar and AA-6 "Acrid" missiles of the MiG-25. **continued on page 156▶**

Above: IA-PVO officers huddled round a "Flagon D". The new wing gives much-enhanced manoeuvrability.
Below: Three "Flagon A" interceptors of the IA-PVO, with "Anabs".
Bottom: The Su-15 has an exceptionally high wing loading.

Sukhoi Su-15 "Flagon F"

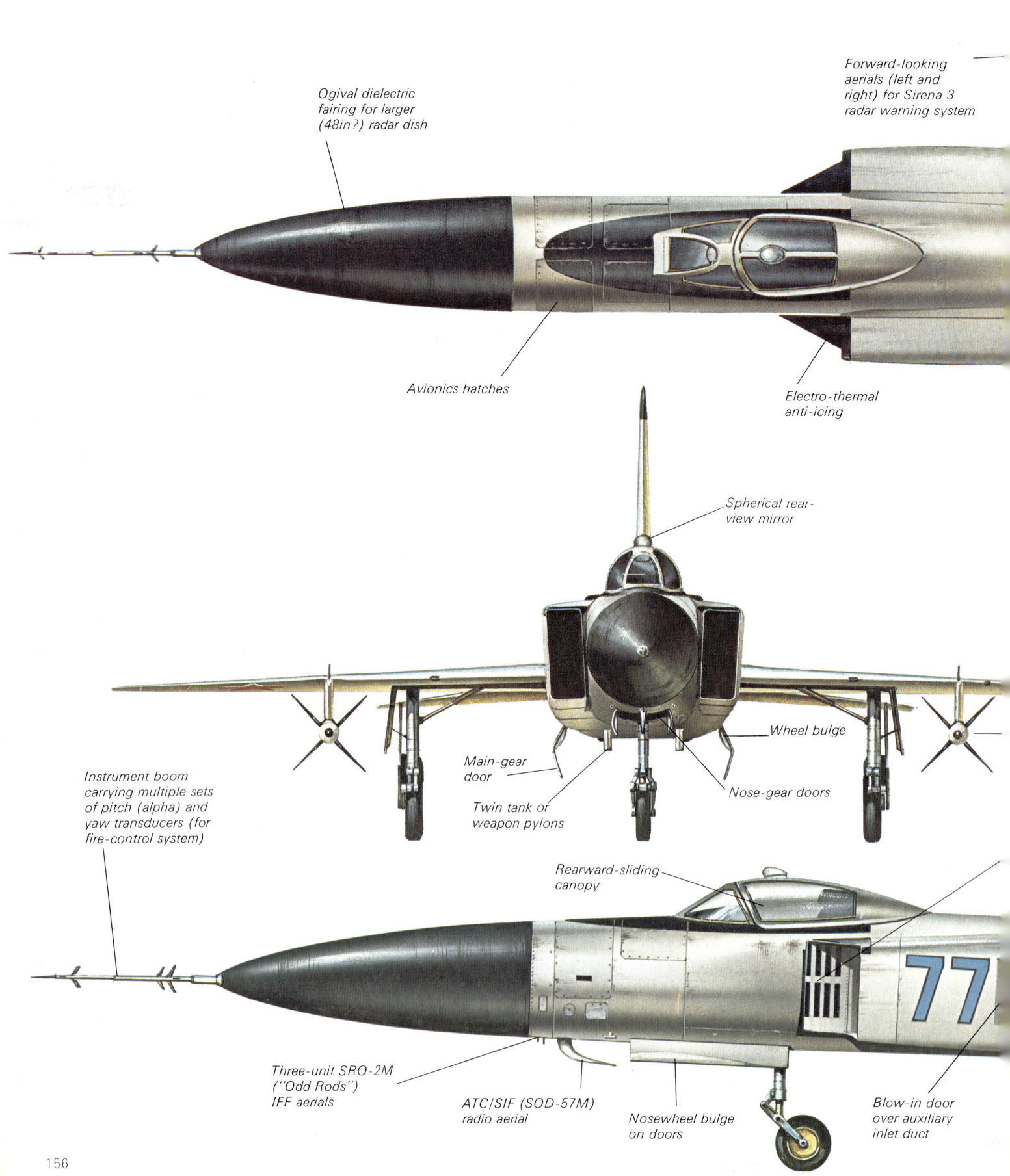

Ogival dielectric fairing for larger (48in?) radar dish

Forward-looking aerials (left and right) for Sirena 3 radar warning system

Avionics hatches

Electro-thermal anti-icing

Spherical rear-view mirror

Instrument boom carrying multiple sets of pitch (alpha) and yaw transducers (for fire-control system)

Main-gear door

Twin tank or weapon pylons

Nose-gear doors

Wheel bulge

Rearward-sliding canopy

Three-unit SRO-2M ("Odd Rods") IFF aerials

ATC/SIF (SOD-57M) radio aerial

Nosewheel bulge on doors

Blow-in door over auxiliary inlet duct

77

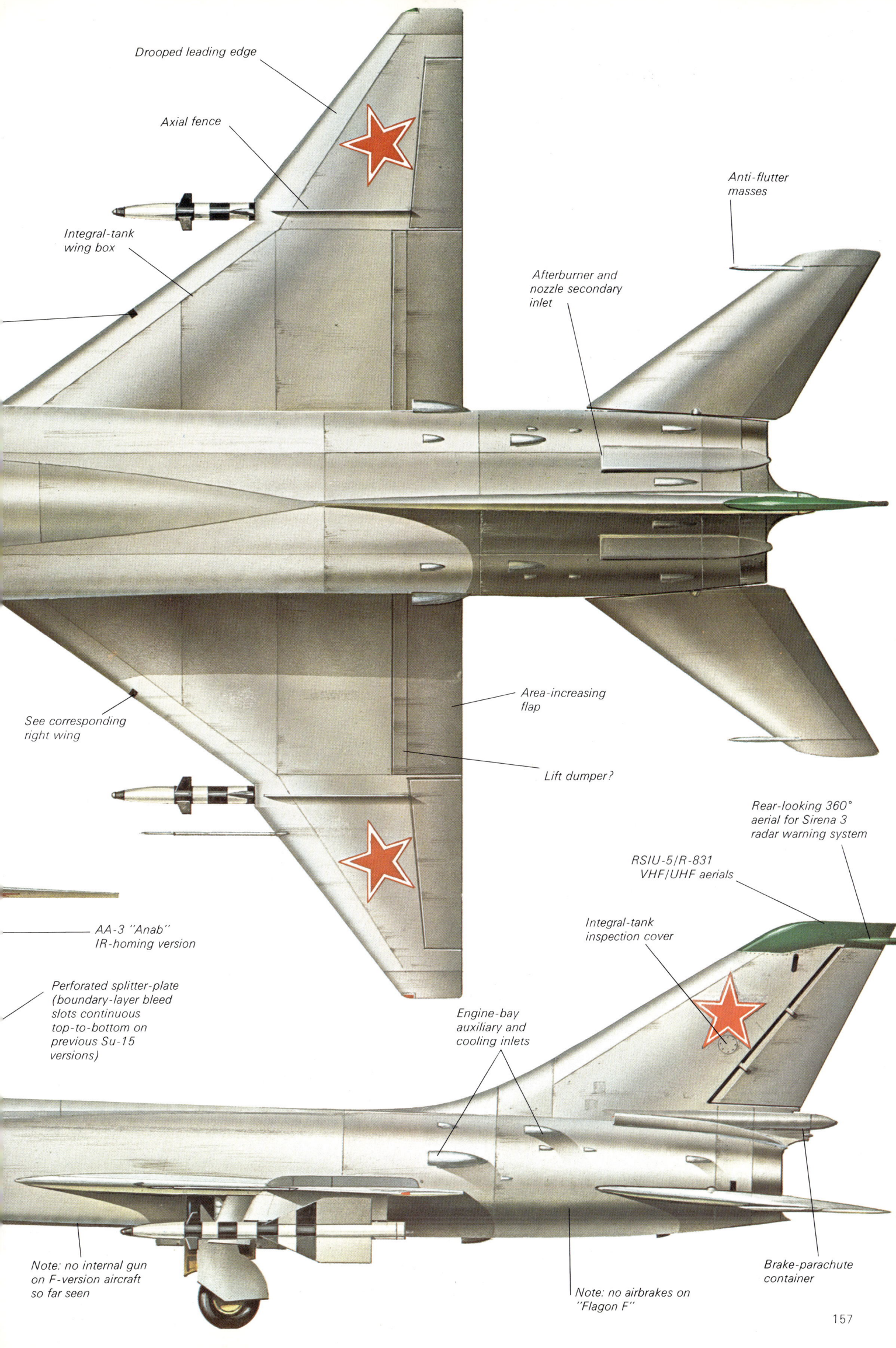

Drooped leading edge

Axial fence

Integral-tank wing box

Anti-flutter masses

Afterburner and nozzle secondary inlet

Area-increasing flap

Lift dumper?

See corresponding right wing

Rear-looking 360° aerial for Sirena 3 radar warning system

RSIU-5/R-831 VHF/UHF aerials

AA-3 "Anab" IR-homing version

Integral-tank inspection cover

Perforated splitter-plate (boundary-layer bleed slots continuous top-to-bottom on previous Su-15 versions)

Engine-bay auxiliary and cooling inlets

Note: no internal gun on F-version aircraft so far seen

Note: no airbrakes on "Flagon F"

Brake-parachute container

157

Sukhoi Su-19

Su-19 versions known to NATO as ("Fencer")

Origin: The design bureau of Pavel O. Sukhoi, Soviet Union.
Type: Two-seat multi-role combat aircraft.
Engines: Two afterburning turbofan or turbojet engines, probably two 24,500lb (11,113kg) Lyulka AL-21F3.
Dimensions: (Estimated) span (spread, about 22°) 56ft 3in (17·5m), swept (about 72°) 31ft 3in (9·53m); length 69ft 10in (21·29m); height 21ft (6·4m).
Weights: (Estimated) empty 35,000lb (15,875kg); maximum loaded 70,000lb (31,750kg).
Performance: (Estimated) maximum speed, clean, 950mph (1530km/h, Mach 1·25) at sea level, about 1,650mph (2655km/h, Mach 2·5) at altitude; initial climb, over 40,000ft (12,200m)/min; service ceiling, about

continued on page 160▶

Sukhoi Su-19 "Fencer"

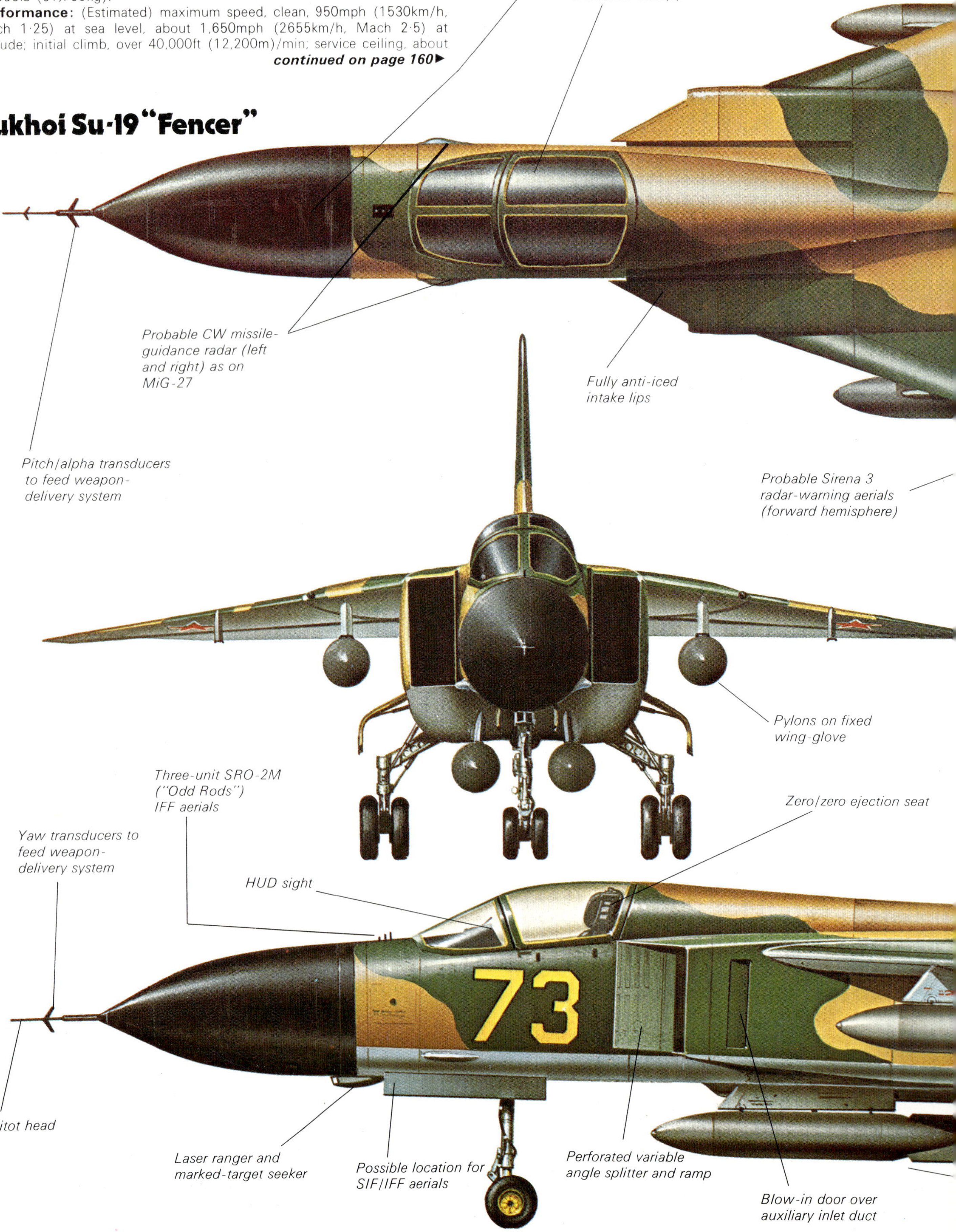

Wing in minimum-sweep (LO, about 16°) position

Advanced radar, probably of pulse-doppler type, for navigation, terrain-following and all-weather weapon delivery (scanner dish size about 50in, 1·25m)

Powerful spoilers/lift-dumpers

Clamshell canopy

Probable CW missile-guidance radar (left and right) as on MiG-27

Fully anti-iced intake lips

Probable Sirena 3 radar-warning aerials (forward hemisphere)

Pitch/alpha transducers to feed weapon-delivery system

Pylons on fixed wing-glove

Three-unit SRO-2M ("Odd Rods") IFF aerials

Zero/zero ejection seat

Yaw transducers to feed weapon-delivery system

HUD sight

Pitot head

Laser ranger and marked-target seeker

Possible location for SIF/IFF aerials

Perforated variable angle splitter and ramp

Blow-in door over auxiliary inlet duct

158

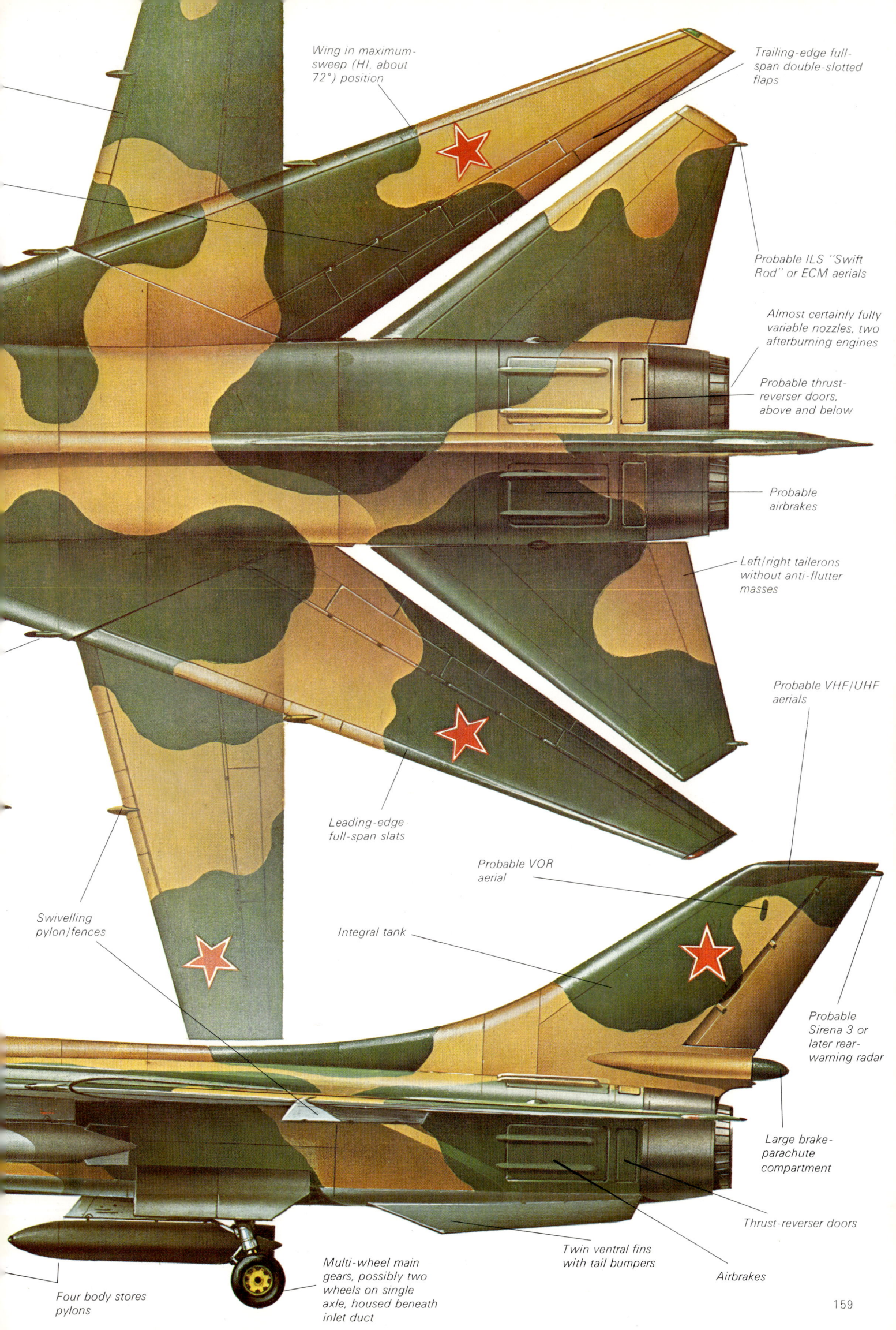

Wing in maximum-sweep (HI, about 72°) position

Trailing-edge full-span double-slotted flaps

Probable ILS "Swift Rod" or ECM aerials

Almost certainly fully variable nozzles, two afterburning engines

Probable thrust-reverser doors, above and below

Probable airbrakes

Left/right tailerons without anti-flutter masses

Probable VHF/UHF aerials

Leading-edge full-span slats

Probable VOR aerial

Swivelling pylon/fences

Integral tank

Probable Sirena 3 or later rear-warning radar

Large brake-parachute compartment

Thrust-reverser doors

Twin ventral fins with tail bumpers

Airbrakes

Multi-wheel main gears, possibly two wheels on single axle, housed beneath inlet duct

Four body stores pylons

►60,000ft (18,290m), combat radius with maximum weapons, about 500 miles (805km); ferry range, over 2,500 miles (4025km).
Armament: One 23mm GSh-23 twin-barrel cannon in lower centreline; at least six pylons on fuselage, fixed and swinging wings, for wide range of stores including guided and unguided air-to-ground or air-to-air missiles.
History: First flight, probably about 1970; service delivery, 1974 or earlier.
User: Soviet Union (mainly FA).

Development: First identified publicly in the West by the Chairman of the US Joint Chiefs of Staff, who described the Su-19 as "the first modern Soviet fighter to be developed specifically as a fighter-bomber for the ground-attack mission", this aircraft will probably be the chief tactical

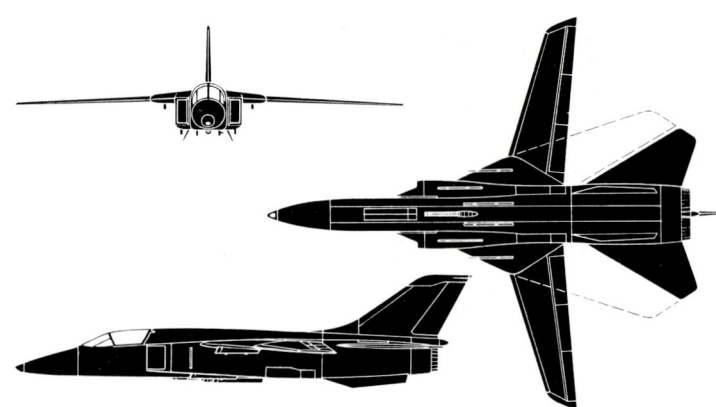

Three-view of Su-19, showing range of sweep (provisional).

attack aircraft of the Soviet V-VS in 1980. Like the rival but much smaller MiG-27, the Su-19 is an extremely clean machine strongly reminiscent of the F-111 and Mirage G, having side-by-side seats and wing and tailplane at the same level, as in the US machine, yet following the French aircraft in general layout. In general capability the nearest Western equivalent is the F-14 Tomcat, which shows just how formidable this aircraft is. Whereas "Foxbat" was on many Western lips in the 1960s, so is "Fencer" a big scare-word in the 1970s. Features of the first service version include a typical Sukhoi tail, but with ventral fins; double-shock side inlets; full-span slats and double-slotted flaps; and very extensive avionics (thought to include a multi-mode attack radar, doppler, laser ranger and very comprehensive EW/ECM installations).

Above: Unlike the splendid colour three-view of the Su-19 on pp. 158–159, this artist's impression is provisional and was based on inadequate visual information.

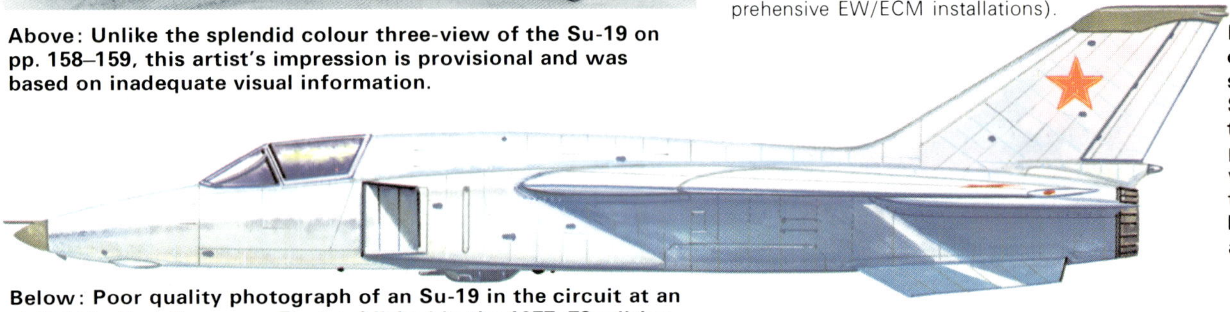

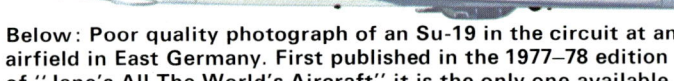

Left: A side view of an Su-19 in service with the Soviet FA. Like the three-view this is provisional and was drawn before the photograph below became available.

Below: Poor quality photograph of an Su-19 in the circuit at an airfield in East Germany. First published in the 1977–78 edition of "Jane's All The World's Aircraft" it is the only one available.

Sukhoi Su-17 and Su-20

Su-17, Su-20 and Su-22; ("Fitter C" and "D")

Origin: The design bureau named for Pavel O. Sukhoi, Soviet Union.
Type: Single-seat attack and close-support aircraft.
Engine: (-17) one Lyulka AL-21F-3 single-shaft turbojet with afterburner rated at 17,200lb (7800kg) dry and 25,000lb (11,340kg) with maximum afterburner, (-20, -22) believed to be AL-7F-1 rated at 22,046lb (10,000kg).
Dimensions (all): Span (28°) 45ft 11¼in (14·00m), (62°) 34ft 9½in (10·60m); length (incl probe) 61ft 6¼in (18·75m); height 15ft 7in (4·75m).
Weights: (-17 estimated, -20 and -22 slightly less) empty 22,046lb (10,000kg); loaded (clean) 30,865lb (14,000kg), (maximum) 41,887lb (19,000kg).
Performance: (-17, clean) maximum speed at sea level 798mph (1284 km/h, Mach 1·05), maximum speed at optimum height 1,432mph (2305 km/h, Mach 2·17); initial climb 45,275ft (13,800m)/min; service ceiling 59,050ft (18,000m); combat radius with 4,410lb (2000kg) external stores (hi-lo-hi) 391 miles (630km).
Armament: Two 30mm NR-30 cannon, each with 70 rounds, in wing roots; eight pylons under fuselage, fixed gloves and swing-wings for maximum external load of 11,023lb (5000kg) including the AS-7 "Kerry" air-to-surface missile (-20, -22, six pylons).
History: First public display at Domodedovo 1967; service delivery, possibly 1970 (-17) and 1972-3 (-20).
Users: Egypt (-20), Peru (-22), Poland (-20), Soviet Union (FA, -17).

Development: A logical direct modification of the somewhat limited Su-7B, the Su-17 has variable-geometry "swing-wings" pivoted far outboard, hinged to a slightly modified -7B centre section with strengthened landing gear. At maximum sweep the trailing edge of the centre section aligns with the outer section, and it carries two shallow fences on each side. At the pivots are large square-fronted fences combined with pylons which

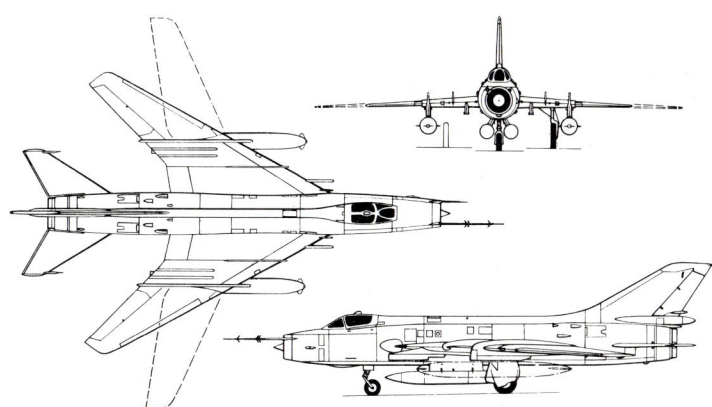

Above: Three-view of Su-20, showing range of wing sweep.

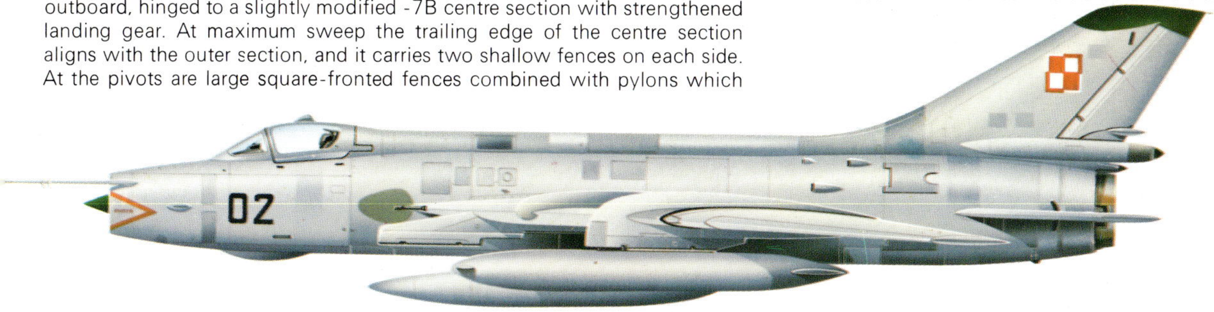

are stressed to carry 2,200lb (1000kg) stores which in the Polish Su-20 are invariably drop tanks with nose fins. The swing-wings carry full-span slats, slotted ailerons and flaps which retract inside the centre section. Compared with the Su-7B the result is the ability to lift twice the external load from airstrips little more than half as long, and climb and level speed at all heights are much increased, even in the lower-powered Su-20 and export Su-22. Equipment in the -17 includes SRD-5M "High Fix" radar, an ASP-5ND fire-control system and comprehensive communications and IFF. Landing performance is so much better than the -7B that a braking chute is not fitted; in its place is the aft-facing aerial for a Sirena 3 radar homing and warning system at the rear of the prominent dorsal spine. "Fitter D" has under-nose radar and laser. Peru's 36 aircraft were to be delivered in 1977.

continued on page 162▶

Above: Su-20 in service with Polish Air Force (wings swept).

Below: On 6 October 1976 the Egyptian Air Force sprang a surprise on foreign observers by including this group of Su-20 variable-sweep attack aircraft in its parade commemorating the October war three years earlier.

Sukhoi Su-17 "Fitter C"

ASP-5ND advanced fire-control weapon-delivery system requires precise air-data measures:
1. Alpha (angle of attack) transducers

Pitot tube

Spherical rear-view mirror

Blow-in auxiliary inlet doors (left and right)

Left and right RSB-70 HF communications aerials

NR-30 30mm cannon (70 rounds)

Walkway

Inboard fence/pylon

Forward-looking Sirena 3 radar warning aerials (left and right)

2. Yaw transducers

Clamshell canopy hinged at rear

Protective blast plate sprayed on skin

SRD-5M "High Fix" multi-mode radar

Auxiliary (pilot's) alpha sensor (anti-iced)

Bulge for retracted nose gear

Levered-suspension nose and main gears

Total of eight (early Su-17, six) pylons, total 11,023lb external load

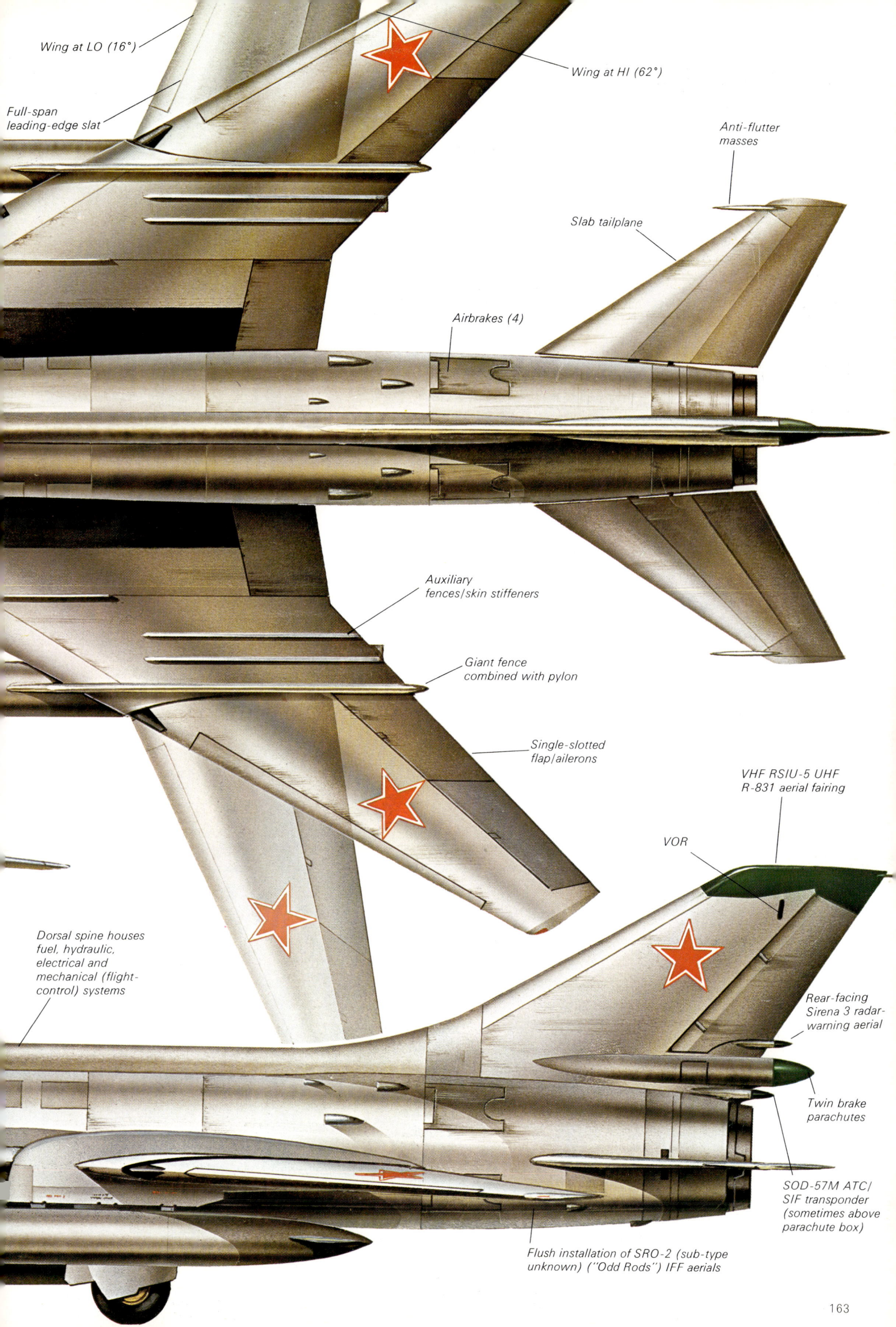

Wing at LO (16°)

Full-span
leading-edge slat

Wing at HI (62°)

Anti-flutter
masses

Slab tailplane

Airbrakes (4)

Auxiliary
fences/skin stiffeners

Giant fence
combined with pylon

Single-slotted
flap/ailerons

VHF RSIU-5 UHF
R-831 aerial fairing

VOR

Dorsal spine houses
fuel, hydraulic,
electrical and
mechanical (flight-
control) systems

Rear-facing
Sirena 3 radar-
warning aerial

Twin brake
parachutes

SOD-57M ATC/
SIF transponder
(sometimes above
parachute box)

Flush installation of SRO-2 (sub-type
unknown) ("Odd Rods") IFF aerials

Tupolev Tu-16

Sub-types known to West as ("Badger A") to ("Badger G") Tupolev bureau, Tu-88

Origin: The design bureau of Andrei N. Tupolev, Soviet Union; built (probably without licence) at Shenyang, China.

Type: Designed as strategic bomber; see text.

Engines: Believed in all versions, two Mikulin AM-3M single-shaft turbojets each rated at about 20,950lb (9500kg).

Dimensions: Span (basic) 110ft (33·5m) (varies with FR system, ECM and other features); length (basic) 120ft (36·5m) (varies with radar or glazed nose); height 35ft 6in (10·8m).

Weights: Empty, typically about 72,750lb (33,000kg) in early versions, about 82,680lb (37,500kg) in maritime/ECM roles; maximum loaded, about 150,000lb (68,000kg).

Performance: Maximum speed, clean at height, 587mph (945km/h); initial climb, clean, about 4,100ft (1250m)/min; service ceiling 42,650ft (13,000m); range with maximum weapon load, no missiles, 3,000 miles (4,800km); extreme reconnaissance range, about 4,500 miles (7250km).

Armament: In most variants, six 23mm NR-23 cannon in radar-directed manned tail turret and remotely-aimed upper dorsal and rear ventral barbettes; versions without nose radar usually have seventh NR-23 fixed firing ahead on right side of nose. Internal weapon bay for load of 19,800lb (9000kg), with certain versions equipped to launch missiles (see text).

History: First flight (Tu-88), believed 1952; service delivery 1954; final delivery (USSR) about 1959, (China) 1975.

Users: China, Egypt, Indonesia (in storage), Iraq, Libya, Soviet Union (AV-MF).

Development: Representing a simple and low-risk approach to the strategic jet-bomber requirement, the Tu-88 prototype was generally in the class of the Valiant but incorporated heavy defensive armament. Technology throughout was derived directly from the Boeing B-29, which Tupolev's bureau had in 1945–53 built in large numbers as the Tu-4. The first ("Badger A") version had blind-bombing radar and glazed nose, and a few were supplied to Egypt and Iraq. The B carried two "Kennel" cruise missiles on underwing pylons and served the AV-MF (Navy) and Indonesian AF. C carried the large "Kipper" stand-off missile on the centre-line, with panoramic nose radar for ship search and missile guidance. D is a maritime reconnaissance type, with comprehensive radars and ECM. E is a photo and multi-sensor reconnaissance type, F is an E with major new ECM and ESM installations, and G is an updated B which launched many missiles against Israel in 1973. Total production exceeded 2,000, and production (without Soviet aid) in China yielded about 60 aircraft by 1975.

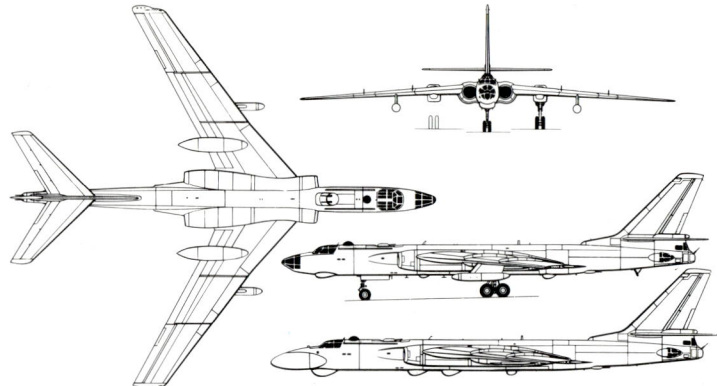

Above: Three-view of Tu-16 "Badger F" with side view (bottom) of "D".

Above: Tu-16 of the AV-MF, photographed on a "Zombie" electronic reconnaissance mission near Britain by a Phantom FG.1 of 892 Sqn, Royal Navy. It is a "Badger D" type.

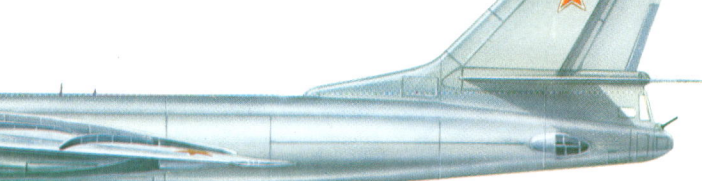

Above: Tu-16 of "Badger D" type, in service with the AV-MF.

Left: A Tu-16 of the "Badger F" type, photographed by a Nimrod of the RAF as it wheels low over the North Atlantic. This type of Tu-16 is visually distinguished by its two small electronic pods carried on pylons beneath the wings. Frequently Tu-16s engaged in ESM (electronic surveillance measures) missions have worked in pairs, the "Badger D" and "Badger F" apparently being complementary. Several versions have been converted as air refuelling tankers, using an unusual wing-tip/wing-tip hook-up method.

Tupolev Tu-20

Tu-95 (Tupolev bureau designation) in versions known to West as ("Bear A") to ("Bear F")

Origin: The design bureau of Andrei N. Tupolev, Soviet Union.
Type: Designed as strategic bomber; see text.
Engines: Four 14,795ehp Kuznetsov NK-12M single-shaft turboprops.
Dimensions: Span 159ft (48·5m); length 155ft 10in (47·50m) (certain versions differ by up to 6ft); height 38ft 8in (11·78m).
Weights: Empty, probably about 160,000lb (72,600kg); maximum loaded (estimate) about 340,000lb (154,000kg).
Performance: Maximum speed (typical "Bear" clean) 540mph (870km/h); service ceiling, about 44,000ft (13,400m); range with 25,000lb (11,340kg) bomb load, 7,800 miles (12,550km).
Armament: Normally six 23mm NS-23 in radar-directed manned tail turret and remote-aimed dorsal and ventral barbettes (defensive guns often absent from late conversions); internal weapon bay for load of about 25,000lb (11,340kg).
History: First flight (prototype) mid-1954; service delivery, 1956; final delivery, probably about 1962.
User: Soviet Union (ADD, AV-MF).

Development: Making use of identical systems, techniques and even similar airframe structures as the Tu-16, the Tu 95 (service designation, Tu-20) is much larger and has roughly double the range of its turbojet predecessor. The huge swept wing, forming integral tanks, was a major accomplishment in 1952–54, as were the monster turboprop engines and their eight-blade 18ft 4½in (5·6m) contraprops. The basic bomber called "Bear A" had a glazed nose, chin radar and gun-sight blisters on the rear fuselage. First seen in 1961, "Bear B" featured a solid nose with enormous radome, refuelling probe and centreline attachment for a large cruise missile ("Kangaroo"). C appeared in 1964 with a large new blister on each

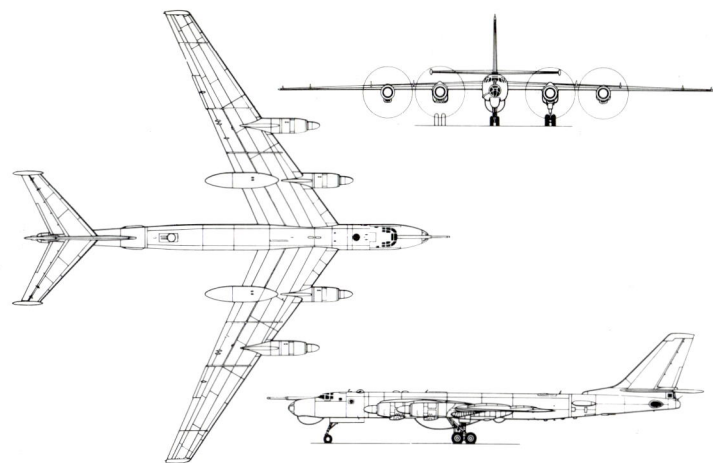

Above: Three-view of Tu-20 (Tu-95) of "Bear D" type.

side of the fuselage (on one side only on B), while D was obviously a major ECM/ESM reconnaissance type with chin radar, very large belly radar, and from 12 to 21 avionic features visible from stem to stern. E is a multi-sensor reconnaissance conversion of A, while F is a recent further conversion with an array of ventral radars and stores bays in place of the ventral guns.

continued on page 166►

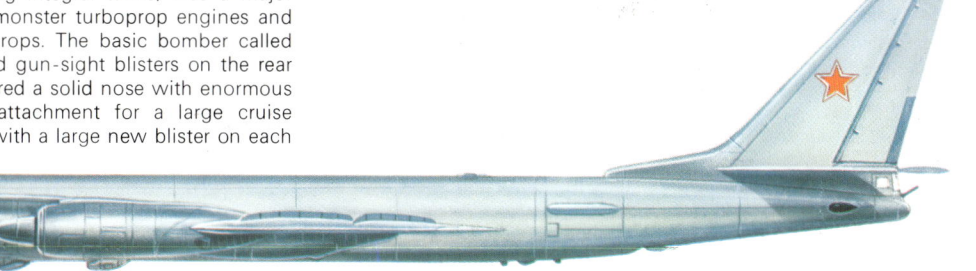

Above: Tu-20 (Tu-95) of the "Bear C" maritime surveillance type.

Above: A monster AS-3 "Kangaroo" air/surface missile drops away from its recess in the belly of a Tu-20 of the "Bear B" sub-type. This is the largest stand-off missile in the world (48ft 11in, 14·9m, long).

Left: A fine picture of a Tu-20 of the "Bear D" sub-type, taken by the pilot of an RAF Lightning north of Scotland. This model helps to direct anti-ship missiles.

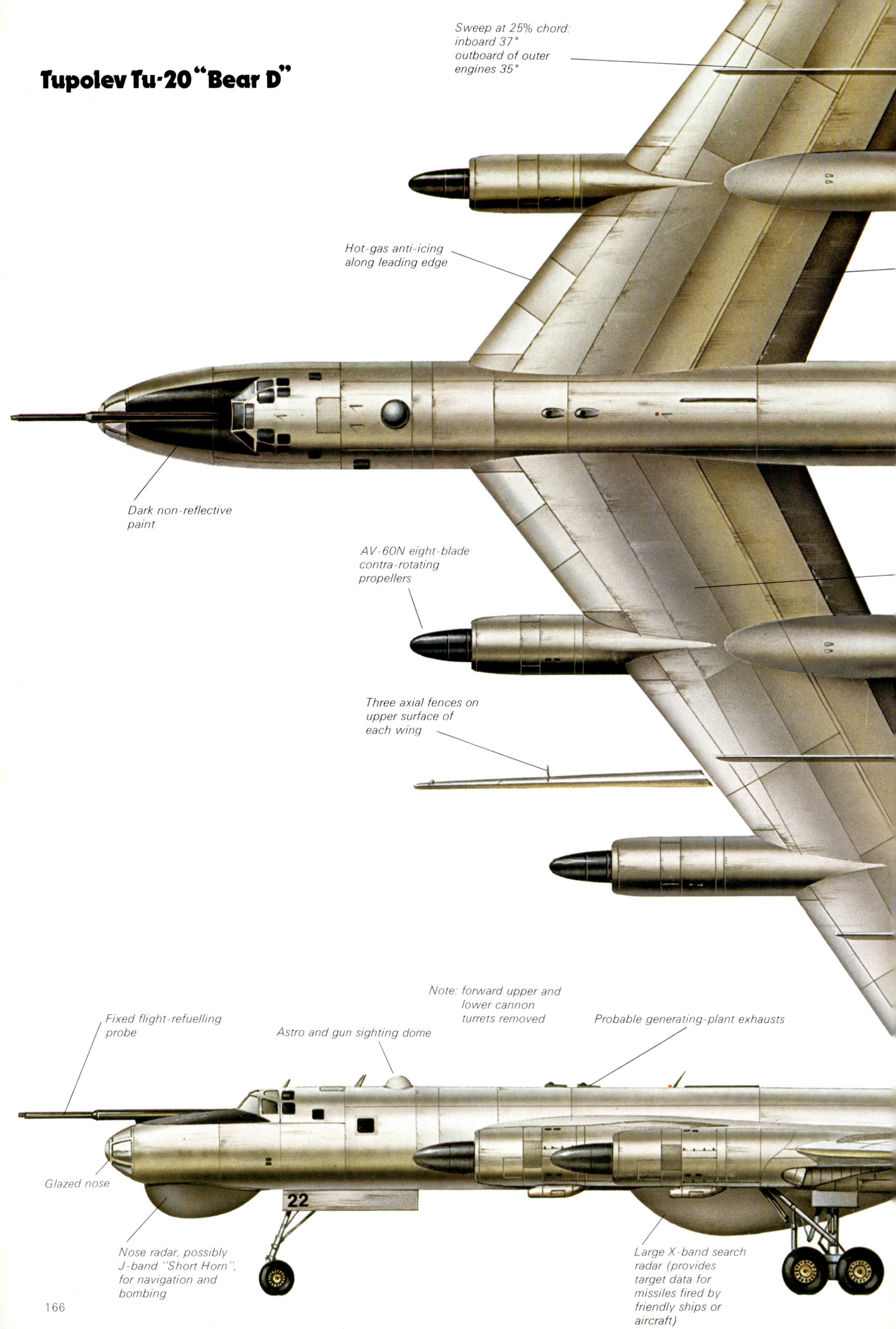

Tupolev Tu-20 "Bear D"

Sweep at 25% chord: inboard 37° outboard of outer engines 35°

Hot-gas anti-icing along leading edge

Dark non-reflective paint

AV-60N eight-blade contra-rotating propellers

Three axial fences on upper surface of each wing

Note: forward upper and lower cannon turrets removed

Probable generating-plant exhausts

Fixed flight-refuelling probe

Astro and gun sighting dome

Glazed nose

Nose radar, possibly J-band "Short Horn", for navigation and bombing

Large X-band search radar (provides target data for missiles fired by friendly ships or aircraft)

22

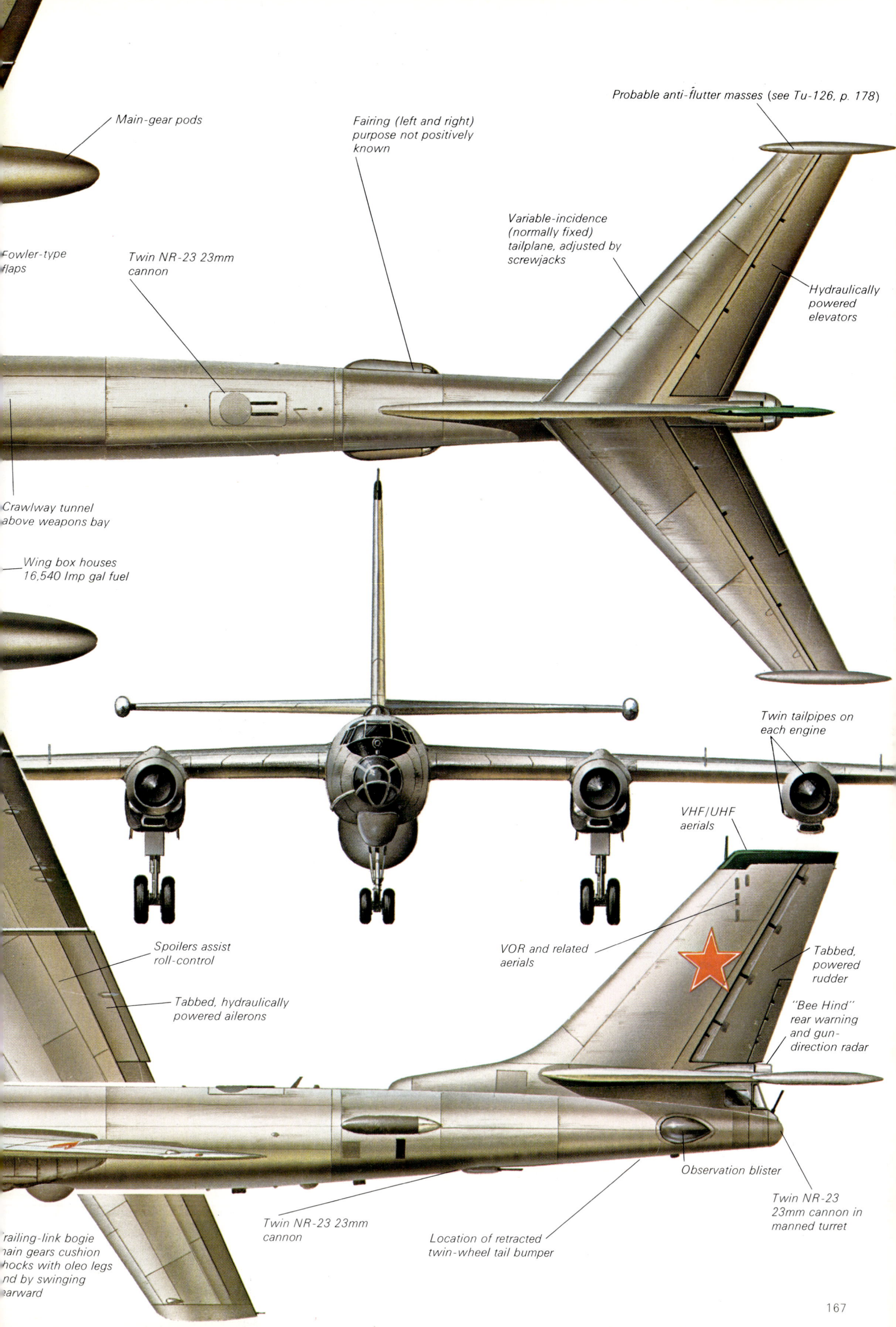

Main-gear pods

Fairing (left and right) purpose not positively known

Probable anti-flutter masses (see Tu-126, p. 178)

Fowler-type flaps

Twin NR-23 23mm cannon

Variable-incidence (normally fixed) tailplane, adjusted by screwjacks

Hydraulically powered elevators

Crawlway tunnel above weapons bay

Wing box houses 16,540 Imp gal fuel

Twin tailpipes on each engine

VHF/UHF aerials

Spoilers assist roll-control

VOR and related aerials

Tabbed, powered rudder

Tabbed, hydraulically powered ailerons

"Bee Hind" rear warning and gun-direction radar

Observation blister

Trailing-link bogie main gears cushion shocks with oleo legs and by swinging rearward

Twin NR-23 23mm cannon

Location of retracted twin-wheel tail bumper

Twin NR-23 23mm cannon in manned turret

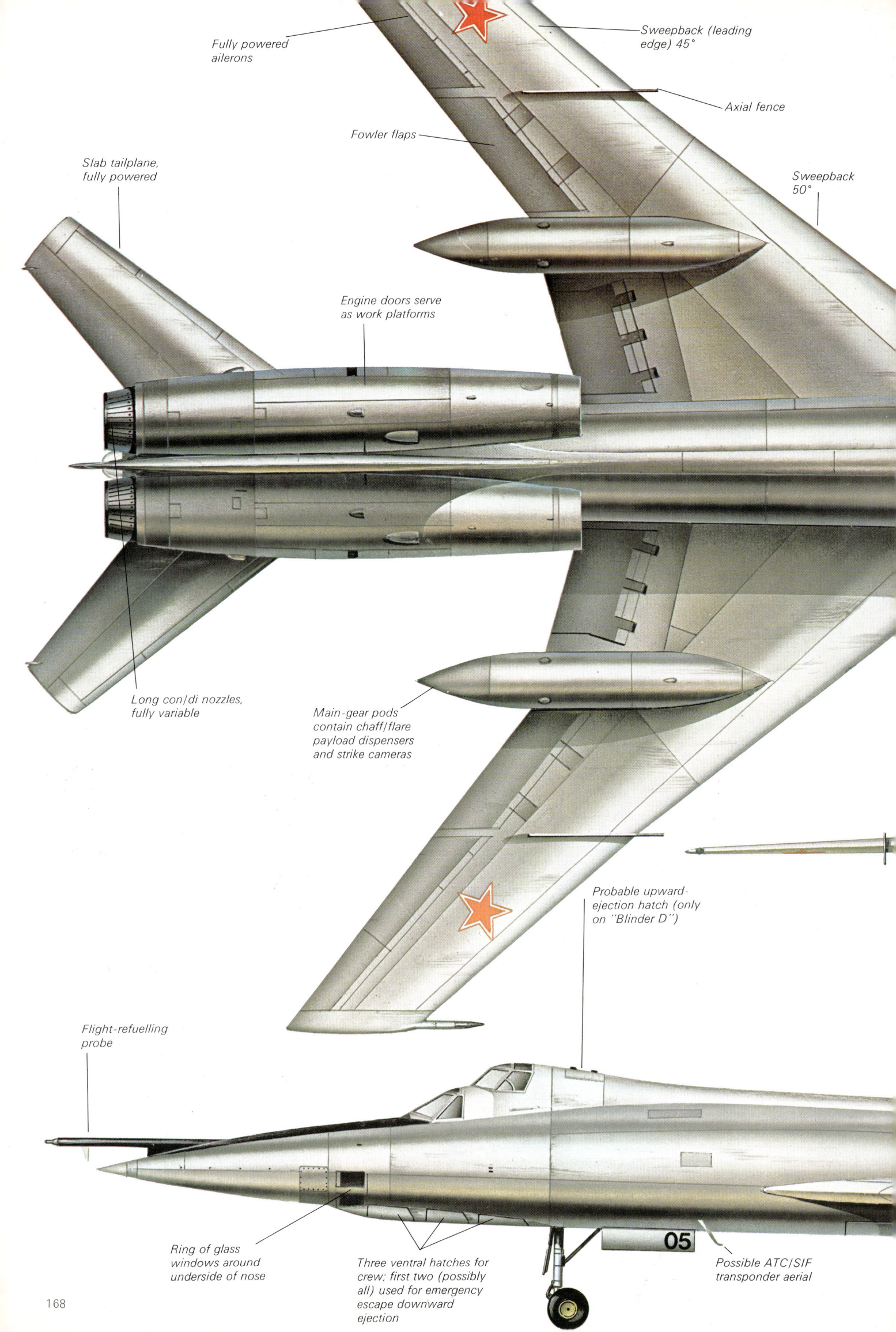

Fully powered
ailerons

Sweepback (leading
edge) 45°

Axial fence

Fowler flaps

Sweepback
50°

Slab tailplane,
fully powered

Engine doors serve
as work platforms

Long con/di nozzles,
fully variable

Main-gear pods
contain chaff/flare
payload dispensers
and strike cameras

Probable upward-
ejection hatch (only
on "Blinder D")

Flight-refuelling
probe

Ring of glass
windows around
underside of nose

Three ventral hatches for
crew; first two (possibly
all) used for emergency
escape downward
ejection

Possible ATC/SIF
transponder aerial

05

Tupolev Tu-22

Tu-22 in versions known to West as ("Blinder A") to ("Blinder D") Tupolev bureau, Tu-105

Origin: The design bureau of Andrei N. Tupolev, Soviet Union.
Type: Originally bomber: see text.

Engines: Two afterburning turbojets, of unknown type, each with maximum rating estimated at 27,000lb (12,250kg).
Dimensions: Span 90ft 10½in (27·70m); length (most versions) 132ft 11½in (40·53m); height 35ft 0in (10·67m).
Weights: Empty, about 85,000lb (38,600kg); maximum loaded, about 185,200lb (84,000kg).
Performance: Maximum speed (clean, at height) 920mph (1480km/h, Mach 1·4); initial climb, about 11,500ft (3500m)/min; service ceiling 59,000ft (18,000m); range (high, internal fuel only) 1,400 miles (2250km).

continued on page 170▶

Tupolev Tu-22 "Blinder D"

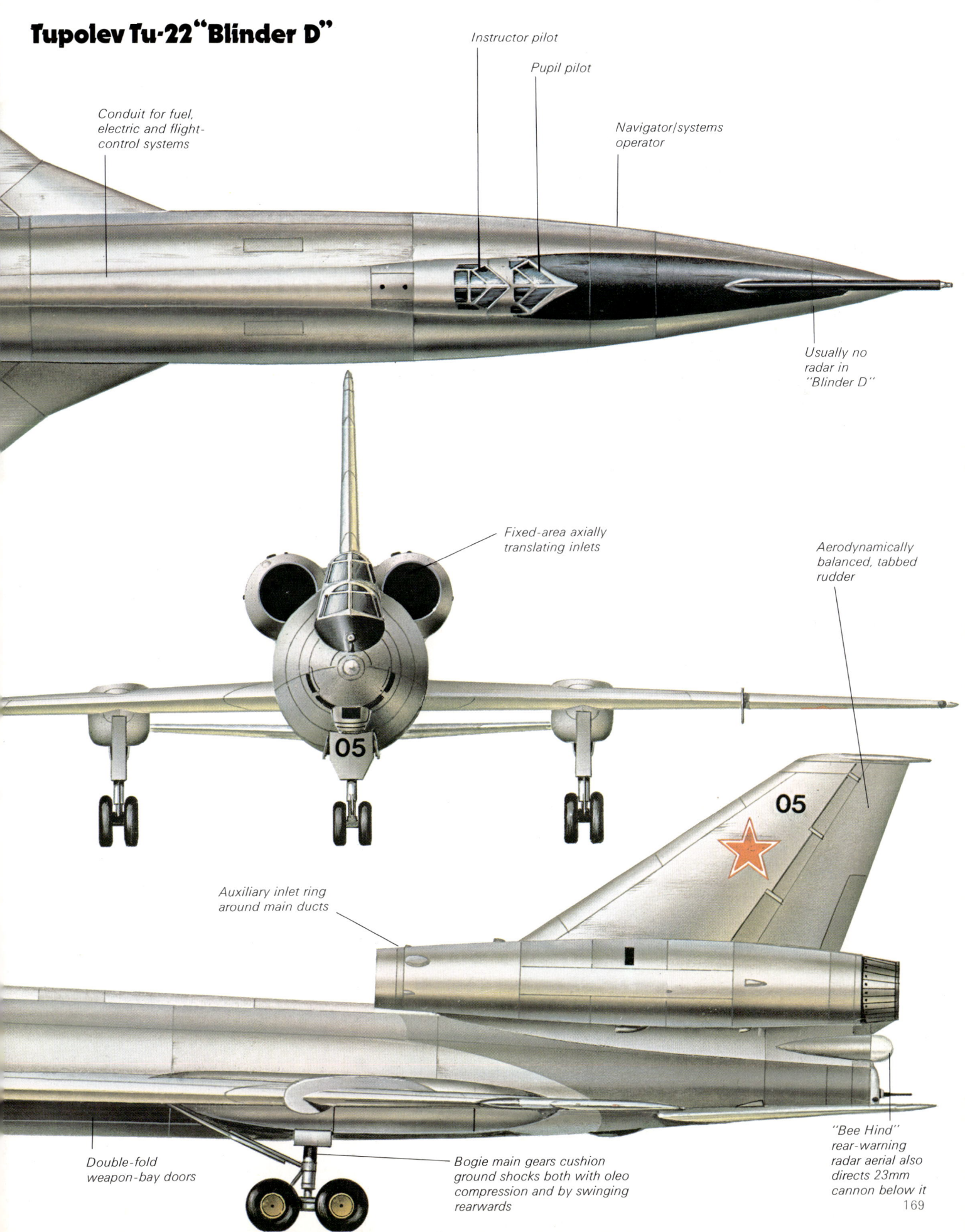

Instructor pilot

Pupil pilot

Navigator/systems operator

Conduit for fuel, electric and flight-control systems

Usually no radar in "Blinder D"

Fixed-area axially translating inlets

Aerodynamically balanced, tabbed rudder

Auxiliary inlet ring around main ducts

Double-fold weapon-bay doors

Bogie main gears cushion ground shocks both with oleo compression and by swinging rearwards

"Bee Hind" rear-warning radar aerial also directs 23mm cannon below it

169

▶**Armament:** One 23mm NS-23 in radar-directed barbette in tail; internal weapon bay for at least 20,000lb (9070kg) of free-fall bombs or other stores, or ("Blinder B") one "Kitchen" stand-off cruise missile semi-recessed under centreline.
History: First flight, well before public display in 1961; service delivery, probably 1963.
Users: Libya, Soviet Union (ADD, AV-MF).

Development: Having an efficient wing closely related to that of the Tu-28P, this supersonic bomber is a large aircraft with a bigger body and higher gross weight than the USAF B-58 Hustler. Typical crew appears to be a pilot, upward-ejecting, and two more members in tandem at a lower level who eject downwards. "Blinder A" was a reconnaissance bomber, seen in

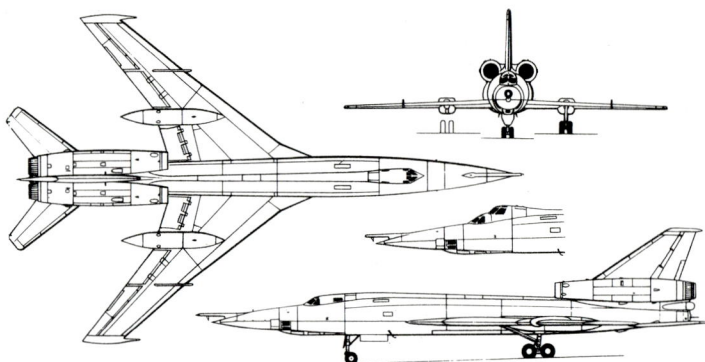

Three-view of Tu-22 "Blinder A" with (inset) nose of "Blinder D".

small numbers. B carried the stand-off missile, had a larger nose radar and semi-flush FR probe. C is the main variant, used by Naval Aviation for over-sea ECM/ESM surveillance, multi-sensor reconnaissance and with limited weapon capability. D is a dual trainer with stepped cockpits. Recent versions appear to have later engines (probably turbofans) with greater airflow. There have been persistent reports of an interceptor version, but this seems unlikely. The abiding shortcoming of the Tu-22 has been limited range, only partially alleviated by flight refuelling.

Above: This Tu-22 is the "Blinder C" multi-sensor reconnaissance version, with at least six bomb-bay cameras and extensive equipment for Elint missions.

Above: Tu-22 "Blinder A" ("Blinder C" is similar).

Below: These Tu-22 supersonic aircraft are from a unit of the AV-MF. They are probably of the "Blinder B" type with weapon bays tailored to the 37ft AS-4 "Kitchen" stand-off missile.

Tupolev Tu-26

Two main versions ("Backfire A") and ("B")

Origin: The design bureau named for Andrei N. Tupolev, Soviet Union.
Type: Reconnaissance bomber and missile platform with probable crew of four.
Engines: Two afterburning turbofans, probably Kuznetsov NK-144 two-shaft engines each with maximum rating of 48,500lb (22,000kg).
Dimensions: Span (15°) 113ft (34·44m), (56°) 86ft (26·2m); length (excluding probe) 132ft (40·23m); height 33ft (10·1m).
Weights: (Estimated) 99,250lb (45,000kg); maximum loaded 231,500lb (105,000kg).
Performance: (Estimated, "Backfire B") maximum speed at altitude 1,520mph (2445km/h, Mach 2·3); speed at sea level, over Mach 1; service ceiling over 60,000ft (18,290m); maximum combat radius on internal fuel 3,570 miles (5745km); ferry range, about 5,900 miles (9500km).
Armament: Internal weapon bay(s) for free-fall bombs up to largest thermonuclear sizes, with provision for carrying two AS-6 "Kingfish" stand-off missiles (often only one) on external wing racks; nominal weapon load 20,800lb (9435kg).
History: First flight ("Backfire A" prototype) not later than 1969; ("Backfire B") probably 1973; entry to service, probably 1974.
User: Soviet Union (ADD, AV-MF).

Development: Owing to the obvious inability of the Tu-22 to fly strategic missions the Tupolev bureau designed this far more formidable aircraft, larger in size and fitted with a swing-wing. "Backfire A" was apparently not a very successful design, with multi-wheel main gears folding into large fairings projecting in typical Tupolev fashion behind the only moderately swept wing. About half the gross wing area was fixed, just the outer portions swinging through a modest arc. Today's "Backfire B", which is believed to have the service designation of Tu-26, has no landing-gear boxes and is improved in other ways, though the details are still largely a matter for conjecture. The large engines are fed through wide inlet ducts which probably pass above the wing; a flight refuelling probe is fitted above the nose, but even without this "Backfire B" has an endurance of some ten hours. The Chairman of the US Joint Chiefs of Staff said in 1974: "It is expected to replace some of both the current medium and heavy bombers and, when deployed with a compatible tanker force, constitutes a potential

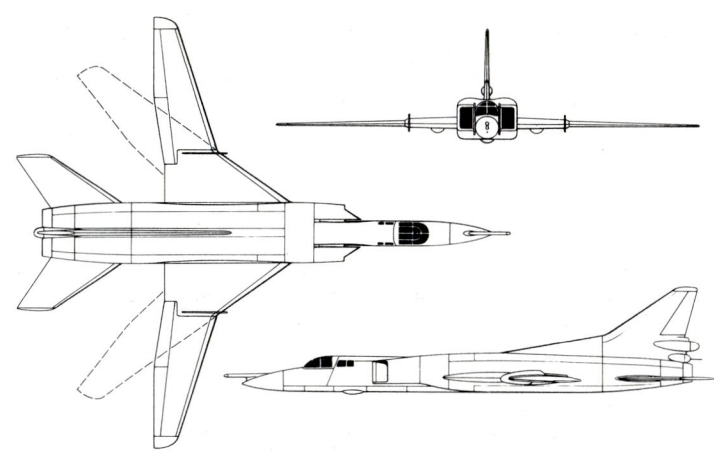

Above: Three-view of (Tu-26?) "Backfire B" (provisional).

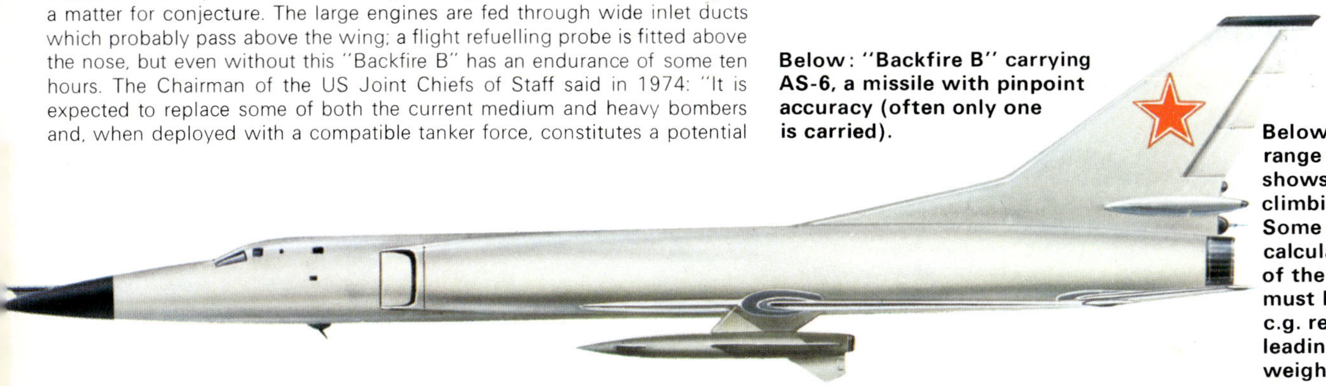

threat to the continental United States." The speed of development is also disquieting to the West, because these aircraft were being encountered on long oversea missions in early 1975. Even in 1977 details of the aircraft were sparse, not even its correct Soviet bureau or service designations having surfaced publicly. It is believed to have a crew of three, a very large radar and extremely sophisticated ECM/EW fits. The internal bomb load has been estimated by the US Department of Defense at the low level of 20,800lb, and the Russian insistence on having a radar-directed tail cannon is believed to have prevailed over those who think such installations a waste of cost and payload. Unusual features include the double-taper outer wings pivoted no less than 19ft from the centreline; another puzzle is where the landing gears are in the main production (B) version. Production rate is estimated at five per month, with 95 in service by the end of 1976 out of a planned total (ADD and AV-MF combined) of possibly 450.

continued on page 172▶

Below: "Backfire B" carrying AS-6, a missile with pinpoint accuracy (often only one is carried).

Below: This long-range telephoto shows a B-model climbing to altitude. Some observers calculate that much of the fuselage must be empty (for c.g. reasons), leading to lower weights and ranges.

Tupolev (Tu-26?) "Backfire B"

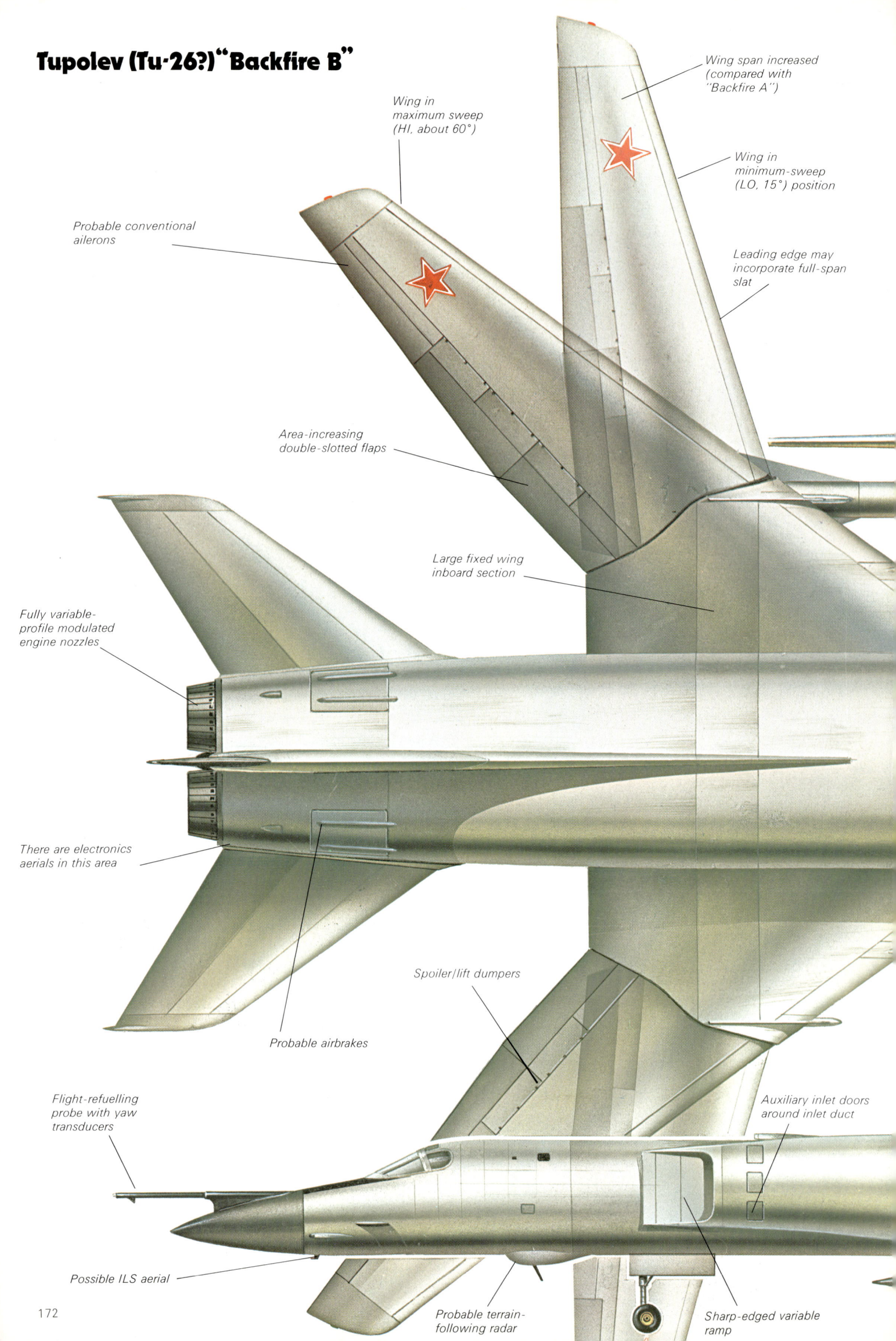

Wing in maximum sweep (HI, about 60°)

Wing span increased (compared with "Backfire A")

Wing in minimum-sweep (LO, 15°) position

Probable conventional ailerons

Leading edge may incorporate full-span slat

Area-increasing double-slotted flaps

Large fixed wing inboard section

Fully variable-profile modulated engine nozzles

There are electronics aerials in this area

Spoiler/lift dumpers

Probable airbrakes

Auxiliary inlet doors around inlet duct

Flight-refuelling probe with yaw transducers

Possible ILS aerial

Probable terrain-following radar

Sharp-edged variable ramp

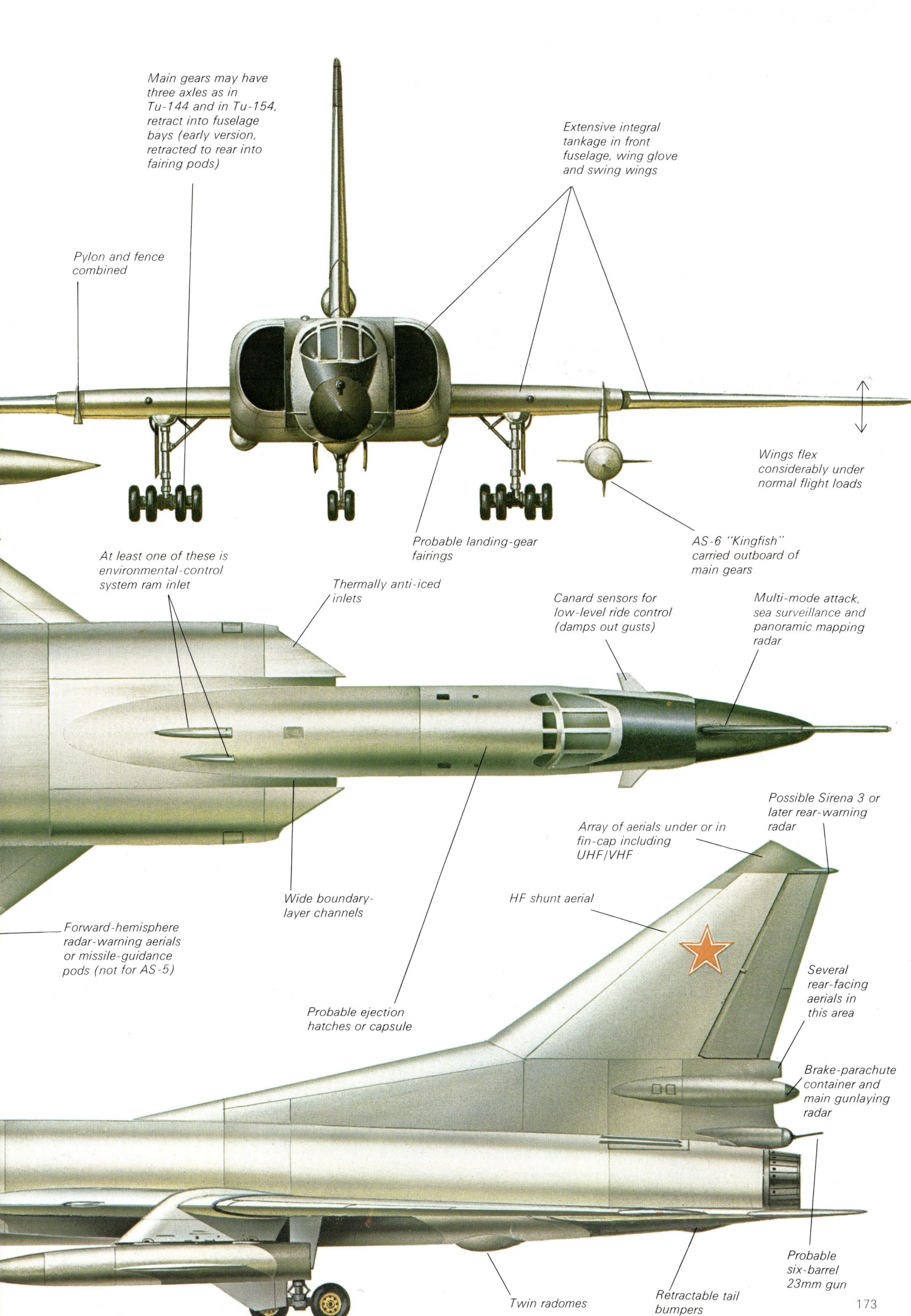

Main gears may have three axles as in Tu-144 and in Tu-154, retract into fuselage bays (early version, retracted to rear into fairing pods)

Extensive integral tankage in front fuselage, wing glove and swing wings

Pylon and fence combined

Wings flex considerably under normal flight loads

At least one of these is environmental-control system ram inlet

Probable landing-gear fairings

AS-6 ''Kingfish'' carried outboard of main gears

Thermally anti-iced inlets

Canard sensors for low-level ride control (damps out gusts)

Multi-mode attack, sea surveillance and panoramic mapping radar

Possible Sirena 3 or later rear-warning radar

Array of aerials under or in fin-cap including UHF/VHF

Forward-hemisphere radar-warning aerials or missile-guidance pods (not for AS-5)

HF shunt aerial

Wide boundary-layer channels

Several rear-facing aerials in this area

Probable ejection hatches or capsule

Brake-parachute container and main gunlaying radar

Twin radomes

Retractable tail bumpers

Probable six-barrel 23mm gun

Tupolev Tu-28P

Tu-28 versions of unknown designation; Tupolev bureau, Tu-102 ("Fiddler")

Origin: The design bureau of Andrei N. Tupolev, Soviet Union.
Type: Long-range all-weather interceptor.
Engines: Originally, two large axial turbojets of unknown type, each with afterburning rating of about 27,000lb (12,250kg), probably similar to those of Tu-22; later versions, afterburning turbofans of about 30,000lb (13,610 kg) each, as in later Tu-22.
Dimensions: (Estimated) span 65ft (20m); length 85ft (26m); height 23ft (7m).
Weights: (Estimated) empty 55,000lb (25,000kg); maximum loaded 100,000lb (45,000kg).
Performance: (Estimated) maximum speed (with missiles, at height)

continued on page 176 ▶

Tupolev Tu-28P "Fiddler"

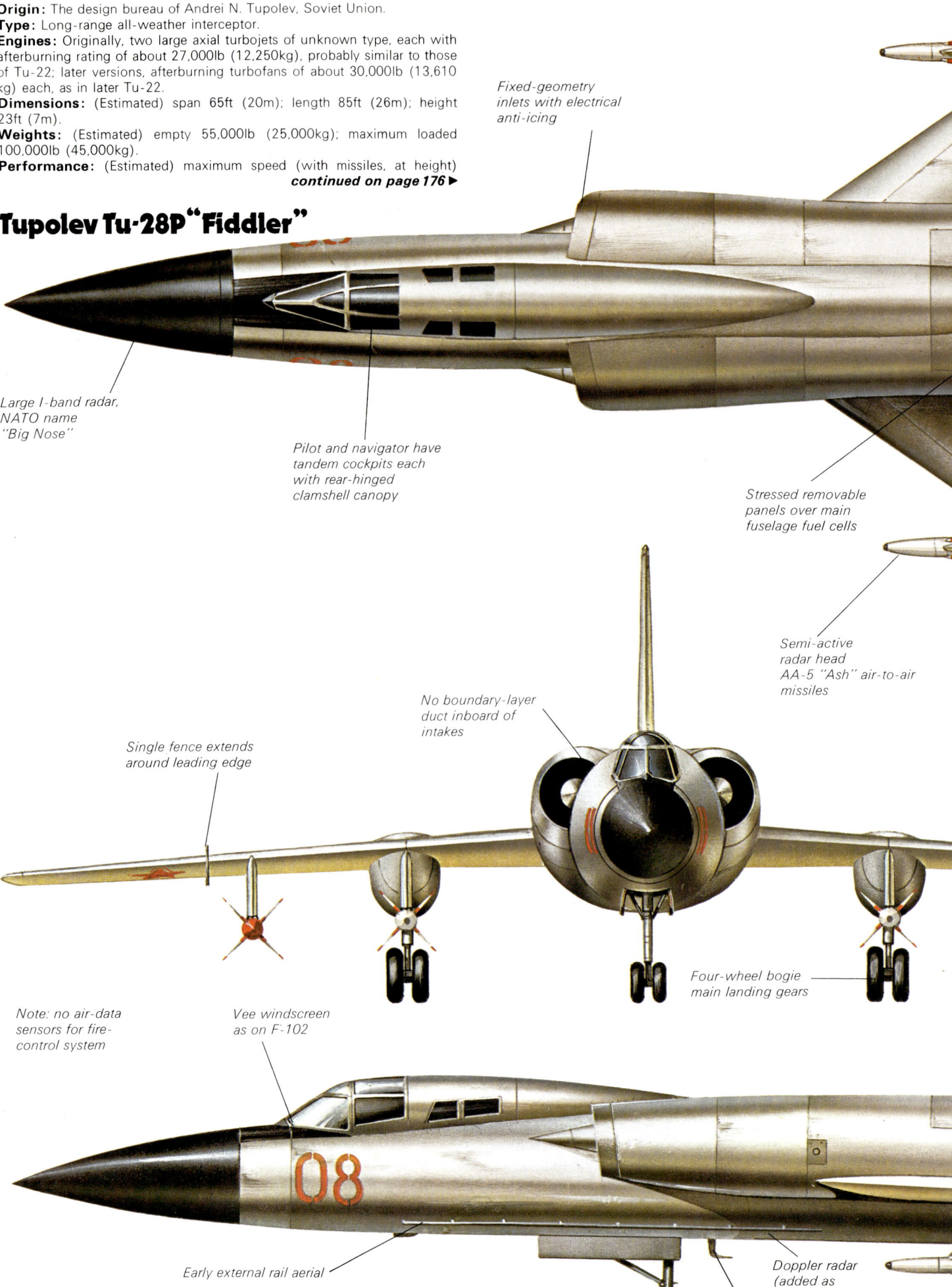

Fixed-geometry inlets with electrical anti-icing

Large I-band radar, NATO name "Big Nose"

Pilot and navigator have tandem cockpits each with rear-hinged clamshell canopy

Stressed removable panels over main fuselage fuel cells

Semi-active radar head AA-5 "Ash" air-to-air missiles

No boundary-layer duct inboard of intakes

Single fence extends around leading edge

Four-wheel bogie main landing gears

Note: no air-data sensors for fire-control system

Vee windscreen as on F-102

Early external rail aerial

Steerable nose gear

Doppler radar (added as modification)

ATC/SIF transponder aerial

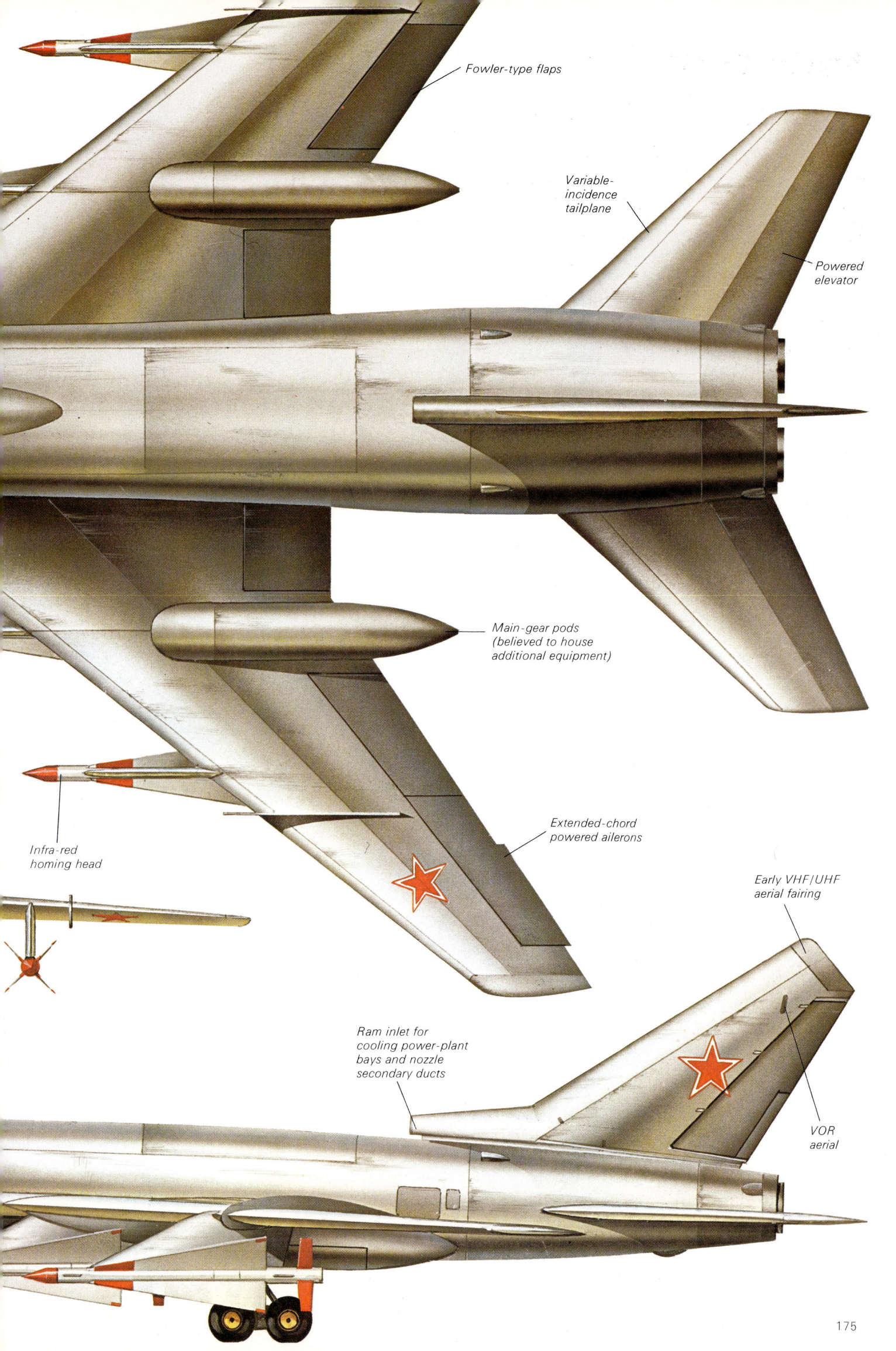

Fowler-type flaps

Variable-incidence tailplane

Powered elevator

Main-gear pods (believed to house additional equipment)

Extended-chord powered ailerons

Infra-red homing head

Early VHF/UHF aerial fairing

Ram inlet for cooling power-plant bays and nozzle secondary ducts

VOR aerial

▶1,150mph (1850km/h, Mach 1·75); initial climb, 25,000ft (7500m)/min; service ceiling (not gross weight) about 60,000ft (18,000m); range on internal fuel (high patrol) about 1,800 miles (2900km).
Armament: No guns seen in any version; mix of infra-red homing and radar-homing "Ash" air-to-air guided missiles, originally one of each and since 1965 two of each.
History: First flight, believed 1957; service delivery, probably 1961.
User: Soviet Union (PVO).

Development: Largest fighter known to be in service in the world, this formidable machine is essentially conventional yet has the greatest internal fuel capacity of any fighter and the biggest interception radar known to exist. It was one of a number of supersonic types produced by the Tupolev bureau with technology explored with the family of aircraft of the late

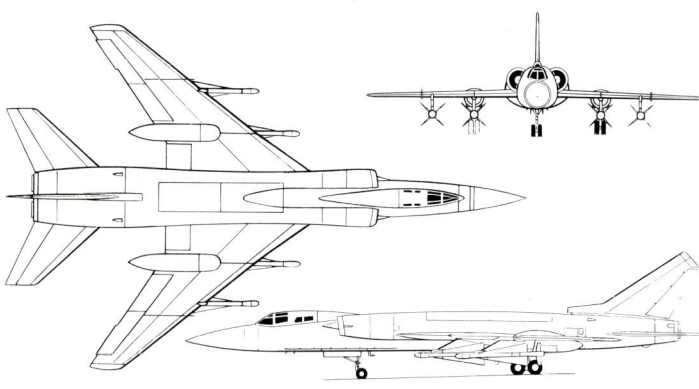

Three-view of the Tu-28P long-range interceptor, with four "Ash" air-to-air missiles.

1950s known to NATO as "Backfin" (another is the Tu-22). Like the others the Tu-28P has a distinctive wing with sharply kinked trailing edge, the outer 45° panels being outboard of large fairings extending behind the trailing edge accommodating the four-wheel bogie landing gears. Two crew sit in tandem under upward-hinged canopies, and all armament is carried on wing pylons. Early versions had twin ventral fins and usually large belly fairings, but these features are absent from aircraft in current service. The Tu-28P would be an ideal strategic patrol fighter to operate in conjunction with the "Moss" AWACS.

Above: This Tu-28 development aircraft was displayed at Tushino in 1961. It had a large ventral fairing (reason unknown), twin ventral fins and only two missiles under its wings.

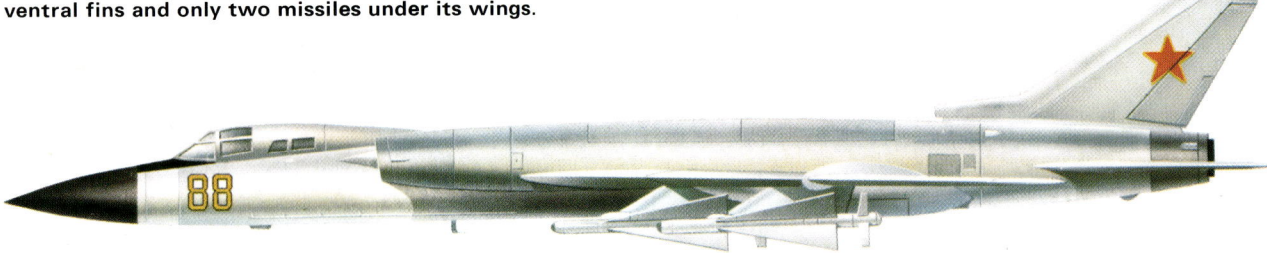

Above: The latest Tu-28P, with "Ash" air-to-air missiles.

Below: Dramatic action shot of a Tu-28P "rippling" away all four of its large air-to-air missiles. Though almost 20 years old as a design, the Tu-28P is still an all-weather interceptor of great capability and in most respects remains the world's largest fighter.

Tupolev Tu-126

Design bureau Tu-126; service designation, possibly Tu-24 ("Moss")

Origin: The design bureau named for Andrei N. Tupolev, Soviet Union.
Type: Airborne warning and control system.
Engines: Four 14,795ehp Kuznetsov NK-12MV single-shaft turboprops.
Dimensions: Span 167ft 8in (51·10m); length 182ft 6in (55·48m), (with FR probe) 188ft 0in (57·30m); height overall 52ft 8in (16·05m).
Weights: Empty (estimate) 198,400lb (90,000kg); maximum loaded 375,000lb (170,000kg).
Performance: Probable maximum speed 500mph (805km/h); on-station height 40,000ft (12,200m); normal operational endurance 18hr; ferry range at least 6,000 miles (9,650km).
History: First flight probably 1962–64; service delivery not later than 1967.
User: Soviet Union (almost certainly IA-PVO).

Development: Tupolev's family of swept-wing turboprops bigger and faster than any others ever put into service began with the long-range bomber Tu-95 (service designation Tu-20). From this evolved the considerably bigger Tu-114 civil airliner and the same-size Tu-114D special transport. The Tu-114 was never used as the basis for a large military freighter, but it was tailor-made for the Tu-126 AWACS (airborne warning and control system). Even examination of photographs indicates that this is a sophisticated and highly developed aircraft. Though details are sparse in the West, it is unlikely that its surveillance radar can quite equal that of the Boeing E-3A. On the other hand there is an element of wishful thinking in the supposed US belief that it is "of limited effectiveness over water and ineffective over land." At least one Tu-126 was detached with its crew to serve with the Indian Air Force during the 1971 fighting with Pakistan. The

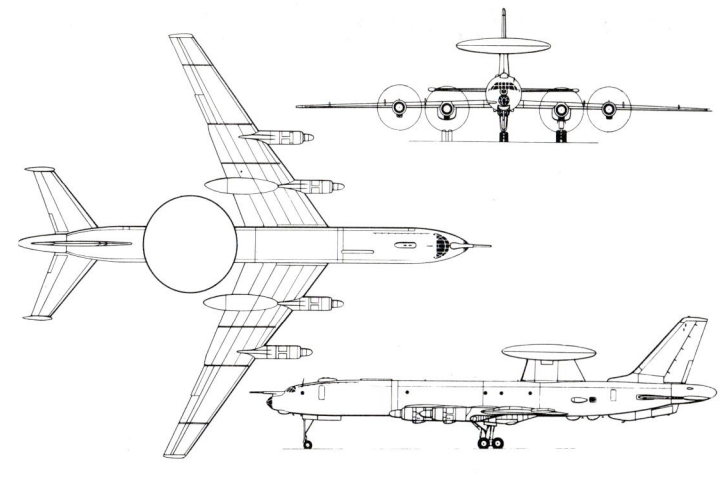

Three-view of Tu-126 "Moss" with landing gear extended.

number in Soviet service in 1976 was put at "at least ten" but ten times that number would be needed to patrol even the main sections of the Soviet frontier unless the only threat was cruise missiles.

continued on page 178▶

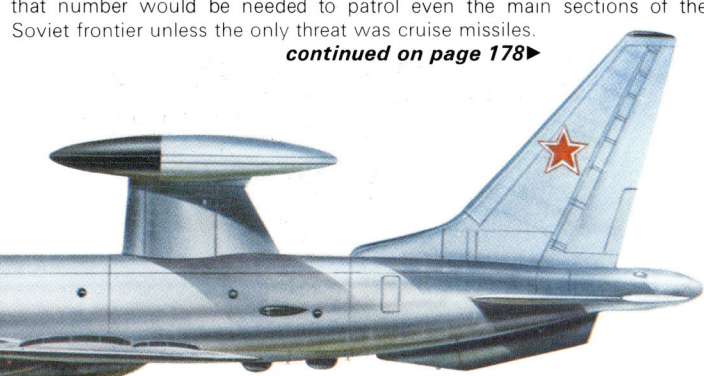

Above: A recent Tu-126.

Below: Enlargement from a Soviet ciné film. The "Moss" force is probably being increased by rebuilding Tu-114 transports.

Tupolev Tu-126 "Moss"

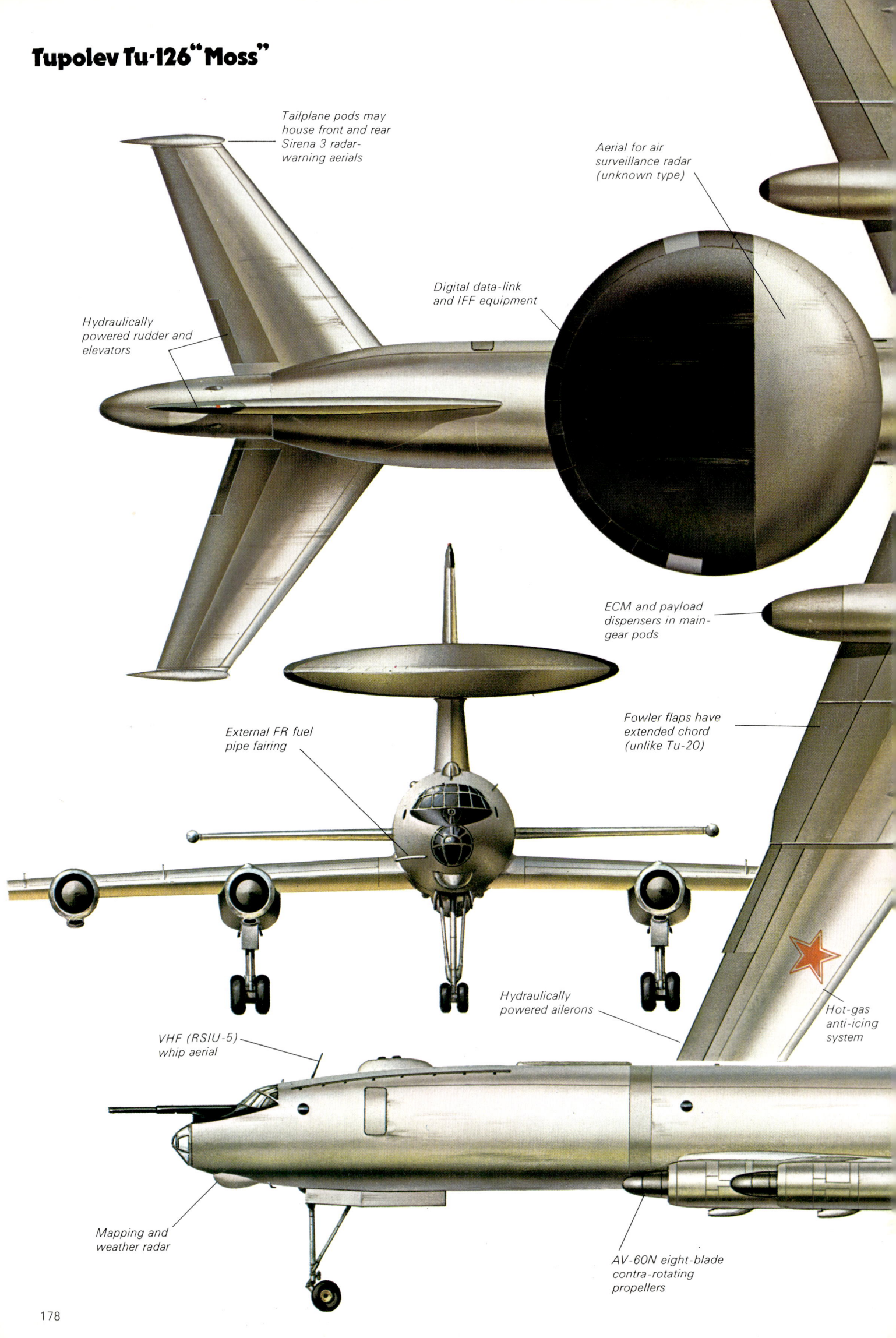

Tailplane pods may house front and rear Sirena 3 radar-warning aerials

Aerial for air surveillance radar (unknown type)

Digital data-link and IFF equipment

Hydraulically powered rudder and elevators

ECM and payload dispensers in main-gear pods

External FR fuel pipe fairing

Fowler flaps have extended chord (unlike Tu-20)

Hydraulically powered ailerons

VHF (RSIU-5) whip aerial

Hot-gas anti-icing system

Mapping and weather radar

AV-60N eight-blade contra-rotating propellers

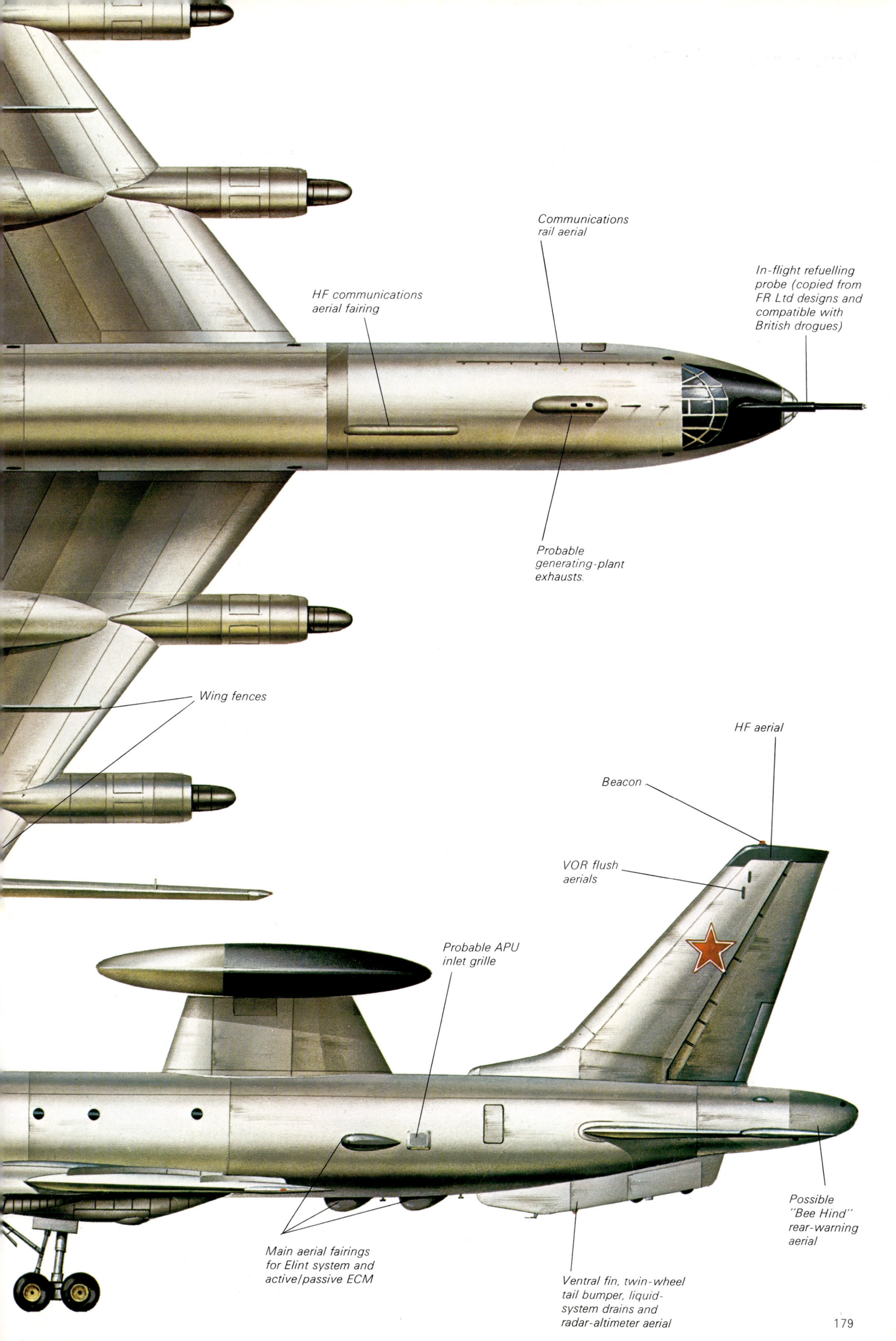

Communications
rail aerial

In-flight refuelling
probe (copied from
FR Ltd designs and
compatible with
British drogues)

HF communications
aerial fairing

Probable
generating-plant
exhausts.

Wing fences

HF aerial

Beacon

VOR flush
aerials

Probable APU
inlet grille

Main aerial fairings
for Elint system and
active/passive ECM

Possible
"Bee Hind"
rear-warning
aerial

Ventral fin, twin-wheel
tail bumper, liquid-
system drains and
radar-altimeter aerial

179

Yakovlev Yak-11

Yak-11 ("Moose")

Origin: The design bureau of Alexander S. Yakovlev.
Type: Basic combat trainer.
Engine: 800hp Shvetsov ASh-21 seven-cylinder radial.
Dimensions: Span 30ft 10in (9·40m); length 27ft 10¾in (8·50m); height 9ft 2½in (2·80m).
Weights: Empty 4,630lb (2100kg); maximum loaded 5,512lb (2500kg).
Performance: Maximum speed 286mph (460km/h); dive limit 368mph (593km/h); stalling speed (landing configuration) 90mph (145km/h).
Armament: Optional machine gun (usually 7·62mm ShKAS) on upper left side of nose; practice-bomb racks under wings.
History: First flight, believed 1946; service delivery, believed 1948.
Users (past and present): Afghanistan, Albania, Algeria, Austria, Bulgaria, China, Cuba, Czechoslovakia, East Germany, Egypt, Hungary, Iraq, Poland, Romania, Somalia, Soviet Union (VVS, DOSAAF), Syria, Vietnam, Yemen and probably other countries.

Development: Never in the limelight, so that even basic data and history are hard to research, this straightforward trainer is still used in vast numbers by the VVS pilot-training schools and by many other air forces around the world. Based on the Yak-9 fighter, though having a totally different fuselage with tandem seats, it has a small wing and thus needs a long take-off run but rolls extremely rapidly. An odd feature is that flaps, landing gear and other powered services are operated by compressed air. The tailwheel can retract but is invariably seen protruding. Czechoslovakia made the Yak-11 as the C-11, and the nosewheel-equipped Yak-11U (used by the Soviet Union only in small numbers) as the C-11U. The direct-injection engine has cooling shutters that can almost seal off the airflow. In 1964 one of a formation of Yak-11s (painted dark green and bearing no markings, but presumably bound for Egypt) forced-landed in Cyprus. It eventually was made airworthy in Britain as G-AYAK, and remains the only example of its type in West Europe (Yak-11s are no longer used by the Austrian AF).

Right: Though probably no longer equipping any unit exclusively, the Yak-11 remains in use in large numbers with all arms of Soviet air power. It is a popular hack and liaison aircraft.

Below: Two Czech-built C-11 trainers, the nearer a civil-registered club machine. No civil C-11s are left in Czechoslovakia today, but military examples are still in air force service in training, towing and various utility roles.

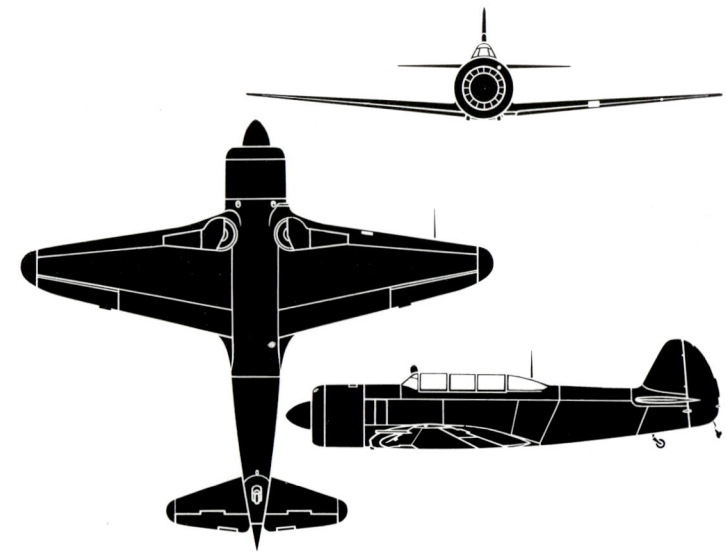

Above: Three-view of standard Yak-11, with rear-view mirror.

Yakovlev Yak-18

Yak-18, 18U, 18A, 18P, 18PM, 18T ("Max")

Origin: The design bureau of Alexander Yakovlev, Soviet Union.
Type: Primary trainer; see text for other roles.
Engine: (18, 18U) one 160hp Shvetsov M-11FR five-cylinder radial; (18A, P, PM) one 300hp Ivchenko AI-14RF nine-cylinder radial; (T) one 360hp Vedeneev M-14P nine-cylinder radial.
Dimensions: Span (18) 33ft 9½in (10·3m), (18U, A and P) 34ft 9¼in (10·60m), (T) 36ft 7¼in (11·16m); length (18, 18U) 26ft 5½in (8·07m), (18A, P and T) 27ft 4¾in (8·35m); height (18, PM) about 7ft (2·13m), (U, A, P, T) 11ft 0in (3·35m).
Weight: Empty (18) about 1,800lb (816kg), (U, A, P) typically 2,259lb (1025kg), (T) 2,450lb (1110kg); maximum loaded (18) 2,469lb (1120kg), (U, A, P) 2,910lb (1320kg), (T) 3,637lb (1650kg).
Performance: Maximum speed (18) 133mph (215km/h), (U) 143mph (230km/h), (U, A, P, T) 186mph (300km/h); range with max fuel (A) 435 miles (700km), (T) 560 miles (900km).
History: First flight 1946, (U) 1955, (A) 1956, (P) probably 1959, (PM) probably 1965, (T) 1967.
Users: China, E Germany, N Korea, Mongolia, Romania, S Yemen, Soviet Union, Syria, probably others.

Development: Most of the primary training of the Warsaw Pact air forces (apart from Poland, which uses the TS-8 Bies) is done in civil or para military schools, and it is to these that the bulk of some 8,000 of these popular and robust aircraft have been supplied. The original Yak-18 had an M-11 with helmeted cowling and tailwheel-type landing gear with the main legs retracting to the rear. The 18U introduced a long nosewheel gear with forward-retracting main legs, while the much more powerful A was cleaned up and had a variable-pitch propeller. The P and PM were refined single-seat aerobatic versions, the PS being a tailwheel derivative leading to today's Yak-50. The T has a wider centre section and a new stressed-skin fuselage with four-seat cabin, suitable for training, ambulance, patrol and similar duties, with wheel, ski or float landing gear.

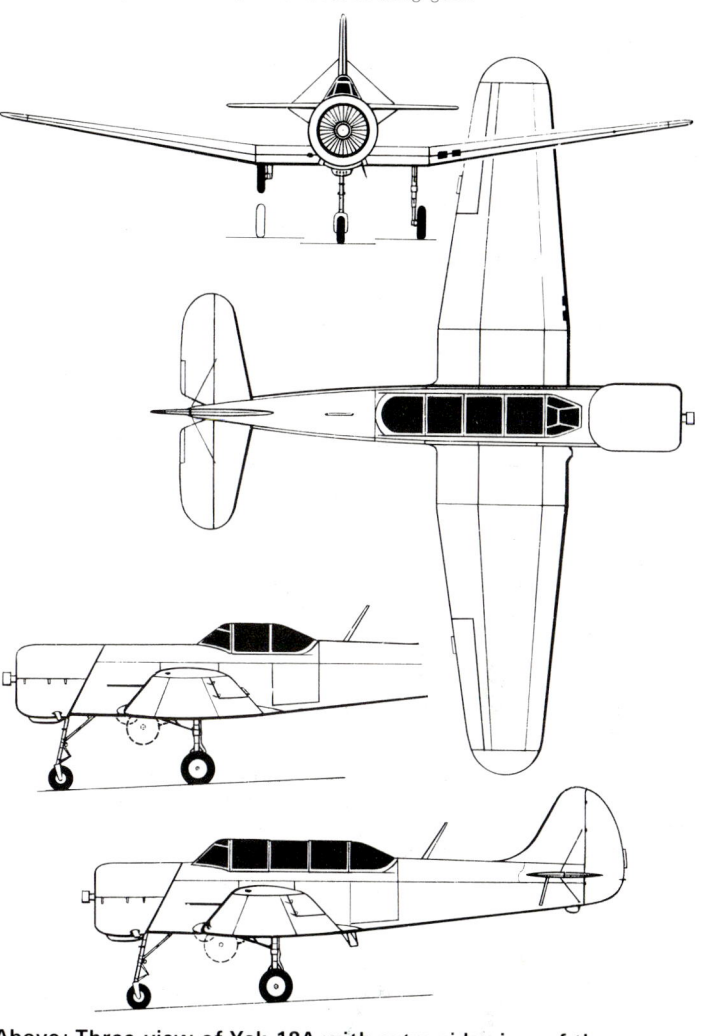

Above: A Yak-18A tandem-seat tricycle-gear trainer of the Soviet Air Force pilot-training organization. Though designed just after World War II the Yak-18 is still used by DOSAAF and Warsaw Pact air forces for pilot aptitude grading and ab initio training.

Below: The Yak-18PM single-seater was developed for the 1966 World Aerobatic Championships, which it won decisively. The two most distant in this line-up were part of the Soviet team.

Above: Three-view of Yak-18A with extra side view of the Yak-18P single-seater. Today there are many models with nosewheel or tailwheel and one to four seats.

Yakovlev Yak-26

Yak-26, -27P ("Mangrove") and ("Mandrake")

Origin: The design bureau of Alexander S. Yakovlev, Soviet Union.
Type: Two-seat reconnaissance (27P, interceptor).
Engines: (26, 27P) Two Tumansky RD-9B or other RD-9 versions rated at from 7,165lb (3250kg) to 8,820lb (4000kg) with maximum afterburner; ("Mandrake") two non-afterburning turbojets, probably RD-9 rated at about 6,000lb (2720kg).
Dimensions: Span (26 and 27P) 38ft 6in (11·75m); (original 27) 36ft 1in; ("Mandrake") estimated at 71ft (22m); length (26) 62ft (18·90m); (27P) about 55ft (16·75m); ("Mandrake") about 51ft (15·5m); height (26, 27P) 14ft 6in (4·40m); ("Mandrake") about 13ft (4m).
Weights: Empty (all) about 18,000lb (8165kg); maximum loaded (26) about 26,000lb (11,800kg); (27P) about 24,000lb (10,900kg); ("Mandrake") possibly nearly 30,000lb (13,600kg).
Performance: Maximum speed (26, 27P, at altitude) 686mph (1104km/h, Mach 0·95); ("Mandrake") about 470mph (755km/h); initial climb, about 15,000ft (4600m)/min ("Mandrake", less); service ceiling (26, 27P) 49,200ft (15,000m); ("Mandrake") about 62,000ft (19,000m); range at altitude (26) about 1,675 miles (2700km); (27P) 1,000 miles (1600km); ("Mandrake") possibly 2,500 miles (4000km).
Armament: (26) one 30mm NR-30 cannon in fairing low on right side of forward fuselage; (27P) small batches with cannon and rockets, then small batches with two missile pylons; ("Mandrake") none.
History: First flight (26) before mid-1956; (27P) before mid-1956; ("Mandrake") possibly 1957.
User: Soviet Union.

Development: Stemming directly from the Yak-25, these aircraft introduced various changes, of which the most significant was afterburning engines in the Yak-27 and 27P. The leading edge was swept very sharply at the root and the trailing edge extended inboard of the longer nacelles to meet the body at 90° and give much greater root chord. The nose was pointed (glazed on the 26 and a radome on the 27P) and in the production aircraft the outer wings were extended beyond the outrigger gear and fitted with drooped extended-chord leading edges. Only the 27 was built in large numbers (NATO name "Mangrove"). The 27P was called "Flashlight C". The high-altitude, unswept "Mandrake", whose proper designation is not known, made overflights in Eastern Asia, the Middle East and along the borders of Communist territory in Europe before being withdrawn from most front-line units. Today a few "sneak" missions are still being made, and it may be that the aircraft making them are remotely piloted (because Mandrake and other Yak twin-jets have been important radio-controlled targets used in Soviet missile tests).

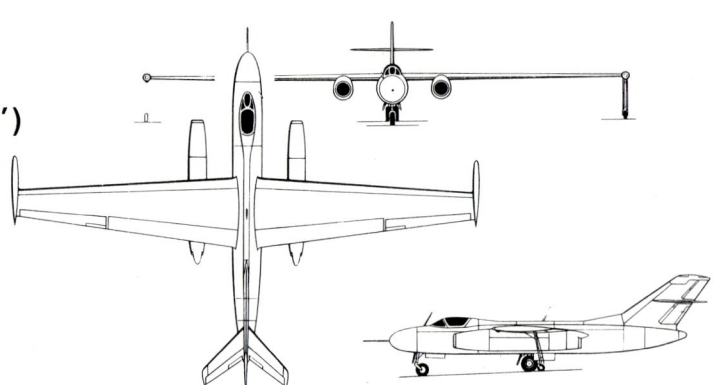

Above: Three-view of (Yak-25RD) "Mandrake" (provisional).

Below: The several Yak-27 sub-types (NATO name "Mangrove") were interim aircraft which led to the Yak-28 "Brewer" family—which look similar but are totally redesigned.
Foot of page: (Yak-25RD) "Mandrake", from Soviet ciné film.

Yakovlev Yak-28P

Yak-28 attack versions, -28P, -28R, -28U ("Firebar"), ("Brewer"), ("Maestro")

Origin: The design bureau of Alexander S. Yakovlev, Soviet Union.

Type: 28 (unknown designations) two-seat attack; (P) all weather interceptor; (R) multi-sensor reconnaissance; (U) dual-control trainer.

Engines: Two Tumansky RD-11 single-shaft afterburning turbojets each with maximum rating of 13,120lb (5950kg); certain sub-types have RD-11-300 rated at 13,670lb (6200kg).

Dimensions: (Estimated) span 42ft 6in (12·95m) (some versions have span slightly less than standard); length (except late P) 71ft 0½in (21·65m); (late 28P) 74ft (22·56m); height 12ft 11½in (3·95m).

Weights: Empty (estimated, typical) 24,250lb (11,000kg); maximum loaded (U) 30,000lb (13,600kg); (others) 35,300–41,000lb (16,000–18,600kg).

Performance: (Estimated) maximum speed at altitude 735mph (1180km/h, Mach 1·13); initial climb 27,900ft (8500m)/min; service ceiling 55,500ft (16,750m); range (clean, at altitude) 1,200–1,600 miles (1930–2575km).

Armament: (Attack versions) one 30mm NR-30 cannon on both sides of fuselage or on right side only; fuselage weapon bay for internal load of free-fall bombs (estimated maximum, 4,400lb, 2000kg); hard-points or pylons between drop-tank attachments and outrigger gears for light loads (usually pod of 55mm rockets); (28P) two "Anab" air-to-air guided missiles, one radar and the other infra-red; in some aircraft, two additional pylons for two K-13A ("Atoll") missiles, both "Anab" then being radar homers; (R) believed none; (U) retains weapon bay and single gun.

History: First flight, before 1961; (production attack and interceptor versions) before 1961; service delivery not later than mid-1962; final delivery, before 1970.

User: Soviet Union (IA-PVO).

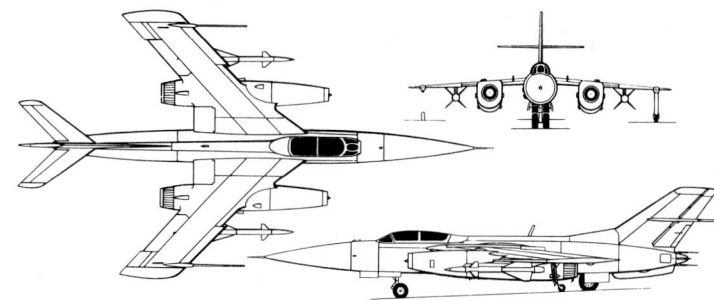

Above: Three-view of the current sub-type of Yak-28P with pointed radome.

Development: Obviously derived from the Yak-25/26/27, the Yak-28 is a completely new aircraft, with high wing of different form, new engines, steerable twin-wheel nose gear and considerably greater weight. Early attack versions had slightly shorter fuselage and shorter nacelles ahead of the wing; many hundreds (possibly thousands) of glazed-nose attack 28s (code name "Brewer") were built, most having been rebuilt as ECM and other specialist tactical machines. The Yak-28P (code name "Firebar") remains a leading interceptor, its "Skip Spin" radar being enclosed in a much longer and more pointed nose from 1967. The 28U trainer (code name "Maestro") has a separate front (pupil) cockpit with canopy hinged to the right. Many 28R versions ("Brewer D"), with cameras and various non-optical sensors, may be converted attack aircraft. Flight refuelling is not fitted.

continued on page 184▶

Above: A long-nose Yak-28P

Below: About to take off, a short-nose Yak-28P lines up on the runway with tailplane at negative incidence to rotate the aircraft about its rear landing-gear truck. This is the ultimate development of the Yak-25 of 1953.

Yakovlev Yak·28 "Brewer C"

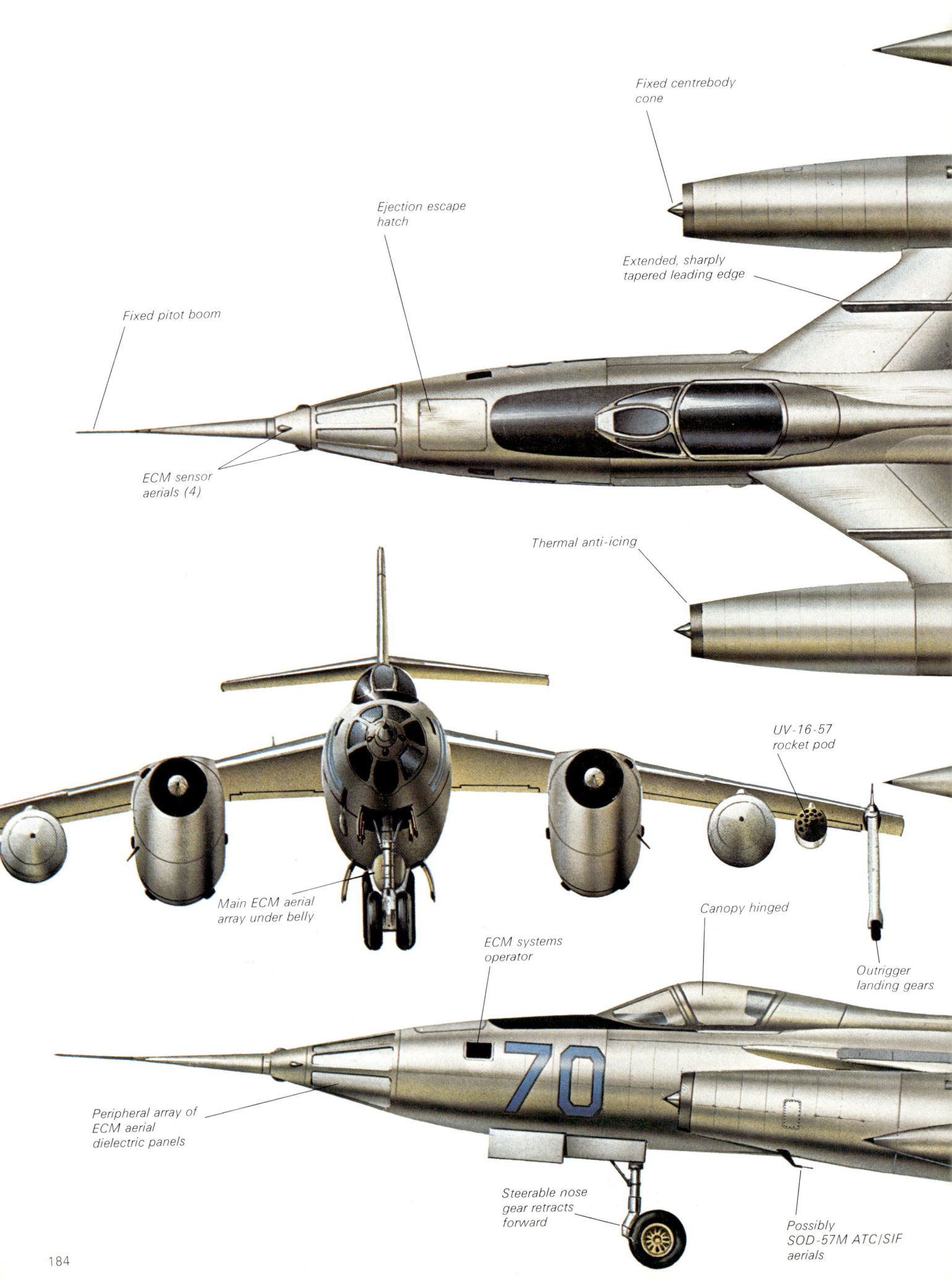

Fixed centrebody cone

Ejection escape hatch

Extended, sharply tapered leading edge

Fixed pitot boom

ECM sensor aerials (4)

Thermal anti-icing

UV-16-57 rocket pod

Main ECM aerial array under belly

Canopy hinged

Outrigger landing gears

ECM systems operator

Peripheral array of ECM aerial dielectric panels

Steerable nose gear retracts forward

Possibly SOD-57M ATC/SIF aerials

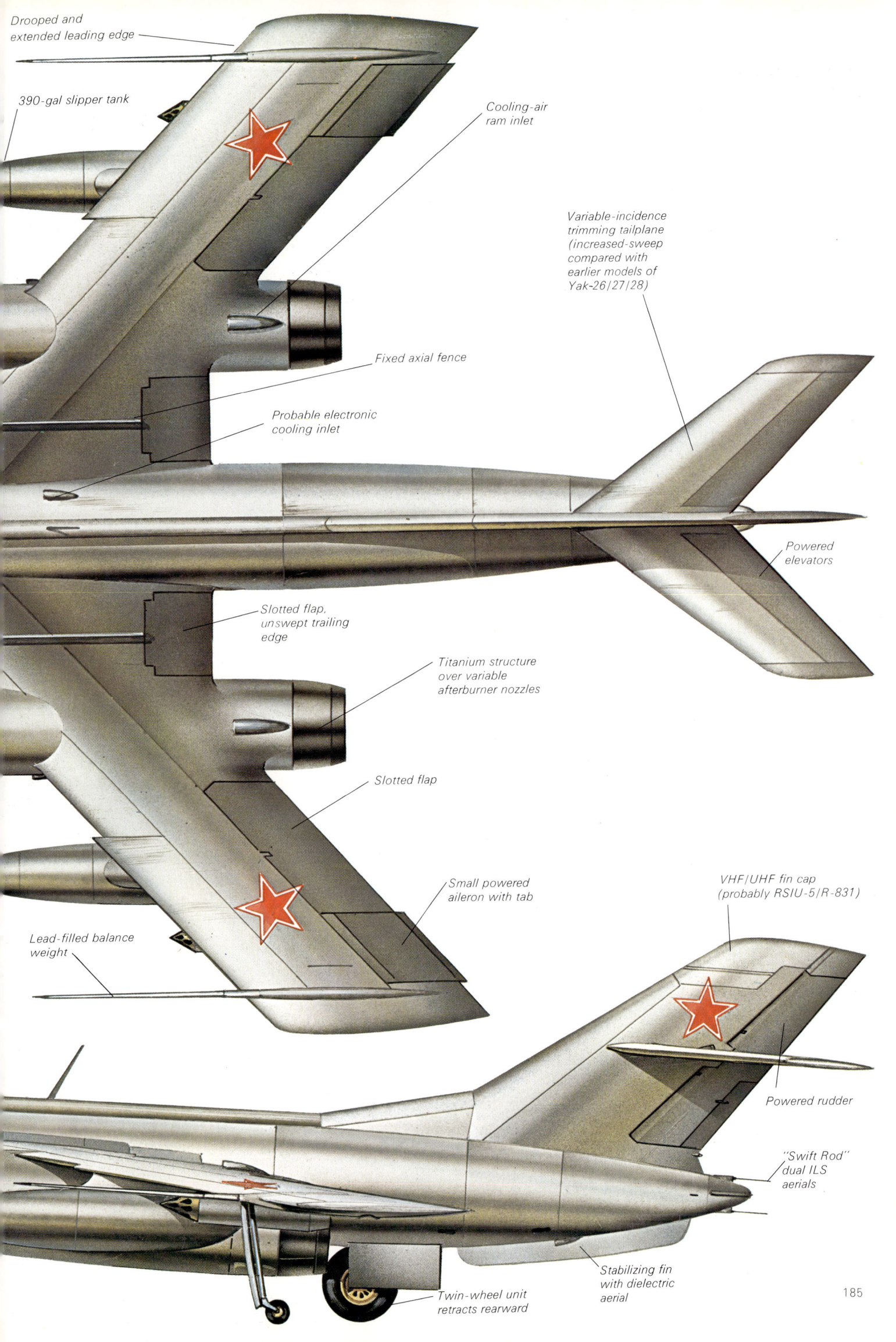

Drooped and extended leading edge

390-gal slipper tank

Cooling-air ram inlet

Variable-incidence trimming tailplane (increased-sweep compared with earlier models of Yak-26/27/28)

Fixed axial fence

Probable electronic cooling inlet

Powered elevators

Slotted flap, unswept trailing edge

Titanium structure over variable afterburner nozzles

Slotted flap

Small powered aileron with tab

VHF/UHF fin cap (probably RSIU-5/R-831)

Lead-filled balance weight

Powered rudder

"Swift Rod" dual ILS aerials

Stabilizing fin with dielectric aerial

Twin-wheel unit retracts rearward

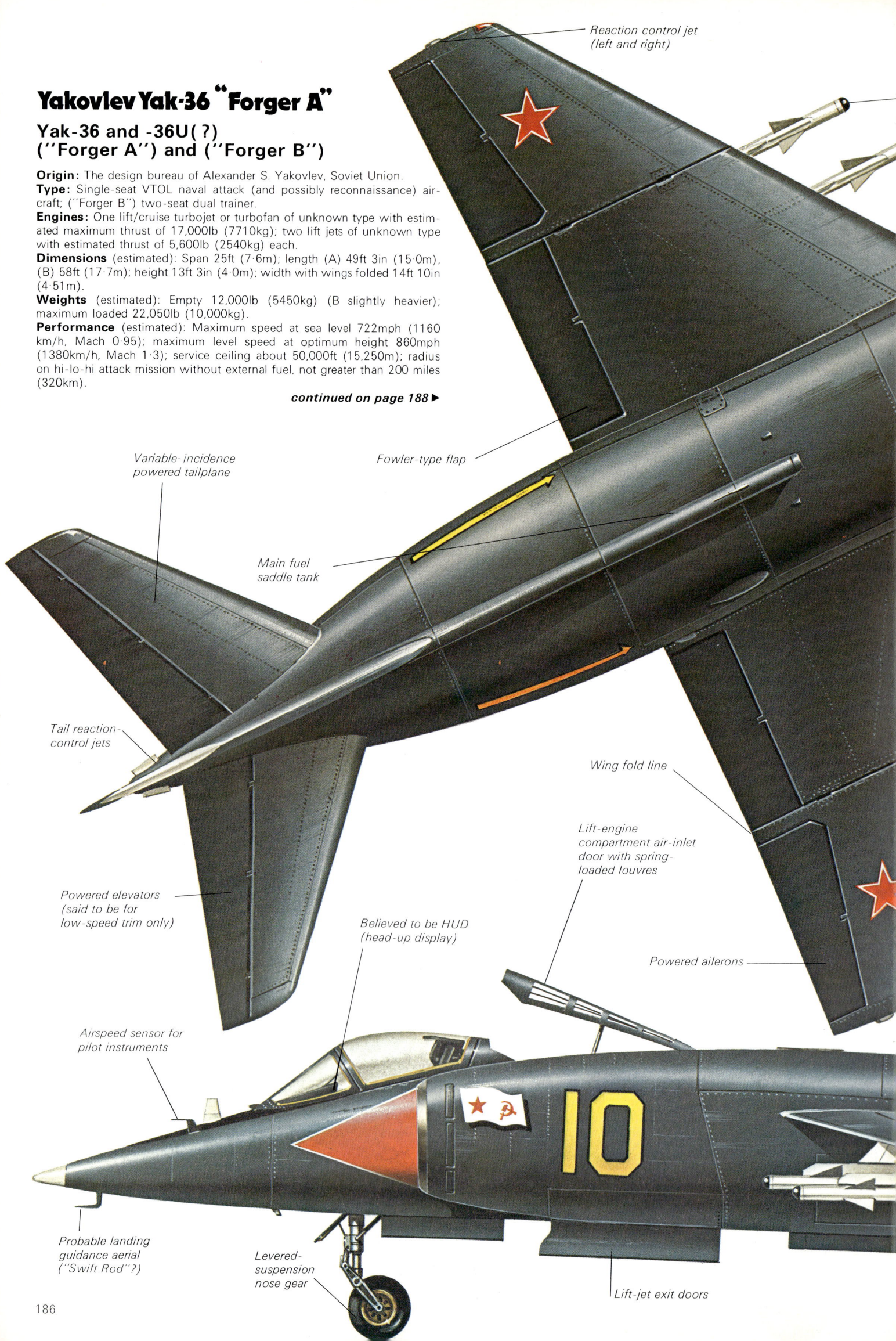

Yakovlev Yak-36 "Forger A"

Yak-36 and -36U(?)
("Forger A") and ("Forger B")

Origin: The design bureau of Alexander S. Yakovlev, Soviet Union.
Type: Single-seat VTOL naval attack (and possibly reconnaissance) air-craft; ("Forger B") two-seat dual trainer.
Engines: One lift/cruise turbojet or turbofan of unknown type with estim-ated maximum thrust of 17,000lb (7710kg); two lift jets of unknown type with estimated thrust of 5,600lb (2540kg) each.
Dimensions (estimated): Span 25ft (7·6m); length (A) 49ft 3in (15·0m), (B) 58ft (17·7m); height 13ft 3in (4·0m); width with wings folded 14ft 10in (4·51m).
Weights (estimated): Empty 12,000lb (5450kg) (B slightly heavier); maximum loaded 22,050lb (10,000kg).
Performance (estimated): Maximum speed at sea level 722mph (1160 km/h, Mach 0·95); maximum level speed at optimum height 860mph (1380km/h, Mach 1·3); service ceiling about 50,000ft (15,250m); radius on hi-lo-hi attack mission without external fuel, not greater than 200 miles (320km).

continued on page 188 ▶

Reaction control jet (left and right)

Variable-incidence powered tailplane

Fowler-type flap

Main fuel saddle tank

Tail reaction-control jets

Wing fold line

Powered elevators (said to be for low-speed trim only)

Lift-engine compartment air-inlet door with spring-loaded louvres

Believed to be HUD (head-up display)

Powered ailerons

Airspeed sensor for pilot instruments

Probable landing guidance aerial ("Swift Rod"?)

Levered-suspension nose gear

Lift-jet exit doors

AA-2 "Atoll" close-range missiles

Two lift jets

Possible radar-ranging aerial for air/air use or in landing on ship

Canopy hinged to right

Fixed air inlet with thermal anti-icing

Blow-in auxiliary inlet doors

Fuselage fuel cell

Folded position of wing

Pylons can carry GSh-23 gun and/or ECM pods

Autostabilization ram-air inlet

UHF/VHF dielectric fin cap

Possible ILS ("Swift Rod"?)

VOR aerials

Tail bumper

Three-unit SRO-2M ("Odd Rods") IFF aerials

Left nozzle (one of two handling entire airflow of main engine)

Armament: Contrary to early reports there appears to be no internal gun; four pylons under the non-folding wing centre section carry gun pods, reconnaissance pods, ECM payloads, bombs, missiles (said to include AA-2 "Atoll" AAM and AS-7 "Kerry" ASM) and tanks. Maximum external load, about 4,000lb (1814kg). (B two-seater) none seen.

History: First flight probably about 1971; service delivery possibly 1975.

User: Soviet Union (AV-MF).

Development: At the 1967 show at Domodedovo a single V/STOL jet-lift research aircraft gave a convincing display of hovering and transitions. Called "Freehand" by NATO, it was at first thought to be the Yak-36, but this is now believed to be the service designation of the combat aircraft carried aboard *Kiev*, the first of the large Soviet carriers (officially classed as anti-submarine cruisers) which also carry ASW helicopters and an unprecedented array of shipboard weapons. The "Freehand", of which fewer than ten are thought to have been built, conducted trials from a specially built platform on the carrier *Moskva*. It provided information to assist the design of the Yak-36, which probably has the same large lift turbofan engine plus aft-angled lift jets behind the cockpit. To take off, the three engines must be used together and a vertical ascent made, the main nozzles being rotated to about 100° to balance the rearward thrust of the lift jets. STOL takeoffs are not thought to be possible, neither is Viffing (vectoring in forward flight) to increase combat manoeuvrability. The design is simple, though one wonders why the wing was mounted in the mid-position instead of the much lighter solution of putting it above the main engine. The latter has plain inlets usually with auxiliary doors as on the Harrier, but supersonic speed at height is judged possible in the clean condition. Other features include Fowler flaps, large ailerons on the folding outer wings,

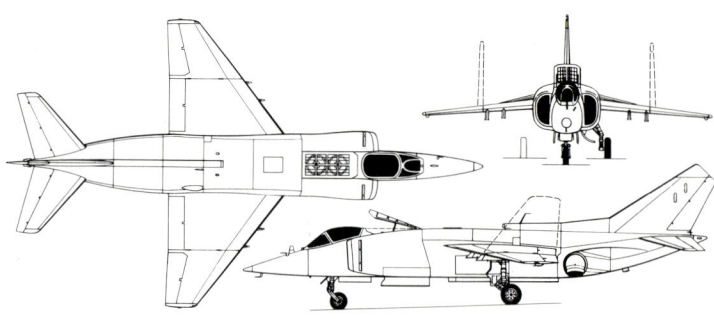

Above: Three-view of single-seat "Forger A" (note wing fold).

wingtip and tail control nozzles, a ram inlet duct in the dorsal spine, rear airbrakes, a large vertical tail with dielectric tip, and a dielectric nosecap probably covering a small ranging radar. The "Forger B" has a completely different tandem-seat nose angled downwards and a lengthened rear fuselage to preserve directional stability. The development squadron aboard *Kiev* on her shakedown cruise from the Nikolayev yard to Murmansk flew intensively, and observers especially noted the repeated precision of take-offs and landings, indicating ship guidance. Even this aircraft is almost certainly an interim type.

Below, top to bottom: Single-seater making precision approach on to deck of *Kiev*; take-off by single-seater with auxiliary inlets (painted flag further aft); and the two-seat version.

Aircraft Designations

The designation of Soviet aircraft (or any other equipment) is an absorbing and complex subject, full of anomalies and exceptions and over-ridden by the fact that the Soviet Union is usually unhelpful by disclosing as little as possible. Where aircraft and engine designations do have to be disclosed, as in world-record submissions to the international ratifying body, the FAI, they appear to be designations invented for the purpose and bearing no apparent relationship to those for the basic aircraft or engine type.

There are many other difficulties. The Soviet Union uses a Cyrillic alphabet quite unlike our own, and while many letters look like a familiar C, V, P or H (for example) they actually have totally different sounds (the obvious aircraft example is seen in the Soviet Union's civil registration letters SSSR, which look like "CCCP".)

Again, the national aircraft industry is grouped into a number of highly competitive "collectives" or design bureaux, named either after its leader or after famous deceased leaders; for example, both Mikoyan and Gurevich are dead but their bureau is still named after them and produces "MiG" combat aircraft. Each bureau has the authority to work out its own numbering system. At one time it was thought that an odd number meant a fighter and an even number a bomber or other type, but there are too many exceptions for this to be workable. Numerous aircraft (not featured in this book) have quite inexplicable numbers much higher than the normal run, while duplications are common. To make life yet harder, the Soviet armed forces (whose main aviation elements are listed below) have their own numbering scheme which bears no evident relationship to those of the design bureau. Thus, MiG prototypes usually have designations beginning with I (see list following), and the familiar designations of MiG aircraft appear always to be those allotted by the services. Tupolev aircraft have all been numbered from Tu-1 (of 1923), and most of the bureau numbers of modern Tupolev types can be paired up with the user-service designation (for example, the Tu-88 has the service designation Tu-16, while the Tu-95 became the Tu-20). An exception to the welcome Tupolev sequence is that civil transports received bureau designations ending in 4 (104, 114, 124, 134, 144, 154) carrying them beyond their "true" places.

The following list is merely a brief guide covering the aircraft in this book and the suffix letters the reader will encounter.

A Usually aerodynamically refined (aerodynamichesky). Also, in addition to use in aircraft not included in this book, a new record-breaking Mil helicopter believed to be an Mi-24 is called "A-10". Western speculation suggested this was the initial letter of the town-location of a new Mil bureau.
B Bomber (bombardirovshchik) and (rarely) other meanings.
bis Soviet use of Latin suffixes (bis, ter, quatro) denotes absence of any obvious helpful suffix-letter, but enough changes to warrant a new designation. Thus MiG-21bis means "MiG-21 Mk 2", though in fact it was preceded by a dozen or more quite distinct developments.
D Long range (dalny, dalnya).
F Boosted (forsirovanny).
FL Boosted + radar or other sensor (forsazh lokator).
I Fighter (istrebitel).
L Search radar or other sensor (lokator).
M Modified (modifikatsirovanny).
NATO names For obvious reasons the Western alliance has had to invent easily spoken code-names for Soviet aircraft, radars and some other equipment. The ASCC (Air Standards Co-ordinating Committee) follows a general rule of assigning English-language names beginning with B for bombers, C for transports (cargo), F for fighters (including attack bombers), H for helicopters and M for all other types (miscellaneous). Sub-types are identified by suffix letters, but these are often not assigned. Of course, there are many cases of mis-identification of role, and in in some cases the code-name has had to be changed.
N Usually Night (nochnoy).
P Many meanings, including all-weather interceptor (perekhvatchik), passenger version (passazhirsky), fire-fighting (protivo-pozharny), and aerobatic (pilotazhny).
PF All-weather interceptor, boosted.
PM Aerobatic, modified.
R Various, including reconnaissance (razvedchik) and jet-propelled (reaktivny) or rocket (raketny).
S Various, but in MiG-19S denotes slab-tailplane (stabilizator).
SPS Blown flaps (sduva pogranichnovo sloya).
T Several meanings including transport (transportny) and torpedo (torpedonosetz).
U Invariably trainer (uchebny), but also strengthened (usilenny) or improved (usovershentsvovanny).
UTI Fighter trainer.
V Helicopter (vertolet), seaplane (vodyanoi) and other meanings.

Glossary

AAM Air/air missile, fired from one aircraft against another.
Ablative Capable of being worn away; ablative skins of re-entry vehicles (such as ICBM nose-cones) erode as they plunge down through the atmosphere and dissipate heat.
ABM Anti-ballistic missile.
Active Describes device emitting radiation, sound waves or other phenomena.
ADD Soviet Union Aviatsiya Dal'Nevo Deistviya, longrange bombers.
Afterburner Device added to rear of jet engine (turbofan or turbojet) in which extra fuel is burned to give extra thrust; in UK often called reheat jetpipe.
AGM Air/ground missile (US designation system).
ALCM Air-launched cruise missile.
Anti-flutter Masses can be attached to parts of high-speed aircraft to damp out flutter (high-frequency vibration).
APU Auxiliary power unit.
ASALM Advanced strategic air-launched missile.
ASM Air/surface missile.
ASW Anti-submarine warfare.
ATC Air-traffic control.
ATO Assisted takeoff.
Attack Combat mission flown against tactical surface targets on land or sea.
Avionics Aviation electronics, ie electronic systems carried in aircraft.
AV-MF Soviet Union Aviatsiya Voenno-morskovo Flota, naval air force.
AWACS Airborne Warning And Control System.
Azimuth Direction in the horizontal plane.
BLC Boundary-layer control, method of increasing lift, reducing lift, reducing drag or improving control by blowing air under pressure from thin slits in aircraft skin.
Bomber Term virtually defunct; originally meant large aircraft that dropped bombs, but today this is done by virtually all combat aircraft, while role of modern bombers is to carry stand-off missiles within range of enemy strategic targets.
Canard Tail-first aircraft, or a foreplane (auxiliary horizontal surface on the nose instead of the tail).
CAS Close air support.
Cassegrain Optical system involving two sets of concave mirrors, used in astronomical telescopes and adapted to radars.
Casevac Casualty evacuation (assumed from land battle).
Chaff Small metal slivers, such as strips cut from roll of aluminium foil, scattered by million by aircraft in hostile airspace to blanket enemy radars.
Chord Distance from leading edge to trailing edge of a wing.
CL Coefficient of lift, a measure of the lift generated by a wing (increased by high-lift devices such as slats and flaps).
CL Ceskoslovenske Letectvo, the Czech air arm
Close support Combat mission flown against surface targets hindering friendly ground forces.
Code name NATO compiles a list of invented names, easily remembered and unambiguously transmitted quickly by radio, for Soviet and Chinese aircraft, missiles and radars. This is because the true designations are either not known or complex. Also called "reporting name".
Coin Counter-insurgent, designed for use against unsophisticated enemy in "limited" or "bushfire" conflict.
Con/di Convergent and then divergent, the shape of the propelling nozzle of a jet engine for supersonic flight.
Countermeasures Equipment and operations intended to nullify or confuse hostile sensors, such as chaff, jammers, decoys; could even include a smokescreen.
Cruise missile Missile that flies to its target like aircraft, with sustained propulsion and lifted by wing.
CW Continuous-wave e.m. radiation (as distinct from pulse).
DA Daln'ya aviyatsya, long range.
Decoy Small aircraft or other object arranged to look like attack or bomber aircraft on hostile radars or other sensors, to confuse or dilute enemy defences.
Delta wing Shaped like triangle in plan, with sharply swept leading edge and almost straight trailing edge.
Development aircraft Aircraft built for flight testing to eliminate faults or deficiencies; may later be brought up to production standard.
Doppler Apparent change in frequency (such as pitch of a note or wavelength of radar signals) due to relative motion between source and observer. Doppler radar can measure velocity of targets, or of aircraft in which the radar is fitted.
DOSAAF The Soviet para-military national organization for sporting flying.
Drogue Device trailed on cable, hose or other filament from aircraft (especially on FR hose, to keep latter steady, pull it out from hose-reel and provide receptacle for receiver's probe).
ECCM Electronic counter-countermeasures (ie, anti-ECM).
ECM Electronic countermeasures, equipment or techniques intended to nullify or confuse enemy electronic sensors such as radars.
Elint Electronic intelligence, mission flown to find out maximum about enemy (or potential enemy) e.m. emissions such as radars, communications, IR, lasers and ECM.
E.m. Radiation Electromagnetic radiation, which includes visible light, radio waves (including radar microwaves) and IR (heat)
ESM Electronic support measures (sometimes electronic surveillance measures), including ECM, Elint and related activities.
EVS Electro-optical viewing system.
EW Electronic warfare, all use of e.m. radiation in war.
FA Soviet Union Frontovaya Aviatsiya, frontal aviation, ie tactical air force.
FAC Forward Air Controller, experienced airborne manager of tactical air strike on surface target.
Fence Thin surface aligned parallel to airflow across top of wing.
FFAR Folding-fin (or free-flight) aircraft (or air-to-air) rocket.
Fighter Combat aircraft intended primarily for destruction of enemy aircraft in the air.
Flare Source of high-intensity light (for night reconnaissance or to assist ground or naval battle).
FLIR Forward-looking infra-red.
FR Flight refuelling.
g Acceleration due to Earth gravity; on Earth's surface bodies experience 1g and appear to weigh their normal amount, but in free fall they experience 0g while in air combat they may be accelerated in tight turns and dive pull-outs to 6g or more, modern fighters being designed to withstand up to 12g.
GSFG Group of Soviet Forces in Germany.
Gunship Helicopter (rarely, light fixed-wing aircraft or military transport) equipped to carry sensors and weapons, usually to participate in land battle.
Hardpoint Part of aircraft strengthened to carry pylon.
Hard target Protected against nuclear blast and radiation.
Head-up-display (HUD) Optical device which projects information and/or pictures on pilot's windscreen, focussed at infinity so that he can simultaneously search sky/ground ahead.
Homing Able to steer automatically towards target or other objective.
HUD Head-up-display.
IA-PVO Soviet Union Istrebitel'naya Aviatsiya Protivo-vozdushnaya Oborona, interceptor force of air defence force.
ICBM Inter-continental ballistic missile (about 6,300 miles, 10,000km).
IFF Identification friend or foe, a radio device.
ILS Instrument landing system.
Inertial Deriving information from gyros and accelerometers of extreme accuracy, able to calculate exact position of aircraft or other vehicle without external information.
Interceptor Fighter designed for finding and destroying hostile aircraft even in bad weather or at night.
IR Infra-red (ie heat).
IRBM Intermediate-range ballistic missile (about 1,730 miles, 2500km).
Jammer EW device emitting such powerful e.m. radiation as to blot out hostile reception on same wavelength(s).
Jato, JATO Jet-assisted takeoff (a misnomer, because it invariably means rocket-assisted).
LABS Low-altitude bombing system, method of delivering nuclear bombs at low level by "tossing" them much higher than the aircraft to increase time available for latter to get clear
Laser Device for emitting beam of coherent (waves in phase) light which can be made intense, focussed precisely and used with receiver at same wavelength.
LLTV, LLLTV Low-light TV, low-light-level TV, TV able to be used in poor visibility (but not on pitch-black night).
Loiter To cruise at economical low airspeed.
LRMTS Laser ranger and marked-target seeker.
LSK Luftstreitkräfte, E. German (DDR) air force.
Mach Scale used for speed of fast aircraft; Mach 1.0 is speed of sound, about 760mph (1223km/h) at sea level (more on hot day, less in winter) and 660mph (1062km/h) at high altitude, thus Mach 1.6 is 60 per cent faster and Mach 2.0 twice as fast.
MAD Magnetic-anomaly detector, sensitive device able to detect local irregularity in Earth's magnetic field due to presence of submerged submarine.
Marked target Target illuminated by e.m. radiation (usually laser) so that attacking aircraft can spot it and missile home on to it.
MARV Manoeuvring re-entry vehicle
MIRV Multiple independently targeted re-entry vehicle (thus, one missile can hit several widely separated targets).
MRBM Medium-range ballistic missile (100–1,000 miles, 160–1600km).
Multi-sensor Equipped with radar, optical cameras and IR to give fullest picture of hostile target, eg to defeat camouflage.
Nadge NATO Air-Defence Ground Environment, the NATO air-defence system.
NATO North Atlantic Treaty Organization.
Ogival Rounded conical nose or curved slender-delta wing having same outline shape.
Oleo Air/oil shock-absorbing strut, as in landing gear.
Passive Receiving but not emitting (human ear is example, but in aircraft usually concerned with e.m. radiation).
PD Pulse-doppler, kind of radar.
Pitot Tube pressurized by forward-facing inlet; gives accurate indication of air-speed.
Pod Streamlined container carrying equipment outside aircraft.
Pre-production aircraft Batch of aircraft built in production tooling but still subject to progressive modifications as result of flight testing and engineering development.
Pressurized Aircraft interior inflated to pressure which, though lower than at sea level, is higher than surrounding air at high altitude, for comfort of crew.
PRF Pulse-recurrence frequency (radar).
Probe Long boom (rod) projecting ahead of aircraft, especially pipe for taking fuel from FR drogue.
Profile Combat mission drawn with distance horizontally and height vertically; attack mission may be hi-lo-hi, as much as possible being flown at high altitude to save fuel but attack being at treetop height to escape radar detection.
Prototype First aircraft built of new type; strictly does not apply to "one-off" experimental aircraft but only to type intended later to be mass-produced, after development is completed.
Pulse radiation E.m. emission in form of succession of bursts, as distinct from CW.
PVO Se IA-PVO.
PWL Polskie Wojska Lotnictze, Polish air force.
Pylon Attachment for external store, usually embodying means for release and positive ejection to throw clear of aircraft.
Radar System using e.m. radiation to detect, locate and track targets.
R & D Research and development.
RAF Royal Air Force (UK air force).
Ram system Pressurized by fast-moving forward-facing inlet.
Receiver In FR, the aircraft accepting fuel.
Reporting name See code name.
Retarded bomb Bomb fitted with airbrakes and/or parachute to allow low-flying aircraft to get clear of burst.
RPV Remotely piloted vehicle aircraft (usually small) flown by human pilot not carried on board.
SALT Strategic-Arms Limitation Talks.
SAM Surface/air missile, fired from ground or ship to destroy aircraft.
Semi-active Guidance system using passive e.m. receiver to home on to target illuminated by external radiation source.
Sensor Device for detecting, and often recording, e.m. and other radiation (optical, radar, IR, magnetic, sound).
SIF Selective identification facility, radio device related to IFF.
Signature Precise characteristics of e.m. or other signal, such as radar echo from particular type of aircraft, which when analysed acts as kind of fingerprint.
Slab tailplane Made in one piece, without separate elevators (US = stabilizer).
SLAR Side-looking aircraft (or airborne) radar.
SLBM Submarine-launched ballistic missile.
Sonobuoy Acoustic device for detecting submerged submarines by sound; active sonobuoy sends out intense pulses of sound and listens for reflection, passive sonobuoy listens for sound generated by submarine itself.
Splitter plate Sharp-edged plate which separates sluggish boundary-layer air (close to aircraft surface) from relatively fast-moving free air rammed into engine.
Spoilers Powered hinged surfaces above wings, opened together to increase drag or reduce lift, and differentially to roll aircraft.
Sqn Squadron
SSBN US code for nuclear-powered SLBM-armed submarine.
SSM Surface-to-surface missile.
Stand-off missile ASM designed to hit target when launched from bomber outside range of enemy defences.
STOL Short takeoff and landing, fixed wing aircraft able to use small rough fields or clearings.
Store Any object carried on external pylon.
Strategic Concerned with attacks on enemy heartlands (cities, industries etc) as distinct from targets associated with surface battles.
Subsonic Below the local speed of sound.
Supersonic Above the local speed of sound.
Sweep Angle at which wings are raked back (often measured at ¼-chord, ie one-quarter of way back from leading edge.
Tactical Concerned with local surface warfare on land or sea.
Taileron Slab tailplanes (left and right) capable of being deflected differentially to roll aircraft, either as primary control or for trimming.

continued ▶

Terrain-following radar Equipment able to guide attack aircraft safely at lowest possible height across enemy territory, missing hills or telephone poles even at night or in fog.

Throw-weight Total mass carried to re-entry by ballistic missile, comprising warhead(s), decoys, RV (re-entry vehicle) and chaff or other penaids (penetration aids).

Transducer Device for converting mechanical strain (or small linear movement) into an electrical signal.

Transponder Radio device which automatically broadcasts a signal when triggered by another (or the same) incoming signal.

Turbofan Gas-turbine jet engine with large fan (similar to multi-blade ducted propeller) generating half or more of total thrust, rest coming from hot core jet that drives fan.

Turbojet Gas-turbine jet engine of simplest kind, generating single jet of hot gas.

Turboshaft Gas-turbine engine delivering all power through shaft, for driving helicopter or other shaft-drive vehicle.

TV Television which in combat aircraft is usually not just passive as in household receiver but active system taking own pictures.

UHF Ultra-high frequency e.m. radiation.

uts Ultimate tensile strength, a measure of structural properties.

Variable-geometry Aircraft able to change shape, especially by varying sweep angle of wings.

Vernier Small rocket used for final adjustment of missile trajectory and velocity.

VHF Very high frequency e.m. radiation (lower frequencies than UHF).

VOR Vhf omni range, a radio navaid.

VTOL Vertical takeoff and landing.

V-TA Soviet Union Voenno-transportnaya Aviatsiya, transport aviation.

VVS Soviet Union Voenno-vozdushniye Sily, combined air forces.

Wire guidance Guidance by electrical signals transmitted from operator through fine wires unreeled from missile in flight.

Yaw Aircraft rotation about a vertical axis, ie change of heading with the wings level.

Index

continued ▶

Picture Credits

The publisher wishes to thank the following organisations and individuals who have supplied photographs for this book. Photographs have been credited by page number; where more than one photograph appears on a page, references are made in the order of the columns across the page and then from top to bottom. Some references have for reasons of space been abbreviated as follows:

Education and Television Films Ltd, London: E and TV Films
Flight International Library: Flight
Ministry of Defence, London: MOD
Official United States Air Force photography: USAF
Official United States Navy photography: USN
Soviet Studies Centre, Sandhurst: SSCS

12: E and TV Films. 13: Rockwell. 16: General Dynamics. 17: E and TV Films. 27: USAF. 28: SSCS. 30-31: USAF. 32: D. Jenkins via H.R. Muir/USAF. 33: Flight. 34: SSCS. 39-40: SSCS. 40/41: J.W.R. Taylor collection. 41-46: SSCS.

46/47: William Green collection 47-50: SSCS. 50: bottom, Novosti. 51: SSCS/Keystone Press Agency. 52-57: SSCS. 60-61: PAA. 62: SSCS. 63: SSCS/PAA. 64-65: PAA. 67-69: SSCS. 71: Interinfo. 72: SSCS. 73: Interinfo. 74/75: J.W.R. Taylor collection. 76/77: *Flug Revue*. 77: SSCS. 78: SSCS. 79: Interinfo/Novosti. 80-81: SSCS/J.W.R. Taylor collection (bottom). 82-89: SSCS. 89: bottom, USAF. 98: Novosti. 99-100: SSCS. 101: MOD. 104: top two, William Green collection/SSCS. 105: SSCS/Aero. 106: PAA/William Green collection. 107: SSCS. 110: Interinfo/J.W.R. Taylor collection. 111: William Green collection. 112: J.W.R. Taylor collection/Interinfo. 113: China News Agency. 115: USN/Novosti. 116: William Green collection/USN. 117: Finland Defence Department/PAA. 118: Novosti/Bill Gunston collection. 119: William Green collection. 120/121: Pakistan Air Force. 123: William Green collection. 126: E and TV Films/William Green collection. 126/127: Flight. 132: Flight. 133: Tass/Flight. 136-137: William Green collection. 138: E and TV Films. 139: Novosti/Interinfo. 142: USN/Interinfo. 143: William Green collection/SSCS. 146: MOD/E and TV Films. 147: E and TV Films. 154: SSCS/E and TV Films/William Green collection. 155: Tass/Novosti/Tass. 160: Interinfo (Elio Torregino)/MOD. 161: Interinfo. 164: MOD. 165: E and TV Films/Interinfo. 170: E and TV Films. 171: J.W.R. Taylor collection. 176: Aviation Week and Space Technology/E and TV Films. 177: E and TV Films. 180-181: William Green collection. 182: bottom, E and TV Films. 183: William Green collection. 188: USN/MOD.